Kamál **"The Diva"** Larsuel-Ulbricht, a self-avowed "movie nut," spearheaded and put the framework of this project together with her amazing collection of historical box-office data. Raised in San Diego and now living in Seattle with her husband and family, she has a special place in her heart for bad musicals, and wants vengeance for horror movies she is forced to watch.

Rose **"Bams"** Cooper, a curmudgeonly sort who, before July 1999, was voted "Most Likely to Hate this Movie"; her time with 3 Black Chicks has made her a born-again believer in the magic of movies. She is a Detroit native transplanted to the wilds of Lansing, Michigan, where she's likely to be seen chasing her husband down the road on her Harley. Though she spends way too much time conquering the Internet, this Chick is all about the written word: her personal motto is "Will Write for Food."

Cassandra **"Cass"** Henry hails from somewhere down deep in the bayou. But don't let her sweet disposition and good ol' Southern hospitality fool ya. She's no pushover. Cass prefers to review older flicks because she believes that contemporary movies are remakes with special effects thrown in. Her only claim to fame is that she was "Carmen" in a school play.

Kamál **"The Diva"** Larsuel-Ulbricht
Rose **"Bams"** Cooper
Cassandra **"Cass"** Henry

 Amistad *An Imprint of HarperCollinsPublishers*

3 **black** chicks
review flicks

A Film & Video Guide With Flava!

HarperCollins books may be purchased for educational, business, or sales promotional use. For information, please write: Special Markets Department, HarperCollinsPublishers Inc., 10 East 53rd Street, New York, NY 10022.

FIRST EDITION

Designed by Shubhani Sarkar

Printed on acid-free paper

Library of Congress Cataloging-in-Publication Data
Cooper, Rose.
  3 Black Chicks review flicks : a film and video guide with flava! /
Rose Cooper, Cassandra Henry, and Kamál Larsuel-Ulbricht.—1 st ed.
      p. cm.
   Includes index.
    1. Motion pictures—Reviews. 2. African Americans in motion pictures.
 I. Title: Three Black Chicks review flicks. II. Henry, Cassandra. III.
Larsuel-Ulbricht, Kamál. IV. Title.
  PN1995 .C65 2002
  791.43'75—dc21
                                                      2002066631

ISBN 0-06-050871-X

02 03 04 05 06 BVG/RRD 10 9 8 7 6 5 4 3 2 1

This book is dedicated to everyone who ever wanted their voices to be heard, but thought no one would ever listen; and to Black artists everywhere who continue to strive for their work to be noticed.

HERE'S TO BEING APPRECIATED.

KAMÁL, ROSE, and CASS would like to acknowledge the following people and groups for their kind inspiration, encouragement, and support:

Lynnette Anthony (hi Mommy!), the Atiba Anthony Family, the Douglas Anthony Family, Auntie V, Phyl Behrer, Sol Bermann, Bill and the Kids, Bones, Cathlene Brady Kubwa Brown, Pat "Hana" Brown, Chris, Michael Cooper, DC, Allison Dean, Diana, Dinette, Tonya Marie Evans, Rachelle Ferrell and Russ Barnes (let's start a revolution y'all!), Tom Goff, Hen, Jim Hill, Kelly Howard, the Arthur Jackson Family, Jean, Jeanine, Cynthia Johnson, Leonard Johnson, Jumbe Jolly, the George Jones Family, Harvey S. Karten, Harriet Keeling, Kera, Jalilah Larsuel, Spike Lee, M. Ford, M. Green, Marcus, Maria, Markie, Mary Margaret, Mat, Mathew, Mike, David Mills, the Milon Mills Family, Mizz Honore, Nancy, Burlinda Radney, Betty Richardson, Ro, the George P. Robbs Family, Mablene Rogers (hi Mom!), Michelle Rogers, Roosevelt Rogers Jr. (hi Daddy!), the Lonny Rollins Family, Michael Segers, Alan Sepinwall, Shani, Terrence Spivey, Gordon Steudler, Tanya Stephens, Stocker, Mr. T., Bev Thomas, Robert Townsend, Frederick Ulbricht (I love you. Thanks for supporting us 100%), the Edgar Ulbricht Family, Uncle "C", ChrisUtley, Apryl Voner, Artis Wixx, Gary Wolcott, Roger Zotti

and

Susan Borden Evans Assoc., Celebration Cinema/Jack Lokes Theaters, Dawn Davis (Thanks for all of your hard work. You get your ghetto pass back.), "Dblink" List, Drizzle.com, the "Fam'lee," Loews Cinema Corporation, Tanya McKinnon and Richard Pope, Motolist, Nancy Locke, all of the women (and Mike) on the NWR List, the OFCS, the Poets Niche, the folks in RBN, the Rosie O'Donnell List, SCAA list, Siskel & Ebert, the folks at Terry Hines and Associates (Keri, Mac, Nancy, and Therese), "The Box," Janet Wainwright and employees, the Wharton Center, our 3BC "Guest Stars," the 3BC "Viewers' Voices" family—and, heck; we thank each other, too. We deserve it.

And last, but not least—Elvis Mitchell for fighting the good fight and for being a nationally known Black critic.

CONTENTS

Introduction   xi

Cheat Sheets: A Practical Guide to Understanding
  3 Black Chicks   xv
The Black Factor
The Brotha Rule
Ghetto Wednesday
The Rating Scale
STS: Spot the Spot

1 **The Blockbusters**   1
Flicks That Made Bank!

2 **Black Gold**   37

3 **Ghettofabulous Flicks**   59
Who Said the 'Hood Ain't Heaven?

4 **When White Folks Dog Each Other**   73

5 **When White Folks Dog Us**   92

6 **In Celebration of Our Culture**   107
Blaxploitation (or What We Call "The Classics")
and Beyond

7 **Lip Smackers**   142
(a.k.a. Date Flicks)

8 **Late-Night Booty-Call Flicks**   171
   For the More Determined

9 **Chick Flicks**   195
   Flicks Where Chicks Rule!

Intermission: A Movie Trivia Quiz   215

10 **Wired for Sound**   217
   You Know You Own the Movie
   and the CD—or Maybe Even the LP!

11 **When Bad Things Happen to White Folks**   233

12 **Funny Bone Flicks**   259

13 **Sci-Fi and Beyond**   289
   Things That Go Bump
   in the Night Way the Hell Out There

14 **Animation**   305
   Who Sez They're Kiddie Flicks?

15 **Independently Thinking**   325

16 **Movies That Just Plain Suck**   343

Appendix: Intermission Trivia Quiz Answers   359

Index of Films Reviewed   363

It started with a simple question: "Why are there no nationally known Black movie reviewers . . . ?" Of course we found out later that there are a few nationally known Black movie reviewers, including Elvis Mitchell; but by then, we were racing down the Internet superhighway with our own unique look at cinema . . . and that "simple" question evolved—and still continues to evolve—into 3 Black Chicks.

Before 3BC took off in early July 1999, Kamál "The Diva" Larsuel and Rose "Bams" Cooper had never met face to face. Living on opposite ends of the country—"The Diva" in Seattle and "Bams" in Lansing—we knew each other only from our typefaces: our shared email messages posted to the "SCAA" Internet list. The SCAA list is a private email group that was started seven years ago by a group of like-minded individuals who seem to run into each other in cyberspace quite often and, as SCAA members tend to do, we were discussing upcoming summer movies with the group, when we both realized that Black movie critics were few and far between in this country. And we had questions . . . Why were there so few critics adding our unique Flava to their reviews? Why was there no one out there dishin' on Our Issues? Like the quandary The Diva found herself in:

You always hear me complaining about the lack of quality Black films. I got to thinking about this. Am I being a hypocrite? I mean, this is the same woman who has seen *Waterboy* about 15 times. Why is it okay for me to spend my money watching a stupid Adam Sandler movie but not okay for me to watch *Booty Call*? I honestly don't know. I guess my reasoning stems from the fact that there aren't very many Black films to begin with. I imagine Hollywood having this quota system. This quota dictates that there can be no more than 10 Black movies in any given year. I asked myself aloud, "Am I being a bit too harsh in judging Black films?"

Who was discussing "The Black Factor"? Why wasn't Alfre Woodard Feelin' the Love from movie audiences? Who the heck told Steven Segal he could act???

Who else was discussing "The Brotha Rule"? Would it kill Hollywood to let the brotha live more than 63 minutes?

Who else was discussing feeling manipulated by *Blow* because the audience is being asked to feel sympathetic toward a drug dealer because he was an "All-American" boy, yet we all know had the character been African-American and selling crack, he would have been painted a thug.

But rather than continue to sit back and complain about what was missing, we decided to take matters into our own hands. Before anyone could tell us "it can't be done," we did it. We put together the framework of the www.3blackchicks.com Web site, watched and reviewed our first movie (*Wild Wild West*, or, as we like to call it, "Wild Wild Mess"—ugh!), and published our individual reviews on the 3BC site. After searching high and low for a Third Black Chick who could ruffle her feathers and feel comfortable in our Chicken Coop, The Diva and Bams found her: Cassandra Henry. Cass makes an appearance as a "Special Chick," which explains why she doesn't have as many reviews in this, our first book. However, look for Cass to figure prominently in our future. The rest, as they say, is History. Ain't modern technology grand?

Yeah, actually, it is. The World Wide Web allowed us to have a voice that traditional media often ignores. Because we know our way around the Web and the Internet, we were able to address a niche, using our writing and technical skills in a way that—a mere ten years ago— would have been unheard of. And 3BC took off; between pounding the virtual pavement to hip Web sponsors, search engines, Black Web hangouts, and telling our friends to tell their friends (and so on and so on and so on), we started making a name for ourselves as Black women who take no prisoners when it came to telling it like it is. Folks everywhere, from Australia to Zimbabwe, came to us for a taste of 3BC Flava;

people of all races, colors, and creeds wanted the real deal on the Silver Screen.

"Hmmm ..." we thought, "why not take this to another level? Why not spread some good ol' Chicks Flava to the printed page, with our own book of 3BC reviews?" Why not, indeed? But we know what you're thinking: "Will this be just another dull collection of white-bread reviews?" C'mon now, would Chicks do that to you? Hecky naw!

* Who else but Chicks would pay homage to "Chick Flicks," help you get your swerve on with our choice of "Lip Smacker" date flicks, and shine the spotlight on "Independently Thinking" indie flicks that you otherwise might never have heard of? Where else can fill you up on "The Blockbusters," musicals, aka "Wired for Sound," and "Blaxploitation Classics"?

* Issues? Yeah, we got 'em; see if you agree with the Issues we have with Hollywood.

* Catch our flow when we take you from the sweetness of Bams's favorite, "Animation," to The Diva's forte, anything with Denzel Washington in it and what she likes to call "The Horrors and The Horrible." And let's be upfront about our biases. We have an unwritten agreement for our 3BC reviews: The Diva watches all the scary movies— Bams can't handle them at all—and, in turn, Bams gets to view assorted kiddie fare. Meanwhile, Cass prefers to review older movies.

* And you can bet that when we tell you about "Movies That Just Plain Suck," you DON'T wanna go there . . .

Our short-term goal is to get you, the reader, to enjoy going to the movies again. Our long-term goal is to get Hollywood to understand that we, the viewer, just won't settle for subpar movies. More to the point, movies cost too darn much. We'll be ding-danged if folks should spend ten bucks to see a movie that neighborhood kids could have made with a camcorder!

But in the meantime, these 3 Black Chicks plan to put Hollywood, New York, London, and Vancouver on notice that the Chicks CyberCafe is open, and we are discussing *you*, so Listen Up!

et us give you a little nudge to help you understand our writing style and viewpoints.

THE BLACK FACTOR

In many of our reviews, we include something we call "The Black Factor." Check out what Bams has to say about it:

"As a Black woman, I see The Black Factor— things that affect me as a 'consumer of color'—in many aspects of life, movies included. Whether from the standpoint of noting Black (and other 'minority') cast and crew members (if any), to the (lack of) focus toward 'people of color' (dag, I hate that term), to the out-and-out antagonistic attitude toward Us (Jar-Jar, anyone?), the Black Factor (BF) is something that plays as much a role in my film enjoyment as any other aspect of the movie itself."

THE BROTHA RULE

The Diva loves to talk about "The Brotha Rule." "The Brotha Rule" is the same as the "Ensign Rule." You Trekkies out there know what I'm talking about (everyone else—just pretend that you do). The only difference is that instead of the red shirt being sent to his/her demise, it's the brotha that gets to check out early. Now The Diva has done extensive research on this phenomenon. She has logged countless hours following this and she believes she has it down to a science.

For starters, the rule does not apply to comedies and dramas. You have to be fleeing someone or something. A giant wave, a sea monster, a space creature, a serial killer, an all-around-nasty villain. You get the picture. If there is one Black man in the central part of the cast, he will die between 45 and 65 minutes of his first appearance. Most often, but not always, he will sacrifice himself for the life of the Caucasian main character.

Now—if there are two Black men, things change a little bit. If he is, say, a security guard or a janitor—you know, someone who is just filler— he'll be gone in less than 20 minutes and usually under 5 minutes. Rent *Mimic* to see a good example of this.

Of course, there are movies that break this rule—not very many, but there are some. And though I make light of the situation, it does bother me. I hope that if I point it out enough, it will cease to exist.

GHETTO WEDNESDAY

Many moons ago, the powers that be decided that the only way to cut down on the violence in urban theaters during the release of Black films was to release the films in the middle of the week. They believed that the people causing the drama would have to go to school the following day so they would not be out running the streets and shooting up movie theaters. This is why most Black films are released in the middle of the week and that's why we have "Ghetto Wednesday." Where applicable, we point out which films were subject to Ghetto Wednesday openings.

THE RATING SCALE

We wanted to come up with something unique to rate our movies. After much deliberation, we decided to use a variation of a stoplight: Here's what the variations mean:

RED LIGHT   "I don't *think* so!"
FLASHING RED LIGHT   "On video only.
                            Maybe."
YELLOW LIGHT   "Ya might wanna slow
                            your roll . . ."
FLASHING YELLOW LIGHT   "Okay—at matinee
                            prices."
GREEN LIGHT   "What are you
                            waiting for?"

STS: SPOT THE SPOT

In this fun game, viewers get points for finding the lone person of color in movies otherwise untainted by melanin, when a sneeze or an untrained eye could convince the average viewer that the movie is race-pure. The point is not to name flix where there are only one or two Black people who play pivotal roles (usually by helping White folks get in touch with their humanity—oh, *The Green Mile, Ghost, Driving Miss Daisy* . . . don't get me started) or comic relief (do the words "Feets, do yo' stuff!" ring a bell?). Pick movies that'll make your friends say, "No way—nobody in that movie ever met a Black person," and prove them wrong. The scoring works like this:

* **15 POINTS** for spotting the one lonely Negro with a nonspeaking part and under 10 seconds of total screen time (hint: practice with Woody Allen's oeuvre. The characters in his 30-plus movies live in that magical version of New York City that hasn't been discovered by more than a dozen Black folks, total—and believe me, they're just passing through!).

* **10 POINTS** for the same thing, except the lonely Negro has a speaking part of no more than ten words—most of which are "Yes'sm," "Nope," "Ma'am?" "Yes, boss," and "YOWZAH!"

* **5 POINTS** for spotting African-Americans standing in for other non-White people—ever take a slo-mo look at the faces on the "braves" in some of those old westerns? "HOW!" is right.

* **50 BONUS POINTS** for movies with ONE White person in a sea of brown (think *Porgy and Bess*). Now no movie in this category has a White person who doesn't speak, but try hard to find one where his ten words don't account for half the plot.

Unlike most games, this one has to end. As long as Hollywood keeps making movies, no matter how long Will Smith and Denzel live, it will always be a challenge to find a single Black face in depictions of the American landscape.

3 **black** chicks
review flicks

It used to be a rarity for a film to make 100 million dollars. The 100 million+ list was dominated by filmmakers such as George Lucas or Steven Spielberg. These days, instead of striving for 100 million, the push is to see who can get there the fastest. *Titanic* closed out Day 11 at 96 million and Day 12 at 104 million. It did have the advantage of opening up during the Christmas holiday season. *The Sixth Sense*, however, made 100 mil in 17 days—without the benefit of a holiday. Likewise, *Spider-Man* and *Attack of the Clones* Made Bank. Check out our reviews of a few movies in the 100-Million-Dollar Club.

Big Momma's House
(2000)

RATED PG-13; running time 98 minutes
GENRE: Comedy
WRITTEN BY: Darryl Quarles and Don Rhymer
DIRECTED BY: Raja Gosnell
CAST: Martin Lawrence, Nia Long, Paul Gia-
    matti, Jascha Washington, Terrence Howard,
    Ella Mitchell

> All of the movies that Martin Lawrence
> has been in since 1992 have grossed a
> combined total of $598,859,831.

THE DIGEST
Malcolm Turner (Martin Lawrence) is a hotshot
FBI agent who can disguise himself to look like
and take over the identity of anyone. He hopes to
catch a convicted bank robber and murderer who
has escaped from prison and is the ex-boyfriend
of Sherry (Nia Long). The money from the bank
robbery has never been recovered and Malcolm is
convinced that Sherry has it. In order to find out
if his hunch is right, he disguises himself as
Sherry's grandmother, Big Momma.

What Malcolm doesn't count on is falling in
love with Sherry and her son. Can he be objective
enough to follow through on this case or will his
heart get in the way?

THE DISH
I can't say that I didn't enjoy this movie. But I can
say that I'm starting to tire of going to watch two-
hour skits of *Martin*, the now-defunct television

show. That's basically what this was. If you've
watched the show, picture a combination of Martin's mom and the old security guard and there
you have *Big Momma*. It's the same ole same. Nia
Long plays the "Nia Long Character"—you
know, the long-suffering girlfriend—and Martin
Lawrence plays, well, Martin.

I can't complain too much. It wasn't a movie
with a bunch of naked hoochies; there was hardly
any violence and there weren't too many curse
words. There are some very funny moments, despite some jokes that kinda fall flat. But, again,
I'm not sorry that I watched it.

THE DIRECTIVE
You really have to suspend reality while watching
Big Momma's House. Ain't no way someone could
pose as my grandma and me not know it—even if
I hadn't seen her in years. Nor could this person
fool her best girlfriends, especially if she saw
them every day. But if you like Martin Lawrence,
you'll like this.

YELLOW LIGHT

The Blair Witch Project
(1999)

RATED R; running time 86 minutes
GENRE: Horror/Thriller
WRITTEN BY: Daniel Myrick and Eduardo Sánchez
DIRECTED BY: Daniel Myrick and Eduardo Sánchez
CAST: Heather Donahue, Joshua Leonard, Michael C. Williams

> *The Blair Witch Project* had virtually no marketing beyond the Internet. It made over 100 million dollars, mostly all on Internet hype

THE DIGEST

The Blair Witch Project is a story about three college students who want to make a documentary about a ghost story. Local legend has it that the Blair Witch is a woman who was kicked out of town some hundreds of years earlier for trying to take blood from children. Ever since then, children and adults mysteriously disappear. If they are seen again, they are dead. Most just vanish, including the students. What we see is the footage the three students shot, which is found a year after they are presumed dead.

The three would-be filmmakers head to a little Maryland town with their cameras going all the time except for when they are asleep. The whole movie is shown from the camera angle of whoever is holding it. The camera jumps and jiggles, causing some in the audience who suffer motion sickness to toss their cookies. It's really interesting, watching the filmmakers lose their grip on reality after wandering aimlessly for days in the forest and constantly being woken up in the middle of the night. Short on food and frustrated, they begin to turn on one another. This movie gives you a peek into the psyche of these individuals during the scariest time of their lives, and it's an interesting peek indeed.

THE DISH

I love having the bejesus scared out of me without the gore. *The Blair Witch Project* did just that. I'm still reeling from this film. It is original and completely scary.

THE DIRECTIVE

The Blair Witch Project cast a spell on this viewer and I loved every minute of it. Some people claim this movie didn't live up to the hype. I disagree. Do yourself a favor and check it out.

GREEN LIGHT

Chicken Run
(2000)

RATED G; running time 85 minutes

GENRE: Animation

WRITTEN BY: Mark Burton, Karey Kirkpatrick, Jack Rosenthal

DIRECTED BY: Nick Park, Peter Lord

VOICES OF: Mel Gibson, Julia Sawahla, Miranda Richardson, Anthony Haygarth, Phil Daniels, Timothy Spall, Lynne Ferguson, Jane Horrocks, Imelda Staunton, Benjamin Whitrow

> *Chicken Run* lost out to *Notting Hill* by 10 million as the highest-grossing British film released in the United States.

THE STORY

Life on the farm is anything but fun for dese hea' chicks in this animated flick.

Tired of being cooped up for the harvesting of her eggs (and of living in fear that the axe will fall the day that her egg-production days are over), Ginger dreams of freedom somewhere out there, away from her oppressors, evil chicken farmer Mrs. Tweedy (Miranda Richardson) and her henpecked husband Mr. Tweedy. Ginger gets little help from her fellow cacklers, since most of them are caught up in the slave mentality that tells them they are destined to live out their lives in captivity. But Ginger ain't havin' it; and with the help of packrats Nick and Fletcher, and Rocky (Mel Gibson), a cocky flying Rhode Island rooster who falls out of the sky and into their roost, Ginger believes she and her chick friends might soon gain their freedom after all.

THE UPSHOT

Chicken Run got the adult-to-children entertainment ratio right, even more so than *Toy Story 2* (see page 323) did—and *TS2* was one of my top 10 flicks of 1999, so you know that's saying a lot. A good mix of clever allusions to war flicks of the past (especially *The Great Escape* and *Stalag 17*), plus quick nods to the likes of *Cool Hand Luke* and Gibson's *Braveheart*, *Chicken* didn't forget to play for the kiddies as well—and it did so without patronizing the children or insulting its older viewers' intelligence. For every adult-type inside joke that went over the wee tots' heads ("bend over and kiss your bum good-bye!"), there was a message that could be easily grasped by the young ones.

Chicken Run was fun to watch, even with its nonbright colors (done purposely, I'd say, to denote a World War II–ish time period, as well as the comparative bleakness of the setting). I can easily compare it to another animated favorite of mine, *A Bug's Life*, in its attention to detail and surrounding environment. And, like *Bug* in its climax, *Chicken* addresses the concept of teamwork, another good lesson for kids to take away. Not a shabby one for us adults either, come to think of it.

The animation technique used in *Chicken Run*—Claymation—worked beautifully; there were only a few moments (primarily when the camera was pulled back for a long shot) that the "drawings" seemed transparent and the scene didn't look natural (as if a chicken with teeth, and hands instead of wings, could possibly look natural). Still, it was head-and-shoulders above the schizo animation mix in *Titan A.E.* (see page 320) with the added benefit of looking less polished (and, therefore, even more believable) in its backgrounds. But as good as the animation was, the voice characterizations were even better. Here, the characters were convincing in their chickdom. More important, the actors seemed to be in touch with their characters; they seemed to be having *fun* with them.

BAMMER'S BOTTOM LINE

A clever, funny flick with a good sense of Brit style, and a surprisingly good (without being overbearingly coy) vocal performance by Mel Gibson. Now, who's up for a two-piece and a biscuit?

GREEN LIGHT

Bams **Dinosaur**
(2000)

RATED PG; running time 82 minutes
GENRE: Animation
WRITTEN BY: There are 10 writers credited with the story and screenplay
DIRECTED BY: Eric Leighton, Ralph Zontag
VOICES OF: D. B. Sweeney, Ossie Davis, Julianna Margulies, Samuel E. Wright, Alfre Woodard, Max Casella, Hayden Panettiere, Joan Plowright, Della Reese, Peter Siragusa

Dinosaur can be considered a flop if you only count U.S. receipts. It cost 200 million dollars to make and only grossed $137,748,063 in the States. After worldwide distribution, however, the total went up to $354,600,000.

THE STORY

After being mistakenly dropped, as an egg, into a group of lemurs—among them, father and group leader Yar (Ossie Davis), mother Pilo (Alfre Woodard), and Zini, a hopeful (hopeless?) bachelor and the necessary comic relief—Aladar the dinosaur is brought up as a member of the lemur family. Aladar and the lemurs' world is changed forever when giant meteors fall onto their island, and they find themselves among other plant-eating dinosaurs, led by Darwin-loving Kron, and his crew, while trying to stay two steps ahead of the dreaded meat-eating Carnotaurs.

THE UPSHOT

Way back when, I fell in love with a movie called *The Bear*, a film that explored the non-animated, non-comical lives of two bears fighting against man and nature. When it finally came out on DVD, I bought it, savoring the memory of having seen a rousing story told without the trickery of singing beasts and wisecracking sidekicks. I mention this because, for a short while, I had a glimmer of a hope that—given the beautifully epic sweep shown in its previews—*Dinosaur* could also tell its tale without smarminess, or at least with the finesse of a *Toy Story*.

And then, the monkeys spoke.

Actually, I'm probably being unfair to *Dinosaur* in comparing it to the cinematic wonders of *The Bear* or the fun enough for an adult (but it's made for kiddies) fare found in *Toy Story*; then again, with the oodles and oodles of dough Disney dumped into this project, you'd *think* they'd remember the number-one rule: make the story interesting.

Instead, they blew their wad on making the pictures look pretty and scripting some awfully pedestrian lines, which were proffered up by good actors like D. B. Sweeney, Ossie Davis, Joan Plowright, and Alfre Woodard—all actors whose talents belie what sounded like mere journeymanism on their parts. Instead of seeing big dinos and silly little monkeys, I found myself listening for familiar voices ("yep, that's Julianna Margulies reading 'Neera,' sounding a whole lot like 'Carol Hathaway'").

The filmmakers seemed to count on children's love of dinosaurs (and, uh, hasn't that fad played out by now?) and all things Disney, to carry the day. But whether or not the movie keeps the kids' hyperactive attention is another story.

BAMMER'S BOTTOM LINE

Dinosaur may have been great eye-candy to look at—and until the monkeys first spoke, it was, indeed, beautiful without distraction. But they forgot to build something into this movie—heart. Fun- and story-wise, the toys in *Toy Story* and the ants in *A Bug's Life* ran circles around the big dino brutes. One thing in its favor—at least there were no singing prehistoric critters.

FLASHING YELLOW LIGHT

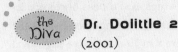

Dr. Dolittle 2

the Diva

(2001)

RATED PG; running time 85 minutes
GENRE: Comedy
WRITTEN BY: Larry Levin (based on stories by Hugh Lofting)
DIRECTED BY: Steve Carr
CAST: Eddie Murphy, Kristen Wilson, Raven-Symone, Kyla Pratt, Jeffery Jones, Kevin Pollack, Steve Zhan (voice of Archie the bear)

> Both *Dr. Dolittle* movies made over 100 million dollars. This is probably why Eddie has escaped Ghetto Wednesday (see page xvi).

THE DIGEST

Dr. Dolittle is back and he is busy beyond belief. Both his human and animal patients have increased 10-fold. He is never at home and it is causing a strain between him and his eldest daughter Charisse (Raven-Symone). She's turning 16 and has a rebellious streak. Mrs. Dolittle understands what her daughter is going through and tries to smooth the waters, but Dr. Dolittle is not quite ready to let his baby go, *especially* when he meets her new boyfriend. Dr. D vows to take his family on a European vacation to the delight of Charisse, but once again, the animals have another plan.

No sooner does Dr. D tell Charisse to plan for a vacation than a raccoon tells him that his presence is required in the forest. There he meets the beaver who tells him that he must help save their homes. An evil developer is clear-cutting the forest and running everyone out of the way. Dr. D reluctantly figures out a way to buy them some time, with the help of his wife. There is one female Pacific bear left in the wild; she is on the endangered species list, but without a male bear in sight, her status is useless. Dr. D manages to find a male bear, but he has spent his life in captivity and must be rehabilitated in order to survive in the wild.

Can Dr. D save the forest by rehabilitating a singing and dancing bear in one month? Will he lose his family in the process?

THE DISH

The plot was rather bland, but there were enough bathroom jokes to keep the kids happy. I'll admit to laughing at them once or twice myself.

Eddie Murphy was the closest to the Eddie Murphy I grew up watching that I've seen in a long time. For me, that was very pleasant. But none of the other actors really stood out.

THE BLACK FACTOR

I got ISSUES. Of course I was *not* thrilled that the jailed bear thugs were Black (and don't tell me that you can't tell). You can tell just as you can tell that the mafia animals were Italian. Why they insist upon reinforcing these stereotypes to children is *beyond* me.

THE DIRECTIVE

Rent it for your kids—though be warned, there are a few curse words—one Saturday and have a blast.

GREEN LIGHT

 ## Double Jeopardy
(1999)

RATED R; running time 106 minutes
GENRE: Thriller
WRITTEN BY: David Weisberg & Douglas Cook
DIRECTED BY: Bruce Beresford
CAST: Ashley Judd, Tommy Lee Jones, Annabeth Gish, Bruce Greenwood

> Double jeopardy—the legal concept, that is—does not work the way the film would have you believe. Parsons would have had to kill him the exact same way and in the exact same jurisdiction.

THE STORY

Libby Parsons (Ashley Judd) finds her Perfect Life turned upside down when she's convicted of killing her husband, Nick (Bruce Greenwood), after a cruise on their boat. Heartbroken, she asks her friend Angie (Annabeth Gish) to adopt her son, Matty, while she does her stretch in the joint. She's too through when she finds out that her so-called friend and her husband played her like a fool—it seems he's not dead after all, and they're making the beast with two backs together. Libby has other plans for them once she's paroled. A fellow inmate tells her that, revenge being a dish best served cold, she has carte blanche to kill Nick when she gets out, because she cannot be convicted twice for the same crime under double jeopardy rules, see.

THE UPSHOT

Okay, let me just get this outta the way: NEVER, UNDER *ANY* CIRCUMSTANCES, PICK UP A BLOODY KNIFE WHEN YOU WAKE UP AND SEE BLOOD 'N' GUTS ALL OVER THE PLACE, DUH!

One more thing: there is NO WAY IN BLOODY HELL that I'd "ride out" a prison term for murder, just to get revenge on the punk who put me in the slam in the first place. I don't care *what* it'd take, I'd be working every day, telling as many people as I could to get my big Black ass outta there!

That said, you've just read the entire set of issues I had with this flick. And minor they were—because other than that, I enjoyed the movie. Yes, it's been done before (shades of *Thelma & Louise* and, especially, *The Fugitive* abound), and Judd seemed overpowered by the always-enjoyable Tommy Lee Jones as her parole officer, but *Double Jeopardy* delivered an action-packed wallop.

One thing that pleasantly surprised me in this movie was the proper use of technology; I can't recall ever seeing computers that looked nearly as authentic as the ones used in this movie. Time after time, we geeks—technology-enhanced persons of good breeding and high

moral fiber—are left to moan and groan at the screen when totally unrealistic output is shown (the scenes in *Mission: Impossible* where Ethan receives pseudo-email come quickly to mind).

BAMMER'S BOTTOM LINE

Not an original, but this treatment is enjoyable, and nobody plays Pissed Off Official quite like Tommy Lee does, but they bet' not make a *Double Jeopardy 2*.

GREEN LIGHT

 **Erin Brockovich**
(2000)

RATED R; running time 131 minutes
GENRE: Comedy
WRITTEN BY: Susannah Grant
DIRECTED BY: Steven Soderbergh
CAST: Julia Roberts, Albert Finney, Aaron Eckhart, Marg Helgenberger, Scarlett Pomers, Peter Coyote, Cherry Jones, Scotty Leavenworth, Gemmenne de la Peña

> The "real" Erin has a bit part as a waitress. Look for her in the beginning when "movie" Erin takes her kids to a restaurant.

THE DIGEST

Erin Brockovich (Julia Roberts) is a twice-divorced mother of three. Unemployed, she has no real skills other than being a mother and "Ms. Wichita." After leaving a job interview, Erin is involved in a car accident, and attorney Ed Masry (Albert Finney) takes on her case pro bono. After they lose the case, one that Ed promised was a no-brainer, Erin finds herself seriously in debt and still unemployed. Finally at her wits' end, she demands that Ed give her a job as a filing clerk in his law office. It's not an easy job. Erin dresses like a hoochie and has a mouth that would make a sailor blush. No one really cares for her. But she doesn't let it bother her and she does her job well.

While investigating a case, she sees some medical records in a real estate case file. She finds out that the gas and electric companies are trying to pull a fast one on the residents of a small town and she sets out to help them.

This is a true story about sacrifice, hope, and trust. Erin has been hurt so often, she doesn't know how to trust anyone. But as she continues to look into the case, she finds that the town residents love and respect her. She's "one of them." This case consumes almost every hour of her life. She even sacrifices time with her family. She misses her baby's first words and first steps. She misses countless dinners and bedtimes. But she has to go on. For the first time in her life people listen to her and she is not willing to give that up.

THE DISH

Enjoyable and uplifting. I really enjoyed seeing Albert Finney. If you grew up when I did, you re-member his talent being wasted on *Wolfen*, *Looker*, and *Annie*. The praise doesn't stop there: Julia Roberts was brilliant.

THE DIRECTIVE

Erin Brockovich is a feel-good movie. I laughed and cried. It's horrible what those residents had to endure. All in all I found it to be a great story, and kudos to the real Erin Brockovich. Even if you don't care for Julia, Erin's story is worth watching.

GREEN LIGHT

 E.T. the Extra-Terrestrial
Anniversary Edition (2002)

RATED PG; approximate running time 120 minutes
GENRE: Science Fiction
WRITTEN BY: Melissa Mathison
DIRECTED BY: Steven Spielberg
CAST: Henry Thomas, Drew Barrymore, Dee Wallace, Robert MacNaughton, Peter Coyote

THE DIGEST

It's not easy being ten years old, especially when you're the middle child and your parents are going through a divorce, as Elliott (Henry Thomas) is learning firsthand. His fourteen-year-old brother, Michael (Robert MacNaughton), has taken on the role of "man of the house" and his six-year-old sister, Gertie (Drew Barrymore), is, of course, the spoiled baby. Elliott is struggling to find his place in his family. All this changes the night he goes outside to pay for a pizza.

On his way back into the house, he hears a noise in the shed. He picks up a ball and throws it into the shed and something throws it back. Scared, he runs back into the house and tries to explain it to his mother, brother, and his brother's friends. After some good-natured teasing, they go outside to investigate, but see nothing.

Convinced that he saw something, Elliott camps outside until he comes face to face with whatever was out there. His patience pays off, and he finds what turns out to be a space alien. What Elliott doesn't know is that this space alien is on the lam, lost and hiding. The alien was collecting plant specimens when some mysterious humans happen upon his group. The group takes off and leaves him behind. The big bad humans know that he is lost, and they try to track him down. Even if Elliott knew all of this it wouldn't matter to him. He has decided to keep the alien, whom he has dubbed E.T., and care for him.

Elliott now has someone who depends on him and needs him and he is going to rise to the challenge even if it means helping E.T. contact his people so he can go home.

THE DISH

The time is June 1982. The place is the Loma Theater in San Diego. I had just celebrated my—ahem—12th birthday. We got up early and got in line at 8 or 9 A.M. for the noon show, opening weekend for *E.T.* The line was curving around the block. There was a juggler keeping us entertained, and because of the heat, drinks were being sold outside. The door opened, we rushed inside, and sat right in the middle. When the cur-

tain came up, the audience became eerily quiet. I don't remember the trailers but I do remember the silence. About 5 minutes later, the movie started. I cried, cheered, laughed, and got scared when I was supposed to. When all was said and done and the screen went black; I briefly was unable to cope with the fact that E.T. didn't exist. I identified with Elliott on so many different levels, so much so, that I needed to have an E.T. of my own. My mother finally went out and bought me an E.T. doll and I spent *hours* playing with that doll and creating a world for him and me that was safe from mean adults. It was, in many ways, my salvation.

So, 20 years later, I ask myself "is there a such thing as a perfect movie and if so, is *E.T.* it?" This was the first time I saw the movie in its entirety since it was on the big screen in 1982. I was terrified that one of my most cherished childhood memories was going to be smashed to pieces. I was going to find all of these flaws. I was going to realize that it was a horrible film *and* I would not longer be able to enjoy it through my childhood eyes. I'd be so disappointed I'd burn my E.T. in effigy. But when the curtains went up, I once again cried, cheered, laughed, and got scared when I was supposed to. I was mad at Mom (Dee Wallace) for separating E.T. and Elliott. I got butterflies in the pit of my stomach each time E.T. made them fly. When all was said and done and the screen went black, once again I briefly was unable to cope with the fact that E.T. didn't exist. I needed him to be real just like when I was 12.

Oh, there were a few things that I noticed, some good, some bad. Henry Thomas's acting was not as wonderful as I seemed to recall. Drew Barrymore is precocious and cute as a button. There were times when the story didn't flow very evenly, and I found myself wanting to know more about Keys and his experiences. I was a little upset about the guns being removed from the new edition. I understand Spielberg wanted to make it more kid-friendly, but part of the wonderment of that scene is knowing how dangerous guns are, and having the audience cheer when E.T. and the kids outwit the bad guys who carry them. Most of all, I realized once again, that I wanted a sequel. Just like the 12-year-old Diva, I need to know that E.T. is doing well and has taken care of himself. I need for him to know that I stayed and I've always been right here.

THE DIRECTIVE

As I mentioned above, *E.T.* was one of my favorite childhood memories. It still is perfect for a family outing.

GREEN LIGHT

(b)*ams* **Gladiator**
(2000)

RATED R; running time 150 minutes
GENRE: Action
WRITTEN BY: David H. Franzoni, John Logan, William Nicholson
DIRECTED BY: Ridley Scott
CAST: Russell Crowe, Joaquin Phoenix, Richard Harris, Connie Nielsen, Oliver Reed, Djimon Hounsou, Derek Jacobi, Spencer Treat Clark, Tomas Arana

> Oliver Reed—"Proximo"—died during the filming of this movie. Apparently, most of his scenes were shot and they only had to do a little bit of tricky camera work to finish the movie. For example, there is a scene at the end where he is kneeling—that is someone else's body in place of his.

THE STORY

Corrupt politicians. High-profile athletes. Blood-thirsty fans. No, it's not business as usual in modern-day America.

It's A.D. 180, and Maximus (Russell Crowe), fearless and beloved general in the Roman Empire, has had a hard 2 years, 234 days, and 1 morning, and he just wants to go home to his wife and son. But Emperor Marcus Aurelius (Richard Harris) has something else in mind for the general. Declaring Maximus "the son I wish I'd had," Marcus wants Maximus to ensure that Rome returns to public rule by taking interim control of the Empire until the Roman Senate can get it together enough to take over.

This does not sit well with Marcus's actual son, the pampered Commodus (Joaquin Phoenix). Feeling cheated out of his rightful place in life, he conspires against Marcus and Maximus to become the next emperor of Rome. Commodus (am I the only one who can't help thinking of a toilet bowl when seeing that name in print?) does bad things that eventually lead to Maximus's being made a gladiator-slave in the servitude of Proximo (Oliver Reed), who teaches Maximus and fellow gladiator-slave Juba (Djimon Hounsou) the rule of thumb of becoming a successful—that is, living—gladiator: "Win the people and you'll win your freedom."

THE UPSHOT

Lions and tigers and Crowe. Oh my.

Hmmm . . . That shorthand synopsis sounds a bit soap-opera-ish, and in fact, elements of the story do bring to mind something along the lines of *All My Decadent First-Century Children.* And a soap isn't the only thing the storyline of *Gladiator* brings to mind. The movie reminded me of any number of things, from NFL players in a stadium to the American Congress to other movies (like Kevin Costner's version of *Robin Hood,* and, of course, classics like *Ben Hur* and *Spartacus*). Mostly, *Gladiator* reminded me just how brilliant and chameleon-like Russell Crowe is as an actor. It's breathtaking to watch Crowe so easily lose himself in his roles, while totally drawing the viewer in and keeping them believing.

That said, the movie suffers most whenever Crowe is not involved in a scene. Certainly, most of the supporting cast is capable, if not strong— Richard Harris in his brief turn as the emperor, Oliver Reed in a meatier role as Proximus, and Derek Jacobi's Gracchus being standouts among them—but the movie seems to crawl along most noticeably in Crowe's absence, as well as when the action stops. That, and the difficult time I had believing that Commodus would last a day as emperor (could he be more whiny?) or that Lucilla would suddenly become powerless and demure in the presence of her rather limp brother, threatened to wreak havoc with my suspension of disbelief . . . until Crowe showed up on the screen again, and everything was made right once more.

And speaking of "action," director Ridley Scott pulled out all the stops to bring it to the viewer, in full, bloody gore. The special effects are seamless and spectacular, never getting in the way of the story. Effects alone don't pay the bills,

though; and the interplay between Crowe and Nielsen, and Crowe and Phoenix, and Crowe and (insert cast member's name here) show the earmarks of good directing on Scott's part.

BAMMER'S BOTTOM LINE

Gladiator has spectacular images, remarkable action, powerful scenery-chewing by Russell Crowe in the lead—on top of a hit-and-miss story presented whenever he wasn't on screen. Oh well; three outta four ain't bad . . .

GREEN LIGHT

the Diva　　Gone in 60 Seconds
(2000)

RATED PG-13; running time 117 minutes
GENRE: Action/Comedy
WRITTEN BY: Scott Rosenberg
DIRECTED BY: Dominic Sena
CAST: Nicolas Cage, Angelina Jolie, Giovanni Ribisi, Robert Duvall, Delroy Lindo, Will Patton, Chi McBride, Scott Caan, Christopher Eccleston, Vinnie Jones, Timothy Olyphant

Producer Jerry Bruckheimer pictures have grossed over 2 billion in the U.S. alone since 1975. His pictures, which include *The Rock, Crimson Tide,* and *Beverly Hills Cop II,* on average make 91 million each. Only 5 of his 23 movies have failed to make at least 20 million.

THE DIGEST

Randall "Memphis" Raines (Nicholas Cage) is the best car thief to ever have graced the streets of Los Angeles. But that was the past. He has happily given up that title after seeing too many friends killed "in the line of duty." Memphis has been spending his days running a go-cart racing track for children. He seems content enough until he gets word that his little brother is in trouble. It seems that Kip (Giovanni Ribisi) has followed in his brother's footsteps; only he botched a job and is now being held by "The Big Evil Guy." If TBEG doesn't get his cars, he is going to kill Kip. Memphis comes out of retirement and gets some of his old crew together with his brother's younger crew to steal 50 cars in one night and save his little brother.

THE DISH

What was most amusing to me was seeing the old school and new school mix it up. The young pups watching the old dogs do things the old-fashioned way, making them see that sometimes less is more. On the flip side, the old dogs learned to respect the young pups when they show them a thing or two about boosting new cars.

Angelina Jolie as Sway is little more than the obligatory "hot chick." And for the most part, I'm tired of the clowning brother. You know, the one that tells stupid jokes and is always acting silly. White folks love him, while we Black folks roll our eyes. But Chi McBride and his counterpart, TJ Cross, a young brother from Kip's crew, had me rolling. Delroy Lindo as the detective "hot on the trail" was decent, but not overly impressive. I was impressed, however, with the '67 Mustang—Memphis's "Eleanor." The one that always gets away.

THE DIRECTIVE

Don't expect an Oscar-winning performance. Just turn your brain off and enjoy the fun ride . . .

GREEN LIGHT

The Grinch
(2000)

RATED PG; running time 105 minutes
GENRE: Children's/Comedy
WRITTEN BY: Peter Seaman, Jeffrey Price (based on the book by Dr. Seuss)
DIRECTED BY: Ron Howard
CAST: Jim Carrey, Taylor Mumsen, Bill Irwin, Molly Shannon, Jeffrey Tambor, Christine Baranski, Josh Ryan Evans, Anthony Hopkins (narrator)

> Rick Baker — Master of Makeup — won an Academy Award for his work on *The Grinch.* Apparently, Universal first complained about the makeup because they couldn't see Jim Carrey. Are all studio department heads on crack?

THE STORY

He's a Mean One: Mr. Grinch.

In this updated version of the classic tale by Dr. Seuss, the Grinch (Jim Carrey) has issues. He doesn't like all the noise that his Whoville neighbors 'round the way make—especially the Christmasy noise they make. The Grinch, frankly, doesn't like Christmas.

This astonishes young Cindy Lou Who, though she's having issues of her own over the commercialization of Christmas. Her father, Lou Lou Who (Bill Irwin), is buying up Christmas stuff left and right, while her mother, Betty Lou Who (Molly Shannon), is in a fierce Christmas light-stringing competition with neighbor Martha May Whovier, leaving Cindy to wonder just what Christmas is about.

The Grinch has no doubts. For him, Christmas is about being tortured by the Whos, a practice that started when he was yet a wee Grinch (Josh Ryan Evans). But this year will be different; this year, the Grinch and his dog, Max, will stop Christmas for good.

THE UPSHOT

Three things you should know about Bammer, before we get started: (1) Generally, remixes grind my gizzard; (2) Jim Carrey and his extremely over-the-top clowning gets on my *last* nerve; and (3) Dr. Seuss was one of the first heroes I had; hell, he spoke for the trees before tree-huggers were even thought of! Mess with him, and somebody's feelings are gonna get hurt.

So, I probably loathed Jim Carrey's remix of Dr. Seuss's cartoon *How the Grinch Stole Christmas,* right? Maybe. Maybe not.

Quite a few things about *The Grinch* were exactly as I thought, and even hoped, they would be: director Ron Howard obviously put a lot of love and care into this project; certainly he and his production team put a lot of moolah into set design and costumes. Narrator Anthony Hop-

kins's sonorous voice lived up to the original cartoon *Grinch* narrator—Boris Karloff's. And the key song—"You're a Mean One, Mr. Grinch"—was updated just enough to be jazzy, but still remained true to the original (okay, I'll admit it: I liked Carrey's version even *more* than the original song. Who knew he could actually sing?). Overall, my hopes that this production would remain true to Seuss's Whoville weren't shattered.

It's where they veered off of Seuss's beaten path that rankled me. That, and Jim Carrey being allowed off-leash without a pooper scooper to clean up behind him.

Many of Carrey's shtick bits should have been edited out. There were far too many times when Carrey just went manic without bringing the viewer with him. Also, for the life of me, I couldn't figure out why they decided to explain why the Grinch grinched. Some stuff just *is;* let it be, I say—especially if you're gonna explain it like this flick did. Further, I like my Whos unspoiled by Y2K sensibilities. Not to mention the big nads it takes for *The Grinch* to preach an anti-commercialism rant—all while your local department store is busy stocking truckloads of "Grinch" tie-in merchandise. Bah humbug, indeed.

THE BLACK FACTOR
Black "Whos"?

I'm sure it can't be easy being a Hollywood Filmmaker. They can be boxed into a "damned if you do/damned if you don't" corner: if they sprinkle a few Blacks (and since We're still the Default Minority, it'll probably remain "a *few* Blacks") in their productions, some folks will scream "TOKENISM!!!" But if they *don't* include Blacks, the scream becomes "WHERE THE BLACK FOLKS AT?"; I don't envy Howard, et al, their decision; and maybe the result should just be seen as the *Grinch* team having taken the high road.

But still: Black "Whos," for me, was about as weird a sight as, say, Black Vulcans.

BAMMER'S BOTTOM LINE
Just call me Mrs. Grinch, I think I'll stick with the original for now.

FLASHING YELLOW LIGHT

Bams Ice Age
(2001)

RATED PG; running time 85 minutes
GENRE: Animation (CG)
WRITTEN BY: Michael Berg, Peter Ackerman, Michael Wilson
DIRECTED BY: Chris Wedge
VOICES OF: Ray Romano, John Leguizamo, Denis Leary, Gorna Visnjic, Cedric The Entertainer, Stephen Root, Kristen Johnson, Jane Krakowski, Diedrich Bader

THE STORY
In the Ice Age, a trio of unlikely compatriots—surly Manfred the Mammoth (Ray Romano), wacky Sid the Sloth (John Leguizamo), and scheming Diego the Sabre-toothed Tiger (Denis Leary)—reluctantly team up to deliver a human baby they call "Pinky" back to its tribe, after Diego's tiger packmates, led by Soto, raid the baby's family's village and chase the baby and mother off into the wilderness.

The threesome have Wacky Adventures along the way, due mostly to Sid's encounters with other creatures like Silvia and Jennifer Sloth (Kristen Johnson and Jane Krakowski), and Carl and Frank Rhino (Cedric The Entertainer and Stephen Root). But the scheming Diego has a wee surprise in store for Pinky and Manfred . . .

THE UPSHOT
One of the funniest recurring bits in *Ice Age* was Scrat, the cute little squirrel, tryin'a get a nut. Unfortunately, except for that recurring bit, not much differentiated this movie from blockbuster

animated flicks of recent years. The opening (and admittedly cute) montage? Been there in *Dinosaur* (see page 5). The (admittedly fun) ice slide? Done that with the rollercoaster door ride in *Monsters, Inc.* (see page 310). The (admittedly funny) Wacky Schmoozing Sidekick? See for example: *Shrek*. (see page 315). Though in that latter case, Shrek himself was head and shoulders cooler than his *Ice Age* equivalent, Manfred.

Contrary to what CBS would like you to believe, Everybody *Doesn't* Love Ray . . . Romano. I found his Manfred to be a complete buzz kill; I vastly preferred Sid (voiced by the brilliant John Leguizamo) and Diego (voiced by the almost-as-brilliant Denis Leary) as a mismatched couple in "the oddest pack I've ever seen." But even I was moved by the scene explaining why Manfred was so surly. My non-loving of Ray aside, that was a fine piece of storytelling, as was the funny—but a wee bit too long—Dodos scene.

The videogame-ish look of *Ice Age* worked to its advantage. Going for a grand fantasy world instead of photorealism (though some images, such as the waterfall, looked incredibly real), *Ice Age* certainly dazzles the eye. But I had issues with the whole layout of the story, from start to finish.

Giving props where props are due, 20th-Century-Fox definitely improved on their previous attempt: 2000's *Titan A.E.* (see page 320)—and all without the irritating production numbers that far too many Disney cartoons force on the audience. But *Ice Age* just felt like a nicely animated copycat, with a bummer of a lead mammoth. Still, if the hoards of kids at Podunkville's sold-out hour-on-the-hour showings are any in-

dication, you can count on a sequel . . . *Ice Age 2: Pinky the Predator.*

BAMMER'S BOTTOM LINE

While this movie is certainly cute enough, there's not enough new stuff in *Ice Age* to make it a must-see. Younger kids might disagree—and who am I to argue with the target demographic? But animation-loving adults who've Seen This Before in movies like *Shrek* and *Monsters, Inc.*, might want to save *Ice Age* for a rainy day.

FLASHING YELLOW LIGHT

the Diva **The Lord of the Rings— The Fellowship of the Ring** (2001)

RATED PG-13; running time 178 minutes

GENRE: Adventure/Drama

WRITTEN BY: Philippa Boyens, Fran Walsh, and Peter Jackson based on the book by J. R. R. Tolkien

DIRECTED BY: Peter Jackson

CAST: Sean Astin, Sean Bean, Cate Blanchett, Orlando Bloom, Billy Boyd, Ian Holm, Christopher Lee, Ian McKellen, Dominic Monaghan, Viggo Mortensen, John Rhys-Davies, Andy Serkis, Liv Tyler, Hugo Weaving, Elijah Wood

THE DIGEST

Thousands of years ago at the dawning of a new age, there are nineteen powerful rings forged and given to the leaders of the races. Three go to the elves; seven go to the dwarf lords; and nine go to the human kings. It is thought that with each race having control over the rings, everyone will live in peace and harmony. What they didn't know is that there was a master ring made—a ring to control all the other rings and thus all of the races. This ring is in the evil hands of Sauron. One by one, he begins to turn the leaders against each other, and one by one he takes control. This leads to an epic battle in which a human prince, Isildur, chops off the ring finger of the evil Sauron and takes the ring from him. Rather than destroy the ring, this prince is taken by the power of it and decides to keep it. Isildur is shortly thereafter slain, and the ring floats to the bottom of a great river where it is eventually found by a little creature called Gollum. It stays in his possession for 2,500 years. Gollum accidentally loses it and it is then found by a hobbit—Bilbo Baggins (Ian Holm).

Bilbo has the ring for about 60 years. His good friend, a powerful wizard named Gandalf the Grey (Ian McKellen), is visiting Bilbo and notices that Bilbo has a magic ring that makes him invisible and figures out it is "The Ring." Gandalf convinces him to give it to his nephew, Frodo (Elijah Wood).

Meanwhile, Gandalf sets out to gather the kings and leaders of the races. They meet at the elf king's palace. Elrond is over 3,000 years old and was present during the battle that cost Sauron his finger and the ring. He knows that the ring must be destroyed and the only place it can be destroyed is where it was made—in the fires of Mordor. Nine people bravely volunteer for the task. These nine people comprise the fellowship of the ring. They set out on their dangerous quest and are pursued by Orcs, Uru-Kai, the Nazgul (the original nine human kings that are now demons), and people they thought they could trust, but who have now turned on them. Can they all survive long enough to complete their task?

THE DISH

I sat for three hours mesmerized by what was on the screen. The story was engaging and the cinematography was astounding; I felt as if I too were on a quest. I've never before been so drawn into a story. But don't expect much in the way of acting. With exception of Sean Astin, who gave the performance of his life, this film is about the story and the scenery.

THE DIRECTIVE

The Lord of the Rings is a must-see, though the Orcs and other evil characters may scare children under ten.

GREEN LIGHT

The Matrix
(1999)

RATED R; running time 136 minutes

GENRE: Action/Science Fiction

WRITTEN BY: Andy Wachowski and Larry Wachowski

DIRECTED BY: Andy Wachowski and Larry Wachowski

CAST: Keanu Reeves, Laurence Fishburne, Carrie-Anne Moss, Hugo Weaving, Joe Pantoliano, Marcus Chong, Gloria Foster, Julian Arahanga, Matt Doran, Belinda McClory, Ray Anthony Parker, Paul Goddard, Robert Taylor

> According to Exhibitor Relations (the people who track these things), *The Matrix* was the biggest Easter opener of all time. It brought in $27,788,331 that weekend.
>
> Another little goody. Supposedly, "the Studio" really wasn't all that excited about the movie and its budget until the directors showed them the first 10 minutes. The first 10 minutes absolutely kicks ass.

THE STORY

Thomas A. Anderson (Keanu Reeves) leads a double life. By day, he's a white-bread software programmer. By night, he spends his time as "Neo," burned-out computer hacker. And it's in his Neo life that he finds out that reality just ain't what it used to be.

Neo is perplexed by a question: "What is the Matrix?" Three "Agents" who might know the answer want to use Neo to crush a resistance group they consider to be subversive and highly dangerous. Meanwhile, Morpheus (Laurence Fishburne) and his team are seeking Neo to help find the answer to *that* question and defeat the powerful, deadly Agents. After The Oracle ordained it to be so, Morpheus believes that Neo is The One who'll save the human race from extinction by the Agents. But does Neo believe in himself?

THE UPSHOT

Though *The Matrix* has been dismissed by some as "New Age spiritual babbling chop-socky," I've always accepted it as it is: pure nads-out fun, with Mondo Cool special effects, great stunts, all the action any testosterone-driven male could ask for, with a lil' sum'n sum'n for us chicks as well. And what can you say about the special effects that hasn't already been said time and again? Not much, except "wow, they're neat."

I'll grant the naysayers that there are a few aspects of this film that, in different hands, would put it in the yellow-light realm—not the least of which is its tendency toward a mumble-jumble of touchy-feely quasi-religion. Other gripes I've heard before are in regards to its pseudo sci-fi and paeans to John "Shoot Everything in Sight" Woo. Truthfully though, the sci-fi stuff whizzed right past me; I found it to be the most boring part of the flick. Well, not "boring," exactly, but certainly not what I was there to see. Nope, in spite of myself and my Cultured Upbringing, I grooved on the gunplay, on the special effects, and most of all, on the "chop-socky." As a bona fide "VirtualFighter" addict, I howled when Neo speed-learned "drunken fighter" style.

One thing that I've *not* heard any real complaints about was the cast involved; all of the major actors seem to fit their roles to a T, even (surprisingly) Reeves himself. Say what you like about the beach boy, but his oft-snickered-at "whoa" only emphasized how *perfect* he was for this role. The almost always excellent Fishburne (we'll forgive him for *Event Horizon*, eh?), and the equally brilliant Pantoliano could recite the alphabet and I'd show up to watch them.

As for the bad guys, Agents Brown and Jones were pretty much straight men for the menacing Agent Smith, played to the hilt by the Aussie actor Hugo Weaving.

BAMMER'S BOTTOM LINE
Hardcore sci-fi folks probably won't take it under their wing, but *The Matrix* had a little something for everyone else to enjoy; certainly I look forward to the sequels. Now if I could only find those damned red pills . . .

GREEN LIGHT

Bams Miss Congeniality
(2000)

RATED PG-13; running time 110 minutes
GENRE: Comedy/Action
WRITTEN BY: Katie Ford, Marc Lawrence, Caryn Lucas
DIRECTED BY: Donald Petrie
CAST: Sandra Bullock, Benjamin Bratt, Michael Caine, Candice Bergen, William Shatner, Ernie Hudson, Wendy Raquel Robinson, Heather Burns, Melissa De Sousa, Diedre Quinn, Asia De Marcos, Steve Monroe

> Rent *Demolition Man* and catch Sandra Bullock and Benjamin Bratt as futuristic cops.

THE STORY
From the time she was a young girl growing up in New Jersey, Gracie Hart (Sandra Bullock) was what's commonly referred to as a "tomboy." Young Gracie felt she had an obligation to protect and serve those who couldn't do so for themselves. Naturally, that obligation led her to become an FBI agent, under no-nonsense supervisor McDonald (Ernie Hudson), who was wary of Hart's hard-edged, gung-ho tactics. His wariness was borne out when rough-and-tumble Hart went against his orders, endangering the lives of fellow FBI agents, including handsomely rugged Eric Matthews (Benjamin Bratt); because of this, McDonald makes Hart cool her jets at her desk.

But when Matthews gets assigned to run his own Ops in pursuit of the terrorist known as the

Citizen, Matthews convinces McDonald to let Hart be used as bait when they learn of the Citizen's next target: the Miss United States Beauty Pageant. Excuse me, I meant "Scholarship Contest." Or so says Cathy Morningside (Candice Bergen), pageant . . . er, contest sponsor, aging ex–beauty queen, and co-host along with the equally aging Stan Fields (William Shatner). The idea is for Gracie to be planted in the contest as Miss New Jersey, alongside fellow contestants. One problem: *this* Miss New Jersey is a slob. Enter Victor Melling (Michael Caine), a pageant consultant with issues.

THE UPSHOT

After being completely underwhelmed by Sandra "Speed" Bullock in forgettable flick-lites such as *Speed 2*, *28 Days*, and the completely unentertaining *The Net*, I figured *Miss Congeniality* would be a total bust. No one was more surprised than I was to hear myself laughing throughout the movie— and at appropriate times, no less! Sandra Bullock was a delight to watch from start to finish. Not since *Speed* has she seemed so Lucille Ball-esque in her mix of roughneck charm and physical humor, blended with a natural beauty that shined even under all the grit.

But contrary to the views of some of my fellow critics, Bullock didn't have to carry this flick alone. She was ably assisted by the almost always brilliant Michael Caine as disgruntled diva-maker Victor Melling, who was flat-out hilarious in yet another good role. The quick-wit sparring between Bullock and Caine was as good a bit of acting, editing, and writing as I've seen in any mainstream comedy in some time. Add Candice Bergen to the mix as an acerbically funny

ex–beauty queen, and Benjamin Bratt as the obligatory stud, and you have a recipe for a purty darn good flick.

Strangely enough, William Shatner's campy pageant queen, Stan Fields, did nothing for me. I went in expecting Shatner to chew up scenery in classic Captain-Kirk-with-a-twist mode, but he fell flat. In fact, other than the need for having a separate groomsman and show host, Shatner's Fields was an unnecessary duplication of efforts; Caine could've more than ably handled playing the host.

THE BLACK FACTOR

The Diva and I often talk about Spot in our reviews—you know, that one Black person that you *know* was included as Diversity Filler, just to show that the lead character has Black friends, too. The Black pageant entrants in *Miss Congeniality*—Miss California (Wendy Raquel Robinson) and Miss New York (Melissa De Sousa, late of *The Best Man*)— showed no signs of Spottage; they looked and acted like they belonged right where they were.

And speaking of De Sousa, look for a funny spotlight on her late in the movie. By that time, I thought all the laughs were over. I was, fortunately, wrong again.

BAMMER'S BOTTOM LINE

Miss Congeniality brought out the humorous best in Sandra Bullock, Michael Caine, and Candice Bergen. I'm no fan of beauty cattle calls . . . er, I mean, pageants . . . but the chicks of *Miss Conge-*

niality made the fictional Miss United States Scholarship Contest a winner.

GREEN LIGHT

The Mummy Returns
the Diva
(2001)

RATED PG-13; running time 130 minutes
GENRE: Adventure
WRITTEN BY: Stephen Sommers
DIRECTED BY: Stephen Sommers
CAST: Brendan Fraser, Rachel Weisz, John Hannah, Arnold Vosloo, Patricia Velasquez, Freddie Boath, Alun Armstrong, The Rock

It was reported that more cliffs had to be digitally added to the tidal wave scene in order to cover up all the spectators who were watching the filming.

THE DIGEST
Over 5,000 years ago, there was a fierce Egyptian warrior named the Scorpion King (The Rock). He was barreling across the land for seven years, taking out anyone who stood in his way, until he was finally defeated. He and his remaining troops retreated and began their long trek across the desert back home, but the elements proved too much for them, and one by one, they perished, leaving the Scorpion King to fend for himself. Facing death, he made a deal to the God Anubis: if he could return and vanquish those that had sent him across the harsh land, he would relinquish his soul to Anubis. Anubis agreed on the condition that the Scorpion King lead Anubis's army.

Fast-forward to the 20th century. Nine fictional years have passed since the first movie, *The Mummy*, and Ric (Fraser) and Evie (Weisz)—whom we last saw trying to save the world by doing away with the dreaded (and mummified) Evil Priest, Imotep—are still very passionate about Egypt. They're also passionate about their son, Alex (Freddie Boath). Evie has been having some bizarre dreams as of late, dreams that have caused her to drag her family back to Egypt and into the various tombs of the dead. Unfortunately, they are not alone.

A mysterious woman that has an uncanny resemblance to Anck-Su-Namun is in the process of digging for the remains of Imhotep. But there is a kink in the process—Evie and her family, who have secured the bracelet of the Scorpion King, which she needs to bring Imhotep back to life. With that, Imhotep will be able to control the army of Anubis and rule the world with Anck-Su-Namun by his side. Anck-Su-Namun takes the one thing Evie would die for, her son, in order to coerce Evie and Ric to turn over the bracelet. How can Evie get her precious Alex back and prevent the destruction of Earth?

THE DISH
Even though there were plot holes big enough to drive a truck through, the special effects kicked major butt. The special effects and the fight scenes made me forgive all the other shortcomings. Word of caution: There is a lot of kissy-face in this movie and I think some kids may, as a result, find parts of the movie a bit boring.

THE BLACK FACTOR
Let me get right to the point: The two people who wanted to kill a child were Black men, and the buffoon was a Black man. I'll just let y'all contemplate that.

THE DIRECTIVE
The Mummy has returned and with a vengeance. Make sure you're there to see him make a mess of Egypt.

GREEN LIGHT

Ocean's 11
(2001)

RATED PG-13; running time 120 minutes
GENRE: Action/Thriller/Crime
WRITTEN BY: Ted Griffin, based on the 1960 screenplay by Harry Brown and Charles Lederer
DIRECTED BY: Steven Soderbergh
CAST: George Clooney, Brad Pitt, Julia Roberts, Casey Affleck, Scott Caan, Don Cheadle, Matt Damon, Andy Garcia, Elliott Gould, Carl Reiner, Shaobo Qin, Eddie Jemison, Bernie Mac

THE DIGEST
Danny Ocean (George Clooney) has just been released from prison and is ready to be a good citizen, or so he told the New Jersey parole board. Yet, Danny isn't out more than a day when he is trying to assemble a crew to hit a casino vault. Not just any casino, mind you, but Las Vegas' Bellagio Hotel's vault, which holds all the money for the MGM Grand, the Mirage, and the Bellagio, the value of which can balloon to $170 million on a night when there is a boxing match in town. So this is Danny's plan: to hit on the night of a big boxing match. But to be successful he has to have the best team and assembles one that includes Rusty Ryan (Brad Pitt), Reuben Tishkoff (Elliot Gould), Frank Catton (Bernie Mac), Linus Caldwell (Matt Damon), Basher Tarr (Don Cheadle), Saul Bloom (Carl Reiner), and Turk and Virgil Malloy (Scott Caan and Casey Affleck). To complicate matters, the Bellagio is run by Terry Benedict (Andy Garcia), the love interest of Danny's ex-wife Tess (Julia Roberts).

So now, Danny has the best of the best. Can the best do it? It's not enough to be able to commit the crime, they have to trust each other and trust that they will all be smart enough not to get caught after the fact.

THE DISH
I just love it when a "smart" film comes along—one that will make you laugh without resorting to bathroom humor, one that keeps you engaged, interested, and wanting more. *Ocean's 11* was all of this and more. It was sort of a throwback to older movies where the characters relied on the brains, good looks, and luck, not their guns. Heck, there was almost zero violence in this movie and absolutely no blood or gore.

I also love it when an ensemble piece works.

The entire cast worked well together. A good share of the credit for this has to go to Steven Soderbergh. His portfolio is filling to the rim with movies that star several high-profile actors and actresses, and each time I've walked away without a sour taste in my mouth. It's apparent that he has a gift for massaging egos and getting the best out of his cast and crew.

In my opinion, there were two stars of this film—Brad Pitt and the state-of-the-art vault. I'm trying very hard to not make any comparisons to the 1960 original, but Pitt was the Dean Martin to George Clooney's Frank Sinatra. Frank was always kinda of serious while Dean Martin was a smart-ass. I loved the chemistry between the two of them. The chemistry between Pitt and Clooney works nicely here as well.

Speaking of chemistry, Julia Roberts and George Clooney set the screen a-smolderin'. (Right about now, I'm ready to sell my mama in order to trade places with Julia. I just want one tiny little kiss. That's all I ask.)

THE BLACK FACTOR
There is a scene where Bernie Mac plays "the race card." Now, I understand it was done to create a diversion. And it was a funny scene. But it still bothered me, because a Black man fails to take responsibility for his behavior and his actions, and instead blames "The Man" for all that is wrong in his life and world. I know that *most* white folks get that this is just a characterization. But, I'm also here to tell you that quite a few don't get it.

THE DIRECTIVE
Ocean's 11 was a sea of good times. (Okay, that was corny . . .)

GREEN LIGHT

the Diva Pearl Harbor
(2001)

RATED PG-13; running time 183 minutes and 17 long-ass seconds
GENRE: Drama/War/Romance
WRITTEN BY: Randall Wallace
DIRECTED BY: Michael Bay
CAST: Ben Affleck, Josh Hartnett, Kate Beckinsale, William Lee Scott, Alec Baldwin, Cuba Gooding Jr., Jon Voight, Mako, Ewen Bremner

Ben Affleck and some cast members took pay cuts to keep the movie within its $135-million-dollar budget. Some of those actor folks get paid too much anyway!

THE DIGEST
Rafe (Ben Affleck) and Danny (Josh Hartnett) have been best friends since they were young boys in Tennessee. The boys learned how to fly using Rafe's father's crop-dusting plane. Now it's 1941 and they are serving in an Army that is just on the brink of war. The United States has not gotten directly involved in the

war going on in Europe, other than to send trained pilots to England to help out the British Royal Air Force, but it's only a matter of time.

Rafe, who lives for flying, volunteers to go to the Continent. This devastates Danny who has always been protected and guided by Rafe. Then there's Evelyn (Kate Beckinsale): a dedicated army nurse, and the love of Rafe's life.

After Rafe leaves, Danny, Evelyn, and their friends are stationed in Pearl Harbor, a paradise surrounded by clear and warm blue water. Everyone is having a good time except for Danny and Evelyn. They both miss Rafe desperately. Rafe and Evelyn write to each other every day and try to keep their spirits up, while Danny, who has always been shy and unsure of himself, throws himself into his work. Eventually, Danny and Evelyn begin a fragile relationship that comes to a screeching halt on December 7, 1941, when the entire population of Pearl Harbor loses its innocence and the United States is thrust into World War II.

THE DISH

I gotta tell y'all that I'm still in awe of the attack on Pearl Harbor. It was very difficult watching it, and not because it was especially gory—because it wasn't—but because we didn't have a clue that we were about to be attacked, and we got our butts kicked. Plus, we all have/had someone in our family who served in WWII and it hits you to see the loss of life.

Now on to the problems I had with the film. It didn't flow evenly, which is a *big* problem when you have to sit for three hours. This script lost momentum about every 30-40 minutes and then would pick up after 10 minutes. Because of the

screeching halts, this is a good movie when it could have been a great one.

THE BLACK FACTOR

Let's talk about Dorie Miller for a moment. His role in the movie wasn't as significant as his role in real life. Dorie Miller was an African-American and a Navy mess attendant. Given that this was 1941, he could not aspire to be more than a cook. He was stationed on the *USS West Virginia* when it was struck by Japanese planes and bombs. He wasn't trained to use weaponry, yet he managed to shoot down two Japanese planes as well as save the captain of his ship. Dorie was awarded the Navy Cross, and was the first African-American to be given this award.

Despite this great accomplishment, the Dorie Miller in this movie, prior to the attacks, was reduced to that of basically a butler trying hard to impress all the white men on his ship by becoming the boxing champ and running around behind the captain desperately wanting his praise. While it was nice to remember him and include him in the movie, it was a disservice to reduce him to no more than the captain's "boy."

THE DIRECTIVE

Pearl Harbor feels like it's five hours long. The actual war wasn't this damn long.

YELLOW LIGHT

The Perfect Storm

(2000)

RATED PG-13; running time 135 minutes
GENRE: Action/Drama
WRITTEN BY: William D. Wittliff (based on the book by Sebastian Junger)
DIRECTED BY: Wolfgang Petersen
CAST: George Clooney, Mark Wahlberg, Diane Lane, John C. Reilly, William Fichtner, John Hawkes, Mary Elizabeth Mastrantonio, Michael Ironside, Allen Payne, Janet Wright, Karen Allen

> The "real" Linda Greenlaw—Mary Elizabeth Mastrantonio's (Lord, woman, will you get a shorter name?) character—had issues with a few of the scenes. She pointed out how it would be impossible to stand, much less walk and climb, up a boom during a force-12 storm. And further, how did the torch stay lit? Amen, Girlfriend, Amen.

THE DIGEST

This movie is about the *Andrea Gail*, a fishing ship and its crew. Billy Tyne (George Clooney) is the captain, Bobby (Mark Wahlberg), Murph, Bugsy, Alfred Pierre, and Sully are the crew. Capt. Tyne is under pressure to bring in a big haul. His last few catches have been poor with barely any profit. Because of this he goes about 300 miles further out to sea than he should. It pays off because he's able to fill his cargo hold to the rim. Unbeknownst to him and the crew, however, a catastrophic weather event is occurring while they are way out to sea. Three different weather fronts are converging on one spot. This will create what is called a perfect storm: Thirty- to fifty-foot waves, a hurricane, winds up to 150 miles per hour, and the *Andrea Gail* is right in the middle of it.

THE DISH

Between this movie and *Chicken Run*, I'm going to be reduced to eating twigs and leaves. I'll tell you what; I had no desire to see how fish are handled. Blech. Then again, that was about the most interesting thing in the whole movie. I swear to y'all that I wrote down "Extremely SLOW!" in my notes at 7:54 and the movie started at 7:40. At more than one point, I was hoping a tsunami would hit me instead of them.

The special effects of the waves were pretty cool and the acting was okay, but this movie would have been a lot more enjoyable if they had gotten rid of the subplots. One subplot had three people stuck in the storm on a sailboat. One woman kept telling the boat's owner that they were in danger, but all he could think about was his boat. Well you know what? Let his ass sink with the boat. Another subplot was the rescue of the rescuers. Boring.

By the way, Karen Allen (Mariam from *Raiders of the Lost Ark*) was one of the women in one of the subplots. It was nice seeing her working again, but Karen, honey, listen to me. Use sunscreen, girl. From now on both you and Mary Elizabeth Mastrantonio should wear SPF-40 and a wide-brim hat.

I'm not cold-hearted; I was saddened by the events at the end of the movie. But other than that, I could have stayed home and watched the *Monkees* movie on VH-1.

THE BLACK FACTOR

There was one Black person in this entire town, a French Canadian named Alfred Pierre (Allen Payne). He spent the first half of the movie lip-locked to a blonde. When they weren't kissing, they were the town joke because they made the ceiling above the local bar shake when they were, uh, intimate. Nice. A Black man is the town joke because of his sexual prowess. Whatever. Other than that, he might as well have not been around. He was always on the fringe.

THE DIRECTIVE

More like "The Perfect Bore." Catch it on HBO.

YELLOW LIGHT

 Planet of the Apes
(2001)

RATED PG-13; running time 117 minutes
GENRE: Science fiction
WRITTEN BY: William Broyles Jr. and Lawrence Konner & Mark Rosenthal. Based on a novel by Pierre Boulle
DIRECTED BY: Tim Burton
CAST: Mark Wahlberg, Tim Roth, Helena Bonham Carter, Michael Clarke Duncan, Paul Giamatti, Estella Warren, and Cary-Hiroyuki Tagawa

THE DIGEST

In 2029, Captain Leo Davidson (Mark Wahlberg) is above Earth in a medical research space station. Rather than flying, he is unhappily spending his time training chimpanzees to fly space pods, so that if the crew comes across something dangerous, they can send a monkey-piloted pod rather than risk the life of a human. When the monkey he has been training is sent to investigate what appears to be a magnetic cloud, and gets lost, Leo defies orders and goes after the monkey. Now lost himself, Leo struggles to keep his space pod together and manages to crash-land in a swamp. He is barely on land when he looks up and sees some primitive-looking humans running from apes. But these are not ordinary apes. These apes ride horses and talk.

Leo is captured with several other humans and is sold into slavery. He catches the attention of three apes. Thade (Tim Roth) is a psycho chimp who leads the military and Attar (Michael Clarke Duncan) is his right-hand man . . . er, gorilla. Thade hates all things human. He hopes to be able to round them up from their villages and kill them all, and Attar is happy to help. Ari (Helena Bonham Carter) is a human-rights activist. She wants an equal yet separate existence. Thade will hear nothing of the sort. Even his love for Ari is not enough to convince him that the humans should be treated um . . . humanely.

Once Ari meets Leo, she is further convinced that she must save the humans. She helps Leo and several other slaves escape. She knows her actions will cause her to lose Leo. But to Ari it's all worth it in the end, because humans and apes just may be able to coexist.

THE DISH

This is one of the worse scripts I've come across in a while. The story itself wasn't that bad, but the dialogue pretty much sucked. However, I still liked almost every minute of this movie. It's low on plot, but high on special effects. And let me tell you, those special effects were something else. I was completely enthralled. The way the primates moved was amazing. So amazing, that I was able to forget about the bad dialogue and just enjoy myself.

In my opinion, the key to enjoying this movie is to visualize the apes as human. If you think of them as human, then some of the stuff they do and say will not seem so weird. But any way you cut it, the tribal humans seemed to be a bit of a waste to me. Other than helping to fight the apes, they seemed rather pointless. This movie was clearly about Leo, Thade, and Ari. Everything else was scene-filler and bra-filler . . . if you know what I mean.

Those of you who have seen the original will appreciate the references made to it in this updated version. You should also appreciate the twist at the end. I have purposely not discussed the racial implications of the various primates/gorillas, their skin color, and level of violence. This has been rehashed and discussed for over 30 years. I can't add anything new or different.

THE DIRECTIVE

Planet of the Apes rocked my world. But don't expect any nontechnical Oscar-worthy performances or writing.

GREEN LIGHT

We are convinced that The Diva is the only one on the planet that liked this movie. She was probably having flashbacks from Mark Wahlberg's Calvin Klein ad and got the two confused. Now if she had managed to remember Marky Mark and the Funky Bunch, she might have sided with everyone else.

And one more note: The Diva would like to give a special award to Estelle Warren for managing to find a Wonderbra on another planet. A planet run by non-bra-wearing apes. Now *that* is resourcefulness.

the Diva

Spider-Man
(2002)

RATED PG-13; running time 121 minutes
GENRE: Action
WRITTEN BY: David Koepp, based on the comic book by Stan Lee and Steve Ditko
DIRECTED BY: Sam Raimi
CAST: Tobey Maguire, Willem Dafoe, Kirsten Dunst, James Franco, J.K. Simmons, Rosemary Harris, Cliff Robertson

THE DIGEST

High school senior Peter Parker (Tobey Maguire) is a shy geek who is picked on by all of the jocks. To make matters worse he is in love with a girl he can't have, Mary Jane Watson (Kirsten Dunst). Mary Jane has been his neighbor since he was six, but she has never seen him as anything more than just the boy next door. Despite all of this, Peter is content. He lives with his elderly Aunt May and Uncle Ben both of whom he loves to death. He also has a best friend in Harry Osborn (James Franco), a filthy rich young man who longs for acceptance from his father, Norman (Willem Dafoe). But Peter's world drastically changes while on a school trip to a science lab.

At this lab, scientists are genetically altering the DNA of spiders. They have taken a different trait from 3 different spiders and created 15 super spiders. The super spider has enormous strength; can leap and jump from amazing heights; has a super strong web; and has the gift of foresight. One of the super spiders gets out and bites Peter on the hand. Overnight, the spider's DNA meshes with Peter's and Spider-Man is born.

Meanwhile, on the other side of town, scientist Norman Osborn, Harry's father, is struggling to keep his government project funded. Desperate, he tries the formula on himself and it causes his personality to split into two—the normal Osborn, and a downright mean and nasty Osborn. With a jet-powered scooter, a green flight suit, and nasty little spheres that hurt people, the Green Goblin emerges and begins to terrorize the city of New York.

Can Peter put his fear and reluctance behind him and stop the Green Goblin or will the citizens of New York perish?

THE DISH

Hot damn! Boy, did I have fun watching this movie. More fun than I've had in a long time. Plot? We don't need no stinkin' plot! It met my expectations across the board. I wanted to be wowed by special effects, to stare at the screen and drool, to laugh and smile—not think. And I did just that.

I've never really read the comic books, but I knew enough about Spider-Man to visualize what it should be like and I could find very little to fault. Tobey Maguire was born to be Spidey. Heck, everyone was cast just perfect and I wouldn't have picked any other actors. Next to Maguire, J.K. Simmons as J. Jonah Jameson and Dafoe as the Green Goblin were the best casting choices.

Between the pacing of the story, Danny Elfman's sweeping soundtrack, and Spidey zooming through New York, the movie had it all. The audience was able to identify with Spidey. And the side effects are so successful, you feel as if you're climbing buildings and swinging through downtown Manhattan.

Sometimes the acting was just way over the top to the point where it was downright corny, luckily that happened rarely. The constant theme and dialogue about being a man almost alienated me, a Diva. I got it the first time, I didn't need to hear it 50 different ways from 50 different people. But beyond that, it was a great treat and well worth the wait.

THE DIRECTIVE

See this movie. Both you and your kids will love *Spider-Man.* There is some cartoonish violence, some sensuality, and 2 or 3 curse words, so I'll leave it up to you. If you can stand a little cheese and a little fluff, there is no reason for you to pass this one up.

GREEN LIGHT

Star Wars: Episode II— Attack of the Clones
the Diva
(2002)

RATED PG; running time 138 minutes
GENRE: Science Fiction/Action
WRITTEN BY: George Lucas
DIRECTED BY: George Lucas
CAST: Ewan McGregor, Natalie Portman, Hayden Christensen, Christopher Lee, Ian McDiarmid, Samuel L. Jackson, Jimmy Smits, Pernilla August, Frank Oz, Ahmed Best, Kenny Baker, Anthony Daniels

THE DIGEST

Before telling you about this installment, I think I owe it to you not to assume that you have seen the previous episodes and explain them a bit. Loosely, in 1977 a movie called *Star Wars: A New Hope—Episode 4* was released. It was a coming-of-age story centered on the fight between good and evil.

In the "Good" category:

- Luke Skywalker, a young man raised by his aunt and uncle who wants nothing more than to go to flight school.
- Obi-Wan Kenobi, a mysterious old man with a mysterious power called "the Force." He is one of the only two remaining good Jedi Masters.
- Princess Leia Organa who has asked Obi-Wan to help her and the rebels fight against the oppressive rule of the evil empire.
- Han Solo who is a two-bit smuggler and his pal Chewbacca, plus two droids—C3PO and R2D2.

In the "Evil" category:

- The emperor, who also has the Force and was a former good Jedi. His power is stronger then Obi-Wan's.
- Darth Vader. The emperor's main enforcer. He too is a former good Jedi with a very strong connection with the Force. He makes sure that the emperor's plans are executed.

Star Wars ends with Luke, Leia, and the others in a huge space battle in which the evil-built and run Death Star—a space station the size of a planet that can blow up any planet in the galaxy—is destroyed, and Darth Vader and his spacecraft are sent swirling into space, leaving room for a sequel.

In 1981, *Star Wars: Episode V—The Empire Strikes Back* is released. The rebel alliance has enjoyed little peace. They are hiding from the evil galactic empire on the ice planet of Hoth. While Leia, with the help of Han Solo, is trying to plan the next move for the alliance, Luke is off to train with Yoda—the last of the good Jedi (the last physically alive, at least) and a Jedi Master who wishes to train Luke to become a Jedi. Yoda and Obi-Wan have determined that Luke has "the Force" just like they do, and just like Darth Vader does. While he is training, Leia and Han get into trouble. Bad debts have followed Han and he is captured by a bounty hunter and sold. Meanwhile, Leia is once again in the clutches of Darth Vader. Luke decides to go help Leia, which is risky because he hasn't finished his training. He rescues Leia and ends up going toe-to-toe with Darth Vader. During this battle Luke loses an arm, and gains some disturbing news about his family tree. Now Leia rescues him and they escape. They vow to find Han Solo and help crush the evil empire once and for all.

In 1983, *Star Wars: Episode VI—Return of the Jedi* is released. Leia has found Han and is trying to rescue him, when she herself is captured. Luke, now the last Jedi in the entire galaxy, rescues them and they go forth with their plans to destroy the evil empire. They land on a planet inhibited by furry little creatures called Ewoks. With the help of the Ewoks, they manage to turn off the shield that protects the new Death Star, and enable the rebel alliance to destroy it. Meanwhile, Luke once again faces Darth Vader, but this time his skills are stronger and he gets the upper hand. Darth and the Emperor are stopped and the alliance is freed.

In 1999, *Star Wars: Episode I—The Phantom Menace* is released. This movie takes us back in time, charting the origin of Anakin Skywalker and Queen Padmé Amidala—Luke's parents. It is revealed that the Trade Federation began what later became the evil empire. They are led by Darth Sidious, a person no one has ever seen, but who is clearly in control. We are given hints that it is, in fact, Senator Palpatine who is Darth Sidious, and it is he who becomes the Emperor whom we meet in the original trilogy. The unsuspecting senators of all of the planets of the galaxy don't know that they are being manipulated, and with each passing year give him more power. Even though a young Obi-Wan is able to defeat Darth Sidious's henchman, Darth Maul, the innocent people of the galaxy are in trouble—they just don't know how much yet. Even the discovery of young Anakin Skywalker, who at 8 shows exceptional talent, can't save them.

Now we are up to the current movie.

About 10 years have passed and young Anakin (Hayden Christiansen) has grown into a fine young man with a powerful connection to the Force. Even his master, Obi-Wan, is a bit in awe of Anakin's potential, but first Anakin must learn discipline. He will never become a true Jedi if he doesn't chill out and be patient. Meanwhile, Amidala (Natalie Portman) who is now a senator, has come to the planet to vote on an important matter. While there, two attempts have been made on her life and Jedi masters, Mace Windu (Samuel L. Jackson) and Yoda (voice by Frank Oz) decide to assign a still-smitten Anakin to watch over her.

While Anakin and Amidala are playing house, Obi-Wan (Ewen McGregor) is investigating the assassination attempts. He goes to a faraway planet and discovers that an outlawed Jedi,

Count Dooku, (Christopher Lee) has enlisted the aid of a bounty hunter named Jango Fett (Boba Fett from the first 3 movies is his son) to build cloned warriors to be used for sinister plans.

Obi-Wan and the Jedi Council know they alone cannot defend the Republic and again give more control to Senator Palpatine, all the while not knowing that he is still manipulating them. Still safe on the planet of Naboo, Anakin and Amidala are falling in love. They haven't a care in the world until Anakin begins to sense something is wrong with his mother. What he discovers pushes him over the edge and he takes one step closer to the dark side.

THE DISH

Damn it, I don't want mushy dialogue and kissing in my *Star Wars*! I thought I was watching *Romeo and Juliet*. I believe I understand what Lucas was trying to accomplish. I think he was trying to show us that Darth Vader really was human once, and that he was capable of more than just evil. Okay—but did he have to prove it by having him utter some of the most inane lines, in the middle of a galactic upheaval, nonetheless? And I must admit that it felt creepy to watch Anakin checking Amidala out like she was a tramp from Mos Eisley.

I *love* the *Star Wars* series and always have, so I understand it, believe me, I do. I just was not feeling this one at all. One thing I'm finding increasingly more difficult to understand is the business with the Trade Federation and why Amidala is on a hit list. She hasn't done anything yet to warrant getting iced, and the whole Trade Federation bit is just murky to me. Lucas will clear it up in the next one. And he has a *lot* of ground to cover in the next, by the way. If you watch the first three movies, you'll know that the next movie is going to either have to be four hours long, or some stuff is going to have to get skipped.

Hayden Christensen didn't do it for me. He was cute and his fight scenes rocked, but he seemed to show too much emotion. He was generally over the top. That was a tad annoying. It was cool seeing Samuel Jackson, with more screen time—and this time he does a much better job of it. He seems to be more comfortable and less in awe over the fact that he has an action figure in the toy store now. Yoda kicked butt—big time.

The scenery was phenomenal. Someone spent a lot of time with the details of the buildings and the atmosphere of each planet. That aspect of the movie left me speechless. I also have to give Lucas props for his mission to show diversity on the screen. I was very pleased with the representation of people of color. Yes, Jar-Jar is back and I hate him even more, but beyond him, I have no new complaints. It's clear that he tried to include everyone.

THE DIRECTIVE

Attack of the mildly engaging plot. I can boil it down to being a cheesy love story taking place in the middle of political upheaval, but the last 45 minutes made it worth every penny. If you're a *Star Wars* fan, you'll want to watch this more than once—so why don't you go ahead and buy the DVD.

GREEN LIGHT

The World Is Not Enough
(1999)

RATED PG-13; running time 105 minutes

GENRE: Action

WRITTEN BY: Neal Purvis, Robert Wade and Bruce Feirstein

DIRECTED BY: Michael Apted

CAST: Pierce Brosnan, Sophie Marceau, Robert Carlyle, Judi Dench, Denise Richards, Samantha Bond, Robbie Coltrane, Desmond Llewelyn, John Cleese, Ulrich Thomsen, Colin Salmon

> Pierce Brosnan—who was born to play Bond—was unable to get out of his *Remington Steele* contract way back when, so we got stuck with Timothy Dalton (*The Living Daylights* and *License to Kill*). We're sure that Mr. Dalton is a nice guy, but he's not high on our list of Favorite Bonds.

THE STORY

The gang's all here—James Bond (Brosnan), M (Dench), Q (Llewelyn) and his new assistant R (Cleese), and Moneypenny (S. Bond)—and they're called on, once again, to save the day, this time, from the ruthless Renard (Carlyle), a kidnapper of oil heiress Elektra King (Marceau).

Renard begins sabotaging the oilfields, so of course Bond has to stop him. Over the course of his investigation, he finds out that Renard has taken an interest in a nuclear disarmament site run by Dr. Christmas Jones (Denise Richards). He goes to check it out and discovers that Renard has stolen some plutonium. Bond must, once again, save the planet, and the only one who can help him is Dr. Jones.

THE UPSHOT

Wow, *that* stunk.

Okay, okay, I'll be fair; anyone who goes to see a Bond (James Bond) movie must equip themselves with three things: one, a tolerance for *extremely* (and purposely) bad puns; two, the willingness to play along with the notion that (wink, wink) the Bond Babes are chosen for something other than their ability to fill their D-cups; and three, the belief that 007 could run/jump/fly/swim/crawl through all sorts of impossible situations and come out with not much more than a broken nail or sprained shoulder—which will be perfectly healed after he, in the tradition of his alter-ego James T. Kirk, beds down every Babe in the flick. Because, mon frere, the hallmark of Bond flicks is that they are filled to the brim with all three. And ya know what? I can diggit. But somewhere down that 19-flicks-in-the-series road, that indescribable Thing that is Bond has become tarnished, leaving in its wake the same ol' same ol'.

Maybe it's because so many other action flicks, good and bad, have raised the bar in one way or another; *Die Hard*, *Speed*, *The Matrix*, and others, have made life after the Cold War a not-so-welcome place for straight-out movie spydom, and without the swaggering, authoritative confidence of a Sean Connery (who Brosnan himself has acknowledged as being *the* Man), or the wink-and-a-smile playfulness, which Roger Moore brought to the fore in his go-round as 007, current-day Bond is left with gadgets, gizmos, and falling-flat puns. And Q's famous gadgets and gizmos were all but absent, so . . .

"Well," I hear ya sayin', "were the Bond Babes any good, at least?" Hate to break it to ya, bub, but—nope. Marceau brought a been-there-done-that feeling to the screen with a bad impersonation of Fatima Blush (Barbara Carrera) in Sean Connery's last 007 movie, *Never Say Never Again;* and if Christmas Jones (Richards) is believable as a Nooclear Scientist, then I'm a bald Scotsman with a heavy brogue.

So, was there *anything* salvageable about *The World?* Yeah, I guess; Brosnan's not hard on the eyes, and he's game enough, though he (like most of the rest of the cast) seemed to be sleepwalking his way to the bank. But sooner or later, Bond (James Bond) will have to face the fact that a cute grin and a throwaway tagline Is Not Enou . . . well, you know the rest.

THE BLACK FACTOR
Not much to go with here; I hear tell that agent Charles Robinson (Colin Salmon) has been present in a couple of Brosnan's 007 movies, but from what we saw of him here, I'd take Bernie Casey as Felix Lighter (as he was in *Never Say Never Again*) any day.

BAMMER'S BOTTOM LINE
Pierce Brosnan is, arguably, the best Bond (James Bond) to come down the pike since Sean Connery. But you don't make it to 19 of anything be-fore the freshness wears off. Perhaps, as with *Star Trek,* somebody should say, "Actually, it *is* enough."

YELLOW LIGHT

Bams Unbreakable
(2000)

RATED PG-13; running time 115 minutes
GENRE: Thriller
WRITTEN BY: M. Night Shyamalan
DIRECTED BY: M. Night Shyamalan
CAST: Bruce Willis, Samuel L. Jackson, Robin Wright Penn, Spencer Treat Clark, Charlayn Woodward

> M. Night Shyamalan once again used Philly as the backdrop for one of his films. He apparently loves his hometown.

THE STORY
Security guard David Dunne (Bruce Willis) is living a broken life. Detached from his wife, Audrey (Robin Wright Penn), seen as something he doesn't believe himself to be by his son, Joseph, and unsatisfied with his life in Philadelphia, David plans to move to New York to start afresh. His plans change, however, when the train that he's a passenger on, derails—and not only is he the sole survivor, he also escapes the accident completely untouched, *physically* untouched, that is.

Elijah Price (Samuel L. Jackson) too is, quite literally, a broken man. Elijah suffers from a birth defect that makes his bones brittle. When neighborhood kids bully him into becoming a hermit in his own home, his mother (Charlayne Woodward) challenges him to not be afraid, offering him a special gift each time he conquers his fears. From that, Elijah takes comfort in the world of comic books, especially those dealing with mythical, superheroic characters. David's life becomes connected to Elijah's in ways David never imagined—and he finds himself believing the unbelievable.

THE UPSHOT

This movie belonged to three people: stars Bruce Willis and Samuel L. Jackson, and writer-director M. Night Shyamalan.

Willis reprises the sensibility toward his character that he had in *The Sixth Sense*, again playing a quiet, confused, world-weary character who has something bubbling just below the surface. Jackson, effusive and commanding as always, provides just that something as the brittle Elijah. The physical manifestations of these characters—David as the strong and silent type, Elijah as a man as fragile as glass—belie their true nature; and in his portrayal of Elijah's inner self, Jackson especially lives up to his powerhouse acting reputation.

Robin Wright Penn was adequate as David's estranged wife, Audrey, though she and Spencer Treat Clark, as their son, Joseph, shared quite a thrilling scene when Joseph, believing his father to be invincible, decides to test just how invincible good old dad might be. I was very surprised to note that the audience I was in *laughed* during this taut scene.

I'm trying to figure out whether that laughter only served to mask our stress and its subsequent relief. I *know* our stunned silence, and near-refusal to leave at the end, was a good indication of the confusion most of the viewing audience felt at that last scene. It felt "off," as if the movie wasn't completely done. That, combined with an ill-advised (and, unless I miss my guess, tacked-on) tag line, brought me right out of the moment. It took a few minutes of sitting still and analyzing what I'd seen in the prior 113 moments before I could get past the somewhat stunning disappointment of feeling I was just talked down to, as if Shyamalan didn't think the audience would get it in the end.

But don't let me spook you: the 113 moments prior were well worth it. If nothing else, *Unbreakable* will make you think about what you've just watched. And, in my book, any time a movie makes you pause to consider, that's most def A Good Thing.

BAMMER'S BOTTOM LINE

M. Night Shyamalan, first with *The Sixth Sense* and now with *Unbreakable*, is fast proving to be the kind of writer-director whose stories bite you right in the ass. Thing about bites, though, is that they are rarely filling. *Unbreakable* is, nonetheless, a helluva tale spun by a master craftsman.

GREEN LIGHT

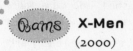 **X-Men**
(2000)

RATED PG-13; running time 140 minutes
GENRE: Action
WRITTEN BY: Tom DeSanto & Bryan Singer, David Nayter
DIRECTED BY: Bryan Singer
CAST: Patrick Stewart, Sir Ian McKellen, Hugh Jackman, Anna Paquin, Famke Janssen, Halle Berry, James Marsden, Ray Park, Rebecca Romijn-Stamos, Tyler Mane, Bruce Davison, Shawn Ashmore

> We firmly believe that Angela Bassett was supposed to be Storm. No dis to Halle, but Angela will always be Storm to us.

THE STORY

In the not-too-distant future, genetically altered mutants will become a "forward leap" in mankind's evolution. And, as has been proven in mankind's past dealings with those seen as different, that evolution will be feared—possibly to the point of extinction.

An orphaned survivor of the Holocaust in Poland, Magneto (Sir Ian McKellen) has no intention of being vulnerable to the whims of mortal men again. Using his powers of literal magnetism, he gathers other mutants of similar mind—including super-strong Sabretooth; the flexible (of tongue and limb) Toad; and shape-shifting Mystique—to gain the upper hand on normal humans before McCarthyite Senator Kelly (Bruce Davison) and his ilk try to legislate the mutants out of existence.

But Magneto and the Bad Mutants have to contend with the X-Men: led by super-psychic Professor Charles Xavier (Patrick Stewart). Despite their ability to cause mutants permanent grief, Professor X still believes in the basic goodness of human beings, and brings in young and old mutants into his School for the Gifted to teach them how to use their powers for good, to best serve humanity.

THE UPSHOT

Let me just say right off the bat that the closest I ever got to *X-Men* comics was (I can't believe I'm confessing this) when I used to read *Betty and Veronica;* that, and watching my sons play the "X-Men" arcade game. I had a passing knowledge of the basic idea of the Super (anti) Heroes, but not much more than your average Chick. I went into this flick with a clean slate, not quite knowing what to expect.

And while I didn't come out with nearly the "wow" feeling that I had from a similar-in-spirit flick—1999's *The Matrix* (page 18)—I can honestly say that *X-Men* was a damned sight better than most of the live-action remakes of cartoons and comics I've had the sorry "pleasure" to witness (*Batman and Robin* and *Rocky and Bullwinkle*). Heck, I can say more than that: I actually *liked X-Men.*

The best compliments I can pay to this movie are that it did not get overwhelmed by its (pretty decent) special effects, and that it provided a good (without being condescending) introduction to a world formerly known only to fans of the comic books and, to a lesser extent, the video games.

X-Men would've been much less successful without the decent-to-good performances of its cast; wherever the writing and direction went lacking (they were, in quite a few places), the actors came through with better-than-expected, honest depictions of their comic-book characters. It would've been all too easy to play it for camp, or go the "Batman" route with overly maudlin performances; to their credit, this mostly aglitter (with obvious exceptions) cast played it straight without being stodgy or overblown.

This first in an apparent series (that "ending" was anything but) was obviously Wolverine and Rogue's story, and actors Jackman and Paquin had the lion's share of the lines and action. They did well, as did Stewart as the hopeful Professor X and McKellen as the very bitter Magneto.

While I did enjoy the movie, I walked away feeling somewhat unsatisfied, and with more questions than answers. Probably much to the delight of the filmmakers, who've set this up as a *Batman*-like franchise. One can only hope that the follow-up flick has a stronger ending than the original *X-Men,* and that it has more staying power as a series than *Batman* did.

BAMMER'S BOTTOM LINE
It ain't rocket science (Hmmm . . . actually, in this case, it might just be) but *X-Men* was a good fun romp for an hour or two; certainly, as a direct-from-the-comics flick, it ran circles around *Teenage Mutant Ninja Turtles.* Not that that's hard.

GREEN LIGHT

in 1939, a Black woman by the name of Hattie McDaniel was nominated as Best Supporting Actress for her role as "Mammy" in *Gone With the Wind*. This was the first time an African-American had been nominated for any Oscar. She went on to win—a feat that was not repeated until Whoopi Goldberg won for her role in *Ghost*.

All told, African-Americans have been nominated 36 times. Of those 36 times we have won eight times: *Gone With the Wind, Lilies of the Field, An Officer and a Gentleman, Glory, Ghost, Jerry Maguire, Monster's Ball,* and *Training Day*. Of these wins, only three—*Lilies of the Field* (for the regal Mr. Sidney Poitier), *Monster's Ball* (for the very deserving Ms. Halle Berry), and *Training Day* (for the superb Mr. Denzel Washington)—were for a Leading Actor win. The rest were all for supporting roles.

There are not 38 movie reviews in this chapter. We have included "the 8" and a cross-section of the remaining 30.

Ali
(2001)

RATED R; running time 160 minutes

GENRE: Drama/Biography

WRITTEN BY: Stephen J. Rivele, Christopher Wilkinson, Eric Roth

DIRECTED BY: Michael Mann

CAST: Will Smith, Jamie Foxx, Jon Voight, Mario Van Peebles, Ron Silver, Jeffrey Wright, Jada Pinkett Smith, Nona Gaye, Michael Michele, Barry Shabaka Henley, Albert Hall, Mykelti Williamson, Giancarlo Esposito, Joe Morton, Michael Bentt, James Toney, Charles Shufford

THE STORY

Michael Mann's interpretation of the life of legendary heavyweight boxing champion Muhammed Ali (Will Smith) spans a very short period in his life and career. Here, we see Ali's life from just before his first title bout—still using his "slave" name, Cassius Clay—with then-champ Sonny Liston (Michael Bentt); his friendship with freelance photographer Howard Bingham (Jeffrey Wright) and Malcolm X (Mario Van Peebles); the dawning of his mutually beneficial relationship with Howard Cosell (Jon Voight); three of his four marriages, to Sonji Roy (Jada Pinkett Smith), Belinda Boyd (Nona Gaye), and Veronica Porsche (Michael Michele); his fight with the "whole United States Government" over his refusal to participate in the draft; his belief in, struggles with, and abandonment by the Nation of Islam and its leaders, Elijah Muhammed (Albert Hall) and his son Herbert (Barry Shabaka Henley); and ending with his as-

sociation with Don King (Mykelti Williamson), and Ali's fight with George Foreman (Charles Shufford) in Kinshasa, Zaire.

THE UPSHOT

My issues with *Ali* are many and far-reaching. First and foremost, I learned nothing new about Ali, either as a legend, a fighter, or private citizen of the world. For young guns like my son, who seem to think that the history of boxing began when Tyson showed up, perhaps this watered-down version of Ali's life will do. But I've seen the Ali documentary *The Greatest*, watched too many hours of ESPN and *Wide World of Sports*, and read too many pages of *Jet* magazine, to be satisfied with the small, relatively meatless chunk Mann presented. A filmed ending that leaves you wondering "hey, what about the rest?" while you are simultaneously grateful that you can finally leave the theater misses the mark, in my book.

Which leads me to my next point: it was far too long for such a condensed period of time. Mann seemed to be in love with his shots, to the point where I became anxious for the story to get on with itself. Scenes such as Ali's first meeting with Sonjy Roi, and Ali's run through the African village, had me dying to scream "We get it, OK? Can we move on now?"

Third, and somewhat related to my original issue with this film, is the notion that Ali could do no wrong. The best heroes, in my view, are those with flaws. This film barely glossed over the significance of Joe Frazier (played by James Toney) to Ali as a champ and as a symbol—and, more to the point, Ali's role in unnecessarily provoking Frazier the way he did before their first fight (they had a guaranteed purse, so his "stoking the fire" added nothing to the amount of money they'd get from a bigger draw). And aside from Ali's off-the-cuff admission about his tendency to chase skirt, and a brief scene with Bundini, you wouldn't really know that Ali had a life outside the ring; sure, others revolved around him, but we never saw Ali really relate to those others, besides Malcolm X (played surprisingly well by Mario Van Peebles).

I didn't have a big problem with Will Smith as Ali here. He obviously deeply admires the man, and does a good job mimicking his speech patterns, especially the more boisterous taunts that Ali was so famous for. In this, Smith excels. But I was never truly convinced in his portrait of Ali; never did I get so caught up that I forgot it was Will Smith As Ali, not an actor, immersed in his part. I blame the material Smith was given to work with, though. He seemed very hamstrung and restricted in this role. But for the love of Pete, why play Ali as if he didn't have a thought running around that pretty little head of his? Which reminds me: whoever plastered on all that goop to try to make Jon Voight look like Howard Cosell, needs their butt whupped. Nona Gaye as Belinda gave an outstanding performance, as did Jamie Foxx as Ali's cornerman Drew "Bundini" Brown. My recommendation? See *Ali*, but don't expect it to be the greatest.

THE BLACK FACTOR

While promoting the film, Mann said Smith was the only actor who could've played Ali. Now, I understand his need to defend his choice of Will Smith; and considering Smith's ability to mimic the champ, and, frankly, his box office status, I even grudgingly accept that choice in the end. But I think Mann is quite wrong. I can think of quite a few young Black actors who could've beat the tar out of Smith's performance, without having to resort to histrionics to do so. And at the top of that list? Terrence Dashon Howard, of *The Best Man* and *Hart's War*. In a way, it's too bad we'll never know what Howard could've done with such a juicy part. On the other hand, given the material available to work with, maybe Mann did Howard a favor after all.

BAMMER'S BOTTOM LINE

Ali does have some bright spots, and it was certainly more than merely average. If nothing else, it will give some young folks the opportunity to learn a little something about a boxing legend who truly earned the title "World Champion."

FLASHING YELLOW LIGHT

Cass Driving Miss Daisy
(1989)

RATED PG; running time 99 minutes

GENRE: Drama

(PLAY AND SCREENPLAY) WRITTEN BY:
   Alfred Uhry

DIRECTED BY: Bruce Beresford

CAST: Morgan Freeman, Jessica Tandy, Dan
   Aykroyd, Esther Rolle, Patti LuPone, Jo Ann
   Havrilla, William Hall Jr., Alvin M. Sugarman

> Who in their right mind names a store
> "Piggly Wiggly?"

CASS'S CLIP

The place and year—1948 in Atlanta, Georgia, which means cotton is king and racism its queen. The contenders in this corner, the uncompromising (and sometimes paranoid) Daisy Werthan (Tandy); and in this corner, the dutiful Hoke Colburn (Freeman). Refereeing disagreements between the two is Boolie Werthan (Aykroyd). Esther Rolle also turns in a fine performance as Daisy's sly-tongued maid Idella.

Daisy's simple statement, "I'm going to the market, Idella," changes her life. Instead of going to the market, Daisy backs her 1948 Packard into her neighbor's yard. Boolie, owner of Werthan Bag & Cotton Co., hires his mama a chauffeur, Hoke Colburn. Boolie explains to Hoke that his mother is a "little high-strung" but that Hoke works for him no matter what his mama says. Hoke compares his instructions to the time when he was a boy on a farm in Macon. He used to "wrestle hogs

to the ground during killing time, and not one hog got away from him." Trouble is, Daisy's no hog but a proud elderly Jewish woman who believes she's still "in control of her abilities" and "nobody's fool." Hoke finally convinces Daisy to let him chauffeur her to the Piggly Wiggly. Hoke calls Boolie from a pay phone across the street from the Piggly Wiggly and tells him, "I just drove your mama to the store . . . She flapped around some, but she's all right . . . It only took me six days, the same time it took the Lord to make the world."

In spite of Hoke's seemingly subservient demeanor, he does more than just drive Miss Daisy around. He teaches this retired teacher the true meaning of racial tolerance during a time when Blacks and Jews were both treated with such disdain. Over 25 years and two cars later, Hoke and Daisy have forged a friendship that has outlasted most marriages.

DA 411

The dialogue written for Daisy and Hoke was outstanding. Their one-line quips were cleverly disguised in compassionate conversations, which led to their inevitable respect for one another.

> ### THE BLACK FACTOR
> Though nominated for an Oscar, Morgan Freeman only won the 1989 Golden Globe award for Best Actor (Musical/Comedy), while Jessica Tandy won both the 1989 Golden Globe award for Best Actress (Musical/Comedy) and the 1989 Oscar for Best Actress. It seems to me not much has changed from 1948 to 1989—if you know what I mean.

CASS'S CONCLUSION

Compassionate and moving, the perfect movie for the whole family.

GREEN LIGHT

Bams Ghost
(1990)

RATED PG-13; running time 128 minutes
GENRE: Romantic thriller
WRITTEN BY: Bruce Joel Rubin
DIRECTED BY: Jerry Zucker
CAST: Patrick Swayze, Demi Moore, Whoopi Goldberg, Tony Goldwyn, Rick Aviles, Vincent Schiavelli

THE STORY

Wall Street hotshot Sam Wheat (Patrick Swayze) and his sculptor girlfriend, Molly Jensen (Demi Moore), have it all: good careers, a huge loft-n-the-hood, the friendship of Sam's co-worker Carl Bruner (Tony Goldwyn), and lots o' love for each other. Alas, it doesn't last: Sam gets mugged and murdered by the swarthy Willie Lopez (Rick Aviles) as Sam and Molly are coming back from the theater one day.

But Sam doesn't simply die: spurred on by the everlasting love he had for Molly, he stays behind as a ghost, trapped between this world and the next. Sam slowly realizes that his murder was no chance accident of fate; he finds psychic Oda Mae Brown (Whoopi Goldberg), and works on

Oda Mae's nerves until he convinces her to tell Molly: "You in trouble, girl."

THE UPSHOT

I've wondered "what the hell" many times in the past when the Academy made their nominations and picked their winners. I've scratched my head so often at their choices, it's a wonder I'm not bald. Still, I just don't get the inclusion of *Ghost* in the annals of Oscar lore. Call it cute or sexy, sweet or funny, or even "fluffy." But "Oscar-caliber"? Maybe it's just me, but I didn't see anything within the 128 minutes of this film that screamed out, "Hey, somebody should nominate this for Best Picture!" "Best Screenwriter," either.

This is not to say that *Ghost* didn't have some redeeming factors. Patrick Swayze's blandness and Demi Moore's hilarious cry-at-the-drop-of-a-hat act aside, they did have a potent chemistry that could melt pottery; Tony Goldwyn proved yet again that he's one of Hollywood's most underrated actors; and Vincent Schiavelli, as the Subway Ghost, spanked Swayze's behind on the acting front. I was none too pleased with the overbearing light=good, dark=bad theme (or did you miss the swarthy Willie Lopez, the "Yuppie Gentrification Saves The Hood" action, or the unintentionally comical light angels, dark devils?), but hey, par for the course.

And at the heart of it all, one Whoopi Goldberg, who turned an otherwise silly movie into her own playground, predating Miss Cleo as a psychic with a heart of gold, and a direct line to the funny bone. Too bad Whoopi was nominated for the wrong movie.

THE BLACK GOLD FACTOR

Take a look at the 1991 Oscar nominations for "Best Actress in a Supporting Role":

Dances with Wolves—Mary McDonnell
Ghost—Whoopi Goldberg
Goodfellas—Lorraine Bracco
The Grifters—Annette Bening
Wild at Heart—Diane Ladd

Granted, a comedy nomination in the midst of all that drama is sure to raise a few eyebrows (just ask Marisa Tomei about My Cousin Vinnie). But I keep going back to the Great Oscar Robbery Of 1986, when The Color Purple and Whoopi Goldberg & company suffered the slings of Oscar's feebleness ... and suddenly, I understand. Whoopi may not have been the best choice for 1991, but if an Apology Oscar was good enough for the likes of Al Pacino, Paul Newman, and other such giants, then hey.

BAMMER'S BOTTOM LINE

Silly and at times laugh-out-loud funny, Ghost may not go down in the annals as everybody's Best Of, and Whoopi Goldberg may have been "given" that Oscar as penance for an earlier snub; but one thing The Whoopster once said still holds true: from now until forever, she'll always be an Oscar-winning Actress. Hey, I ain't mad atcha, girl; you go.

FLASHING YELLOW LIGHT

Bams Glory
(1989)

RATED R; running time 122 minutes
GENRE: Historical war drama
WRITTEN BY: Kevin Jarre (based on the letters of Robert Gould Shaw)
DIRECTED BY: Edward Zwick
CAST: Matthew Broderick, Denzel Washington, Cary Elwes, Morgan Freeman, Jihmi Kennedy, Andre Braugher, John Finn, Bob Gunton, Cliff De Young

THE STORY

Robert Gould Shaw (Matthew Broderick), a Union Army officer, was the son of wealthy New England abolitionists. Not content to bide his time on the sidelines while the Civil War raged on, Shaw took the opportunity to command the Army's first all-Black regiment, the 54th Regiment. Shaw recruits his friend Cabot Forbes (Cary Elwes) to become a major, while their friend Thomas Searles (Andre Braugher)—a free Black man raised in New England—becomes the 54th's first volunteer. They are soon joined by the rebellious Southerner Trip (Denzel Washington in his first Oscar-winning performance), wise older soldier John Rawlins (Morgan Freeman), and the stuttering Jupiter Sharts (Jihmi Kennedy).

But the men of the 54th must wage an uphill battle. As if hard-nosed Irish sergeant major (John Finn) wasn't enough, they also face resistance and outright prejudice amongst white enlisted men, barbaric, bigoted ex–slave owning Colonel Montgomery (Cliff De Young), a near-return to slave conditions from an unfeeling General Harker (Bob Gunton), and the threat of instant execution by Confederate soldiers of any Black man found in Union uniform—or of any White officer leading them.

THE UPSHOT

One of the things I remember having been said about the movie *Color Purple* when it first hit was that a director like Steven Spielberg couldn't possibly translate Alice Walker's story the way a Black director could. I'm probably in the minority again, but I don't remember Spielberg's White perspective having significantly affected that movie—certainly not to the extent director Edward Zwick's seems to have in *Glory*.

Of course, there's a difference in the focus of the aforementioned movies: Alice Walker, author of the novel *Color Purple,* is a Black woman, who told a story ostensibly about Black people from her perspective as a writer. By contrast, *Glory* is a military story based on the letters of Colonel Robert Gould Shaw, a White officer living in a White man's world. And, as they say, history is told through the eyes of the conqueror.

Still, from where I sit, there's an overwhelming feeling that there's something missing in this story; a gap that comes from having a tale told by a distant observer of life rather than its active, affected participants. But while Shaw was, in his own words very much a distant observer of the Blacks under his command, I fail to see why a movie based even on his words would need to be told with such hesitancy. *Glory* should've been infused with much more of Denzel Washington's in-your-face characterizations, and much less of Matthew Broderick's I-don't-belong-here feints.

Don't misread me: I've long thought that Broderick is a fine actor (though he completely fumbles his New England accent here). But it's clear throughout *Glory* that the actor and his character are vastly outmatched by all around him. Even the understanding that Shaw was a Captain Youngblood, a Boy in the presence of Men, couldn't spare this viewer the sense that Broderick was chosen more for his "star power" (having come from *Ferris Bueller's Day Off* and *Biloxi Blues* prior to this movie) than for his appropriateness for a role that might've been better served by casting an unknown actor instead. In a sense, Broderick's boyishness was negated by his "star power," to the *slight* detriment of the story.

"Slight," I say, because overall, the film excelled on many levels. A rousing portrait of the evil that men do—even to their "allies," a great character study advanced by the likes of Denzel Washington, Morgan Freeman, John Finn, and Andre Braugher amongst many others, a soaring musical score (which, I couldn't help but note, is also used in my favorite TV show, *Iron Chef*), and Oscar-winning cinematography by Freddie Francis, all serve *Glory* quite well. But still, there's that nagging feeling that there could've been something more added to the mix.

THE BLACK GOLD FACTOR

Washington's trip (no pun intended) to the Academy's podium was well earned, and a long time coming. Hell, the man's single, meaningful tear should've won its own Oscar. But I'm also reminded that besides Morgan

Freeman (who, coincidentally, was nominated that year as Best Actor for *Driving Miss Daisy*, ultimately losing to Daniel Day-Lewis in *My Left Foot*), there's another strong Black actor who didn't get righteous props then, and to this day, still doesn't fill nearly the amount of screen time he deserves: Andre Braugher, one of the best actors alive, period. Braugher, the powerhouse behind the criminally unheralded TV drama *Homicide: Life on the Street*, added a needed reminder to *Glory* that We were not then, as We are not now, A Monolith, a single voice speaking from a single experience.

Cass Guess Who's Coming to Dinner
(1967)

UNRATED: running time 108 minutes
GENRE: Drama
WRITTEN BY: William Rose
DIRECTED BY: Stanley Kramer
CAST: Sidney Poitier, Spencer Tracy, Katharine Hepburn, Katharine Houghton, Beah Richards, Roy Glenn, Isabel Sanford

This was Spencer Tracy's last film.

BAMMER'S BOTTOM LINE
As good as it was, *Glory* remains one of those "Blacks as subjects" films that I think might've been better served with more Black voices behind the scenes. I commend director Edward Zwick and writer Kevin Jarre for what they did with this story, but I wonder what glorious levels of Black-and-White consciousness might've been raised with one of Us at the helm.

GREEN LIGHT

CASS'S CLIP
John Wade Prentice (Sidney Poitier) is a thirty-seven-year-old doctor. Joann "Joey" Drayton (Katharine Houghton) is a college graduate. John is Black and Joey is White. They meet in Hawaii, fall in love, and get engaged. *Guess Who's Coming to Dinner* tells the story of this 1960s couple's dilemma of convincing their parents—Katharine Hepburn and Spencer Tracy play Joey's parents, and Beah Richards and Roy Glenn play John's—to approve their interracial marriage.

DA 411
Every time I see *Guess Who's Coming to Dinner*, I am thoroughly entertained. The parental performances by Spencer Tracy, Katharine Hepburn, Beah Richards (who was nominated for a Best Actress award), and Roy Glenn are outstanding. Their acting convinced me that had they been faced with this same situation in real life, they would have given their children realistic advice

about the obstacles they would certainly face as an interracial couple in the late 1960s. Nevertheless, I just didn't sense any real passion between John and Joey. I'm willing to bet that Sidney and Katharine weren't allowed to *act* passionate because of censors and studio execs!

CASS'S CONCLUSION

Tonight's menu—Appetizer: Marinated racist ideology, with a sprinkle of liberalism. Entrée: Bigoted principles crushed with tolerance. And Dessert: Fresh new ideas topped with acceptance. Then, *Guess Who's Coming to Dinner?* "The Glory of Love"!

GREEN LIGHT

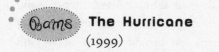

Bams The Hurricane
(1999)

RATED R; running time 146 minutes

GENRE: Drama

WRITTEN BY: Armyan Bernstein (based on the book by Rubin "Hurricane" Carter)

DIRECTED BY: Norman Jewison

CAST: Denzel Washington, Vicellous Reon Shannon, Dan Hedaya, Deborah Unger, Liev Schreiber, John Hannah, Debbi Morgan, David Paymer, Harris Yulin, Clancy Brown, Rod Steiger, Garland Whitt

THE STORY

A strong contender for the middleweight boxing title during the '60s, Rubin "Hurricane" Carter's (Denzel Washington) hopes were dashed when he and John Artis (Garland Whitt) were sentenced to three life terms and imprisoned for 20 years for murders they didn't commit. This is his story, and it is also the story of an unlikely group of folks from Canada (one, by way of Brooklyn): Lesra Martin (Vicellous Reon Shannon), a young Black teen from Brooklyn, being home-schooled in Toronto by three White Canadians—Lisa Peters, Sam Chaiton, and Terry Swinton. By a strange twist of fate, Lesra finds a book written by Rubin about his unjust imprisonment, and he is so moved by it and his fervent belief in Rubin's innocence, that he convinces the Canadians to help him set Rubin free. But not without a fight: they come up against pure evil in the form of detective Vincent Della Pesca (Dan Hedaya), a dirty, racist cop who's been after Carter for years, and does all he can to see that Rubin remains locked up.

THE UPSHOT

Let me get this out of the way: Denzel Washington, Vicellous Reon Shannon, and Dan Hedaya were outstanding in this film. Washington we've seen go "all-out" before, so his strong performance didn't surprise me at all. Hedaya is one of those character actors that you know you've seen a million times, but can't put your finger on where exactly; he's played funny (*Cheers*) as well as straight drama (*Nixon*), but never before has he sent chills down my spine as he did here. Shannon really impressed me in the strangest of ways: every time he spoke, I said to myself, "his voice and his body don't match." For some reason, I kept expecting to hear a "softer" voice, but sure enough, his heavy Brooklyn accent came through each time. Beyond that, Shannon's portrayal of Lesra's passionate belief in Rubin, and in his place in Rubin's life, astonished me—and will hopefully move him beyond the obligatory thug roles that he has played so frequently in the past.

The story itself, though moving, felt somewhat hollow. Though of course Rubin couldn't know what became of John Artis while they were both in prison, I felt short-changed by the offhand mention of him throughout the film. I also got somewhat dizzy during the flashback/flash-forward sequences. Further, the boxing scenes were beautifully shot in black and white, but they felt cut-n-pasted on. And one has to wonder how, after Rubin's lawyers Myron Beldoc (David Paymer) and Leon Friedman (Harris Yulin) spent ten years on a case that was heard by two juries, the Canadians could come along and, well, see for yourself. Still, in spite of its padding (a half-hour could've easily been excised from this movie, with little detriment), *The Hurricane* spins a good tale; fractured, in places, but still told reasonably well.

Besides the performances of the three leads mentioned above, most of the other cast seemed pretty mute. Liev Schreiber as Sam Chaiton was almost invisible in a role that should have provided ample opportunity for him to shine. Unger and Hannah (as Lisa Peters and Terry Swinton, respectively) were almost as marginal. And what a wasted opportunity the movie's powers that be made in not using Clancy Brown to his fullest potential; he's played prison guards enough before that casting him as Jimmy Williams, the "guard with a heart" (but not much to do), made little sense to me. But not as little sense as the casting of Rod Steiger as Judge H. Lee Sorokin. He was just more flotsam.

The use of period music throughout the film was an excellent idea, even Bob "Damn, I Can't Sing!" Dylan's song "Hurricane" which was written during the time when Dylan, along with a few other celebrities (Ellen Burstyn and Muhammad Ali included), was trying to get Rubin set free. Their involvement (or lack thereof) over time was a key point made by Beldoc, when Lesra and the Canadians came to confront him in what Beldoc surely saw as guilty White liberalism at its worst.

Guilty White liberals make an easy target. They seem to come in like a whirlwind, upset the status quo, do what they seem as the right thing for those poor heathens whom they deem worthy of their patronage, and leave after their guilt is assuaged, right? Well, maybe. And maybe the three guilty White liberals from Canada took pity on both Rubin and Lesra, and by helping them, purged themselves of their guilt long enough to look back at their lives and feel they've done good—much to the consternation of those other poor heathens left behind in their wake who weren't so lucky as to gain the favor of those guilty White liberals. Maybe that's the way some see it.

To those "some," ask yourself this: is Rubin still in that prison? Anyone who thinks—and it has been suggested—that 3 Black Chicks should be ashamed of not slamming *The Hurricane* for deifying those White Liberals can, pardon my French, *baise mon belle noire âne*.

THE BLACK FACTOR

Actually, since the BF is pretty clear in this flick, consider this space "The White Factor." And let's go one step further: since Della Pesca's (and those like him) rabid racism needs no explanation, let's examine the "Guilty White Liberal Factor," shall we?

BAMMER'S BOTTOM LINE

Padded in spots (especially those involving the "Danger!" the Canadians were in), *The Hurricane* is, overall, a powerful story featuring bravura performances by Washington, Shannon, and Hedaya that should not be missed.

FLASHING YELLOW LIGHT

the Diva   Jerry Maguire
(1996)

RATED R; running time 138 minutes
GENRE: Drama
WRITTEN BY: Cameron Crowe
DIRECTED BY: Cameron Crowe
CAST: Tom Cruise, Cuba Gooding Jr., Renée Zellweger, Regina King, Bonnie Hunt, Jonathan Lipnicki

Jerry Maguire cost 50 million dollars to make. It took in 61 million at the end of its third week in theaters. It ended up bringing in $153,952,592. As of Summer 2002, it is number 91 out of the 250 top grossing films of all time (not adjusted for inflation).

THE DIGEST

Jerry Maguire (Tom Cruise) is a hotshot sports agent for Sports Management International. Their clients are the movers and shakers of the sports world and they all know it. SMI employs 33 agents who represent just over 1,200 clients. Sounds impressive, right? Well according to Jerry, that's the problem. After talking to the young son of an injured hockey player, Jerry has an epiphany. It occurs to him that what is missing from his job is the one-on-one care his clients deserve. The personal touch, if you will. He wants to hearken back to a time where you nurtured your clients and gave them your complete attention. Jerry writes this down in a mission statement that he gives to the entire company. Both he and his mission statement are lauded and applauded—for about a week. Then his boss decides to give him what he wants—less clients—by stealing all of Jerry's and firing him.

Jerry is left with one client, Rod Tidwell (Cuba Gooding Jr.) a wide receiver with an attitude. Rod wants endorsements and more money. He knows that a good receiver only has about a ten-year shelf life; he is on year five and wants to make sure that his wife and kids are cared for.

Other than Rod, Jerry has one person in his corner—Dorothy (Renée Zellweger). Dorothy is a single mother and a hopeless romantic. She idolizes Jerry and is so impassioned by Jerry's memo that she also leaves the company to help build up his business. She is normally so sensible and responsible, but when he's around, all that goes out the window. Dorothy is nothing if not strong, and she is determined to help Jerry be successful in business and in love—with her.

THE DISH

If there is one thing I can say about Cameron Crowe it's that he can write. No question about it. His dialogue is always engaging and interesting and he builds wonderful characters. Renée Zellweger was absolutely refreshing. In her turn as a single mother, she was endearing and believable. It was heartwarming to see the love she had for her child, Ray (Jonathan Lipnicki). Lest you think that I've forgotten about Tom Cruise, I haven't. While he was obviously the most commanding presence on the screen, the movie belonged just as much to the supporting cast as to him. I didn't see anything new from Cruise, who, once again, played a sensitive cute guy. The two strongest and completely overlooked actors were Bonnie Hunt as Dorothy's loving and overprotective older sister, and Regina King as Rod Tidwell's strong and determined wife, Marcie. These two women deserved to be showered with accolades.

THE BLACK FACTOR

First things first. Cuba deserved his Supporting Actor Oscar for this role—the third time in history that it was given to a Black man. And, as you may recall, Cuba's Oscar acceptance speech was almost as memorable as his performance.

THE DIRECTIVE

With 35 nominations to its credit, *Jerry Maguire* is a cute film and worth the rental.

YELLOW LIGHT

 Lady Sings the Blues
(1972)

RATED R; running time 144 minutes
GENRE: Drama
WRITTEN BY: Chris Clark, Suzanne De Passe, William Dufty (book), Billie Holiday (book), Terence McCloy
DIRECTED BY: Sidney J. Furie
CAST: Diana Ross, Billy Dee Williams, Richard Pryor, Virginia Capers, J. T. Callahan

> This was Diana Ross's first acting role, and she won the 1972 Golden Globe for "Most Promising Newcomer." She was nominated for an Oscar but lost to Liza Minnelli, who won for her role in *Cabaret*.

THE DIGEST

Belittled by her aunt and harassed by the male clients at the house of ill repute where she works as a cleaning girl, Elenora Holiday (Diana Ross) dreams of escape. That escape unfortunately comes in the form of lost innocence when she is raped and sent to live with her mother in New York.

Her mother can't take care of her, and so sends her to live with a church friend of hers. She instructs Elenora to do the cleaning for this woman's boarding house and in exchange she'll have a place to stay. Unbeknownst to her mother, this "boarding house" is actually a "cat house," and once again Elenora is surrounded by prostitutes and johns. Elenora tries her best to not get involved in this lifestyle. Her dream is to sing, but after being turned down time after time, she gives in and starts turning tricks.

Her foray into the oldest profession in the world is short-lived. She quickly gives it up and lands a job singing in a club. Billie "Lady Day" Holiday is born. It's 1933 and, at age 18, she is sitting on top of the world, making a decent living and doing what she wants to do more than anything—singing. She catches the eye of Louis McKay (Billy Dee Williams—jeez, that man is fine), a local numbers-runner who is enchanted by her demeanor. Louis isn't the only one who notices her. Reg Hanely wants her to tour with his all-White band. Itching for success, she agrees, and it is the beginning of her end. Trying to keep up with the hectic pace, she starts drinking heavily and eventually turns to heroin as a pick-me-up. Before long, Lady Day is beyond the point of no return.

THE DISH

This is Motown's version of jazz great Billie Holiday's life. Be warned that they took many liberties with her story, and while the major themes are true, this is pretty much a work of fiction. Now some of the fault lies with Lady Day herself. She wrote a book about her life and she told it how she saw fit, and the screenplay is based on the book. I tell you this not to slam the movie, but I don't want you to walk away expecting this to be the true story of a music icon.

I have found new respect for La Diva Ross. Not so much for the acting skills she displayed in the film, but the risks she took in telling Billie's story. I mean, she is a Diva's Diva, and here she is, rolling around in a straightjacket with no makeup on and her hair screaming. She looked like a ThunderCat and that, children, is *bold*.

Kidding aside (well, she did look like Lion-o from the ThunderCats, so I'm not really kidding), she really did "put her foot in it." She made me believe that she was an addict. I felt her pain when she faced racism in the South. She was outstanding and deserved the Oscar nomination that she received. Billy Dee was awesome, particularly in scenes where he expressed concern over her drug use. My heart broke watching him absorbing her pain. Richard Pryor had little screen time and didn't add much to the film.

Not all was perfect. The story needed some serious work. The time line they chose to use didn't jive with reality, and as such, her career was glossed over and her comeback is thrown together and shown in the last five minutes. In reality there are 12 years between her drug arrest in 1947 and her death. The way the movie tells it, girlfriend is dead within a year.

I can understand not wanting to do a whole movie about her downward spiral and eventual death, but it's criminal to cover her middle years and not include Count Basie, Louis Armstrong, and Glenn Miller—all famous musicians who were central to her life.

THE DIRECTIVE

I'm singing the blues because Boss Ross was robbed. She should've won the Oscar. Rent *Lady, Sings the Blues* and *Cabaret* and see for yourself.

GREEN LIGHT

Lilies of the Field
(1963)

UNRATED; running time 92 minutes

GENRE: Drama

WRITTEN BY: William E. Barrett (novel), and James Poe

DIRECTED BY: Ralph Nelson

CAST: Sidney Poitier, Lilia Skala, Lisa Mann, Isa Crino, Francesca Jarvis, Pamela Branch, Stanley Adams, Dan Frazer, Ralph Nelson

"Consider the lilies of the field, how they grow; they toil not, neither do they spin . . . " Matthew 6:28. KJV.

CASS'S CLIP

Lilies of the Field opens with Jester Hairston's famous "Amen" song playing in the background as Homer Smith (Sidney Poitier), a Black man, travels alone in his station wagon (home-on-wheels) in the Arizona desert going nowhere special. His radiator overheats and he stops at a nearby farmhouse for some water. What Homer doesn't know is that this stop will not only change his life but the lives of those whose spiritual beliefs need to be quenched by faith.

Homer drives up to the farmhouse and makeshift convent housing five German nuns: Mother Superior Maria (Lilia Skala), Sister Gertrude (Lisa Mann), Sister Agnes (Isa Crino), Sister Albertine (Francesca Jarvis), and Sister Elizabeth (Pamela Branch). When Homer asks Mother Superior for some water for his radiator, she takes this as a sign that God has answered her prayers. As he fills his radiator, Mother Supe-

rior thankfully says, "God is good. He has sent me a big strong man." Homer sarcastically replies, "He didn't say anything to me about sending me anyplace. I was just passing by." Homer and Mother Superior's initial meeting is just the beginning of their battle of spiritual wits. And their journey together doesn't end until Mother Superior can persuade Homer to build a chapel. However, there are a few minor snags holding up this divine project—(1) a reluctant angel (Smith) who wants to be paid for his labor; and (2) no money to buy the necessary bricks and supplies. But God, the real architect/contractor-in-charge, will use these two quarrelsome souls to galvanize a small Arizona community into building more than just a chapel.

DA 411

Based on William E. Barrett's novel of the same name, *Lilies of the Field* is a wonderful movie that delivers subliminal messages about the power of prayer and faith without being preachy. There are several memorable scenes, particularly those where Homer tries to teach the nuns English and sings the song "Amen." (Jester Hairston's voice was dubbed in as Sidney Poitier's singing voice for this song.) But Poitier's delivery of one-liners—from "That's a Catholic breakfast, one egg" to "If you're still listening, could you put some meat on the table" are what makes this movie unforgettable. Lilia Skala's portrayal of Mother Superior only works in conjunction with that of Sidney Poitier's Oscar-winning performance as the charismatic drifter and handyman Homer Smith. Poitier was also awarded the Silver Bear for Best Male Acting from the Berlin International Film Festival.

CASS'S CONCLUSION

The story centers on building a chapel, but the conflict between Homer and Mother Superior makes watching *Lilies of the Field* heaven sent.

GREEN LIGHT

Monster's Ball

(2001)

RATED R; running time 111 minutes
GENRE: Drama
WRITTEN BY: Milo Addica, Will Rokos
DIRECTED BY: Marc Forster
CAST: Billy Bob Thornton, Halle Berry, Peter Boyle, Heath Ledger, Sean Combs, Coronji Calhoun, Mos Def

THE STORY

"Loss" is a theme that runs rampant in *Monster's Ball*. Leticia Musgrove (Halle Berry) lost her husband Lawrence (Sean "Puffy" Combs) 11 years ago when he was convicted and sent to prison. He's now awaiting execution, while she is on the verge of losing her job and her house. Their son, Tyrell (Coronji Calhoun), experiences the loss of his father through the loss of his own power to control his obesity. Unfortunately for Leticia, her losses have just begun.

As has Hank Grotowski's (Billy Bob Thornton), a second-generation prison guard whose father, Buck (Peter Boyle), retired from the very prison where he works. Hank has just lost his mother and has only the routine of doing his job in a precise, lockstep manner to see him through the day. Hank's and Buck's loss of racial tolerance affects Hank's son, Sonny (Heath Ledger), and Sonny's friend Ryrus (Mos Def). But when Sonny mishandles his role in the execution of Lawrence, a chain of events leads to even more losses for the Grotowski family.

An unlikely set of circumstances throws Hank and Leticia into the same orbit. How they handle what they've lost—and what they might find—is the issue at hand.

THE UPSHOT

Let me say it for the record: I was simply wrong in all those reviews before. Halle Berry, you are, indeed, the real deal.

From start to finish, Berry rendered my previous "Yeah, she's pretty, but she can't really act" statements null and void. Many will talk about her nude scenes in the same tittering tones as they—we—did about her breastesses in the far inferior *Swordfish* (88). Apples and oranges; the two movies aren't even in the same universe as far as I'm concerned. Here Berry's nudity is completely relevant, even if director Marc Forster did seem to get carried away with his love for stark camera angles when the film went there and throughout this film (in general).

The pain, and eventual redemption, that passed between Berry's and Thornton's characters was palpable; when Hank told Leticia "I felt you," I said to myself, "Damn, I did too."

As I said above, it's very easy to draw ugliness like Hank's hateful father in broad strokes, though an actor the caliber of Peter Boyle at least makes it interesting to watch. But Hank's ugly nature is a little harder for us to handle; we want to sympathize with him, to root for what we know is the good in him—even when he's already shown us something less than good. Thornton, who I once thought would be limited to quirky roles, continues to impress me with his strength and range.

And talk about a tale of two woeful sons! Tyrell, as Coronji Calhoun wasn't given a break, not even in Leticia's grief; and poor Heath Ledger—who hasn't quite mastered the art of making an Aussie tongue sound Southern—was little more than a sacrificial lamb. The audience couldn't make much of an emotional investment in either of them, nor in Ryrus, played by rapper-poet Mos Def. I have a feeling that most of his story was left on the cutting-room floor. Too bad Puffy/Piddy/Whatever's laughably bad scenes weren't on that floor instead. Sorry, but the man was grossly outclassed by everyone around him.

As far as dirt being slung at easy Southern Good Ol' Boy targets goes, the writers mostly held themselves in check. Still, they and director Forster did swing their Whiffle bat more than they should've, bopping us with symbols like Hank's hankering for black coffee and chocolate ice cream (eaten with a white plastic spoon, no less). It is to the cast's enduring credit they were able to overcome the director's zealousness for us to see the Ugly Monsters of Racism, by bringing out the humanity in even the worst of their characters instead.

THE BLACK FACTOR

I know—I've said some pretty harsh things about Halle "Revlon" Berry before. And I know—I've said the following before, about movies and actors who weren't as deserving of the recognition as I once thought. But I've never meant it more than I do now: If Halle Berry hadn't received *at least* an Oscar nomination for her performance in *Monster's Ball*, then there is truly no justice. Not because she's Yet Another Black Actor who might have been dissed, but because she was too good not to have been One Of The Five. And if there were five others equally worthy, then dammit, they would have had to add another seat. She definitely deserved a seat at the table—but how glorious to be at the head of it.

BAMMER'S BOTTOM LINE

Now more than in anything since *Boomerang*—yes, that far back, and yes, that movie—Halle Berry's riveting performance in *Monster's Ball* has convinced me that she's the genuine article. Beautiful without meaning to be, vulnerable without trickery, emotive without melodrama . . . Berry brought it all to the table. And that Billy Bob fella wasn't half bad himself.

GREEN LIGHT

Cass | An Officer and a Gentleman

(1982)

RATED R; running time 122 minutes
GENRE: Comedy, Drama, Romance
WRITTEN BY: Douglas Day Stewart
DIRECTED BY: Taylor Hackford
CAST: Louis Gossett Jr., Richard Gere, Debra Winger, David Keith, Robert Loggia, Lisa Blount, Lisa Eilbacher, Tony Plana, Harold Sylvester, David Caruso, Grace Zabriskie, Tommy Peterson

CASS'S CLIP

An Officer and a Gentleman opens with Zach Mayo (Gere) looking out the window of a sleazy hotel. As Zach pulls back the blinds, the light from the window exposes the naked bodies of his father, Byron, and a woman in bed. It's apparent that Zach is accustomed to his father's behavior and he nonchalantly bends down to wake him up from a drunken stupor. Zach flashes back to the time when he moved to Manila to live with Byron after his mother committed suicide. Because Byron was an unfit parent, Zach grew up alone fending for himself as they traveled from port to port. When Zach tells Byron that he has enlisted in the Navy to become an aviator, Byron tries to discourage him. Zach leaves knowing that his relationship with his womanizer, alcoholic father is irreconcilable.

Zach arrives at the Naval Academy with a smug attitude, which instantly clashes with Sergeant Emil Foley (Louis Gossett Jr.). Foley tries to intimidate the new recruits by barking out orders. If they survive, "The prize at the other end," he says, "is a flight school education worth one million dollars." However, for 13 weeks, their lives belong to Foley and half of the recruits will DOR (Drop on Request) before graduating to the next level. Foley attempts to belittle Mayo. Is Mayo up to the challenge?

Foley also advises the recruits about the local girls who only have one thing in mind—"marrying a naval A V I A T O R." Meet Paula Pokrifki (Debra Winger) and her sidekick Lynette Pomeroy, two women with their faces on "Please Marry Me" posters. Both are searching for love and a way out of working at a dead-end factory job. Zach and his buddy Sid Worley (David Keith), hook up with Paula and Lynette at a dance on the base. In the end, after 13 weeks of running around obstacle courses and withstanding Foley's verbal and physical abuse, Zach and Paula fall in love on "no where else to go" highway.

In essence, *An Officer and a Gentleman* deals with two kinds of love—self-love and romantic love. Zach, a college graduate who has no clue how to live or love unselfishly, will learn from the two most pivotal people in his life: his father, who showed him the type of man he did not want to be, and Sergeant Foley, who teaches him how to be a real man.

DA 411

The best scenes in *An Officer and a Gentleman* are between Richard Gere and Louis Gossett Jr. Their relationship evolves from hate to genuine respect. Louis Gossett Jr's. Oscar-winning performance as the strict, no-nonsense drill sergeant, Emil Foley, is what makes this move realistic and enjoyable to watch. Debra Winger's performance is, at best, mediocre. Call me crazy, but has anybody else even felt less love or passion between a couple than Winger and Gere? The remaining cast members, David Keith, Lisa Eilbacher, Tony Plana, and Harold Sylvester, were enjoyable if only because they pull at our heartstrings as we cheer them on, hoping that they will make it through the 13 weeks of training. (I'd like to give a special shoutout to New Orleans native, Harold Sylvester—Perryman—a fine stage actor as well.)

CASS'S CONCLUSION

Even though the Hollywood ending is predictably corny, it really does work for *An Officer and a Gentleman.* Just substitute the prince on a white horse with a naval officer, and a damsel in distress with a factory worker, then add Joe Cocker's "Up Where We Belong" love song, and Zach and Paula can live happily ever after.

GREEN LIGHT

(*Bams*) The Shawshank Redemption

(1994)

RATED R; running time 142 minutes
GENRE: Drama
WRITTEN BY: Frank Darabont (based on the short story by Stephen King)
DIRECTED BY: Frank Darabont
CAST: Tim Robbins, Morgan Freeman, Bob Gunton, William Sadler, Clancy Brown, Gil Bellows, Mark Rolston, James Whitmore, Frank Medrano

THE STORY

The Shawshank Redemption begins in the late 1940s, when Andy Dufresne (Tim Robbins), a once successful banker, is sentenced to two life terms in Shawshank Prison for the murder of his wife and her lover. Andy has a difficult time in prison, initially: when the "bull queer" Sisters, led by Bogs Diamond (Mark Rolston), aren't busy harassing him, the Warden (Bob Gunton) and his ne'er-do-well Captain (Clancy Brown) are making Andy's life almost as miserable.

As time goes by, Andy adjusts to his circumstances, with the help of fellow inmate Red (Morgan Freeman). Red is the man you can "go to if you need it"—whatever "it" is. Red, Heywood (William Sadler), and old-timer Brooks Hatlen (James Whitmore) are amazed that despite his surroundings, Andy can still "keep hope alive." That is, until young gun Tommy Williams (Gil Bellows) comes along and rattles Andy's cage.

THE UPSHOT

There's nary a misstep in this movie. Oscar-nominated director-screenwriter Frank Darabont introduced those of us not very familiar with Stephen King's writing to King's gentler side (Darabont's slow, easy way of unfolding this story was a grand precursor to his similar treatment of another of King's works, *The Green Mile*, see page 183).

Cinematographer Roger Deakins, nominated for his work in *Fargo*, *O Brother Where Art Thou?*, and *The Man Who Wasn't There*, also received a well-deserved nomination for his camerawork in *Shawshank*. As the wife of a prison guard, I could certainly appreciate Deakins's sweeping shots of the prison, including a terrific overhead shot early on in the movie.

But it is the acting that keeps me watching *The Shawshank Redemption* over and over again. The film's secondary characters—like the Hank Williams–loving Heywood, sadistic Captain Hadley, deceptively cool Warden Norton, and even the tortured Fat Ass (played by Frank Medrano)—provide strong support and flavor to the mix.

And, leading them, all are Morgan Freeman as long-timer Ellis Boyd "Red" Redding, and Tim Robbins in a vastly underappreciated turn as the ever-hopeful Andy Dufresne. Freeman does an outstanding job of portraying Red's growing pessimistic view of the toll constant confinement takes over the years, while Robbins gives Andy an almost otherworldly quality, a sincerity that never lets you see the actor behind the character. That Robbins wasn't also nominated for an Academy Award along with Freeman, was downright criminal.

I've heard grumblings from a few detractors that say *The Shawshank Redemption* wasn't realistic in its depiction of prison life as pertains to Black and White prisoners; that there's no way that Red and Andy would be so close, and that there would be much more segregation evident. Get over it, I say. Everything isn't always so black and white.

THE BLACK GOLD FACTOR

The Oscar competition for Best Actor in a Leading Role in 1995 was pretty stiff:

Forrest Gump—Tom Hanks
The Madness of King George—Nigel Hawthorne
Nobody's Fool—Paul Newman
Pulp Fiction—John Travolta
The Shawshank Redemption—Morgan Freeman

With *Forrest Gump* being the juggernaut that it was, it's not too surprising that Tom Hanks won the prize that year; Freeman was great in *Shawshank*, but not even he could stop Hanks's train from rolling in for the second year in a row (after *Philadelphia*). Still, "run Forrest, run!" jokes and "Bubba Gump" restaurants notwithstanding, I do believe Morgan Freeman, Tim Robbins, and *The Shawshank Redemption* got the last laugh: after all, you don't see Forrest running every other day on TNT, do ya?

BAMMER'S BOTTOM LINE

I don't know if there's any such thing as a "perfect" movie; but for my money, *The Shawshank Re-*

demption comes close enough for horseshoes. The writing, the directing, the acting, and the cinematography . . . everything fell into place as if by magic. Maybe that's not too far from the truth.

GREEN LIGHT

Bams Training Day
(2001)

RATED R; running time 122 minutes
GENRE: Drama/Action
WRITTEN BY: David Ayer
DIRECTED BY: Antoine Fuqua
CAST: Denzel Washington, Ethan Hawke, Scott Glenn, Eva Mendes, Snoop Dogg, Dr. Dre, Harris Yulin, Raymond J. Barry, Cliff Curtis, Emilio Rivera, Tom Berenger, Charlotte Ayanna, Macy Gray

THE STORY
LAPD cop Jake Hoyt (Ethan Hawke) is excited about his new gig as an undercover narcotics officer; still naive, Hoyt believes he can make a difference in the War On (Some) Drugs, and he's eager to prove himself to his new boss. Said boss—one Alonzo Harris (Denzel Washington), wants Hoyt to prove himself, all right; but not in the way Hoyt thinks.

Hoyt quickly discovers that Harris is, at best, a rogue cop playing by his own rules, seemingly only answering to his own code of street con-

duct. And at worst, Harris is a completely corrupt cop, taking advantage of the power his badge and shield affords him. Not to mention the dirty money he comes by. Hoyt has to decide, and decide quickly, just how far into the dirt he'll let Harris drag him.

THE UPSHOT
Sure, there were other actors populating this movie—Scott Glenn, Harris Yulin, Tom Berenger, Emilio Rivera, and Cliff Curtis, just to name a few (Snoop Dogg counts too, I reckon; my jury's still out on Macy Gray and Dr. Dre in the "actor" category). But make no mistake: this picture belonged to Denzel Washington and Ethan Hawke. For better or for worse.

For me, it's the second half to two-thirds of this picture that make up the "for worse." Like in *Full Metal Jacket* before it, the "training" bits of *Training Day* were riveting. Denzel Washington was at his over-the-top thug-life finest. Even when he was obviously trying too hard to be Down (did someone buy Denzel a copy of *GhettoSpeak 101*?), Washington's wolfish narcotics cop was fascinating to watch—and cringe at—in all his raw power. Ethan Hawke as rookie undercover cop Jake Hoyt, in training mode, complemented Washington nicely; even as Alonzo Harris became progressively nastier, and Hoyt settled into wary pupil status, the lessons on surviving in this big bad world were great to watch.

The longer this film went on, the more the sheer mass of my suspended disbelief weighed me down, however. Scene after scene after endless boggling scene had me silently screaming over how incredibly doofus Hoyt had to be to get caught up in Harris's madness to such an extent. By the time the overwrought, obligatory Crime Doesn't Pay mishmash of *Bonnie and Clyde* and the "tollbooth" scene from *The Godfather* went down, I was anxious to Exit Stage Right.

Don't get me wrong: my gripe isn't so much with the actors (though Washington's bad mix of Scarface and Nino Brown got on my last nerve) as it is with the story itself.

BAMMER'S BOTTOM LINE

Even if every frame was an accurate representation of Life On The Mean Streets, *Training Day* strains credulity and doesn't inspire empathy for the characters.

YELLOW LIGHT

Cass What's Love Got to Do With It?
(1993)

RATED R; running time 113 minutes
GENRE: Drama
WRITTEN BY: Tina Turner and Kurt Loder
DIRECTED BY: Brian Gibson
CAST: Angela Bassett, Laurence Fishburne, Cora Lee Day, Jenifer Lewis, Phyllis Yvonne Stickney, Rae'ven Kelly, Sherman Augustus, Terrence Riggins, Chi McBride, Vanessa Bell Calloway, Khandi Alexander, Penny Johnson and Rob LaBelle

CASS'S CLIP

What's Love Got to Do With It? is based on Tina Turner's autobiography, *I, Tina*. Tina's birth name is Anna Mae Bullock. Anna's mother, Zelma, leaves her husband to escape his escalating abuse, and abandons Anna with her mother, a traumatic event that ultimately resurfaces and defines Anna/Tina's self-worth. In 1958, Anna moves from Nutbush, Tennessee to St. Louis, Missouri to live with her mother and sister Alline, after her grandmother dies.

One night Alline takes Anna to the Club Royal, where Ike Turner and the Kings of Rhythm are performing. Ike invites Anna onstage. Dumbfounded by her voice, he convinces Anna that he can make her a star. Ike changes Anna's name to Tina, forms the Ike and Tina Turner Revue, and their exhausting cross-country touring schedule begins. Ike and Tina become romantically involved, she gets pregnant, and they have a quickie wedding in Mexico. Now, Ike controls all their money, and Tina's every move.

After the success of their hit song "Fool in Love" Ike spends lavishly, and his cycle of mental and physical abuse against Tina begins. Tina makes excuses for Ike's psychotic temper because she doesn't want to abandon him like her mama abandoned her.

A former backup singer, Jackie, introduces Tina to the doctrine of Buddhism and teaches her how to chant. Chanting and meditating center Tina and allow her to see her life more clearly. Tina's turning point comes when she and Ike are in the limo on their way to a hotel in Texas. The brutality of this attack is the straw that finally breaks Tina's back and she fights back. Tina and Ike stroll into the hotel, both a bloody mess, and check in. When she comes out of the bathroom after examining her bruises, Ike is passed out on the sofa. She leaves that hotel and runs across the highway into a Ramada Inn. Tina tells the hotel manager, "I'm Tina Turner. My husband and I had a fight. I have 32 cents and a Mobil credit card in my pocket. If you would give me a room, I promise I will pay you back." In the face of what seems a humiliating moment, Tina stops making excuses for her past and her abusive husband, and takes control of her destiny.

DA 411

Angela Bassett and Laurence Fishburne were superb as Ike and Tina Turner. Even though Angela's physique was a bit too muscular for my taste, she really embodied the soul of Turner. We hear Tina's voice singing throughout the movie, but Angela's mimicking mannerisms and lip-synching are flawless. Laurence's portrayal of Ike is also believable. I was convinced that Laurence would kick my ass if I didn't do exactly what he told me to do. I was never a big Tina Turner fan until I saw *What's Love Got to Do With It?* The musical arrangements combined with the perfectly choreographed dances woven together with Tina's powerful story changed my mind.

CASS'S CONCLUSION

What's Love Got to Do With It? is not just a typical rage-to-riches story. It's about the power of self-preservation and SELF-LOVE.

GREEN LIGHT

ho said the 'Hood ain't heaven? It wasn't us Chicks, that's for sure. We know that you don't have to have been born in the Ghetto to be Ghetto-fabulous; you don't even have to be Black. Just look at Auntie Mame, for instance . . .

All About Eve
(1950)

RATED G; running time 138 minutes

GENRE: Drama

WRITTEN BY: Joseph L. Mankiewicz and Mary Orr

DIRECTED BY: Joseph L. Mankiewicz

CAST: Bette Davis, Anne Baxter, George Sanders, Celeste Holm, Gary Merrill, Hugh Marlowe, Gregory Ratoff, Barbara Bates, Marilyn Monroe, Thelma Ritter

THE DIGEST

Theater critic Addison DeWitt (George Sanders) is at an award ceremony, watching Eve Harrington (Anne Baxter) accept her award for Best Stage Actress and marveling at how she got there when just a year or so prior, she was nothing more than "your greatest fan." Don't misunderstand Addison, he has no sympathy for the people Eve stepped on to get to the top. In fact, he rather admires her for how she did it, but he is wondering if she is going to turn on him. With a wit that only he possesses, he begins the story.

Margo Channing (Bette Davis) shines in her role as a grand diva of the stage. She is surrounded by her best friend, Karen Richards (Celeste Holms); Karen's husband, Lloyd Richards (Hugh Marlowe), who is also the director of all of her plays; writer Bill Simpson (Gary Merrill); and her faithful secretary, Birdie (Thelma Ritter), all of whom tolerate her histrionics and outbursts.

So. Who is Eve? Eve is Margo's biggest fan. She's seen every performance of Margo's current play. She even waits outside of the stage door just to catch a glimpse of Margo. Karen finally notices Eve one day and, with the hopes of humbling Margo somewhat, she manages to get Eve into Margo's dressing room.

Eve then tells a sad sob story that elicits pity from everyone but Birdie, who can see right through Eve. They discount Birdie and bring Eve into their fold. But was it a mistake?

THE DISH

Eve was a special kind of Ghetto; she was something else. Mind you, this movie is 50 years old, so what was scandalous then would be pooh-poohed now. Consequently, some of the stuff she does loses its punch. What doesn't lose its punch, however, is the brilliant writing. This movie has some of the wittiest dialogue I've ever heard and *this* is what makes it a classic. Not to mention the fact that Bette Davis is in rare form as a diva with an acid tongue. George Sanders stood out as well, matching barb for barb with Bette Davis. I was pretty much glued to the screen.

Eve wasn't doing anything that a good ass-kicking wouldn't fix—it should have been called "All About a Beat Down."

THE DIRECTIVE

All About Eve is the perfect movie to put on one Saturday afternoon.

GREEN LIGHT

A Raisin in the Sun
(1961)

RATED: Unrated; running time: 128 minutes
GENRE: Drama
WRITTEN BY: Lorraine Hansberry
DIRECTED BY: Daniel Petrie
CAST: Sidney Poitier, Ruby Dee, Claudia Mc-
Neil, Diana Sands, Ivan Dixon, John Fiedler,
Louis Gossett Jr., Stephen Perry, Joel Fluellen,
Louis Terrel, Roy Glenn

CASS'S CLIP

A Raisin in the Sun is the story of Lena Younger and her family—her son, Walter Lee, his wife Ruth, and their son Travis; and her daughter, Beneatha. They live in a small apartment on the South side of Chicago. In the 1950s they struggle with racism, dignity, family values, and their dreams coming to fruition. The Youngers' lives are changed when Big Walter dies and leaves Lena $10,000 from his life insurance policy. Lena wants to use the money to buy a house for the family and pay for Beneatha's medical school tuition. Walter desperately wants the money to start his own business—a liquor store.

The day the check arrives, the real drama begins. Walter believes his status as head of the household is threatened when Lena won't give him the money. Ruth and Beneatha wholeheartedly believe the money is Lena's to spend as she pleases. Therefore, Lena puts a down payment on a nice house in a white neighborhood.

Harsh words are spoken and the pressure comes to a head. Lena sees how dejected Walter feels and she gives the rest of the money to him to do as he pleases. The most powerful scene is moving day. It's then that they learn that Walter invested the money in a pipedream gone bad. With his entire family's dreams squandered, Walter makes one last desperate attempt to get some of the money back, but regains his self-worth and family's respect with one act of defiance.

DA 411

Lorraine Hansberry's 1959 Broadway play and subsequent 1961 movie *A Raisin in the Sun*, was inspired by Langston Hughes' poem *Harlem* (which is sometimes referred to as *A Dream Deferred*). I'm sure that Lorraine Hansberry drew from her own personal experiences of growing up in Chicago in the 1950s as an outline for *A Raisin in the Sun*.

Sidney Poitier's depiction of the downtrodden Walter Lee Younger is brilliantly believable. Claudia McNeil, Ruby Dee, and Diana Sands are equally gifted actresses. Their strong-willed, yet supportive portrayal of the Younger women is so authentic, it's hard to believe they're acting. This talented ensemble cast gave a riveting performance, which still holds true some 40 years later.

I could go on and on about how much I loved seeing *A Raisin in the Sun* for the umpteenth time. I could go on and on about how it rekindled memories of my parents teaching me how to deal with racism. But I won't. Instead, I'll muse on my and my family's own deferred dreams and hope the movie inspires you to do the same.

CASS'S CONCLUSION

In 1959, *A Raisin in the Sun* won the New York Drama Critic's Circle Award as the best play of the year. However, *A Raisin in the Sun* is more than just a play or movie about the Youngers' receiving a $10,000 inheritance, it's about how family dynamics are forever changed by money. Whoever said that this was just another play or movie never walked in the shoes of a Colored, Negro, Black, or African-American.

GREEN LIGHT

Cass Auntie Mame
(1958)

UNRATED: running time 143 minutes
GENRE: Dramedy
WRITTEN BY: Patrick Dennis (novel); Jerome Lawrence (play); Betty Comden, Robert E. Lee, Adolph Green (movie)
DIRECTED BY: Morton DaCosta
CAST: Rosalind Russell, Forrest Tucker, Coral Browne, Fred Clark, Peggy Cass, Joanna Barnes, Lee Patrick, Willard Waterman, Robin Hughes

CASS'S CLIP

The sometimes-questionable custodial antics Mame Dennis (Rosalind Russell) adopts to raise her lovable nephew, Patrick Dennis (Roger Smith), is the main premise behind the Broadway play and subsequent movie *Auntie Mame*. Auntie Mame serves up *life* like an all-u-can-eat buffet. Her "life's a banquet, and most suckers are starving to death," philosophy is how she plans to raise Patrick.

There are far too many characters running in and out of Mame's apartment to single them all out. But just to mention a few, there's Mame's nerdy (and many times the butt of the joke) sec-

retary, Agnes Gooch. Then there's Mame's side-kick and best friend, Vera Charles, who is game to do anything Mame comes up with as long as there's a martini involved. Add to the mix Patrick's detestable fiancée, Gloria Upson, who is wonderful with her so-called socialite imperson-ation, and the freeloading Brian O'Bannion who is hired to assist Mame in writing her memoirs. The only book I think O'Bannion ever wrote was *How to Get Paid Freeloading*.

The final laugh-out-loud scene is the dinner party Mame throws for Patrick's soon-to-be in-laws, the Upsons. Mame plans to expose them as regular folks putting on airs just to be accepted by high society. Mame's intentions are good; she wants to save Patrick from spending the rest of his life with phony people who only care about his money and not him. However, her plan goes a bit haywire.

DA 411

Auntie Mame was loosely based on Patrick Den-nis's memoirs and his life with his own Auntie Mame. Rosalind Russell's comedic timing and quick-witted, fast-talking banter with everyone who is lucky enough to cross her path are truly masterful. What I really admired about Mame as a character was Patrick Dennis's depiction of a fiercely independent, devil-may-care type of woman during this era.

CASS'S CONCLUSION

If you can't beat them, at least keep them laugh-ing. Everyone should have his or her own Auntie Mame.

GREEN LIGHT

 **Double Take**
(2001)

RATED PG-13; running time 88 minutes
GENRE: Action/Comedy
WRITTEN BY: George Gallo (based on the story by Graham Greene)
DIRECTED BY: George Gallo
CAST: Orlando Jones, Eddie Griffin, Gary Grubbs, Garcelle Beauvais, Andrea Navedo, Edward Herrmann, Daniel Roebuck, Sterling Macer Jr., Benny Nieves, Vivica A. Fox

THE STORY

Daryl Chase (Orlando Jones) is a successful Wall Street banker who stumbled across some funny money that is somehow tied to the Mexican corporation he, his assistant Shari (Vivica A. Fox), and his boss C. A. (Edward Herrmann) are trying to do business with. Pretty soon, Daryl discovers that he's being set up to take a fall. When the frame job turns into a charge of murder, he "borrows" the identity of the one person who might be able to help him—a street hustler named Freddy Tiffany (Eddie Griffin)—and, on the advice of FBI agent T. J. McCready, heads to Mexico. But, as Daryl soon finds out, appearances can be deceiving.

THE UPSHOT

It's clear from the start that the story in *Double Take* is secondary to its main purpose, which is, primarily, to showcase the talents of its stars: stand-up comedian Eddie Griffin and comic actor Orlando Jones. In this sense, it worked, at least partially, especially as pertains to Jones.

I've seen Orlando Jones in a few previous roles: as one of the funnier players in the otherwise dull *Replacements* (see page 159), as the Black guy (uh, sorry about that) in *Bedazzled* (see page 261); and, yes, as the comic relief in some 7-Up commercials. But in *Double Take*, Jones impressed me much more than in anything else I've ever seen him in—to the point where *Double Take* gets a flashing-yellow-light rating solely on the strength of his participation. Jones's Daryl Chase was that rarity of Black comic skit characters: he was as believable playing Mr. Wall Street (importantly, without the unneeded sellout Uncle Tom overtones) as he was the Schlitz Malt Liquor-seeking hoodie rat. The refreshing thing about his character in Wall Street—mode, is that Jones portrayed him as a smart, ambitious, but realistic—and still Old School—achiever. In other words, Chase was everyday Black folk.

Even given my lowered expectations, however, there's still a limit on the amount of wiggle room I'll give a flick, "low-brow" or not. Eddie Griffin quickly reached that limit. Unlike Jones, Griffin *never* made me believe he was anything but the "nigga"-spouting street clown he portrayed from the start. Maybe I shouldn't be too hard on the brotha—after all, he is more a stand-up comedian than a bona fide actor—but hey, I calls it as I sees it. And as I sees it in *Double Take*, Griffin's welcome was worn out before the end of the first act. He lacked the charm of a Jamie Foxx or the depth of an Eddie Murphy; and without much substance to work with, the flash he had quickly dulled.

As expected, the supporting cast members were primarily in place to provide Jones and Griffin with characters to bounce their shtick off of, though Garcelle Beauvais as Chase's sultry lingerie-model girlfriend Chloe, and especially Andrea Navedo as the multifaceted Maque Sanchez, gave more than one might predict of female leads in an action comedy. Strangely enough, Vivica A. Fox, the one cast member who *might've* added more to the *Double Take* stew, makes an early exit. Bad move, guys. Of the remaining cast, even a veteran character actor like Edward Herrmann seemed like so much flotsam and jetsam floating in a lifeless sea—though "Delores"—Freddy's lap dog—provided an unexpected chuckle or two of her own.

If it seems like I hated this movie, I really didn't; *Double Take* never went very far with me, but it did have its moments, and, truthfully, Griffin *did* improve over time (once Freddy stopped playing Street and spouting "nigga," he was tolerable). *Double Take* just wasn't my cup o' tea.

I just hope Hollywood casting agents start sending Orlando Jones scripts that allow him to showcase his acting and comedic skills without always and only requiring him to Act Black (or their warped idea of Black). Here's hoping Jones allows his potential to be challenged even further, regardless of the shortsightedness of those who would typecast him. Fingers crossed.

BAMMER'S BOTTOM LINE
I tried hard to keep my—can I make it plain?—"boy, I hope White folk ain't diggin' this clown" knee-jerk sensitivity in check. I truly did. And I genuinely liked Orlando Jones here in *Double Take;* with a minimum of over-the-top posturing, his Daryl Chase won me over, easily convincing me that Jones's talent runs deep. But there's only so much "nigga"ing I can take. And, along with

it, only so much of the clowning Eddie Griffin.

FLASHING YELLOW LIGHT

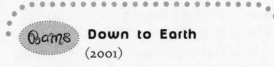

Down to Earth
(2001)

RATED PG-13; running time 95 minutes
GENRE: Comedy
WRITTEN BY: Louis C. K., Lance Crouther, Ali LeRoi, Chris Rock (based on the 1978 screenplay "Heaven Can Wait" by Elaine May and Warren Beatty)
DIRECTED BY: Paul Weitz, Chris Weitz
CAST: Chris Rock, Regina King, Mark Addy, Frankie Faison, Eugene Levy, Chazz Palminteri, Greg Germann, Jennifer Coolidge, Wanda Sykes

THE STORY
The pitch probably went a lil' sum'n like this: "There's this guy, see, who's a frustrated jock, when this gang of angels—let's call them Mr. King (Chazz Palminteri) and his bumbling assistant Keyes (Eugene Levy)—takes him from this earthly veil a few years before he was due. The frustrated jock grumbles about this, so the angels put him in a dead quarterback's body, and he goes on to win the pro championship and lives happily ever after!"

"What's that? Warren who? Heaven Can What?" OK, never mind. How about we make him a mediocre *Black* comic! And let's name him Lance Barton (Chris Rock) and put him into the body of a rich white guy Wellington, and have Lance the inner guy try to squeeze up on Suntee (Regina King) the Social Activist . . . but Suntee—who can only see the White outer guy—hates Wellington the Rich White Guy because he keeps ignoring her Activator . . . er, Activism. And for kicks, let's say Wellington is a lard-butt whose slutty wife (Jennifer Coolidge) sneaks around with Wellington's skanky lawyer Sklar (Greg Germann) to plan Wellington's murder . . . and hey, for more giggles, let's have Lance—in Well's body but with his Ghetto mindset fully in place—not only win over the hearts and minds of his sassy maid Wanda (Wanda Sykes) and uptight Brit butler Cisco (Mark Addy), but also bop up and down the mean streets of New York blasting jungle music and attracting attention from the natives, who'll have no part of Wellington the Rich White Guy emulating their musical stylings and cultural traditions! Yeah, that'll be FUNNNEEE!"

THE UPSHOT

You ever feel like you really, really wanted to sneeze—I mean really, *really* wanted to sneeze—and no matter how hard you tried, you just couldn't do much more than let out an insincere snort or two?

Substitute "laugh" for "sneeze" in the above sentence, and you'll know how I felt while watching *Down to Earth*.

Man, this flick was bad, almost painfully so. I laughed a few times, but always in isolated, "that was a cute gag," circumstances. I spent most of the time wondering about

how We can be so hypocritical at times (see the "Black Factor" for more on this), why anyone would bring their young child to witness Rock's typically foul mouth, and whether or not someone at the WB would get the bright idea to make this movie into a weekly series.

I snickered at Wanda "watch me twist my neck" Sykes's antics, but I saw a lot of the gags (including the Black-man-and-a-taxi) coming from miles away. Most of all, I felt sorriest for Regina King (Suntee? As my bud Jim Hill would say, render unto me a break) and Frankie Faison (Whitney), who seems to get enough steady work as the Sidekick, The Comic Relief, or The Street Hustler, but whose true talents aren't showcased nearly as much as they should be. As for the Rock man himself, I have no such remorse for him; he'll get a big enough paycheck for this one.

THE BLACK FACTOR

Take away my Ghetto Pass if you must, but surely I can't be the only one who thinks it's the ultimate in hypocrisy for Us to get all offended and sh . . . tuff when White comics crack on Black folks using the same language that *Black* comics use, can I? Yeah yeah yeah, "only family can dog" . . . I've heard it all before. What. Ever.

BAMMER'S BOTTOM LINE

Down to Earth was a prime example of why I hate remakes. If *this* is what your movies are gonna look like, Chris, stick with stand-up. You're a whole lot funnier on stage than in lame flicks like this one.

YELLOW LIGHT

How High
the Diva
(2001)

RATED R; running time 89 minutes
GENRE: Comedy
WRITTEN BY: Dustin Lee Abraham
DIRECTED BY: Jesse Dylan
CAST: Method Man, Redman, Obba Babatundé, Mike Epps, Anan Maria Horsford, Fred Willard, Lark Voorhies, Essence Atkins, Chuck Davis

THE DIGEST

If you have a problem, Silas P. Silas (Method Man) has some herb that will cure it. He is so good at fixing ailments that his best friend, Ivory (Chuck Davis), encourages him to become a doctor. He knows that Silas can succeed in college, he just has to find the will. Meanwhile, in another part of town, Jamal King (Redman) has just been kicked out of junior college. His mother is through and berates him until he promises to take his THCs (Testing for Higher Credentials).

Back on the other side of town, Silas's best friend, Ivory, has tragically died. Silas takes his ashes and plants them with some marijuana seeds—it becomes the "special weed." Two months later, he shows up to take his test and pulls up next to Jamal. Both are trying to calm their nerves by getting high. One has the light and the other has the weed. A match made in heaven. They light up Silas's special best friend weed and start puffing. Miracle of all miracles . . . Silas's best friend shows up as a ghost and vows to help them pass the test and succeed in school, by cheating for them. It works, and they land at Harvard. Once in Harvard, they merely have to light up the special weed and Ivory appears to help them.

They are met with hostility by Dean Cain (Obba Babatundé) who sees them as bad examples of Black people and wants them gone at all costs. The campus jock Bart (Chris Elwood)—with his racist behind—has also decided to make their life horrible. They take it in stride. This works out perfectly until someone steals the precious plant. Can they succeed on their own?

THE DISH

Silas and Jamal can't succeed on their own, and I think that was the most disappointing aspect of this movie for me. Had they been able to buckle down, study, and pass their classes, the movie would've been redeemed. The portrayal of the women was also horrendously disappointing. Jamal's girlfriend is the daughter of the vice president of the United States and she wants a thug for a boyfriend. Meanwhile, Jamal's mother, Lauren, talks to him like to a dog and lets herself be bullied by a jackass. What kinds of messages are these? This movie was laced with horrible stereotypes and pathetic characterizations of Blacks, Whites, and Asians.

Before you think that I'm totally without a sense of humor, I did laugh at Mike Epps's character: the pimp called Baby Powder. But that's not enough to justify this mess making it to the screen.

THE DIRECTIVE

This movie reminded me of *The Disorderlies* in that I loved it when I was twelve; I look back on it now and wonder if I was on crack, myself. *How High* should've been called How Low.

RED LIGHT

---

the Diva Kingdom Come
(2001)

RATED PG-13; running time 93 minutes
GENRE: Comedy
WRITTEN BY: David Bottrell and Jessie Jones
DIRECTED BY: Doug McHenry
CAST: Whoopi Goldberg, Loretta Devine, LL Cool J, Jada Pinkett-Smith, Vivica A. Fox, Anthony Anderson, Darius McCray, Toni Braxton, Cedric the Entertainer.

THE DIGEST

How do you plan a funeral for someone that nobody liked? Daddy Slocum has passed on and now the family must come together and deal with the pain he caused when he was alive. Bud Slocum was, as his wife Raynelle (Whoopi Goldberg) puts it, a mean and ornery old cuss. So much so, she wants "Mean and Ornery" on his headstone. But before she can even think about dealing with the headstone, she needs to deal with her kids.

Ray Bud (LL Cool J) is a hardworking man trying his best to support his much-adored wife, Lucille (Vivica A. Fox). Yet every day is a struggle for Ray Bud, a recovering alcoholic. He has to deal with the lack of love from his father, plus he and his wife are unable to start a family. After several miscarriages, they've given up. On top of all of that, it looks like he is the only one financially able to make sure that Daddy Slocum has a decent funeral, because once again his brother Junior is broke. Junior (Anthony Anderson) can't seem to win for losing. He is married to loud-mouthed Charisse (Jada Pinkett-Smith) and the father of three boys. Charisse is a Ghetto shrew. She never lets him forget that she was the catch, not him, and she could have been married to a very rich relative of his. When she's not reminding him of all his failures, she's belittling him. But she is nothing compared to Aunt Marguerite (Loretta Devine).

Aunt Marguerite is a Christian woman; she reads the Bible every day and leads a Christian life, except that she is verbally abusive to her son Royce (Darius McCray). She fears that he will wind up in jail like his brother. Well, she never misses an opportunity to call him some form of Satan. It's enough to wear you out and Raynelle *is* worn out. Can she keep her family together or must she just watch everything fall apart around her?

THE DISH

Interesting, though not as good as I had hoped. Some of the acting was mediocre at best, and there were quite a few holes in the plot. The main

problem may be that the screenwriters had difficulty converting what was originally a play into a
movie. There are lots of things you can get away
with in a play that you cannot in a movie. For example, if you introduce a character in a play, that
will not be on stage, you give as much explanation as possible so the audience doesn't get confused. They failed to do this in the movie. There
were two major characters in the movie that were
never shown but were constantly talked about,
leaving too many loose ends.

I thought Whoopi was great. She just sat
there and let everyone tear up everything around
her, but she was a voice of reason and wisdom
when she felt it was needed. Loretta Devine, Toni
Braxton, and Vivica Fox were also very good, especially Toni in her first screen role. She has potential. Jada Pinkett-Smith's character really got
on my nerves. I couldn't deal with the constant
screeching. LL gave it a good shot and, for the
most part, he was pretty decent. The problems I
had with this movie could've been solved with a
script rewrite.

THE DIRECTIVE

Even though *Kingdom Come* is not the greatest
movie, we need to support our small films.

FLASHING YELLOW LIGHT

the Diva Nutty Professor II: The Klumps

(2000)

RATED PG-13; running time 105 minutes
GENRE: Comedy
WRITTEN BY: Barry W. Blaustein & David
Sheffield and Paul Weitz & Chris Weitz
DIRECTED BY: Peter Segal
CAST: Eddie Murphy, Janet Jackson, Larry Miller,
John Ales

THE DIGEST

We're back at Wellman College. This time, Professor Sherman Klump (Eddie Murphy), with the
help of a colleague and fiancée Denice Gaines
(Janet Jackson), has discovered a youth serum.
The problem is that it only works for a few seconds. Dean Richmond (Larry Miller) doesn't care,
and sells it for 150 million. Meanwhile, Sherman
is having problems keeping his alter ego, Buddy
Love, under control, and this wreaks havoc in his
life, most notably in his life with Denice.

THE DISH

The best part of the movie was Sherman's interaction with his family, though Murphy's
Grandma stole the show. It's really like you are
watching six different actors, though, when you
see all of them together. It was also wonderful
seeing Janet back on the screen though I was
more than annoyed that she spent most of her
time either laughing or crying. No real depth.
Granted, it is a comedy, but it's been seven years
since her last film and I wanted a "wow!"

As with the original, we were treated to crude
fart jokes and projectile hamster turds. The sex

jokes, however, were funny because they were coming from Grandma. You'll see what I mean.

THE DIRECTIVE

Nutty Professor II is amusing, but not rolling-in-the-aisle funny.

FLASHING YELLOW LIGHT

Dams Our Song
(2000)

RATED R; running time 95 minutes
GENRE: Drama
WRITTEN BY: Jim McKay
DIRECTED BY: Jim McKay
CAST: Kerry Washington, Anna Simpson, Melissa Martinez, Marlene Forte, Raymond Anthony Thomas, Rosalyn Coleman, Carmen Lopez, Tyrone Brown, Kim Howard, Juan Romero Jr., Lorraine Berry, Natasha Frith

THE STORY

Our Song is a simple—but not mindless—story of three young friends in Crown Heights, Brooklyn, during one hot summer. Lanisha, Maria, and Joycelyn are members of the Jackie Robinson Steppers, a marching band that's highly respected and supported in their neighborhood. And the bandleader, Mr. Miller, works hard to keep it that way, keeping the members motivated to be the best they can be.

Each of the girls' family members support them in varying degrees: Lanisha's mother, Pilar, and father, Carl, seem to be right behind Lanisha, whereas Maria and her mother, Rita, and numbnut brother, Alex, have some serious issues; and Joy's mother, Dawn, seems more intent on having a good time on the streets than in helping her daughter grow up. And even the strong bond the girls have as friends is threatened when Joy pulls away and gets closer to her new Stepper friends Kim and Keisha.

THE UPSHOT

As a movie critic, I try to stay objective about what I'm watching but involved enough to give a reasoned opinion. But as a member of the human race and of one of its subsets—namely, Black Folk—I sometimes make presumptions. I started watching this movie with any number of expectations, presumptions, and prejudices, mainly revolving around its inner-city setting and subject matter. In the notes I made while watching *Our Song*, there are comments such as "I bet a beatdown is coming next," or "I bet Character X turns out to be a major drug dealer." Many of my presumptions about what makes a 'Hood Flick, were (ahem) shot down.

Our Song surprised me at nearly every turn, however quietly. The lack of "Big Dramatic Events!" was somewhat unnerving, probably because I have become conditioned to expect exactly that from mainstream movies. Yet another surprise for me was how natural the main characters appeared, as did the charm and talent of the young actors playing them. Melissa Martinez (Maria), Anna Simpson (Joycelyn), and especially Kerry Washington (Lanisha) had a strong film presence that is all the more amazing considering that this was the first feature film for each of them. They were able to seemingly effortlessly blend humor with drama, diminishing neither. All three are definitely worth looking for in the future; I just hope that mainstream Hollywood doesn't lock them into dead-end Welfare-Mama-Crackhead-*NYPD Blue*—type roles—I'm not holding my breath.

The lasting impact of *Our Song* is that it is an everyman's film, about the everyday life of young folks in a particular corner of the world. No gritty plot points, no patron saint to come rescue the poor 'hood rats, no big drama for your mama— and that's the point. The circumstances might be different, the shading might change, the mood music might be in a different key—but the groove of *Our Song*, whether on the streets of New York, in the suburbs of Colorado, or on the street where *you* live, might just be universal.

THE BLACK FACTOR

I know it's not PC to draw attention to our differences, but the Jackie Robinson Steppers did things differently from their White counterparts. I live for the day when a funked-up marching band like the fabulous Steppers becomes the rule instead of the exception. Pardon my lack of racially neutral words here, but I think a little non-gladiator color might do American sports audiences some good. And no, premanufactured Boy Bands don't count.

(OK, that address is 3blacknon-gladiator-Bams@3blackchicks.com just use the subject line "HOW *DARE* YOU SAY THAT BLACK FOLK ARE DIFFERENT FROM WHITE FOLK! WE'RE ALL THE SAME UNDER THE SKIN! KUMBAYA, MY LORD!!!," so I'll know where to file it).

BAMMER'S BOTTOM LINE

Do something different this weekend: check out *Our Song*, a film that reminds you that the little things in life count as much—if not more—as the big dramatic stuff. Yes, even in the 'Hood.

GREEN LIGHT

the Diva   **Sparkle**
(1976)

RATED PG; running time 98 minutes
GENRE: Ghettofabulous Musical
WRITTEN BY: Joel Schumacher (D'oh!)
DIRECTED BY: Sam O'Steen
MUSIC BY: Curtis Mayfield
CAST: Irene Cara, Lonette McKee, Dwan Smith, Mary Alice, Philip Michael Thomas, and Dorian Harewood

THE DIGEST

Effie is trying to raise her three teenaged daughters in 1950s Harlem, which isn't easy. Because she is a single parent, she is not home as often as she would like to be. She's a maid for a rich White family and sometimes she must stay late to handle dinner parties. As a result, the girls are responsible for themselves.

The girls don't give her much trouble. Sister (Lonette McKee), the eldest, is fast; she's already running around with men. In fact, one of her suitors has given her a ring that cost $17 dollars and has a real diamond chip in it. Next up is De-lores, middle girl. As middle children tend to do, she sinks into the background. It doesn't help that she looks different from her sisters. She has smooth and pretty brown skin, the color of a "Hershey's Kiss." She has short, manageable hair, while both of her sisters have long tresses and so-called "good hair." And, finally, there's Sparkle, the baby girl. She has taken on the role of helpmate and peacekeeper. She adores her older sisters and her mother. She will do any-thing to keep them happy. All the while, she is cultivating a relationship with a young man from the neighborhood, named "Stix" (Philip Michael Thomas). Stix—who, besides being Sparkle's boyfriend, is an aspiring musician—and Sister's latest boyfriend, Levi, have a great idea. They have time on their hands and the girls can sing, so why not form a singing group? The five of them form "The Hearts" and they start touring the local clubs for amateur night and before you know it, they are a local hit. And that's when the prob-lems start. Can the girls work through their prob-lems and remain a family or will semi-fame destroy them?

THE DISH

I couldn't get enough of this movie. I've seen it about 300 times. I'm most in love with Curtis Mayfield's soundtrack: "Giving Up," "Look Into Your Heart," "Jump," and "Giving Him Some-thing He Can Feel." Classic Curtis Mayfield . . . Ghetto anthems. But I have to mention the shock I suffered when I noticed that Joel Schumacher, a White screenwriter who also wrote *The Wiz*, wrote this movie.

THE DIRECTIVE

Sparkle puts a sparkle on my day whenever I see it.

GREEN LIGHT

Bams　Willy Wonka and the Chocolate Factory

(1971)

RATED G; running time 100 minutes
GENRE: Musical/Fantasy
WRITTEN BY: Roald Dahl (based on his book)
DIRECTED BY: Mel Stuart
CAST: Gene Wilder, Jack Albertson, Peter Os-trum, Roy Kinnear, Julie Dawn Cole, Leonard Stone, Denise Nickerson, Paris Themmen, Nora Denney, Ursula Reit, Michael Bollner, Diana Sowle, Gunter Meisner, David Battley

"Wonkamania" continues to influence gen-erations of its watchers. Two of its char-acters have reached pop-icon status: Veruca Salt has a band named after her, and Mike Teevee was a character on ABC's *ReBoot*.

THE STORY

Charlie Bucket (Peter Ostrum), a po' Ghetto chile, is doing the best he can to avoid The Man and hi . . . oops, sorry, wrong Ghetto Movie de-scription.

Charlie lives in a one-room shack with his widowed mother (Diana Sowle) and both sets of grandparents—all four of whom are bedridden and have slept in the same bed together, without once getting up, for twenty years. When Charlie hears that local chocolatier Willy Wonka (Gene Wilder) is sponsoring a Golden Ticket giveaway for something wonderful, Charlie manages to get a ticket! Now Charlie and his fellow tribe members—glutton Augustus (Michael Bollner) and his mother, Mrs. Gloop (Ursula Reit); spoiled brat Veruca Salt (Julie Dawn Cole) and her rich daddy (Roy Kinnear); gum-chewing Violet (Denise Nickerson) and her salesman father (Leonard Stone); and constant television-watcher Mike (Paris Themmen) and his teacher mother (Nora Denney)—must survive before Wonka's evil candy rival, Slugworth (Günter Meisner), gets them voted off the island á la *Survivor*.

THE UPSHOT

I'm not exaggerating when I say that, emotionally speaking, *Willy Wonka and the Chocolate Factory* is my bestest, most favoritest movie of all time. Where else would you find Dr. Seuss's warped cousin, White people who are so hungry that a loaf of bread is considered a feast, and references to torturing children that *aren't* subject to nationwide boycotts? Only *Willy Wonka* can bring you dialogue like this:

Reporter (asking Mike about television): "You like the killings, huh?"

Mike Teevee: "What do you think life's all about?!?"

And you wanna talk dancing and singing Oompa Loompas? Come on, ya gotta love them! *Willy Wonka* has something to please every age level: candy for the kiddies, sarcasm for the adults, flashbacks to mind-altered states for the druggies.

Wilder played Wonka as a slightly sarcastic Dr. Seuss, something I don't think I caught as quickly when I was a child, but certainly noticed—with a grin—as an adult. But I liked Albertson most as a representative of four people who never got up out of bed for 20 years—if that ain't Ghetto, I don't know what is. Cole stole the show away from the other five kids with her brilliantly bratty Veruca Salt. That she made me want to smack Veruca upside her spoiled little head means Cole hit the bull's-eye (with "Dad" Roy Kinnear providing the arrow). Her song "I Want It Now" could be the theme song for a whole generation of Nintendo-PlayStation-DVD-MP3-soaked kids. And as Charlie's teacher Mr. Turkentine, David Battley takes a small role and wrings so much laughter out of it, it's almost scary.

The writing wasn't consistently sharp; I didn't much care for the weaker "Mike Teevee" portion of the tour (Wonka's fiery speech to Charlie and Grandpa Joe was really the only thing that registered for me in the last part of the movie). And I'd still like to know just how so many Americans managed to live in that obviously Bavarian village during that period. But these small annoyances in no way negated the magnificent art direction, wonderful music by Anthony Newley and Leslie Bricusse, or Mel Stuart's inspired directing.

BAMMER'S BOTTOM LINE:

Willy Wonka and the Chocolate Factory is 60 percent Ghettofabulous, 55 percent psychedelic, 20 percent Pythonesque . . . and 100 percent good.

GREEN LIGHT

hat can we say about this section that isn't covered in the title? We originally intended to call this chapter "When White Folks Hit Each Other." We had just come off a round of movies where White folks were kicking the living tar out of other White folks. Then we noticed that there were quite a few movies out there that show White folks straight-up dogging one another—a movie where someone does some foul stuff to another person but doesn't necessarily visit physical harm on the other person. It just made sense to combine the two categories. Movies like *Fight Club* and *American Beauty* are two great examples of the types of movies this chapter will cover.

Bams American Beauty

(1999)

RATED R; running time 119 minutes
GENRE: Drama
WRITTEN BY: Alan Ball
DIRECTED BY: Sam Mendes
CAST: Kevin Spacey, Annette Bening, Thora
Birch, Wes Bentley, Mena Suvari, Peter Gal-
lagher, Chris Cooper, Allison Janney, Scott
Bakula, Sam Robards

> Kevin Spacey is a wiz at impressions; his
> best are of Johnny Carson, Al Pacino, and
> our personal favorite, Christopher Walken.

THE STORY

Lester Burnham (Kevin Spacey) is a fortysome-
thing burnout whose daily highlight is the time
he spends alone each morning in the shower. He
feels as trapped by his now-loveless marriage to
his wife, Carolyn (Annette Bening)—a mediocre
real estate agent who can't quite see past the
plastic liners on her furniture—as she feels
trapped by him. Lester seeks a new life through
bodybuilding exercises, as suggested to him by
gay neighbors-lovers Jim (Scott Bakula) and Jim
(Sam Robards)—arguably the most "normal"
residents of their little town. Carolyn, meanwhile, seeks mentorship, and a wee bit more,
from real estate king Buddy King (Peter Gallagher). Equally trapped in their misery is their
daughter, Jane (Thora Birch); and as if normal
teen angst wasn't enough for her, she also has to
deal with her father's men-o-pausal attraction to

her very blond (and she knows it) cheerleader
friend Angela Hayes (Mena Suvari).

And behind door number two . . . the Fittses,
Watchers Of Life: dope-dealing loner Ricky
(Wes Bentley) watches Jane and her family
while he tapes them via camcorder. The bulldog
Colonel Fitts (Chris Cooper) watches son Ricky
turn into a zombie under his cold and austere
paternal regiment. And all-but-brain-dead-
mother Barbara (Allison Janney) watches life go
by in a haze of her own nonexistence.

True poster families for Dysfunctions 'R' Us.

THE UPSHOT

Beauty lives up to its Oscar hype. There's little
doubt that these are people you wouldn't normally want to associate with every day—but, in
fact, probably do: Is flabby, unmotivated Lester
really unlike sloppy Joe Down The Street? Doesn't
Carolyn remind you of that obnoxious Avon Lady
that keeps ringing your doorbell just as you're sitting down to dinner? And face it: if Jane hasn't
started bringing guns to Public School 101, she
probably will soon. Yes, America: these *are* the
people in your neighborhood/in your neighbor-
hood/in your neigh-bor-hood . . .

And look closer yet: beyond its portrait of dysfunctional suburbia in all its ugliness, *Beauty* has
humor, glimmers of hope, wonderful cinematography, and, above all, kick-ass performances
throughout. As Lester, Kevin Spacey is magnificent. Spacey lights up the screen in nearly every
scene he's in, and he's equally convincing both as
a burnout and as a rejuvenated weightlifter. The
rest of the cast is also good, though on a somewhat lesser scale. Annette Bening gives an Oscar-
worthy performance as Carolyn, proving yet

again her range as an actress. And though most reviewers trumpeted Thora Birch as angry, angsty daughter Jane, my favorites among the supporting cast are Chris Cooper as the colonel, and especially Wes Bentley as Ricky. I'm sure we haven't heard the last of either of them.

For me, the sign that a director has done his or her job well is that I notice *something* behind the acting, but don't quite know what that something is. This was borne out in *Beauty*, with Sam Mendes's "unseen" touches adding icing to a well-baked cake. One scene in particular in which I finally figured out why I was so mesmerized came when Jane and Lester were seen talking through a kitchen window; though I heard and saw what was going on, I also noticed the row of bottles filled with colored liquid, which in turn made me notice the intricate use of light and shadows throughout the scene. I had to snap out of it so I wouldn't miss the forest for the proverbial trees.

BAMMER'S BOTTOM LINE

If *American Beauty* does for Dysfunctional Suburbia what *Fatal Attraction* did for . . . uh, Dysfunctional Suburbia . . . Hmmm . . .

GREEN LIGHT

the Diva

Boiler Room

(2000)

RATED R; running time 117 minutes
WRITTEN BY: Ben Younger
GENRE: Drama
DIRECTED BY: Ben Younger
CAST: Giovanni Ribisi, Vin Diesel, Ben Affleck, Jamie Kennedy, Scott Caan, Ron Rifkin, Nicky Katt, Nia Long, Taylor Nichols, Tom Everett Scott

Actor Scott Caan is the son of actor James Caan.

THE DIGEST

Seth (Giovanni Ribisi), contentedly makes a good living running a card game from his apartment. One night he starts a late-night game for an old friend and his associate, Greg (Nicky Katt), who plunks down a fat roll of money. Seth is intrigued. Greg senses this and he likes Seth's spunk, so he invites him to interview for a position at his stock firm. Seth is a bit cautious but he is thrilled to be going legit. He wants nothing more than to please his father, a federal judge who hates Seth's "home business," and worries that his career will end if he is associated with his son. Hoping to mend his relationship with his father, Seth goes for it.

Seth proves to be very good at getting folks to part with their money. Not only is he good at making money, he has also attracted the attention of the receptionist Abby (Nia Long). This causes tension between Seth and Greg because

Greg is used to being the shining star and Abby is his ex. Greg is extremely jealous and gives Seth a hard time, but Seth and Abby begin to build a relationship anyway.

Eventually, Seth starts to notice a few things that don't add up and realizes that he is actually scamming people when he thought he was legit.

THE DISH

Boiler Room was disgusting. Forty White guys were running a stock scam on other White guys, and in the process making millions of dollars. What's disgusting? Well, they were pigs. For one, they had no respect for Black folks, especially the "Nigger Rich"—those who make all kinds of money but still live from paycheck to paycheck. Secondly, they had no respect for women: "we do not pitch the bitch," meaning they don't sell stocks to women. And lastly, they thought it was cool and funny to pretend to be Black and talk like someone out of the 'hood. "Shooooot niggah, you be trippin'. Pass the muddah fuggin weed, beatch." In the theater, I was the only Black person watching, and I was beyond upset to hear White folks laughing at the mockery.

The entire soundtrack is rap music, which I assume is part of rebelling against the system. In fact, in the opening monologue, the main character quotes Biggie Smalls. According to Biggie, it's about making fast money. You can sell crack or you can have a wicked jump shot. Seth Green has opted to sell "White-boy crack"—stocks. This movie reminded me of *Fight Club* without all the violence—White male angst and anger. If the moviemakers thought the message was about getting a piece of the pie by bucking the system, I saw it as a bunch of spoiled rich White guys sat-

isfying their every whim—be it drugs, cars, homes, food, or women. And, of course, the other message was dealing with parental relationships, which anyone can understand.

Were there any redeeming qualities in this movie? One or two: I was touched by Seth's devotion to his father. He was doing all of this to earn his father's love, affection, and respect. That much I could relate to.

Why haven't I mentioned Ben Affleck? Well, because all he did was pop up now and then to cuss out the new recruits and belittle them. While he said a few amusing things, he was a waste of space.

THE BLACK FACTOR

Once again, Nia Long plays the long-suffering Black woman. I'm so tired of her getting stuck as the Girlfriend, where she is always on the fringe of the story. I was through—y'all hear me—*through* when Seth asked her for some chocolate loving. AND I was unbelievably through when she called him on his assumption that she was taking care of her sick grandma 'cause her mama was a crackhead. Oh yeah, *that* stereotype. Anyway, Abby reveals that she has to deal with the sexism and racism because she makes 80 grand a year, which is enough to care for her ailing mother. Please! We don't all have sick parents at home. And we all weren't raised by our grandmothers. My mama raised me and she is not locked up in my extra bedroom . . . sick. I would have been more impressed if Abby were socking that money away to open her own business.

THE DIRECTIVE

If I want to watch folks sit around and berate each other and dog women while making millions of dollars, I'll watch WWF. Don't bother.

RED LIGHT

the Diva Blow
(2001)

RATED R; running time 120 minutes

GENRE: Drama

WRITTEN BY: David McKenna and Nick Cassavetes (based on the book by Bruce Porter)

DIRECTED BY: Ted Demme

CAST: Johnny Depp, Penelope Cruz, Franka Potente, Rachel Griffiths, Paul Reubens, Max Perlich, Ethan Suplee, Ray Liotta

> You might know Paul Reubens a little better by his stage name: Peewee Herman.

THE DIGEST

It is said that 90 percent of the cocaine that flowed into the United State in the '70s and '80s had to pass through George Jung's hands first. This movie attempts to show how an average American boy goes from "Leave It to Beaver" to drug kingpin.

George Jung (Johnny Depp) watched his father struggle and his mother berate his father for their lack of money, and swore he would never be poor again. By the time he was 20, he had moved out of his Massachusetts home to California. There he found an abundance of beautiful women and dope. His best friend, Tuna, (Ethan Suplee), figures there is a demand for weed and they could supply it. That way they could stay high all of the time, make money, and not have to work. George finds the local supplier, Derek Foreal (Paul Reubens), and strikes up a deal with him. Before long they are making a killing.

This works out perfectly until George gets busted and spends two years in jail. This turns out to be a blessing in disguise because there he meets Diego Delgado who, it turns out, has a cocaine connection. Diego knows Pablo Escobar, the head of the Colombian drug cartel, who has been looking for an American connection.

This partnership affords George all of the things he has always wanted: a beautiful trophy wife (Penelope Cruz), a child, millions of dollars, a nice home, and cars. It is also the beginning of his descent.

THE DISH

Hmmm. I had a few issues with this movie. While George Jung was high-rolling, so was I. I was vicariously caught up in his life, but when things went South, I got bored. Now, it can be argued that this was a very well-written piece of material since I was so caught up in the hype with George. But it can also be argued that the script just fell apart halfway through the movie. I think the latter was closer to the truth than the former. Depp put in a solid performance, as did Liotta and Cruz.

THE BLACK FACTOR

This movie pissed me, as a Black woman, off, because the movie attempted to manipulate me into having sympathy for George Jung, portrayed as an all-American boy who, because of his mother's hangups, decides to sell drugs. But that's okay because he never hurts anyone, so, ethically, it's all good. Whatever.

Everyone wants to point at the urban areas and blame Blacks for the crack epidemic. What about this dude? Cocaine was barely on the West Coast until he opened up the connection in 1976. When I say he moved *tons* of cocaine, I'm not exaggerating. Fifty kilos is equal to 110 pounds; he moved/sold 150 kilos in 36 hours, and this was his first California shipment. Imagine what it was like three months later.

Now, had this been a story about a Black crack dealer, what do you think the reaction would have been? Do you think the crack dealer would have been called lazy and shiftless because he didn't want to actually work? Or do you think he would have been called a brilliant entrepreneur, like George?

THE DIRECTIVE

The last half of the movie blew.

YELLOW LIGHT

Fight Club
(1999)

RATED R; running time 139 minutes
GENRE: Drama/Action
WRITTEN BY: Chuck Palahniuk (novel), Jim Uhls
DIRECTED BY: David Fincher
CAST: Brad Pitt, Edward Norton, Helena Bonham Carter, Meat Loaf, Jared Leto

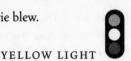

Try to Spot the Spot in this one. You'll get 15 points.

THE DIGEST

Edward Norton plays "The Narrator," and he tells his story via a long flashback and voice over. The Narrator suffers from insomnia. Sometimes going four or five days without sleep. He begins looking for a support group for his condition and happens upon a group of men who are suffering from testicular cancer. By the end of a session, he opens up and cries, and sleeps better than he has in months. So he becomes a support group junkie. He pretends to have various illnesses so he can get his emotional release and sleep. This works fine until he notices that a woman (Helena Bonham Carter) is attending all of the same meetings he is. This unnerves him. He feels that his space has been violated and he becomes an insomniac again. All that changes when he meets Tyler Durden (Brad Pitt, who was looking miiighty nice).

THE DISH

I'll cut to the chase. I hated this damn movie. I hated it with a passion. When I saw the previews, I thought, "If I want to see a bunch of White guys beat up on each other, I'll stay home and watch hockey." I should have stayed home. In all my years of going to the movies, I have only walked out on two: *Hellraiser* and *Fight Club*. In fact, when I was through with this film, so were about six other people. But I'm the only fool to have returned to the theater. It's not a badly acted movie; from a purely technical standpoint, it's a very good movie. So why did I leave? Because of the gratuitous violence. I was sick of seeing broken bones and beat-up faces. Perhaps it was just too controversial for me.

I used to kid myself by thinking I could handle "guy films." I've seen *Natural Born Killers*. I've seen *Reservoir Dogs*. Not my favorites, but I was cool. That wasn't the case with this movie. My moment of realization came early on in the movie, when all the guys were laughing at a particular scene and my face was scrunched up like I was sucking on a lemon. It seemed every time I was disgusted, the men in the theater were laughing. Maybe it's a macho thing. Then again, maybe I just couldn't identify with this movie at all. I'm not a disenfranchised White man. I'm not looking for someone to lead me nor am I looking for something to belong to.

THE DIRECTIVE

I wouldn't waste my hard-earned money on this mess.

RED LIGHT

Bams Magnolia
(1999)

RATED R; running time 195 minutes
GENRE: Drama
WRITTEN BY: Paul Thomas Anderson
DIRECTED BY: Paul Thomas Anderson
CAST: Jason Robards, Julianne Moore, Tom Cruise, Jeremy Blackman, Michael Bowen, William H. Macy, Philip Baker Hall, Melinda Dillon, Melora Walters, John C. Reilly, Philip Seymour Hoffman, Emmanuel Johnson, Henry Gibson, Alfred Molina, Miguel Perez, Denise Woolwine, Luis Guzmán, Felicity Huffman

> Philip Baker Hall has been in 24 movies since 1988 (often bit and uncredited parts), including *The Rock*, *Air Force One*, and *Enemy of the State*. His movies have made over a billion dollars, combined, to date.

THE STORY

Hellifi know. Near as I can call it, the story of *Magnolia* centered around:

Earl Partridge (Jason Robards)—At the end of his life's journey, he wants to make things right with his estranged son;

Linda Partridge (Julianne Moore)—Once in it only for the money, she's surprised to find she's actually in love with her dying husband;

Frank Mackey (Tom Cruise)—Glib, macho TV guru Frank is a smooth operator with the chicks, but is caught up short by family drama;

Stanley Spector (Jeremy Blackman)—A child prodigy and quiz show star, the one thing Stanley doesn't know is how to reach into his father's heart;

Rick Spector (Michael Bowen)—A prime example of an empty man living vicariously through his progeny;

Donnie Smith (Willliam H. Macy)—Former boy genius, his world is slowly crumbling around him, but he holds on to his fantasies of a perfect love;

Jimmy Gator (Philip Baker Hall)—Quiz show host Gator is a straight-and-narrow kinda guy . . . but only if you don't look too closely;

Rose Gator (Melinda Dillon)—A real "stand by your man" kinda gal, Rose is about to learn more than she ever wanted to know about Jimmy;

Claudia Wilson Gator (Melora Walters)—Tired of living the literal high life, Claudia just wants the truth to be known;

Officer Jim Kurring (John C. Reilly)—The unassuming LAPD officer is hit with the bop gun when he least expected it: on a routine investigation;

Phil Parma (Philip Seymour Hoffman)—Rough-and-tumble male nurse, he works hard to see that Earl Partridge's final wishes come true;

Dixon (Emmanuel Johnson)—Young street poet whose words provide the backdrop for the twisted story of the people in his neighborhood.

Hope that helps.

THE UPSHOT

There were some High-Falutin' Reviewers who went on and on about how brilliantly unflawed a piece of art *Magnolia* was; about how it totally changed the way they see filumms; about how

they came away with a catharsis that was better'n a good scromp on a hot summer's day. To those High-Falutin' Reviewers, I say, next time that pipe goes around, Just Say No.

Which is to say that was a weeeird farkin' movie.

Magnolia sets its story up at the start by telling three tall tales—otherwise known as "Urban Legends"—as if they were real ("strange things happen all the time," the earnest narrator tells us). I was lost until the final act, at which point, I realized it was all one big Urban Legend. Not that having that knowledge made the movie gel as a whole, but it at least moved it squarely into the "fantasy" genre, thus moving the Disbelief Suspension Bar up a notch or three. But I find I *still* cannot tell you, dear reader, what *Magnolia* was about—save redemption, forgiveness, weird teeth, and the power of a few frogs (well, more than a few, but I'm just sayin').

What was most intriguing about *Magnolia* was how, in its jump-cut way, it was kind of a morality play with skits and sketches. It was interesting to see one character (Earl) at the end stages of his sickness, and another (Jimmy Gator) at the beginning of his. Likewise, has-been ex–quiz-boy Donnie Smith could easily provide a mirror image to current quiz boy Rick Spector, a potential has-been himself—unless some strange thing occurs, perhaps?

Throughout the very long movie, we learn something about one character, only to learn something similar about the next. Yet we never really get to know *any* of the characters. Even at 195 minutes, there seems to be no time for full character development, by design or because of the large ensemble cast, there is no real feeling for the characters, except for Tom "This Is For The Oscar, Y'all!" Cruise's admittedly good performance as Frank Mackey. Cruise's Mackey is a talk show host gone radically wrong, an unattached-sex-is-everything hawker who seems to be the embodiment of vengeance for all those fellas who have grown tired of women who cry "all men are dawgs!" In Mackey's world, the dawgs rule ("protect the cock . . . and pursue the cunt!" is his mantra), and indeed, he is Top Dawg. Only when a reporter brings him to his knees by bringing up his past, do we see that he's just a scared little boy behind his cocksure bravado.

Most of the other characters are played as one-dimensional to serve their storyline's purpose. But—surprise, surprise—someone else comes along to steal the show. Two someones, in fact: John C. Reilly's portrayal of officer Jim Kurring was a centerpiece to this movie, one that, in my eyes, steered all the other stories to their conclusions. The second someone was Henry Gibson as Thurston Howell (!). Gibson and Macy seem to be from the same school of acting, but here, Gibson was the teacher; he schooled Macy somethin' fierce. Though Macy is one of my favorite thespians (and a primary reason for me seeing this flick), I was disappointed by his acting; I never got the feel for his Donnie, and found him more *pathetic* than *sympathetic*.

Given the right frame of mind (and a nap beforehand, perhaps) *Magnolia* can be enjoyable enough. As long as you're not particularly picky about movies having a discernible beginning, middle, and end.

THE BLACK FACTOR

Strange that Our representation in *Magnolia* comes via three characters: the uncredited Marcy, a big, loud Black woman who defines the mindset "Crime Makes You Stupid"; Dixon, a young boy who communicates best by rapping; and Denise (Denise Woolwine), a female reporter so seemingly unreceptive to Frank Mackey's charms (or he to her potential) that he undresses down to his skivvies in front of her—and she, the safe nonsexual Black female, doesn't even blink.

But maybe that's just me, noticing things.

BAMMER'S BOTTOM LINE

Difficult to completely understand, and uneven though it were, *Magnolia* gets props for thinking different ("farkin' weeeeird," I think I called it). If you look closely enough, however, at the individual tales, it's not really all that earth-shatteringly different. Except for the frogs.

GREEN LIGHT

Mickey Blue Eyes
(1999)

RATED PG-13; running time 112 minutes
GENRE: Comedy
WRITTEN BY: Adam Scheinman and Robert
   Kuhn
DIRECTED BY: Kelly Makin
CAST: Hugh Grant, James Caan, Jeanne Tripple-
   horn, Burt Young

> As the movie ends, "THE THE END" is dis-
> played on the screen. This refers to
> Frank's restaurant, The La Trattoria, which
> translates to The The Trattoria.

THE STORY

Description from the official Web site:

". . . in which Hugh Grant, as Michael Fel-
gate, elegant, debonair Englishman, falls in love
with his wonderful girlfriend Gina, as played by
Jeanne Tripplehorn, and is welcomed with open
arms by Frank, her father, as played by James
Caan. In time, however, Michael begins to realize
that becoming part of Gina's family may indeed
mean becoming part of The Family."

Hookay. Now, Bammer's turn:

. . . in which Hugh Grant once again plays
Hugh Grant; aided and abetted by Jeanne Tripplehorn, who came *this* close to convincing me
that she wasn't yet another warm place to put it,
and James Caan, who looked *way* tired and really
shouldn't try to sing again.

Or something like that.

THE UPSHOT

The "Bumbling Englishman in a Foreign Land"
bit has been done so many times before that it
has become a parody of itself; here in the States,
pre-Hugh Grant, it was done to death by Rowan
Atkinson, and before him, Dudley Moore.

Difference is, *they* were funny.

Here's the plot: English art auctioneer wants
to marry Noo Yawk inner-city schoolteacher, who
doesn't want to tell him that her dad is part of the
mob. He soon meets her father and his Crew anyway. Wackiness Ensues. That's pretty much it.
You can fill in the blanks and cook this stew yourself easily by taking the previews you've undoubt-
edly seen, adding a liberal amount of stereotypes
you've heard about Italians and the mafia, sprinkling it with all the stereotypes you've heard
about Englishmen, and mix well.

Mickey Blue Eyes is, to me, a prime example of
what Hollywood muscle can do for you: throw
enough star power and enough dough at a movie,
and you can get away with damn near anything.
And a wee bit o' nepotism—in the guise of being
the producer's husband (or is that the star's wife?
Hmmm . . .)—don' hurt none, either.

OK, OK, it wasn't all *that* bad. In fact, my
gripe isn't that it was necessarily *bad,* but that it
just wasn't all that *good.* It was potential wasted;
and I *hate* wasted potential. I really did enjoy
Dudley Moore (his *Arthur* was marvelous), and
Hugh Grant could, if he tried, have that same
kind of Flava. But why should he try? As long as
audiences keep paying to see him play himself,
over and over, who needs to stretch? *He* does; because he'll learn, sooner or later, that *cute* only
takes you so far.

I heard myself laughing at one or two scenes

(the one with the Chinese restaurant owner was pretty funny; the scene with the dueling burials was cute, I admit; and the Ritchie character was like something out of a whole different movie), but one or two funny scenes do not a funny movie make.

BAMMER'S BOTTOM LINE

I treasure my hard-earned dollar enough to be discerning about my movie choices. I am, admittedly, hard on flicks, but big names or not, some things just should not be seen, or heard. And unless you're a big Hugh Grant fiend ... uh, I mean, fan ... *Mickey Blue Eyes*, my friends, is one of those things.

YELLOW LIGHT

Bams Mystery, Alaska
(1999)

RATED R; running time 119 minutes
GENRE: Dramedy
WRITTEN BY: David E. Kelley, Sean O'Byrne
DIRECTED BY: Jay Roach
CAST: Russell Crowe, Hank Azaria, Mary McCormack, Burt Reynolds, Colm Meaney, Lolita Davidovich, Maury Chaykin, Ron Eldard, Ryan Northcott, Michael Buie, Kevin Durand, Scott Grimes, Leroy Peltier, Adam Beach, Joshua Silberg, Regan Sean O'Brien-Macelwain, Cameron Bancroft, Jason Gray-Stanford, Brent Stait, Rachel Wilson, Beth Littleford, Megyn Price, Judith Ivey, Michael McKean, Stephen Hair, Mike Myers, Little Richard

> Spot the Spot.
> It won't be hard. Consider this one a gift.

THE STORY

Baseball may be "America's pastime," but for the residents of Mystery, Alaska, hockey's the only game in town. They live and breathe for the Saturday Game, in which the best townsmen play each other on Mystery's frozen-over pond. The whole town supports them in this. To say that they are team boosters is an understatement; they *thrive* on the Saturday Game.

The current lineup of players include team captain and town sheriff John Biebe (Russell Crowe), whose place on the team is threatened by up-and-coming teen phenom Stevie Weeks; Skank Marden, whose name mirrors his reputation; Connor Banks , the best player on the team and a pretty good grocer; "Tree" Lane—one guess why he has that name; "Birdie" Burns, a youngster out to prove himself worthy in the eyes of his teammates and father; and the kick-butt Winnetka Brothers Ben and Galin. Such is a source of pride for being picked by the town fathers to play in the Saturday Game, that those who have never been picked—like stern Judge Walter Burns (Burt Reynolds)—tend to become bitter about it; and those who are picked, have trouble envisioning life after hockey.

Charles Danner (Hank Azaria) was one ex-local who didn't get into the game, though; teased by the locals for his inability to skate, he left Mystery for the Big City, becoming a big-shot writer and producer. His positive story in *Sports Illustrated* about the Mystery boys buzzes up the townsfolk. But when the article convinces the New York Rangers hockey team to come to Mystery and play the boys, will Mystery's hometown pride turn their "dignity and illusions" into bittersweet reality?

THE UPSHOT

Besides snow and hockey, *Mystery, Alaska* also has an abundance of something else: heart. More akin to *The Natural* than to *For Love of the Game* (see page 148), the tale told in *Mystery* has a true down-home feeling to it that Kevin "Aww Shucks" Costner couldn't touch with kid gloves.

I enjoyed *Mystery* a lot more than I would've expected initially, given that I'm no hockey fan. That I'd dig Russell Crowe (See *Gladiator*) was a no-brainer, but the inclusion of Ron Eldard threw me for a loop. I haven't much liked him since his days in NBC's *ER* and I was completely prepared to dislike him here. Didn't happen. In fact, I can't remember a single character in this movie who didn't work for me; they *all* seemed to fit, and made the movie all the better for it.

The best word I can use to describe the feel of *Mystery*'s characters is "real." From the townspeople to the players to the wives and their children, it never felt like a Hollywood fantasy of what Alaskans would be like. The actors portrayed their characters in a nonpatronizing manner, without the Noble Savages haze that a Costner (I keep coming back to him) film, for instance, would've added to it. In fact, the only noticeable phonies in this film were the outsiders—the "New York Rangers," Michael McKean's character (I was wrong: there was a character that didn't work for me), and especially the television group (make that *two* characters: the mistakenly cast Mike Myers as a joke of a sports announcer).

There were far too many characters in this movie for me to make note of, as I usually do; but, surprisingly for such a large cast, they blended well. Crowe, my favorite chameleon, was good in an almost-but-not-quite clichéd role. Like his character, John Biebe, Crowe carried the banner for his fellow actors by the strength of his portrayal; and like Biebe's teammates, each of the actors supported Crowe with their specialized skill. Likewise, David E. Kelley's writing and Jay Roach's directing were good—again, leaving behind the clichés and stereotypes for the most part—and the breathtaking cinematography (shot in Alberta, Canada) was beautifully done.

THE BLACK FACTOR

You'll note above that singer (um) Little Richard was included in the cast. You probably wonder why. When I saw his scenes, so did I.

BAMMER'S BOTTOM LINE

The only mystery to me is why wasn't *Mystery, Alaska* more popular when it was released?

GREEN LIGHT

 **The Patriot**
(2000)

RATED R; running time 165 minutes
GENRE: Action
WRITTEN BY: Robert Rodat
DIRECTED BY: Roland Emmerich
CAST: Mel Gibson, Heath Ledger, Joely Richardson, Jason Isaacs, Chris Cooper, Tchéky Karyo, Trevor Morgan, Lisa Brenner, Bryan Chafin, Skye McCole Bartusiak, Tom Wilkinson, Rene Auberjonois, Logan Lerman, Adam Baldwin, Beatrice Bush, Mika Boorem, Mary Jo Deschanel, Shan Omar Huey, Gil Johnson, Jay Arlen Jones, Jamieson Price, Hank Stone, Kristian Truelsen, Mark Twogood, Joey D. Vieira, Grahame Wood, Peter Woodward

> Mel Gibson was paid 20-25 million dollars for this picture.

THE STORY

1776. A time of upheaval and revolution in these (not quite) United States of America.

Widower Benjamin Martin (Mel Gibson) is a man who has known war and no longer wants any part of it; he just wants to farm, make rocking chairs, and be left alone to raise his seven young children. His eldest son, Gabriel (Heath Ledger), doesn't understand Ben's pacifistic mood, and wants to join the Colonials to fight against the evil British Empire and that old tax baron King George. After the Evil British Colonel William Tavington (Jason Isaacs) wreaks havoc on Ben's family and land, Ben leaves his youngest children with their aunt Charlotte (Joely Richardson), so he and Gabriel can join forces with Regular Army Colonel Harry Burwell (Chris Cooper) and French Army officer Jean Villeneuve to create a militia to go up against Tavington and the Slightly Less Evil General Cornwallis (Tom Wilkinson).

THE UPSHOT

"Manipulative" is the word I keep coming back to when I think about *The Patriot*. It's not enough, it seems, that this movie was released around the Fourth of July; Independence Day roun' dese hea' parts. No—"we must forcefully remind The Uhmerkin Public," the filmmakers seemed to say, "that Gibson . . . uh, blue-eyed Benjamin Martin," was a true American hero, by having him wave the flag meaningfully at every opportunity! And hey, while you're at it, have a few of his friends and family members die slow heroic deaths with the camera trained on their faces for a god-awful long time, whydoncha? And ooh yeah, that image of Mel, baby, running boldly into battle with just that battered flag, *that'll* hit 'em where it hurts, eh?"

Bah. Just tell me the story, dammit; let *me* decide when and where to cheer for them, eh? I don't need no friggin' equivalent of a laugh track, spattered into so many manipulative scenes. Bad moviemakers. Bad, bad moviemakers.

In all fairness, though, *The Patriot* latches on to its singlemindedness and never lets go; at least it's not wishy-washy in its dogged determination to make the viewer love Benjamin and his family for being epic heroes. And don't get me wrong: not having had to ever do much heavy fighting outside of the time Judy hit me in the stomach with a two-by-four when I was 13, I'm *not* saying that war ain't really hell; I'm sure it is that and much more. What I *am* saying, however, is that the audience doesn't need to be battered upside the head with the Whiffle bat to get that point.

The Patriot didn't move me at all. Actually, it did: it moved me from being sympathetic to the cause of a young—and, let's be honest, White—nation getting its legs under itself, to being cynical and critical of the values held by that same nation that *The Patriot* tried to whitewash over: the way it treated its non-White citizens; the folks that were somehow forgotten in "We The People."

THE BLACK FACTOR

We The People. Hold These Truths To Be Self-Evident. All Men Are Created Equal. That is, "we, the White male landowners, see it that way—about us." All others need not apply.

It was this undeniable truth about the establishment of "a more perfect union"—that its people were only "created equal" if and only if they were White male landowners—that grated me most about *The Patriot* and its whitewashing-over of its colorful tale. If the folks behind this movie had not addressed It (slavery: the big It) at all, then fine. I wouldn't have had an issue with their overlooking of that big It. But they addressed It. Badly. Shame on 'em, I say.

A little truth goes a long way; but *The Patriot* couldn't seem to face up to the realities of its own time *this* late into the moviemaking game (well past the time when the filmmakers could've claimed ignorance about such

things). And that—much more than the fact that I never caught the name of the Black slave character, only knowing him from his introduction as "my nigra"—is what finally brought *The Patriot*'s house of cards tumbling down for me. In all its flag-waving, it seemed to forget that even back then, these States weren't as United as the Founding Fathers claimed they were.

History, it seems, *does* tend to repeat itself.

BAMMER'S BOTTOM LINE

Call me cynical, call me anti-American, whatever; but I hate feeling manipulated, and that's *exactly* how I felt watching *The Patriot*. I went into this movie with an open mind, hoping to learn something more about what made the early revolutionaries in these, yes, great United States, tick. I came out of it with contempt for what I had just been put through. And that's *never* A Good Thing.

YELLOW LIGHT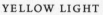

Sleeping with the Enemy
(1991)

RATED R; running time 99 minutes
GENRE: Thriller
WRITTEN BY: Nancy Price (novel); Ronald Bass (screenplay)
DIRECTED BY: Joseph Ruben
CAST: Julia Roberts, Patrick Bergin, Kevin Anderson

CASS'S CLIP

Martin and Laura Burney live opulently in a beautiful beachfront home and appear to be happily married. Laura is a gorgeous, obedient wife. Martin is a fiendish, obsessive-compulsive, abusive husband. If Laura doesn't alphabetically arrange the canned goods in the pantry, or perfectly straighten the bathroom towels on the racks, Martin smacks her around. Martin also sadistically enjoys forcing Laura to have sex as a sign of his *affectionate* control.

To escape Martin's abuse, Laura fakes her drowning death, changes her name to Sara Waters and relocates to a quiet community. Initially, Sara/Laura finds tranquility in Iowa. She even becomes smitten with the local college drama instructor Ben Woodward, because he's genuinely gentle and kind.

Meanwhile, Martin finds out that Laura secretly took swimming lessons at the YMCA. Martin's hunt for the truth and Laura's whereabouts sets up a predictable anti-climactic showdown between Martin and Laura.

DA 411

Sleeping with the Enemy takes a stab at addressing domestic violence. However, I have problems with the *do they really think we're that stupid* scenes. For example, Laura secretly takes swimming lessons at the YMCA but puts her real name and information on the emergency card. Or, Laura takes every precaution to fake her death but *flushes* her wedding ring down the toilet. Can you imagine all the stuff you've flushed down the toilet suddenly reappearing months later? Or, that Laura suspects Martin has discovered her whereabouts because the cans in the pantry of her new home are neatly stacked.

For the record, even though I make light of some of the flaws in *Sleeping with the Enemy*, I believe the overall message is to empower women about the subtleties of domestic violence. Ethnicity, money, or status do not prevent a woman from being abused. And, on some level, perhaps it's successful.

> While faking your death and leaving is an option . . . so is "The Burning Bed."

CASS'S CONCLUSION

If *Sleeping with the Enemy* gives just one woman the courage to leave an abusive relationship, then I recommend seeing this otherwise mediocre movie.

YELLOW LIGHT

Swordfish

(2001)

RATED R; running time 120 minutes

GENRE: Action/Drama

WRITTEN BY: Skip Woods

DIRECTED BY: Dominic Sena

CAST: John Travolta, Hugh Jackman, Halle Berry, Don Cheadle, Camryn Grimes, Vinnie Jones, Sam Shepard

Halle Berry is married to singer Eric Benet. (That's "Buh-nay").

THE DIGEST

Stanley Jobson (Hugh Jackman) just got out of prison for a cyber crime, and as part of his punishment, he can't see his daughter or touch a computer. All of that changes the minute Ginger (Halle Berry) walks into his life. Her employer, Gabriel Shear (John Travolta), has offered to pay Stan a hundred thousand dollars just to meet him. With that kind of money, Stan can quit his dead-end job and fight for his daughter.

Little does Stan know, the 100K doesn't come easy. He has to hack into a government computer in 60 seconds or lose his life. Meanwhile, the FBI agent who put Stan away in the first place, Agent A. D. Roberts (Don Cheadle), is on his tail.

THE DISH

One of the best lines in this movie is spoken early on by Gabriel Shear—"You know what the problem with Hollywood is? They make shit." Unfortunately, *Swordfish* is not exactly exempt from

that statement. While it's not the worst movie I've seen, it left a lot to be desired. Quite frankly, they didn't blow up enough stuff to make up for the crap they called a plot. I wasn't feeling the whole bus thing, because well, I've seen *Speed*. And the American public needs to understand that the code used to create computer programs doesn't render in 3D and pretty pictures. It's lines and lines of words and numbers. Not little DNA sequence-building blocks, which really annoys the geek in me.

Halle did show her boobies. They were perky, but she could have chosen a better movie in which to do it. If I were her, right about now I'd be saying, "I can't believe I let the girls come out to play in that turkey of a movie."

The standout in the film was Don Cheadle. Without him, the movie would have been completely worthless. It is because of him and the hostage scene that I've decided not to give this movie a red light.

THE DIRECTIVE

If you are just dying to see Halle's Berries then rent *Swordfish*; all others can swim right past it.

YELLOW LIGHT

Qams The Talented Mr. Ripley
(1999)

RATED R; running time 139 minutes

GENRE: Drama

WRITTEN BY: Anthony Minghella (based on the novel by Patricia Highsmith)

DIRECTED BY: Anthony Minghella

CAST: Matt Damon, Jude Law, Gwyneth Paltrow, Philip Seymour Hoffman, Cate Blanchett, Jack Davenport, James Rebhorn, Sergio Rubini, Philip Baker Hall, Stefania Rocca

> This movie is based on a book series by Patricia Highsmith.
> There are 5 other books in the series.

THE STORY

Tom Ripley (Matt Damon) experiences a life-altering situation after sitting in as a piano player for the day for a friend. Upon seeing him in a Princeton jacket (lent to Ripley by his friend), wealthy shipping magnate Herbert Greenleaf (James Rebhorn) assumes that Ripley went to school with his son, Dickie Greenleaf (Jude Law). When Ripley fails to deny that, the elder Greenleaf hires him to find the younger Greenleaf in Italy—where Dickie, in Herbert's eyes, is wasting his time lollygagging about whilst playing jazz (mere noise, to Herbert's ears)—and bring him back to America. And thus, Ripley spins a web of deception and murder, drawing in Dickie's fiancée, Marge Sherwood (Gwyneth Paltrow); Dickie's friend and fellow layabout Freddie Miles (Philip Seymour Hoffman); Meredith Logue (Cate Blanchett), a so-cialite whom Ripley misleads early on; and Marge's mysterious companion, Peter Smith-Kingsley (Jack Davenport), who also knows Meredith. To maintain the lifestyle to which he swiftly becomes accustomed, the sleight-of-hand game Ripley plays on Dickie's trusting father soon turns into a deadly game of cat-and-mouse.

THE UPSHOT

It's simple, really: if you were a poor nobody who could get away with lying and swindling your way across 1950s Italy with a rich nobody pseudo-saxophonist and his rich nobody friends all living the Lifestyles Of The Sick And Shameless, you'd kill to keep that life, wouldn't ya?

I'll say it straight, no twist: I rankled at viewing yet another foray into the lives of poor little rich kids who were "terribly misunderstood." Oh, boo friggin' hoo. I couldn't stand to see Matt Damon getting over on a toothy smile and an earnest act (almost every Matt Damon movie, with the possible exception of *Dogma*, seems as if it came off the same assembly line). This almost made me show this movie The Hand (minus a few fingers).

My biggest Issue with *Ripley* was that it seemed to be cold and unfeeling, all smoke and mirrors—intentionally, from the character's viewpoint, to be sure. Except for Law and the fabulous Hoffman (who would make a perfect Mr. Howell if, godforbid, They ever decided to remake *Gilligan's Island*—shudder), there seemed to be little substance beyond all the style of the Italian scenery and the "beautiful" actors. It wasn't until I realized that the characters' lack of substance was the point (or, at least, one of them), that I was able to dig it.

Still, the things that worked for me worked well, including the movie's love affair with classic jazz and the attention to detail for Italy of the 1950s. Once I got past my distrust of Damon's acting abilities, I was able to see that the crux of the hollowness rested squarely with the character of Ripley, and that his depravity need not be shown in big! bold! Wes Cravenesque strokes to be sufficiently chilling.

THE BLACK FACTOR

A loyal 3BC observer (Karen) wrote an insightful note that serves as "The Black Factor" for this movie:

"*The Talented Mr. Ripley* is a very good, kind of creepy movie. Matt Damon shed that all-American boy image with this movie, playing a very confused, messed up young gay man in 1959, at a time when being gay or being anything other than a straight White male was a lot more than just uncool.

This movie kind of reminded me of a White version of *Native Son;* meaning, the way the main character weaves this web that he really can't get out of (and the fact that the first bad thing he does is in self-defense . . . as you realize later, while the second bad thing done is deliberate).

I kept thinking that instead of Ripley being gay it would have been a real interesting movie if it turned out that he was Black and passing for White or something. Ask yourself if you were mistaken for someone else and that mistake benefited you, how would you react? The movie was really about pretending to be something you're not and the consequences of that action. I thought it was great, made my skin crawl but it was great."

BAMMER'S BOTTOM LINE

The Talented Mr. Ripley isn't the kind of movie you'd want to see if you're looking for something easy to watch; indeed, the supposed splendor of Italy belies the deceptive nature of the principal characters involved in this film. But as a study of the tangled web we weave when first we practice to deceive, and of the lengths one must go to maintain a house-of-cards lie, *Ripley* stands head and shoulders above many of the "easy listening"–type flicks out there.

FLASHING YELLOW LIGHT

the Diva **U-571**
(2000)

RATED PG-13; runnning time 115 minutes
GENRE: War/Action
WRITTEN BY: Jonathan Mostow and Sam Montgomery and David Ayer
DIRECTED BY: Jonathan Mostow
CAST: Matthew McConaughey, Bill Paxton, Harvey Keitel, Jon Bon Jovi, Jake Weber, Erik Palladino, Matthew Settle, David Keith

Matthew McConaughey was arrested a few years ago for smoking weed and playing the bongos in the nude . . . in his house. Now, if the man wants to dance around with a joint hanging from his mouth and Mr. Winky bouncing around, we say let him!

The Top 10 Reasons Why I Will Never Be A Sailor on A Sub

#10   Where am I going to plug in my curling iron?

#9   Where am I going to take a bath?

#8   Where am I going to store all my candles and bath salts?

#7   My wide behind won't fit through those tiny-ass doorways.

#6   My wide behind won't fit on those tiny-ass cots they call beds.

#5   I cannot sit upright on my "bed" and pamper myself.

#4   I'm too precious to share my "room" with 50 people.

#3   No evidence of a freezer to store my Reese's Cups.

#2   I'd just as soon not have to chase my food back and forth across the table.

#1   Even in an underwater tin can, one cannot escape cockroaches.

THE DIGEST

Andrew Tyler (Matthew McConaughey) is a young lieutenant who is loved and respected by the crew of U-571, but he doesn't have what it takes to captain his own submarine. Love and respect is not enough. You need to be able to make split-second decisions that could save lives and you need to do so without hesitation. Tyler is not quite there. But that all changes when he and the rest of the crew are called off of their liberty pass and sent on a very "hush-hush" mission. There is a disabled German submarine floating in the ocean and they have been asked to board that sub and secure an Enigma.

They decorate their sub to resemble a German supply ship and they have to beat the real German supply ship that is en route to the damaged one. What follows is a cat-and-mouse game between this boat and the German Navy.

THE DISH

I felt the same way I did after watching *Rules of Engagement* (see page 366)—there are too many movies in this genre. *U-571* failed to "wow" me. Everyone gave solid performances, but again, we've seen it before.

My biggest disappointment with this movie was that it was very dark. Consequently, I couldn't see, which made matters more complicated. I had problems hearing, as well. The music often drowned out the dialogue. On subs, apparently, one's voice can be heard through the walls, so the crew whispers a lot. So we've got dialogue being whispered and a music score swelling over what they're saying—all of which makes for a lackluster moviegoing experience.

THE DIRECTIVE

U-571 almost sinks.

YELLOW LIGHT

5

When White folks in the movies aren't too busy running from Giant Tomatoes or trying to save small towns from radioactive animals or trying to destroy themselves, they manage to set aside some time to dog us Black folk. This chapter's reviews touch on movies in that vein. Also in this chapter, we will introduce you to the "Magical Negro." This is a Black person who "makes everything all right" for the White folks involved in the story.

Along Came a Spider
(2001)

RATED R; running time 123 minutes
GENRE: Thriller
WRITTEN BY: Marc Moss (based on the book
   by James Patterson)
DIRECTED BY: Lee Tamahori
CAST: Morgan Freeman, Monica Potter, Michael
   Wincott, Jay O. Sanders, Penelope Ann
   Miller, Mika Boorem, Michael Moriarty

THE DIGEST

Dr. Alex Cross (Morgan Freeman) is back and
this time he is going after a kidnapper.

It's been seven months since Dr. Cross lost
his partner. He feels totally responsible for her
death because he was in charge of the sting operation that got her killed. He is still at home,
feeling sorry for himself, when the phone rings
and snaps him out of his self-pity. The call he receives is from one Gary Soneji. Gary has managed to infiltrate a private school that educates
the children of senators and dignitaries, and he
has kidnapped the daughter of Senator Rose,
Megan.

Dr. Cross finds himself in the center of the
investigation along with Secret Service Agent
Jezzie Flannigan (Monica Potter), the agent on
duty when Megan was taken. Agent Flannigan
feels personally responsible for Megan's kidnapping and she feels she must find her at all costs.
With the help of Alex, she should be able to face
her own demons while finding Megan in the
process.

THE DISH

Oh boy. I have to be honest, I'm a big fan of the
James Patterson books featuring Alex Cross.
Consequently, I'm biased. If you have read the
book upon which this movie is based, you will
not be happy with it. Gone are the psychological
head games between Soneji and Cross, which
added suspense to the book. Also gone is the relationship between Alex Cross and his two young
children. The most enjoyable scenes in the book
series are his interactions with his kids. These
scenes also provided us with a glimpse of Alex
Cross's intensity and dedication to finding
Megan. In the book, he understands what the
Roses are going through, because he is a parent
himself.

Nonetheless, not all was lost. I was pleasantly
surprised with Mika Boreem, who plays Megan.
She was a scrappy little 10-year-old. I was also
pleased with Michael Wincott and his interpretation of Gary Soneji. Otherwise, give or take a couple of nice plot twists, *Along Came a Spider* is very
low on thrills and chills.

THE DIRECTIVE

I wish *Spider* had brought a plot along
with it.

YELLOW LIGHT

Art of War
(2000)

RATED R; running time 120 minutes
GENRE: Action
WRITTEN BY: Wayne Beach
DIRECTED BY: Christian Duguay
CAST: Wesley Snipes, Anne Archer, Michael Biehn, Maury Chaykin, Marie Matiko, Donald Sutherland, Cary-Hiroyuki Tagawa

THE DIGEST

Shaw (Wesley Snipes) is a special covert operative for the United Nations. He's virtually invisible; he does his job without being seen. In most assignments, his boss Eleanor Hooks (Anne Archer) has the "by any means necessary" philosophy. For the most part, it boils down to threats and blackmail, but there is a hint that it will go beyond that, if necessary. The goal of her team is to make the Secretary of the United Nations, Douglas Thomas (Donald Sutherland), look good and make sure the best interests of America are upheld.

Shaw is tired of life as a nonexistent man. He is ready to retire, but his boss convinces him to do one more very simple operation: putting a bug on a Chinese dignitary. Simple enough until there is a shootout that makes Shaw a fugitive.

With the help of a Chinese interpreter, Julia Fang, Shaw sets out to clear his name with the Chinese Triad and FBI hot on his tail.

THE DISH

Hmmm. Well, it was pretty run-of-the-mill, with a standard falsely-accused/must-clear-name sto-ryline. The one bright spot was Agent Cappella (Maury Chaykin). He is such an old hat that he doesn't even need to cover his nose and mouth from the stench of death. He also figures out early on that Shaw is innocent, even though he is leaving a trail of dead bodies. His wry-and-dry delivery of lines cracked me up.

I'm usually all over a Wesley Snipes action flick, but ya know . . . this one wasn't that thrilling. It might be because I spotted the stunt man more than once. Don't get me wrong. You won't find my ass jumping off of buildings either, but I like to stay unaware of the stunt people. I like to stay ignorant of the whole moviemaking process, in general. I prefer not to know that it's not magic on the screen.

Oh, one more thing I need to mention. I played one of my favorite games, "Spot The Zit On Wesley," and I'm happy to report that I only found one or two very small ones. I guess Wes gets nervous or stressed when making movies, because he always has a big huge zit somewhere. He also has lost some weight and tightened up. He looked good.

THE DIRECTIVE

Tough one. If you just must see Wesley, then rent it right away. For everyone else, it's pretty weak as far as action movies are concerned, and you'll probably figure out early on who is behind everything. Should've been called *The Art of Boredom*.

YELLOW LIGHT

Birth of a Nation
the Diva (1915)

UNRATED; running time 180 minutes (yes,
    that's right, three damn hours)
GENRE: Historical/War drama
WRITTEN BY: Based on the novel *Clansman* by
    Thomas Dixon
DIRECTED BY: D. W. Griffith
CAST: Lillian Gish, Mae Marsh, Henry B.
    Walthall, Miriam Cooper, Mary Alden, Ralph
    Lewis, George Siegmann

> Official records weren't kept in a standard
> fashion when this movie was released—
> because of this, *Variety* stopped including
> this movie in its top-grossing lists. How-
> ever, the numbers bandied about are that
> it made anywhere from 18 million to 50 mil-
> lion.

THE DIGEST

Elsie Stoneman (Lillian Gish) is the much-
adored daughter of the very liberal Northerner,
Austin Stoneman (Ralph Lewis). But this doesn't
deter Ben Cameron (Henry Walthall), the Southern friend of Elsie's brothers. Ben has never met
Elsie, but he carries her picture with him and
pines away for her. He is sure that one day he'll
marry her, but then war breaks out and he must
go defend the way of the South. Elsie's brothers
also join the war and fight for the North. They
meet the Camerons in battle, but remember their
friendship and spare them. Eventually, Ben is
wounded and sent to a hospital in the North.

Elsie's brother sends word that Ben is on the way
and she is to take care of him. It is here that their
love blossoms.

Meanwhile, the South falls.

Ben goes home to see his beloved South in
shambles and overrun by "Negroes" in control of
everything and completely supported by Elsie's
father who, upon the death of Abraham Lincoln,
has become very powerful. He has elevated a mu-
latto, Silas Lynch, to the rank of lieutenant governor of South Carolina. He doesn't care about
equality for his people but for the advancement of
himself and his supporters. The newly freed
slaves control the South Carolina House of Rep-
resentatives and they want "equal rights, equal
politics, and equal marriage." Most of all Silas
Lynch, who has decided that he wants Elsie in
Equal Marriage.

While Silas is singlehandedly tearing down
the South by allowing the Black soldiers to
scare people off the street, Ben is getting more
and more restless. While on a walk, he notices
two White children running away from a group
of Black children. The White children hide under a white sheet and the Black children, now
scared, run away. Thus, the Klan is born. It is
now up to the Klan to restore order and restore
the South.

THE DISH

After the opening credits, we are presented with
this:

"A PLEA FOR THE ART OF THE
MOTION PICTURE
    We do not fear censorship for we have
no wish to offend with improprieties or

obscenities, but we do demand, as right, the liberty to show the dark side of wrong, that we may illuminate the bright side of virtue—the same liberty that is conceded to the art of written word, that art to which we owe The Bible and the works of Shakespeare."

Well, they sure the hell offended me. I freely admit that I didn't see what the big deal was at first. The first 90 minutes were pretty tame. Oh Lawd, but the last 90 minutes were a doozie!

I don't know where to begin. Early on in the movie, I was starting to understand how it made American Film Institute's Top 100. It was a vast undertaking. Artistically speaking, that is. Forget about the content. I was impressed with D. W. Griffith's craftsmanship. But there is no amount of craftsmanship that can make up for the final 90 minutes. Period. Black folks being beaten, dragged, abused . . . and liking it. Images of Black men lusting after White women; eating chicken during legislative session; the "loyal" slaves ratting out the free slaves and calling them "crazy niggers," all the while dancing every chance they got.

The only purpose of this movie was to scare White folks into further oppressing Black folks. If this movie is to be believed, the minute any Black person gets power, the good White women of America will be ravished and roving bands of angry "Negroes" will run White citizens off the streets.

I'm not sure that I've ever been more disgusted with a movie in my life.

THE DIRECTIVE

Birth of a Nation and Death of the Dignity of Black folks. If you have a burning desire to be insulted for 90 minutes, then by all means, check *Birth of a Nation* out.

3 RED LIGHTS

Blade II
(2002)

RATED R; running time 108 minutes
GENRE: Action/Horror
WRITTEN BY: David S. Goyer
DIRECTED BY: Guillermo del Toro
CAST: Wesley Snipes, Kris Kristofferson, Ron Perlman, Leonor Varela, Norman Reedus, Thomas Kretschmann, Donnie Yen, and Danny John Jules

THE DIGEST

Let me give you a little background from the first movie so you'll have a clearer understanding of what is going on. Blade is a Daywalker. A vampire bit his mother while she was pregnant, thus, Blade has all of the strengths of the vampires and none of their weaknesses. Silver, sunlight, and garlic have no effect on him. He has a vampire's super-human strength; he could even bite someone and make them a vampire if he so chooses. He hates what he is and hates the vampires for making him one of them. Now on to the story.

Two years have passed since Blade went up against Deacon Frost (*Blade*, 1999) and he is still in Europe looking for his best friend and mentor, Whistler (Kris Kristofferson). Whistler has survived the vicious attack that ended with his sporting a bite from a vampire. Meanwhile, Blade has hooked up with Scud (Norman Reedus), and Scud has been responsible for making all the groovy weapons that Blade needs to fight the vampires.

While Blade is scouring Europe looking for Whistler, a new breed of vampire has arisen, called a Reaper. This breed has an unquenchable thirst, and as a result, they do not stop at humans; they are attacking other vampires as well. Attacking them to devour them. If the victim manages to survive, they become Reapers themselves. Their numbers are increasing exponentially.

This has terrified the ruling houses of vampires and they have appealed to Blade for help. They want Blade to lead an elite tactical unit of vampires whose mission is to hunt the Reapers down and kill them. One problem—this unit, called the Blood Pack, had a previous assignment. That assignment was to hunt down Blade and kill him. How can he fight off the Reapers *and* make sure that his own team doesn't try to kill him when he isn't looking?

Whew!

THE DISH

Okay, I'll get straight to the point. I've looked at this movie two ways.

1. Blade is bad and if you mess with him, he will 'F' you up.

Looking at from this standpoint, this movie rocked. Plenty of action, special effects, kick-ass stunts. *Blade II* had it all and I did not want for

more. I was on the edge of my seat or hiding behind my hands. I was in complete awe of Wesley Snipes. Hell, all of the actors, and their ability to flip, jump, fight, bounce off walls, was admirable . . . I was a happy camper.

2. *Blade* is like any ole other movie out there. This is where *Blade II* failed.

The supporting acting was poor. I guess most of the budget went toward effects. The dialogue was uninteresting. David Goyer wrote *Blade,* so one would assume that he is not new to the nuances of the characters, therefore it was surprising to me that the jokes seemed forced and Blade's classic one-liners were missing or fell flat.

Everything that made *Blade* work was gone in this sequel. Part of the magic of the first *Blade* was that the first 10 minutes grabbed you and pimp-slapped you to attention. After watching Blade completely and thoroughly kick ass, you couldn't help but be hooked. Also gone was an evil nemesis: in *Blade,* Deacon Frost was evil. You wanted Blade to kick the living tar out of him. There wasn't one character in *Blade II* who elicited those feelings. And finally, I just wasn't feeling the whole Reaper thing. This enemy just didn't create the chaos that Deacon Frost did. I actually felt sorry for the main Reaper dude.

THE DIRECTIVE

If I based my rating on special effects and kick-assness—*Blade II* would clearly get a green light, but given all the problems, I think Blade took that little sword of his and tore up the plot.

YELLOW LIGHT

The Bone Collector
(1999)

RATED R; running time 128 minutes

GENRE: Thriller

WRITTEN BY: Jeremy Iacone (based on the book by Jeffery Deaver)

DIRECTED BY: Phillip Noyce

CAST: Denzel Washington, Angelina Jolie, Queen Latifah, Michael Rooker, Luis Guzmán, Ed O'Neill, Leland Orser, John Benjamin Hickey

> Denzel is fine even when only his head and one finger move.

THE DIGEST

Lincoln Rhyme (Denzel Washington) is a hot-shot forensics investigator and captain of his division within the NYPD. No one can work a crime scene better than he can. He is at the top of his game when tragedy strikes. While investigating the death of a police officer, a piece of roof support breaks away and comes crashing down, nearly cutting Lincoln in half. This leaves him paralyzed from the shoulders down and suffering from seizures so severe that he may become a vegetable at any time. Lincoln is a very proud man, but given all of this he has decided that he no longer wants to live . . . until a serial killer emerges to challenge him.

Enter Officer Amelia Donaghy (Angelina Jolie). She is a patrol officer who wants to work in youth services, and is just biding her time until there is an opening. She is walking her beat when

a call comes in about a little boy finding "something." At the scene of the crime, she begins to clear the debris and discovers that a prominent New York citizen has been killed. Homicide and forensics specialists descend upon the site. All of them are members of Lincoln's former team. They know that they are dealing with something out of the ordinary, and a few officers, without full consent of the new captain, go visit Lincoln and ask for his help.

Lincoln is more focused on dying than on helping out. He is very impressed with Officer Donaghy's work, however, and decides to pitch in. A very angry and reluctant Donaghy becomes his legs for him. He walks her through investigating the crime scene and directs her on how to do it correctly. Lincoln is back to his old self and running a tight ship.

THE DISH

I have this "thing" for Denzel Washington and Stevie Wonder. Don't ask. It is therefore safe to say that Denzel can do no wrong with me when it comes to movies. In fact, if I ever find an email address for Denzel, you'll probably see me on the evening news crying for my mama as they lock me up for cyber-stalking. That man makes my toes curl. My shameless bias notwithstanding, this was a very good movie. Not great, but really good.

The movie has some slows spots, but moves at lightning speed toward the not-so-surprising ending. Queen Latifah as Lincoln's nurse is refreshing. She plays her part like that of a mother proudly watching her child come out of a shell. Michael Rooker plays a convincing jerk, as Lincoln's coworker Cheney. Cheney is now the captain of the division and he is extremely insecure and jealous. Angelina Jolie's portrayal of a very vulnerable yet strong officer reminded me of Clarice Starling, the heroine in *The Silence of the Lambs*. Throughout the movie, you watch her character grow under the care of Lincoln. Their relationship goes from adversarial to respectful, with a strong hint of attraction.

Even though it's a thriller about a serial killer, you never really see the people being killed; you have to sort of use your imagination. I also enjoyed the humor that was laced throughout the movie. It broke the tension. I liked how we were able to see the characters develop and I liked the ending with Denzel. You'll see what I mean. My chief complaint is that sometimes the thrills weren't delivered.

THE DIRECTIVE

I highly recommend this film to people who like *Silence of the Lambs* and *Fatal Attraction*. While there aren't any similar plot points to *Fatal*, it has the same ability to make your heart race and scare you.

GREEN LIGHT

---

the Diva **Bring It On**
(2000)

RATED PG-13; running time 115 minutes
GENRE: Comedy
WRITTEN BY: Jessica Bendinger
DIRECTED BY: Peyton Reed
CAST: Kirsten Dunst, Jesse Bradford, Eliza Dushku, Gabrielle Union

> We have a little cheer for this movie . . .
> U-G-L-Y—you ain't got no alibi . . .

THE DIGEST

Set in an uppity school in San Diego called Rancho Carne (Meat Ranch), these privileged teenagers know nothing outside of the world of cheerleading. When their notorious and fearless leader, Big Red, graduates, she passes the torch to Torrance Shipman (Kirsten Dunst) who must continue the proud winning streak of taking Nationals the last six years in a row.

When they have to replace an injured cheerleader, their world comes tumbling down. They replace her with a "street-smart" (she knows where an inner-city school is—that's about the extent of her street smarts) girl named Missy Pantone. Missy is from Los Angeles and right away recognizes that the cheers they are doing were actually stolen from a Black high school—East Compton High. Torrance refuses to believe her until Missy shows her first hand. The East Compton Clovers, lead by Isis (Gabrielle Union), know that their cheers have been stolen. Big Red used to show up with a camcorder with no shame in her game. It never mattered before, because the Clovers couldn't afford to go to Nationals. But now that Isis is at the helm, she is determined to go all the way to the top and makes that very clear.

Torrance is distraught. She must do the right thing and stop using the Compton cheers, but they only have three weeks to learn new routines. What's she to do?

THE DISH
Ya know, the expression "guilty pleasure"—that's what I felt while watching and enjoying this movie. It was mindless fluff, and fairly amusing.

Of course, I had issues. The whole "save the inner-city kids" theme grated on my nerves. And here's another: Who in their right mind would name their children Jenelope and LaFred? I can't even be mad, because Black folks do have the tendency to make up some foul names. I knew some sisters who were named Peaches, Princess, and Pumpkin. These were their legal first names, presented to them upon birth. But I digress.

THE DIRECTIVE
It's superficial and juvenile, but mildly funny. Of course the Compton Clovers tore it up. If you can dig that, then rent it. If you can't dig that then you might want to pass.

YELLOW AND FLASHING-RED
LIGHTS

 The Diva

The Legend of Bagger Vance
(2000)

RATED PG-13; running time 130 minutes
GENRE: Drama/Comedy/Romance
WRITTEN BY: Steven Pressfield (novel), Jeremy Leven (screenplay)
DIRECTED BY: Robert Redford
CAST: Will Smith, Matt Damon, J. Michael Moncrief, Charlize Theron

THE DIGEST
In 1917, Rannulf Junuh (Matt Damon) was the best golf player in the South. Savannah, Georgia, was boiling over in anticipation that Junuh would take them far and wide. Junuh had all that he could hope for—a game he loved, adoration from the townsfolk, and the heart of Ms. Adele Invergordon (Charlize Theron). Then World War I beckoned and Savannah sent their prized possession to represent the South. It took him 10 years to come home, and when he did, he was a changed and broken man.

Meanwhile, Adele has never married and has drowned her sorrow in being an active socialite. In 1928, she has thrown herself into making the best golf course in the South. She succeeds in doing just that, then the stock market crashes. She decides to sell everything she owns to raise ten thousand dollars that she'll give away as first prize in a golf tournament on her course. She convinces the top two golfers, Bobby Jones and Walter Hagen, to participate in the tournament. The town agrees to support her only if their representative is from good ole Savannah. This, of course, means Junuh.

Well, that's all fine and dandy, but Junuh doesn't want to do it. He is just as happy being drunk. It takes a precocious 10-year-old named Hardy Greaves (J. Michael Moncrief) and a stranger named Bagger Vance (Will Smith) to finally talk him into it.

THE DISH

There are a lot of Magical Negroes in Hollywood . . .

Initially, I was ready to blast the film because it was another case of a Black person being the caretaker of a White person. I was going to rip this movie to shreds because it had all the happy Whites and Coloreds living harmoniously in Savannah. In 1928? Please. Had Bagger walked up to folks in 1928 Savannah and started taking control of the situation, Bagger would have been swinging from a tree for being an uppity Negro. But then I thought about it some more and, I think, had the depiction been accurate, I probably would have complained then too. I probably would have said that race had no business being part of a golf movie.

So, I'm falling back on my fail-safe rule: If I notice that my butt hurts from sitting, then the movie isn't keeping me engaged. I noticed for the last hour of the movie that my butt hurt and I had to keep shifting in my seat.

So, what happened to *The Legend of Bagger Vance*? I can't quite put my finger on it. The acting wasn't bad, the script wasn't bad, the movie wasn't bad. It just didn't impress me. What *did* impress me was J. Michael Moncrief, the young boy who plays Hardy Greaves. I really dug him. I was also impressed with how Southern the people of Savannah are. That was a hoot. It just didn't all knit together.

THE DIRECTIVE

Rent it if you are a golf nut.

YELLOW LIGHT

Men of Honor

(2000)

RATED R; running time 125 minutes
GENRE: Drama
WRITTEN BY: Scott Marshall Smith
DIRECTED BY: George Tillman Jr.
CAST: Robert De Niro, Cuba Gooding Jr,. Aunjanue Ellis, Charlize Theron, David Conrad, Michael Rapaport, Hal Holbrook, Powers Boothe, Holt McCallany, Joshua Leonard, Glynn Turman, Carl Lumbly, Lonette McKee, David Keith

THE STORY

Based on a true story, *Men of Honor* starts in Sonora, Kentucky, in the 1940s. Mac and Ella Brashear live off the land as sharecroppers. As hard a life as it is for them, they want much more for their son; Mac insists that his boy stay in school, not stay home and work the land with them. But when times get hard, the son has no choice but to quit school and help his father. When the son, Carl (Cuba Gooding Jr.), grows up, he enlists in the Navy, hoping to do the thing he loves best—dive—and make his father proud of him. As Carl leaves home, Mac admonishes him to keep his eyes on the prize. The memory of his father's words, and his own determination, stay deep in Carl's heart.

But the '60s aren't much better for a young Black man in the minimally desegregated military. Brashear soon realizes that while President Truman ordered the Navy to let Blacks *in*, the Navy neither had to *like* it—nor did they have to allow Blacks to do anything but, in the words of Chief Floyd (Glynn Turman), "be a Navy cook, a White officer's valet, or leave the Navy." Brashear, though, has other plans. Chafing against rules that apply unfairly to Blacks, Brashear's brash actions impress Captain Pullman (Powers Boothe) of the USS *Hoist* enough that he is allowed to serve as a Search-and-Rescue swimmer—though Brashear quickly learns that he still won't be fully accepted by his fellow seamen, or by the Navy, for some time to come.

This point is driven home after he convinces Pullman to transfer him to Navy Diving School, under the command of Master Chief Billy Sunday (Robert De Niro), a hard-drinking, tough SOB Sunday who, like the rest of the military, has no love for "uppity" Blacks.

THE UPSHOT

Past the story itself, past the history, past the drama of it all, *Men of Honor* is a beautifully shot and acted film, showcasing the many talents of its director, George Tillman Jr., and stars Cuba Gooding Jr. and Robert De Niro (my Lord, can that man act his butt off!). It stands up there with the likes of *Remember the Titans* as one of the best films of 2000, if only on the merits of those three alone.

Gooding first caught my eye in his introductory role in John Singleton's *Boyz 'n the 'Hood*. His Denzel Washington impersonation in *Boyz* only hinted at his ability to strike at the heart of his movie characters, but loud tripe like *Chill Factor* left a bad taste in my mouth for Cuba. Good to see that he's back on the right track in *Honor*, playing a heroic figure with enough personal ambition to keep his Carl Brashear human. And though Billy Sunday is an amalgamation of many of the men the real Carl Brashear served under, De Niro plays Sunday with a fierceness I'm starting to think only De Niro is capable of; neither too melodramatic nor over-the-top. De Niro's Sunday was a character you could love to hate and hate to love, all at the same time. Tillman's direction gave Brashear's story an epic sweep, all the while ensuring that it remained a personal story about what drove Carl to be the best.

Of the supporting cast, actor Michael Rapaport must, again, be noted. Rapaport's talent has been unsung for far too long. This is the third film I've seen him in recently (the other two being *Bamboozled* and the otherwise-unmentionable *Lucky Numbers*), and each time he's stood out among the crowd in noteworthy performances. His solid turn in *Honor*, then, was expected but nonetheless appreciated. Somebody get this man a leading role! (Yeah, I know; but *Zebrahead* was a long time ago . . .)

Acting aside, the story itself cannot be ignored. It's "easy" to make a movie about the Black struggle for equality in America, and simply point at the racist White people and institutions and say "Bad, bad people! Bad, bad institutions!" That *Honor* went deeper than that, went further past Brashear's struggles with racism and told a more full story about Brashear's struggles with *himself*, truly elevated this movie above the pack. The shame of it all is that it takes movies like *Men of Honor* and HBO's *Tuskegee Airmen* to teach some of us—me included—about many of "Our Firsts," notably, our nonsporting and nonentertainment firsts.

THE BLACK FACTOR

I grouse a lot about the state of mainstream Black Cinema in the States; and though it still walks on wobbly legs, looking back at the year 2000, I recall many good projects starring, and helmed by, talented Black actors, actresses, writers, and directors. George Tillman Jr., director of *Honor* and *Soul Food*, can certainly be counted amongst those talented folks; and with *Men of Honor*, he raises the stakes significantly. The question is not "Will Tillman's name be added to the list of America's most talented *Black* directors?"; the question is "Will Tillman's name be added to the list of America's most talented *directors*, period?"

BAMMER'S BOTTOM LINE

Men of Honor was an inspiring tale of one man's triumph over adversity; and on the larger scale, a wonderful way to honor our nation's war heroes, even those who had to be dragged, kicking and screaming, toward a truly integrated military.

GREEN LIGHT

Remember the Titans
(2000)

RATED PG; running time 113 minutes
GENRE: Drama
WRITTEN BY: Gregory Allen Howard
DIRECTED BY: Boaz Yakin
CAST: Denzel Washington, Will Patton, Wood Harris, Ryan Hurst, Donald Adeosun Faison, Ethan Suplee, Hayden Panettiere, Catherine Bosworth, Jerry Brandt, Craig Kirkwood, Neal Ghant, Ryan Gosling, Stuart Greer, Earl Poitier, David Jefferson, Burgess Jenkins, Lucinda Jenney, Kip Pardue, Nicole Ari Parker, Brett Rice, John Michael Weatherly, Scott Miles, Gregory Alan Williams

THE STORY

Virginia, 1971. Desegregation and forced busing made many Whites upset and displaced longtime winning White high school football coach Yoast (Will Patton) from his job, when what originally started out as an assistant coach position under Yoast for Black football coach Boone (Denzel Washington), turned out just the opposite: Boone was to take over as head coach for the newly-integrated Titans football team.

Yoast was somewhat hesitant at first to be assistant coach under a person with less experience than him. And the surrounding neighborhood, parents, students, and others, made it clear in no uncertain terms that Boone, and "his people," were unwanted there.

Boone, however, had big plans; plans that included making the young Black *and* White athletes truly come together as a unit by putting them through boot camp–type training, enforcing interracial socialization, and lots of hard work. And maybe, just maybe, the Titans—the student players as well as the ill-at-ease coaching staff—could pull a victory or two out of their collective hats, in spite of themselves.

THE UPSHOT

Once again, I'm here to praise Denzel Washington. That Denzel would give good show is almost a no-brainer; with the exception of a few miscues early on (*Carbon Copy*, anyone?), Washington's career has been filled with solid, and sometimes awe-inspiring, performances. His Coach Boone is no exception; funny at times (the "offsides" bit near the end had me crackin' up) and almost always intense, his was a topnotch performance.

The actors making up the Titans team were also very good, though, alas, too numerous to name in this small space. Standouts were Ryan Hurst as team captain Gary "Jerry" Bertier, one of the first White players to see the light; Wood Harris as "Big Ju," one of the first *Black* players to also be thus enlightened; Donald Adeosun Faison as Petey, and Ethan Suplee as Louie Lastik, the big loveable lug—both actors playing funny without going overboard. Along with the soft-spoken Will Patton as the go-along-to-get-along Coach Yoast, these actors came together in a way that made the cheering audience really believe they became a cohesive team.

But the shocker for me came with the interplay of Hayden Panettiere as Sheryl Yoast (Coach Yoast's daughter) and Krystin Leigh Jones as Nikki Boone (Coach Boone's daughter). Typically, the cute factor in young actors would be turned up to epic proportions in these types of conquering he-

roes flicks, but not so here. Indeed, they sparkled in their scenes together, and were funny and heartwarming without being overly smarmy (and Panettiere should get special recognition for matching Washington in intensity. She was out there!).

Remember the Titans makes no apologies for its feel-good bent. The music was obviously picked for its inspirational value, and the mending of racial fences might've come across as too trite in a lesser movie; certainly, it takes more than a good round of the dozens to bring people together as brothers. Yes, this was a feel-good setup from jump. But hey, ain't nuttin' wrong with feelin' good. Go rent it, and get some "Feel Good" of your own.

THE BLACK FACTOR

It's easy to pick the overt, cross-burning, white-sheet-wearing, racists out of a crowd, point at them, and assure the viewing audience that Yes, Those People Are Racists. It's much harder, I think, to see that racism doesn't just wear a White face, and isn't always a one-way street. Much harder, I think, to admit that racism will always be there until the mindset that creates an US versus a THEM, begins to be erased by creating a WE. *Remember the Titans* looked at the WE for a time, in a way that's not often shown in mainstream flicks; here's hoping that other movies will pick up where it left off.

BAMMER'S BOTTOM LINE

For a PG-rated Disney flick, *Remember the Titans* did a decent job of addressing the race issue; it did lay it on too thick at times, and not thick *enough* at others. I've seen better attempts, but I've also seen much worse; and at least it pinned the tail right on the major cause of racial hatred: ignorance. Think on that. And while you're thinking, see this movie. It'll make you feel good.

GREEN LIGHT

Bams **Rules of Engagement**
(2000)

RATED R; running time 123 minutes
GENRE: Drama
WRITTEN BY: Stephen Gaghan (based on the story by James Webb)
DIRECTED BY: William Friedkin
CAST: Tommy Lee Jones, Samuel L. Jackson, Bruce Greenwood, Guy Pearce, Ben Kingsley, Blair Underwood, Anne Archer, Philip Baker Hall, Nicky Katt, Hayden Tank, Amidou, Mark Feuerstein, Dale Dye, Jihane Kortobi

THE STORY
Colonel Terry Childers (Samuel L. Jackson), a highly decorated, no-nonsense field Marine, is assigned to "baby-sit" Ambassador Mourain (Ben Kingsley) and his family during a protest by Yemeni citizens at the Yemen Embassy. He sends the terrified ambassador and his family on their way, and proceeds to try to get the situation under control. But something goes terribly wrong; when the protesters start shooting and killing Marines, Childers orders Captain Lee (Blair Underwood) to give the order to the Marines to "waste the motherf—ers" under the "rules of engagement"—policies and procedures put forth by the U.S. President and Secretary of Defense that allow U.S. military forces to take actions they deem necessary to protect themselves from hostile forces.

National Security Advisor Bill Sokal, needing a scapegoat to take the focus off the government's part in the death of 83 Yemeni citizens, demands that Childers be court-martialed for murder, and brings in Major Mark Biggs (Guy Pearce), a very capable military lawyer who has spent more time behind a desk than behind a rifle, to prosecute the case. Knowing what he's up against, Childers seeks out newly retired Colonel Hays Hodges (Tommy Lee Jones), with whom Childers served a tour of duty in Vietnam in 1968, saving Hodges's life when he was under severe fire by the enemy. Hodges, however, doesn't have the confidence in himself that Childers has; seeing himself as only a "shot-at Marine" and a very weak lawyer, Hodges reluctantly takes Childers case—but soon discovers that things in this case may not be as they seem.

THE UPSHOT
If you had told me before I watched this movie that there was even the most remote chance that I'd damn near fall asleep while watching anything starring acting powerhouses Samuel L. Jackson and Tommy Lee Jones, I would've laughed in your face. You'll notice I'm not laughing. The onus for this rests squarely on the shoulders of three men: director William Friedkin and actors Samuel L.

Jackson and (to a somewhat lesser extent) Tommy Lee Jones. Friedkin lost me early on. Once that camera of his started looking like something straight out of *NYPD Blue*, I knew it would be a struggle to take this movie seriously. Of course, it doesn't help that *Rules* has a very derivative, been-there-done-that feeling. It suffers from the comparisons with *A Few Good Men*, *Courage Under Fire*, and *Platoon*.

The normally explosive Jackson had exactly three moments of powerful clarity: the first was his vintage Samuel L. "motherf—ers" outburst; the second was the obligatory fight scene between friends (Childers and Hodges)—which led to Childers blurting out the clichéd "you're nothing but a drunk!" (which itself led to my rolling my eyes and groaning in dismay at the cliché); and the last was the also obligatory, though still enjoyable, courtroom scene where Major Biggs confronted him about the original outburst. In every other scene, Jackson could've been played by his stunt double, and I wouldn't have noticed. Jones fared a little better. Though he played against type in his portrayal of a colonel without command—of himself, primarily—he did show a few moments when his strong acting skills were brought to the fore. But these moments were too few and far between, though.

In a nutshell, I never once felt any real chemistry between Jackson and Jones; any feints toward Childers and Hodges supposed friendship rang hollow, and everything between Childers' outburst and the completely flat and unimaginative ending felt like so much filler, with the outcome of the trial a foregone conclusion. The outrageous epilogue only added insult to injury, but by that time I was more than ready to quickly exit, stage right.

The supporting cast, had they been used to the extent of their abilities, might have made this movie somewhat more bearable. Ben Kingsley playing a cowardly ambassador? Hey, that had legs; why didn't they explore it more? Blair Underwood as a captain asked to order the execution of what he thought were innocent citizens? What a subplot! Hmmm . . . but he's out of the movie almost as quickly as he was there. Philip Baker Hall as the senior General Hodges, playing against Jones as Hodges Jr. Talk about your generation gap! Talk about your clash of titans between Hall and Jones! Talk about a waste of potential.

There were a few bright spots, however: as the "unfeeling" prosecutor, Guy Pearce's Major Biggs made more of his part than was probably written in the script. Pearce, along with Anne Archer in her turn as the ambassador's wife, and Hayden Tank as her convincingly frightened son, showed the only real emotion in this otherwise linear movie.

BAMMER'S BOTTOM LINE

Rules was disengaged. If I hadn't seen the neutering of two of the biggest bulls in the acting arena today—Tommy Lee Jones and Samuel L. Jackson—with my own two eyes, I wouldn't have believed it was possible. Who'da thunkit?

YELLOW LIGHT

ince the beginning in Hollywood movies have dealt with the plight of White folks. Their trials and tribulations. Their ups and downs. Until the late '60s and early '70s, there was no such thing as Black cinema. Sure, there were Black movies (*Green Pastures, Cabin in the Sky, Stormy Weather*), but they were few and far between. Then "The Classics" came along. Black folks flocked to the theater and these movies made mad money.

How can you not love blaxploitation flicks? Where else can you find brothas getting back at "The Man" while driving a "stankin lankin" (that would be a Lincoln Continental)? Where else can you see a sistah "knuckle up" and beat the tar out of someone without killing herself in her platform shoes, or, if she really needs to handle her business, pull a gun out of her Afro? Where else can you see a brotha stroll up with a woman on each arm and two behind him? Where else will you find a main character with his/her own theme song? (Remember, halfway through *Coffy*, her theme music goes, ". . . Coffy, you're in danger, girl?" Indicating homegirl had a problem.)

There are some issues, though. Women were dogged, and if the brotha had a White woman, especially if he was dominating her, he was something to behold. Someone would get called a nigga, a ho', or a bitch in a second. Sistahs would get pimp-slapped every half a second. But not all of these films were about pimpin' and killin'. Some very thought-provoking dramas came out of this genre as well as some harmless comedies. It lasted about eight years, but Black cinema has never been the same. An interesting side note: most of these movies were written and directed by Jewish men. Hmm . . .

This chapter also celebrates African-American culture. Movies about Our Folks and movies by Our Folks—the good, the bad, and the stank.

(Preach, Diva.)

A Piece of the Action
(1977)

RATED PG; running time 135 minutes
GENRE: Dramedy
WRITTEN BY: Timothy March, Charles Black-
well
DIRECTED BY: Sidney Poitier
MUSIC BY: Curtis Mayfield
CAST: Sidney Poitier, Bill Cosby, James Earl
Jones, Denise Nicholas, Hope Clarke, Tracy
Reed, Titos Vandis, Frances Foster, Sheryl Lee
Ralph, Eric Laneuville, Edward Love, Ernest
Thomas, Dianne Dixon, Jason Evers, Larry
Beecham, Ja'Net DuBois, Gammy Burdett,
Wonderful Smith

(Note: for organizational purposes, the Bill
Cosby-Sidney Poitier "trilogy" is listed here
in alphabetical order; but to follow my flow,
you might want to read them in chrono-
logical order: first *Uptown Saturday Night*
(see page 139), then *Let's Do It Again* (see
page 130), and finally *A Piece of the Action*. Or not —Bams)

THE STORY
Once again, our heroes find themselves in a tight
spot, and they have to do a lot of wiggling to get
out. Here, they play Manny Durrell (Sidney
Poitier) and David Anderson (Bill Cosby), two
high-end thieves who are found out by retired
cop Joshua Burke (James Earl Jones). Burke uses
the evidence he has against the men to blackmail
them into spending six weeks volunteering as
teen job counselors at a community center run by
Leila French (Denise Nicholas)—with the alternative being "volunteering" at Joliet prison.

Manny and David ain't havin' it, though; desperate to rid themselves of the attitude-laden
"gorillas" they're forced to counsel—including
jokester Gerald, sensitive Willie, and a very angry
Barbara (Sheryl Lee Ralph, in a powerful performance)—they try to scheme their way out of
their predicament. Meanwhile, Mr. Bruno, the
mobster on whom Manny and Bea (Frances Foster) worked their last con, is out to catch a thief—
and may just use Manny's girlfriend Nikki (Tracy
Reed) as bait.

THE UPSHOT
Seeing the more serious side of a Cosby-Poitier
collaboration was initially heartening, leaving me
to hope that this movie would soar above *Uptown
Saturday Night's* superficiality, and even *Let's Do It
Again's* nicely done comedic spin. Alas, it was not
meant to be. *A Piece of the Action* tries to be too
many things at once and therein lies the rub.
There was a comedy angle, a suave criminal angle,
a dramatic social statement angle ... but only one
angle was completely realized.

On the comedic side of things, *A Piece* failed
the most. Throughout this picture, I got the uneasy feeling that I was being asked to laugh *at*,
not *with*, the characters. This would've been fine,
had Poitier and crew not also taken on the heav-
ier, dramatic story. But it was too much to get into
a laughter groove, only to have the dramatic elements thrust in my face. And that whole unfunny
in-laws subplot involving Nikki's family could've
been excised from the movie with no ill effect; it
stuck out like a sore thumb. Likewise, the suave
criminal bits were just too few and far between to

be very meaningful; except for use as plot advancement, the situation with Cosby and Poitier as big-time burglars and James Earl Jones as the ex-cop who snares them didn't play well at all. And as far as it goes, *I Spy* aside, Bill Cosby just doesn't work as stud muffin material to me.

It was the dramatic social statement angle that was most compelling for me; the most immediate and true-to-life. As a child of the '70s, I remember classes with students just like the ones depicted in *A Piece*, where clowning was rewarded, failure was expected, and crabs-in-a-barrel syndrome was the norm. But as bad as that sounds, I also remember that fights were done by fist—if it got that far. Back in the day, we kids mostly circled each other, shoulder-to-shoulder, until we got dizzy or someone let the combatants save face by distracting their attention.

Could *A Piece of the Action* be made today? On the one hand, I can't picture it, not with the knuckleheads who have caused so much pain and heartache in the younger generation's lives. Any modern-day remake would probably have a shootout in the first frame, over some piddling issue. And on the other hand, I *can* see it—but only in yet another White-savior-saves-the-poor Ghetto-chillrun form. Either way . . . no thanks.

BAMMER'S BOTTOM LINE:
Just when I thought I had the Cosby-Poitier modus operandi down, they went and pulled a dramatic switch on me. The jumbled result wasn't as successful overall as *Let's Do It Again*, but on a personal level . . . I can diggit.

FLASHING YELLOW LIGHT

Baby Boy
(2001)

RATED R; running time 129 minutes
GENRE: Drama
WRITTEN BY: John Singleton
DIRECTED BY: John Singleton
CAST: Tyrese Gibson, Omar Gooding, A. J. Johnson, Taraji P. Henson, Snoop Dogg, Tamara LaSeon Bass, Ving Rhames

Tyrese's big break was playing the young man "sangin'" on the bus in a Coke commercial.

THE DIGEST
Jody (Tyrese) has two kids by two different women; no job; no car; and lives at home with his mother. Yet, despite all of his trifilance, "he got game," lots of game. His mother is always bailing him out when he gets in trouble, especially from "baby mama drama." He jumps from woman to woman, yet his son's mother, Yvette, takes him back every time. But all of this is about to change. Jody decides that he is going to start boosting clothes to make ends meet. Before you know it, he is rolling deep in money. With the money flowing in, you'd think that Jody would get his act together, but he doesn't. He is still at home with his mother.

He doesn't neglect his children, however, spending as much time with them as he can. Though not a constant presence in their lives, he is determined to be there for his kids since his father wasn't there for him.

Meanwhile, Jody's 36-year-old mother Juanita (A. J. Johnson), has found a new love. A reformed O. G. ("Old Gangsta" or "Original Gangsta," depends on who you ask) from the old school, Melvin (Ving Rhames), has come a-callin' and Juanita is sprung. She is ready to start her life again and Melvin moves in. Melvin tries in his own harsh way to be a father figure for Jody, but Jody ain't havin' it. As far as Jody is concerned, he is the man of the house and Melvin is over-stepping his bounds. Melvin and Jody antagonize one another until there is so much tension that a fight breaks loose. Juanita is torn between her man and her child, but any decision she makes is bound to be the wrong one.

THE DISH

Despite myself, as I watched the movie, I found myself justifying, excusing, and accepting all of the stereotypes and issues I fight against: the negativity, the foul language, the belief that everyone in the 'hood is a miscreant and nothing good comes out it. All of this was present in this movie, but I still liked it. Maybe it's because I looked at the film and saw the life of these few people represented—not the Black community as a whole. Maybe it's because what I saw on the screen is what I expected from people who are/were gangbangers and people who grew up in that environment. This very well could be my own stereotype coming into play. I know that not everyone who grows up in South Central is "Rodney," "Sweet Pea," or "Do Dirty." Nor do all the women excuse trifilin' behavior and choose men over their children like Juanita, Yvette, and Peanut.

My sympathies aside, I did have issues. The plot was weak, there were many loose ends, and many characters were not fleshed out enough. Beyond all of my issues, what I saw was a story of a young man struggling to be a man when he hasn't had any male guidance at home. A story about babies having babies then not knowing how to juggle motherhood and womanhood, a story about immature people making poor decisions and lacking the skills that only come with maturity to cope with their poor decisions. It's a vicious cycle.

Snoop played the part of a complete and total thug very well. There was nothing to like about him. Heck, I wanted to beat his ass. Tyrese did very well portraying a young man who is trying his best to be a man but is too weak to take care of himself. Taraji P. Henson's Yvette seems to only know how to express anger and sexual gratification. She's so busy telling Jody to grow up she fails to see that she has some growing to do herself. A. J. Johnson pleasantly surprised me. I remember her as Sharane in *House Party*. A. J. looked *good* and played her role credibly. Even though her character was a bit one-dimensional, I felt her pain when she couldn't get her man and her son to get along. Last but not least, Ving Rhames. Now this brotha scared me. He looked like he would stick you with a shiv in a second. Ving has also been working out. Rent *The People Under the Stairs*, you will see a very skinny Ving Rhames with a Jheri Curl. After you see him then, you'll understand my shock.

Baby Boy is no *Boyz N the Hood*, and I was saddened to see that not much in the 'hood has changed in John Singleton's eyes, but nonetheless I'm glad he took us back to his 'hood for another glance.

THE DIRECTIVE
Baby Mama Drama in da 'Hood.

FLASHING YELLOW LIGHT

 **Bamboozled**
(2000)

RATED R; running time 136 minutes
GENRE: Drama (forget what the genre-labelers are sayin'; this ain't no comedy.)
WRITTEN BY: Spike Lee
DIRECTED BY: Spike Lee
CAST: Damon Wayans, Savion Glover, Tommy Davidson, Jada Pinkett-Smith, Michael Rapaport, Mos Def

> You are about to read the most schizophrenically lengthy review I have ever written—which, ironically, marries it perfectly to the movie being reviewed: Spike Lee's controversial *Bamboozled*. Here we go . . .

THE STORY
Black TV writer Pierre DeLacroix (Damon Wayans) is charged by the White producer of the Continental Network Systems station Mr. Dunwitty (Michael Rapaport) to come up with an all-Black comedy show that will boost CNS's ratings. But when the "streetwise" Dunwitty rejects the Harvard-educated DeLacroix's plans to create

"the next Cosby show," DeLa, along with his assistant, Sloane Hopkins (Jada Pinkett-Smith), decides to create a show so offensive he'll get out of his contract.

Inspired by homeless Black street tap dancer Manray (Savion Glover) and his partner, Womack (Tommy Davidson), DeLa and Sloane come up with the most heinous show imaginable—*Mantan the New Millennium Minstrel Show*, in which Manray and Womack would play Mantan and "Sleep n' Eat" respectively. Described as "Two Reeee-aaaal Coons," they would both be made up in blackface ("Black actors in blacker blackface"). Manray and Womack, being in a state of poverty, agree to this, but DeLa is ultimately undone when, to his surprise, not only does the "nigga"-spouting Dunwitty love the concept, the American TV audience eats it up. Sloane and DeLa have a hard time living with this—but not as hard a time as Sloane's brother Julius, a.k.a. Big Black Africa (Mos Def), a member of the Mau Mau rap group. He takes issue with the "comically" blackened minstrels at the same time as he and his fellow malt liquor–guzzling, self-righteous Mau Maus use the word "nigga" as much if not more than the minstrels themselves.

THE UPSHOT
Initially, *Bamboozled* worked for me on many levels. But I was utterly disappointed when it just kept repeating itself without saying anything new, eventually running out of juice well before it was over. Had I stopped watching it at a certain point, I might've declared it a masterpiece. As it is, I can neither fully praise nor fully denigrate this movie. Funny thing is, *some* Black folks will

try to take me to task for that very thing ("*Bamboozled* was dope! you Oreo traitor!" . . . *Bamboozled* was wack! you Bougie traitor! Can't win for losing.)

As a visionary tale, *Bamboozled* knows few equals. Spike Lee nailed many of the dysfunctional issues Black folks in America have as a People, as well as *the* issue itself: what exactly does it mean to be Black in America? Is DeLa less Black than Julius because Julius is "keepin' it real"? Is Dunwitty—clearly a Caucasian—*more* Black than DeLa because Dunwitty considers himself "street?" Is the White Mau Mau Blacker than *all* of them? And when it gets right down to it, is there even such a thing as one single "Black Culture"?

Though Lee's targets were many, and wide (and, depending on who you ask—for instance, Hollywood's Finest Black Comedy Stars, many of whom loudly questioned Lee's "right" to do this movie—just plain off-base), I found his aim fairly accurate, for the most part. Too many of Us indulge in "nigga"-slinging, malt-liquor drinking, empty mau-mauing—even mentally separating Us into "Blacks" and "Negroes" (or, telling it like 'tis, "Niggers"). *Bamboozled* spoke to many of the things I've long felt were cultural ills with Us here in this so-called Melting Pot, particularly, his examination of the most heinous ill being that We gladly supply the cork, and willingly apply the ugly blackface, to Ourselves.

But—and this isn't a small thing—being a Visionary is only half the battle; to have a successful movie, one must also have successful acting and directing, a tight storyline, and cohesive editing. And that is where *Bamboozled* ultimately failed. Granted, a Spike Lee Joint

doesn't always follow the moviemaking blueprint of your standard motion picture. He is known for his weird jump cuts, the unnatural-feeling scenes, and the strange editing. But this film couldn't afford Lee's quirks. Further, the in-your-face storyline on top of the unbelievability of both Mantan's and Sleep n' Eat's instant revelations and Damon Wayans's bizarre choice of a one-dimensional portrayal of DeLacroix almost killed the joy of seeing the aforementioned issues addressed on the big screen.

Great acting by Jada Pinkett-Smith, Michael Rapaport, and an interesting turn by rapper Mos Def as Big Black Africa, could not overcome Lee's lack of tight focus, the far-too-easy "instant" acceptance of the minstrel show by the audience, the completely incredible "payoff" involving the Mau Maus and Mantan (my eyes truly rolled), or Wayans's just plain bad acting—and worse, the *bad* decision to let him do the narrative voiceover. The "jolly nigger"-type collectibles and the Black actors of the past who did what they had to do—and having done so, *allowed* — a Spike Lee, a Damon Wayans, et al, to be where they are today—should have supplied the final narrative. Too bad they weren't really allowed to speak.

BAMMER'S BOTTOM LINE
Conceptually, *Bamboozled* is something that Spike Lee should be applauded for. Would that the finished product were as great as the concept behind it. It pains me to say that. I desperately wanted to love this movie for both its message and the talent behind it. The message came through loud and clear; but judging *Bamboozled*

on its creative merits alone, we *have* been hood-winked.

GREEN LIGHT

A green light for what visionary Spike Lee tried to Say; but . . .

FLASHING YELLOW LIGHT

. . . A cautionary yellow light for the way director Spike Lee Said it.

Spike, I gotta go with what DeLa's mama said about him: You disappoint me.

The Best Man
(1999)

RATED R; running time 118 minutes
GENRE: Romantic comedy
WRITTEN BY: Malcolm D. Lee
DIRECTED BY: Malcolm D. Lee
CAST: Taye Diggs, Nia Long, Morris Chestnut, Harold Perrineau Jr., Terrence Dashon Howard, Sanaa Lathan, Monica Calhoun, Melissa De Sousa, Victoria Dillard

> Writer-Director Malcolm D. Lee is a cousin of Spike Lee's.

THE DIGEST

In this ensemble cast we have Jordan (Nia Long), an ambitious and driven producer for BET, and Quentin (Terrence Dashon Howard), a jack-of-all-trades and master of none. He can play the hell out of a guitar and charm any lady. (He also steals the show. He had the entire audience rolling.) Lance Sullivan (played by that tall drink of water Morris Chestnut) is the star running back for some New York football team. Murch (Harold Perrineau) is a shy guidance counselor who has a law degree but prefers to work with children. Shelby (Melissa DeSousa), Murch's overbearing bougie girlfriend (another scene stealer). Robin (Sanaa Lathan), Harper's long-suffering girl-friend, and finally Mia (Monica Calhoun), Lance's bride-to-be. All of them, with the excep-tion of Robin, went to college together and they are still very close. They are gathering in New York to take part in Lance and Mia's wedding.

Harper Stewart (played by Taye Diggs who one of my girlfriends said she'd pay $6.50 to watch him make toast for two hours. I'm still cracking up) has just written his first book and early buzz is that it's good. Harper allowed Jordan to have an advanced copy of the book. She was supposed to read it and return it to him. Instead, she passes it on to Murch who reads it and then passes it on to Shelby. By the time Harper gets to New York, everyone but Mia and Lance have read it. They all love the book; the only problem is; as much as Harper denies it, the characters in the book fit his friends to a T, but they all handle it good-naturedly. The fact that the book was passed around normally would not be a big deal, but the book hints at an affair that may or may not have been perpetrated by the best man.

THE DISH

Run, do not walk to rent this excellent movie. You'll find yourself cheering and clapping during the opening credits alone. This is a *great* film! It was refreshing to see normal, upwardly mobile Black folks. No one did anything illegal, although I swear Quentin was high. I've heard this film called "The Wood 2." There is no comparison other than there are four male friends and Taye Diggs was in both. This movie is about trust, love, honesty, respect, as well as "true blue" friendships.

Parents, this movie is rated "R" and with good reason; please watch this one without the kids. And, as always, the "n" word was used a bit over much, as was the "b" word. There is some nudity, cursing, and a very small dose of violence as well.

THE DIRECTIVE

See it twice, folks, it's well worth it. Besides, we really need to support our films. And in what other movie can you find such an illustrious cast doing "The Smurf," "The Running Man," "The Roger Rabbit," and "The Electric Slide?" Plus they played "Treat 'em Right" by Chubb Rock as well as some Stevie Wonder. How can you not want to see *The Best Man*?

GREEN LIGHT

Bams **Black Belt Jones**
(1974)

RATED R; running time 87 minutes
GENRE: Action (Comedy?)
WRITTEN BY: Alex Ross, Fred Weintraub, Oscar Williams
DIRECTED BY: Robert Clouse
CAST: Jim Kelly, Gloria Hendry, Scatman Crothers, Eric Laneuville, Alan Weeks, Andre Philippe, Malik Carter, Vincent Barbi

THE STORY

Oh. My. God. I'm sorry, I'm still in shock. What I *meant* to say was, *Black Belt Jones* stars Jim Kelly as—who else?—Black Belt Jones, SuperBad Cop And Ladies Man.

Mob boss Don Steffano (Andre Philippe) wants to own prime land being developed by the city for a civic center, but Pop Byrd (Scatman Crothers) and his karate school are right in the center of the property Steffano wants. Pop's school keeps young guys like student Quincy and teacher Toppy in good mental and physical condition (and, apparently, in their uniforms 24-7), but Steffano doesn't care; he wants the land, and uses any means necessary to get it. Steffano calls in his marker on Pinky, a local pool hall thug who holds a $1,000 IOU from Pops, which Pinky uses to bully Pops into giving Steffano the dojo. When Black Belt Jones and Toppy foil that plan, Pinky and fellow henchman Big Tuna (Vincent Barbi) take it to the next phase and . . . (resist the urge to type "yada yada yada," Bammer. Oops.) . . . and Pop's SuperBad daughter Sydney (Gloria Hendry) joins Black Belt Jones and . . .

Wackiness—along with lots of bad acting, Afros that should be registered as lethal weapons, terrible special effects, broken things that are supposed to be glass but look like a bad grade-school science experiment, and Scatman Crothers as you've never seen him before—ensues.

THE UPSHOT

Just between you and me . . . the people behind *Black Belt Jones* were just riffin', right? Surely, they weren't being serious! I mean, Jim Kelly, an ex–international karate champ, was a baaaad mofo in *Enter the Dragon*. He has worked with the Master, Bruce Lee; he should've known better than to take on this role which had him doing moves that made him look like he just took his first white-belt class, badly emulating Bruce Lee and his trademark "karate yell." Fine, everybody wanted to be like Lee, so I can't dog the brotha for trying. And all that *Mystery Science Theater 3000*–worthy "acting" was good enough for an hour or so of incredulous belly laughs, so it can't all be bad, I reckon. But—my Lord—*somebody* tell me they weren't serious, eh?

BBJ touched on every silly, bad martial arts stereotype in the book, from the SuperStud Black Hero to the SuperBad Hot Mama, on through to the Greasy Tom Villain—and, of course, the combination funeral home/karate dojo. You ain't seen nuthin' until you see a karate demonstration done to the beat of a grieving choir. But nothing, absolutely nothing, beats a badly toupeed Scatman Crothers as a karate man. I swear I almost lost it.

Okay, I get it. This movie is a parody. It has to be. Let me live in my state of denial, please. Otherwise, I won't be able to sleep at night.

BAMMER'S BOTTOM LINE

Black Belt Jones deserves a red light for its hideousness but a green light for its pokefunatability. Averaged out, a yellow light it is.

YELLOW LIGHT

the Diva — Black Caesar
(1973)

RATED R; running time 87 minutes
GENRE: Action/Thriller
WRITTEN BY: Larry Cohen
DIRECTED BY: Larry Cohen
MUSIC BY: James Brown
CAST: Fred Williamson, Gloria Hendry, Art Lund, D'Urville Martin, Julius Harris, Minnie Gentry, Philip Roye, William Wellman Jr., James Dixon, Val Avery

THE DIGEST

Tommy Gibbs (Fred Williamson) is a shoeshine boy with ambition. He helps out the mob with a hit and gains their trust. He is asked to run an errand and what happens changes Tommy's life forever.

Unbeknownst to Tommy, he is delivering a payoff to a bigoted cop named McKinney (Art Lund). McKinney insists that Tommy stole some of the money and beats him down with a nightstick. The beating results in Tommy's leg being irreparably damaged and Tommy being sent to prison on some trumped-up charges. But Tommy is tough, and tells his friend Joey, the neighborhood nerd to go to school and learn how to make and keep money.

Tommy does about 13 years in the pokey. He comes out with a limp, dressed to the nines. The first thing he does is pull off a bold daylight hit for the mafia. This lands him on the payroll and eventually puts him in a position to demand, and get, a neighborhood of his own to run. Tommy is living high off the hog. But, of course, it can't last too long. As fast as he has risen he is falling. Tommy is too bold and too arrogant. His business associates turn on him and they take his most trusted friends with them. Pretty soon, Tommy is on his own, but he's not going quietly and he's not going alone.

THE DISH

Black Caesar fu . . . messed . . . me . . . up. It was deep . . . real deep.

No matter how Tommy ages, he is still a little boy trying to please his mother and impress people. Not having had a father figure and being in jail from about age 14 to age 27, he behaves as a man the only way he knows how. He accrues power and lets money corrupt his mind. The entire time I was watching *Black Caesar*, all I could think about was the movie *Scarface* (1983). They were so similar it's unnerving.

The supporting cast is strong, particularly Art Lund as McKinney. *Black Caesar* wouldn't have been half the movie it was without the James Brown soundtrack: the Godfather of Soul singing the theme music for the Godfather of Harlem.

THE DIRECTIVE

Anyone who has the slightest bit of interest in the '70s should put *Black Caesar* on the top of their list. *Black Caesar* is a cut above the typical blaxploitation films.

GREEN LIGHT

Cass **Black Heat**
(1975)

RATED R; running time 92 minutes
GENRE: Action/Blaxploitation
WRITTEN BY: John D'Amato and Bud Donnelly
DIRECTED BY: Al Adamson
CAST: Timothy Brown, Geoffrey Land, Tanya Boyd, Jana Bellan, Russ Tamblyn, Darlene Anders, Regina Carrol, J. C. Wells, Neal Furst

CASS'S CLIP

Black Heat opens in the desert with an arms-for-drugs swap between crook Guido and foreign rebel Ramirez. Las Vegas undercover cops Kicks Carter and Tony try to thwart their corrupt business transactions.

Meanwhile, the Hunt Room, a typical Blaxploitation nightclub, serves as the popular hot spot where Kicks and Tony meet their girlfriends, Stephanie and Terry, for drinks and listen to their friend Val sing. Stephanie is a struggling TV reporter. Terry is an employee at a securities commission and a compulsive gambler. The Hunt Room is also one of the locations where owner

Fay and Ziggy, her flunky thug, run an illegal gambling operation.

When Guido, Fay, and Ziggy cook up a scheme to make lots of money, they use Terry as bait. Faye pays Terry's $15,000 gambling debt in exchange for information on the whereabouts of a messenger carrying $25,000 in negotiable securities. Fearing for her life, Terry finally tells Val and Stephanie her dilemma. Stephanie instructs Terry to give Ziggy and Faye the information they want and she'll film the whole thing as evidence for Kicks. Stephanie follows and films the messenger's kidnapping, shooting, and the dumping of his body. She shows Kicks the tape, which sets up the big anticlimactic desert showdown between Kicks and the bad guys.

DA 411

Black Heat is your typical jive-talkin', car-driving-off-the-cliff, staged-fight movie. What made this plotless *Black Heat* even worse was: (1) Kicks and Terry's passionless lovemaking scenes; (2) a senseless (plotwise) gang rape; and (3) Fay's lesbian advances to Terry after she paid off Terry's gambling debts.

CASS'S CONCLUSION

BorING (with a capital ING)! *Black Heat* wasn't even lukewarm.

RED LIGHT

Bams · The Brothers
(2001)

RATED R; running time 106 minutes
GENRE: Romantic comedy/Drama
WRITTEN BY: Gary Hardwick
DIRECTED BY: Gary Hardwick
CAST: Morris Chestnut, D. L. Hughley, Bill Bellamy, Shemar Moore, Gabrielle Union, Jenifer Lewis, Tamala Jones, Susan Dalian, Tatyana Ali, Julie Benz, Clifton Powell, Vanessa Bell Calloway, Marla Gibbs, Angela Brooks

THE STORY

The Brothers literally starts with a bang, as Dr. Jackson Smith (Morris Chestnut) recounts to his therapist (Vanessa Bell Calloway) the nightmares he has of a mysterious woman in bridal attire coming after him with a gun. And, speaking of brides, Terry Wright (Shemar Moore), one of Jack's running buddies (a group of four professional Black men who call themselves "the Brothers") announces that he's about to jump the broom with his girlfriend of two months, BeBe Fales (Susan Dalian). The Brothers are underwhelmed by this news, especially lawyer Brian Palmer (Bill Bellamy), who's never met a Black woman without issues—listen closely and you can almost hear the Black Sista 3-Snaps-Up from Angela Brooks as the spurned judge—and thus looks to a White woman (Julie Benz) to fulfill his needs. And speaking of not having one's needs fulfilled, fellow Brother Derrick West (D. L. Hughley) is also not quite enthusiastic over Terry's news. Derrick speaks from experience, as his wife, Sheila (Tamala Jones), refuses to, as the youngsters say, "give Derrick brain," or to entertain thoughts of letting D's mother (Marla Gibbs) live with them.

Jack also has intimacy issues, stemming from the way his father (Clifton Powell) abandoned his feisty mother (the wonderful Jenifer Lewis), leaving them and his wacky sister, Cherie (Tatyana Ali), to fend for themselves. But Jack's world is about to be turned upside down, as he meets and falls for freelance photographer Denice Johnson (Gabrielle Union); Denice *seems* normal enough at first glance, but like most of the women in the Brothers' lives, she has a skeleton in her closet, too.

THE UPSHOT

In numerous reviews of *The Brothers,* some mainstream critics complained that it's "just another flick in the same vein as *The Best Man* and *The Wood* and the films in this genre of young Black professionals seeking romance, etc."

Yeah, Lord knows we need to get back to the days when the only Black man in a movie played the obligatory thug. What's that now? Five "Professional Black Man/Woman Seeks Fulfillment And The American Dream—Just Like Their White Counterparts" movies to UMPTEEN "Hoodrat/Thug/DrugDealer/SkantchHoe/Pimp/ Ig'nant Shuffling Sambo . . ." flicks?

Even with my eyes rolling at my fellow critics, it pains me to say that *The Brothers* was too derivative of the much better *Best Man.*

This is not to say that there weren't some good-to-great performances in *The Brothers.* Morris Chestnut, as always, put in solid work as Jackson (even though his character's main conflict made absolutely no sense to me), and had wonderful chemistry with Gabrielle Union as Denice. D. L. Hughley had me rolling as the sexually frustrated Derrick West, and put me in mind of, strangely enough, Burgess Meredith in *Grumpy Old Men* (made more evident by the outtakes shown at the end). And Jenifer Lewis once again ran away with a movie, in a role (the mother) that was probably supposed to suppress her power, but you might as well ask the sun not to shine as to try to tuck away Lewis's abilities to bring It.

But Bill Bellamy was disappointing here. Ditto Shemar Moore, who stood there looking as pretty as he wanna be, but added little to the movie itself. In his case, though, I fault the writing and directing more than the actor. Where Bellamy was given *too much* to do, Moore simply wasn't given the tools he needed to make Terry much more than a bad plot device.

My biggest gripe? It's not so much that women, as a gender, get blasted in *The Brothers*— hey, some of my sisters *deserve* the thrashing— but that putting a penis on a skreech doesn't improve the skreech. Apparently, Terry McMillan doesn't have the corner on Black gender-bashing. Writer-director Gary Hardwick had the beginnings of a good idea. But he let it get away from him, failing to support his idea with a solid storyline, believable back story, or straightforward character development. What started out as a near-copycat of *The Best Man* ended up as *Waiting to Exhale* in drag, with an implied Oedipal conflict thrown in for "good" measure.

BAMMER'S BOTTOM LINE

Though I'd take a thousand *Brothers* over one more Black Gangsta flick any day, *The Brothers,* because of its miscues, lack of direction, and derivative nature, gets a flashing yellow light. Even the solid performances by Morris Chestnut, Gabrielle Union, Jenifer Lewis, and the hilarious D. L. Hughley didn't compensate for all that was amiss.

FLASHING YELLOW LIGHT

 Bucktown
(1975)

RATED R; running time 94 minutes
GENRE: Crime/Drama
WRITTEN BY: Bob Ellison
DIRECTED BY: Authur Marks
CAST: Fred Williamson, Pam Grier, Thalmus Rasulala, Bernie Hamilton, Art Lund, Tierre Turner, Carl Weathers

THE DIGEST

Duke Johnson (Fred Williamson) steps off a train and into hell when he lands in Bucktown to bury his brother, Ben. His first sight of the city is two White cops beating a Black suspect. In light of that, he just wants to collect Ben's belongings and get back to a more civilized city. Unfortunately, all of Ben's property is in probate, so he has to stay for at least 60 days.

Since he has time to kill, the locals convince him to reopen Ben's bar—"Club Alabam." Things are running smoothly for about 10 minutes when a group of White cops show up and demand a nightly take of the profits. If he doesn't cough up some money, they'll give him compelling reasons as to why he should cooperate. Duke gives them his answer by promptly beating their asses. He then storms the police captain's office and fills him in on the blackmail that his officers are running. It is at this point that the captain gives him the subtle threat that what happened to his brother could happen to him. Duke is confused. He thought his brother died of natural causes. Well, sorta. After he was beat and left outside for dead, he died from exposure. Duke is very upset that none of the locals told him. He is especially upset with Aretha (Pam Grier), Ben's girlfriend and a waitress at the club. She has been downright rude to Duke for no real reason. She starts to feel guilty and shows up at his house to apologize, at which point the police show up and shoot up the house.

Now Duke is really mad. He calls home for reinforcements. His best friend, Roy (Thalmus Rasulala), brings three hardcore brothas with him and they clean up the town. But Duke doesn't count on Roy and the thugs liking the setup the sheriff had, and now they want a piece of the action. They take over where the sheriff left off—shaking down all the local businesses.

Can Duke save the town and his friendship?

THE DISH

You go in knowing that it's not going to be the best movie ever made, but a slightly plausible plot would have helped. Plot holes aside, Pam Grier was underused and wooden. Fred Williamson looked like he was trying not to laugh. Tierre Turner as the young orphan Steve was the most animated actor, and he provides some of the most interesting moments. Perhaps the irony of the movie title says it all.

THE DIRECTIVE

If you happen to come across *Bucktown,* grab it, but I certainly wouldn't go on a mission to find it.

YELLOW LIGHT

---

the **Diva**   **Coffy**
(1973)

RATED R; running time 90 minutes
GENRE: Action
WRITTEN BY: Jack Hill
DIRECTED BY: Jack Hill
CAST: Pam Grier, Booker Bradshaw, Robert Do-Qui, William Elliott, Allan Arbus, Sid Haig, Barry Cahill, Lee de Broux, Ruben Moreno, Lisa Farringer, Carol Lawson, Linda Haynes

THE DIGEST

Ms. Coffin (Pam Grier)—no first name— known as Coffy by her friends and family, is a woman bent on revenge . . . by any means necessary. Her precious 14-year-old sister is strung out on smack/heroin, and Coffy is none too pleased. When she is not working the graveyard shift as a nurse, she is ripping through Los Angeles taking out the lowlife dope dealers putting smack on the street. Sometimes she has to use her body; most times she uses her mind. She ends up as one of King George's girls. He is a pimp and a small-time pusher, but he has a direct connection to the man supplying all of the dope.

When she's not working or killing folks, she is spending her time with her best friend, an over-worked cop named Carter, and with her main man, Howard Brunswick, a local councilman. Eventually she makes a mistake and it all comes to a head. Can she survive going up against the mob all by herself?

THE DISH

Coffy is too tough. As the tagline says, "They call her Coffy and she'll cream you!" *Coffy* was a lot of fun to watch, even though it was formulaic. A sellout; drug dealers; "The Man"; and boobies everywhere. Five minutes didn't go by without some woman's "naughty pillow" hanging out. Though there wasn't one decent performance it was excellent for the purpose it served—escapism and a chance to see a strong Black woman whipping much ass.

THE BLACK FACTOR

After watching this movie, I clearly understand the Pam Grier mystique. Smart and pretty, she is not afraid to bare all. I can also now understand how important her roles were to Black people, even though they were just fluffy roles and the same ole same. Black men were able to see a beautiful Black woman on screen—one that wasn't just a roll in the hay for some White mobster, and Black women were able to see an independent strong woman.

THE DIRECTIVE

Invite a few friends over and pop *Coffy* into the VCR. Would you like a little Coffy with your beatdown?

GREEN LIGHT

Cornbread, Earl and Me
(1975)

RATED PG; running time 96 minutes

GENRE: Drama

WRITTEN BY: Leonard Lamensdorf (based on the novel by Ronald Fair)

DIRECTED BY: Joseph Manduke

CAST: Laurence Fishburne, Rosalind Cash, Moses Gunn, Bernie Casey, Madge Sinclair, Stack Pierce, Thalmus Rasulala, Tierre Turner, Keith Wilkes, Antonio Fargas, Logan Ramsey, Vince Martorano, Charles Lampkin, Stefan Gierasch

THE STORY

Cornbread, Earl and Me is kind of a misnomer; "Earl" (Tierre Turner) doesn't really have much to do with it, and "Cornbread" (Keith Wilkes) only peripherally more. "Me"—that is, Wilford Robinson (Laurence Fishburne at 13)—is really the central character.

Like the rest of the people they grew up with in the 1970s, Will and Earl greatly admired Nathaniel "Cornbread" Hamilton for his basketball skills, and for his generally positive outlook on life. Cornbread was due to go off to college in a few weeks, and almost everyone who knew him was proud of him, and supported him in his efforts. Back in the days when everybody's parent was your own, Cornbread and his crew were as comfortable hanging out with his parents, Leona (Madge Sinclair) and Sam (Stack Pierce), as they were with Mr. Fred (Charles Lampkin), owner of the corner store. Will and Earl also had the support of Will's mother, Sarah (Rosalind Cash), though her boyfriend, Charlie (Thalmus Rasulala), preferred spending more time with Sarah than with the boys.

Getting by financially was a struggle, to be sure; but as a social unit, life in the 'hood, was good. It was a good time to be a young man with prospects and talent—until outside influences, that is, got in the way. . . . Cornbread's problems with One-Eye (Antonio "Huggy Bear" Fargas), a local numbers-runner, were nothing compared with a case of mistaken identity made by police officers John Golich (Vince Martorano) and Larry Atkins (Bernie Casey).

THE UPSHOT

Some movies age well, some don't. *Cornbread, Earl and Me* definitely belongs in that "don't" category. On a purely dramatic basis, *Cornbread* was surprisingly bad; I say "surprisingly," considering the number of talented actors attached. Individually, I guess the cast had their moments; from Madge Sinclair and Thalmus Rasulala, to the late Rosalind Cash and Moses Gunn (attorney Ben Blackwell), there were brief glimpses of the (as BET would put it) "Black Star Power" they were able to bring to roles in many of their later films. But taken as a whole, the scenes felt forced and choppy, the actors stiff, and the production rather amateurish.

There were two notable exceptions. Bernie Casey, as a cop who wanted to do good in his community but felt betrayed by those who would turn on him, impressed me in this strong and silent (but mad as hell and not gonna take it anymore) role. I was genuinely surprised to see his character, and not the White cop, as the primary source of racial bigotry (actually, *class* bigotry). Clearly, though, Laurence Fishburne stole the show. Shades of the tremendous acting ability that movie audiences would come to know in his later films were visible here in *Cornbread*. In fact, I got a kick out of watching some of the earlier raw displays of power in his Will, displays that I've enjoyed watching mature into subtle nuance in films like *Always Outnumbered, School Daze,* and *Boys N the 'Hood.*

I wish the director, the writer, and the rest of the creative talent had had the same fire in the belly that Fishburne seemed to have. Alas, it was not to be. I was ready to just let it go, to just roll with this movie as a remnant of a less demanding time in Black cinema, up until the very lame, completely bogus, "what the hell was *that*?" ending. I found myself gaping at the screen, jaw dropped, at what the audience was expected to believe vis-à-vis the film's resolution. By the movie's end, I had to write off *Cornbread* as a theatrical loss for me.

THE BLACK FACTOR

This movie may have not aged well in many ways, but in many others, it's ageless. To see just how far We *Haven't* Overcome, consider that it's now 26 years later, and America is still dealing with the trap of welfare, racial profiling, corrupt cops—and Black men being shot down in the streets because of objects that "look" like a gun. Close your eyes, and you might hear "Diallo" instead of "Cornbread." Unless you're the NYPD, of course.

BAMMER'S BOTTOM LINE:

Cornbread, Earl and Me limps dramatically, but it soars as a statement about the society we lived in then—and still live in now. You'll enjoy watching a young Mr. Fishburne.

YELLOW LIGHT

Cass Eve's Bayou
(1997)

RATED R; running time 109 minutes
GENRE: Drama
WRITTEN BY: Kasi Lemmons
DIRECTED BY: Kasi Lemmons
CAST: Samuel L. Jackson, Lynn Whitfield, Debbi Morgan, Jurnee Smollett, Meagan Good, Jake Smollett, Diahann Carrol, Lisa Nicole Carson, Roger Guenveur Smith, Vondie Curtis-Hall, Ethel Ayler, Branford Marsalis, Carol Sutton

CASS'S CLIP

Eve's Bayou is shown through the eyes of Eve Batiste, who reminisces about the summer of

1962 and the secrets of her family, which are finally dredged up from the Louisiana bayous. "I was 10 years old when I killed my father," Eve says. Finding out how and why Eve killed her father is where the story begins.

In the opening scene, we are invited to a summer party at the beautiful home of Dr. Louis and Roz Batiste. We are greeted at the door with the laughter of a few uppity Blacks and the provocative dancing of Matty Mereaux, Louis Batiste's special friend. The Baptiste's children, Cisely, Eve, and Poe, have stayed up way past their bedtime getting into grown folks business. During the party, Louis and Matty slip away to fool around, only to be caught red-handed by Eve. Louis tries to sweet-talk Eve into believing that she didn't see what she saw. She's not convinced and confides her suspicions in Cisely. Cisely, Daddy's favorite little princess, isn't blind to her father's womanizing ways, yet she also tries to paint another picture for Eve to believe.

Several subplots involving everything from voodoo to sibling rivalry are woven into a twisted tale of deception and betrayal, and combine to tell a tale that shows how family secrets must be unearthed so that the living can go on living.

DA 411

Every time I have seen *Eve's Bayou* since its release in 1997, I am intrigued at how the story unfolds through the beautiful cinematography of the lush Louisiana bayous. The superb acting and interpersonal relationships between Jurnee Smollett (Eve) and Debbi Morgan (Mozelle, the clairvoyant medium), is why I keep watching *Eve's Bayou* over and over again. (I strongly believe that Ms. Morgan should have been nomi-nated as Best Supporting Actress for her performance instead of Lauren Bacall in *The Mirror Has Two Faces*.) The other cast members meshed well together, making it even more convincing that they were a family in crisis. But what I thoroughly enjoy about *Eve's Bayou* is that Kasi Lemmons wrote about a Black middle-class family instead of a Black family living in poverty struggling to make ends meet. Not that middle-class families don't face financial hardships, but it was nice to see us in a favorable environment and not on a plantation or in the Ghetto.

CASS'S CONCLUSION

I love it when a good story is captured through cinematography. If you add the strong performances of Samuel L. Jackson, Lynn Whitfield, Meagan Good, Jurnee Smollett, Debbi Morgan, and Diahann Carrol to a concoction of voodoo hexes, *Eve's Bayou* makes for a good pot of gumbo.

GREEN LIGHT

Finding Forrester
(2000)

RATED PG-13; running time 137 minutes
GENRE: Drama
WRITTEN BY: Mike Rich
DIRECTED BY: Gus Van Sant
CAST: Sean Connery, Rob Brown, Anna Paquin, F. Murray Abraham, Busta Rhymes, Matthew Noah Word, Michael Nouri

THE STORY

A young Black teen from the Bronx, a scholar-athlete? Whoda thunkit? Apparently, not many people, including Jamal "J" Wallace (Rob Brown), who hid his book smarts away in the classroom from his crabs-in-a-barrel friends, choosing instead to shine on the basketball courts, a straight-C student doing only enough to get by so his friends won't dog him out for being the bookworm that he really is. About the only ones who knew that Jamal was more than the sum of his class grades were his mother (April Grace) and underachieving brother, Terrell (Busta Rhymes). That is, until J's high standardized-test scores catch the attention of school administrators, including admins from a private prep school which—oh yeah, by the way—happens to have a basketball team that might be helped out by J's roundball skills.

Another force enters into J's life: the force he and his running buds know as "The Window" (Sean Connery), a legendary recluse who lives above the b-ball court they play on, and watches them play. On a dare from his friends, J breaks into The Window's apartment, but after being spooked by him, J drops a backpack full of his writings. From this, their mentorial friendship begins, and soon after, J learns something extraordinary about The Window.

THE UPSHOT

Someone mentioned to me that he felt this movie "glossed over the African-American world it attempted to present, in favor of a didactic agenda." Here's my take on it; consider this "The Upshot" and "The Black Factor," all tied up in one big bow.

A lot of people will think "Hmmm . . . Yet another 'White Man Saves The Ghetto Boy Flick'; still others will see the film, and partway through it, think "Hmmm . . . Yet Another 'Magical Negro' Flick." But I saw something different. I saw a tale of the harms that are caused by giving in to peer pressure, and in letting someone else decide who you are and what you're capable of. And yes, it was a somewhat didactic tale—but one that was refreshingly free of so many of the stereotypical characters that make me cringe. The Bronx kids that Jamal hung out with *were* round-the-way boys, yes, but their "double dog dare" was more reminiscent of *A Christmas Story* than of *Menace II Society*; their 'hood had a '70s-kinda "just boys hangin' out" groove that my old neighborhood had, with a '90s feel to the surrounding environs. And it was fitting that the person who would hold J down most was not his pressuring peers, but instead his envious and bitter *teacher*. What's worse than the pressure your peers put upon you to not perform, if not the unexpected hindrance put upon you by someone who should be *helping* you?

Ignore Anna Paquin (Claire) and Busta

Rhymes (Terrell) if you can; neither one belonged in this movie. Ignore also the pretty bad writing from Mike Rich; there was fair little of the native Bronx dialect to be found in this movie, and some of the words put into the characters' mouths were laughable to hear. But aside from those false starts, *Finding Forrester* resonated. Director Gus Van Sant kept me watching for his touches throughout; and Sean Connery and newcomer Rob Brown made a dynamic duo, overcoming the somewhat stilted dialogue Rich wrote for them. It was as much a treat to hear that Scottish brogue wrap itself around the phrase "you the man now, dog" as it was to watch Brown's Jamal get all up in the Professor's face—literally.

BAMMER'S BOTTOM LINE

A movie that used music like an exclamation point, and visuals that told of a cinematographer and a director in love with their vision of the world, *Finding Forrester* went to a place that few movies go. This movie, particularly the interaction between young J and his needy mentor, warmed me greatly.

GREEN LIGHT

Cass Foxy Brown
(1974)

RATED R; running time 94 minutes
GENRE: Action/Crime drama
WRITTEN BY: Jack Hill
DIRECTED BY: Jack Hill
CAST: Pam Grier, Antonio Fargas, Terry Carter, Peter Brown, Katheryn Loder, Harry Holcombe, Juanita Brown, Bob Minor

CASS'S CLIP

The two men in Foxy Brown's life are on the opposite ends of the law: (1) Link (Antonio Fargas), her brother, is a two-bit hustler who owes the crime bosses a wee bit of cash; and (2) Michael (Terry Carter), her undercover narcotics agent boyfriend, who had plastic surgery to alter his appearance to avoid a hit out on his life. One will betray Foxy and one will die.

Even after Foxy saves Link's jive ass from being kicked by two goons, he saves his own neck and tells the crime bosses Michael's whereabouts. Michael is gunned down and dies in Foxy's arms.

Now it's payback time, Foxy Brown–style—'70s lingo, thugs-on-the-car-hood chase, gratuitous sex and violence, and a final kick-yo-ass action sequence to tie up all the unnecessary loose ends—and heads are gonna roll 'cause somebody done killed her man. (I think it was Foxy Brown who said it first: "Vengeance is mine!") Dub in the Foxy's theme music, and QUIET on the set.

DA 411

With films like *Black Mama, White Mama* (1972), *Coffy* (1973), *Scream, Blacula, Scream* (1973), and *Bucktown* (1975), Pam Grier is the undisputed Queen of the Blaxploitation genre. What would a Pam Grier movie be without her Angela Davis Afro hairdo, skintight pants, and slinky halter dresses? When da Man is outta git ya and Shaft and Superfly are busy restoring Blaxploitation justice 'n da 'hood, who ya gonna call? Foxy Brown, of course. Why? Because she's a bad muth#$%. Shut yo mouf.

CASS'S CONCLUSION

If you want to see Pam Grier dole out some kick-ass justice, nobody does it better than Foxy Brown! Or, as she says, "Death is too easy for you bitch. I want you to live."

GREEN LIGHT

---

the Diva   **Friday Foster**
(1975)

RATED R; running time 89 minutes
GENRE: Action
WRITTEN BY: Arthur Marks
DIRECTED BY: Arthur Marks
CAST: Pam Grier, Yaphet Kotto, Godfrey Cambridge, Thalmus Rasulala, Eartha Kitt, Jim Backus, Scatman Crothers, Ted Lange, Tierre Turner, Carl Weathers

THE DIGEST

Friday Foster (Pam Grier) is a model-turned-photographer for *Glance* magazine. She is raising her little brother, Cleve (Tierre Turner), who—for 10 years old—is the best hustler on the block. She is also trying to thwart the advances of the local lovable pimp who is trying to get her to join his stable. Beyond all of that, she manages to constantly get in trouble on every assignment because she can't leave well enough alone, which is bothersome to her boss who has no choice but to send her on a sensitive assignment. Blake Tarr, the world's richest Black man, is a notorious hermit. *Glance* has the goods on his flight itinerary and Friday is sent to the hangar to snap some pictures of him.

While she is there, she becomes a witness to an assassination attempt against him. Things only get worse when she finds out that one of the would-be assassins is her best friend's man. She recruits her friend, private investigator Colt Hawkins (Yaphet Kotto), to help her figure out what is going on. After some investigating, it seems like there is a plot to kill all of the Black folks in power. It's a race against time. Can they save the Black leaders of America?

THE DISH

The Evil Plot stretched the very elastic borders of imagination and credibility. Everything but the kitchen sink was thrown into this movie.

Every time I turned around, someone was dying while trying to explain something to Friday, and they never quite got it out with their dying breath. After a while I was screaming at the screen, "Just spit it out . . . damn!" It couldn't end soon enough.

THE DIRECTIVE

Friday Foster is not good enough for any day of the week. And if it's Grier's boobies that inspire you, there's not a whole lot of action from Pam in this one.

RED LIGHT

Harlem Nights
(1989)

the Diva

RATED R; running time 118 minutes
GENRE: Action/Comedy
WRITTEN BY: Eddie Murphy
DIRECTED BY: Eddie Murphy
CAST: Eddie Murphy, Jasmine Guy, Richard Pryor, Redd Foxx, Danny Aiello, Michael Lerner, Della Reese, Stari Shaw, Arsenio Hall, Lela Rochon, Desi Arnaz Hines II

Harlem Nights was Eddie Murphy's directorial debut.

THE DIGEST

Sugar Ray (Richard Pryor) has a little speakeasy in Harlem. Nothing fancy, really a little hooch, a little gambling, a little booty. He is mild-mannered and tries to keep things on an even keel—then Quick (Desi Arnaz Hines II) shows up. About 8 years old, Quick runs errands for Sugar Ray. One night, Quick comes in to make a delivery and an angry patron who doesn't like children, confronts him. He says that children give him bad luck and wants Quick to leave. Quick refuses, the patron loses in craps, and wants his money back. In fact, he decides that he wants all the money and holds a knife to Sugar Ray's neck to get it. Well Quick handles the business and kills the patron, Ray finds out that Quick doesn't have any parents and he takes him under his wing. A partnership is forged from that day forth.

1938—20 years later—and the speakeasy has grown into a full-fledged nightclub. The gambling has gone from a crap table to multiple crap tables run by Bennie Wilson (Redd Foxx), and card games. The hooch has gone from the bathtub and jelly jars to a huge bar with waitresses and every kind of drink under the sun. No more women turning tricks here and there. Now there is a brothel and Madame Vera (Della Reese). Sugar Ray is so successful that he has come to the attention of a local mobster—one that is losing his clientele to Sugar Ray. This mobster, Bugsy Calhoun (Michael Lerner), wants a piece of the action.

Said mobster sends his lackey Tommy Smalls (Thomas Mikal Ford) and his mistress Dominique La Rue (Jasmine Guy) to check out the establishment and get close to Quick (Eddie Murphy). But Quick and Sugar Ray smell a rat and they set a plan in motion to take care of Bugsy once and for all.

THE DISH

How can you not love this movie? Yeah, the plot is weak and everyone has a potty mouth, but it's still funny. Beyond the comedic value, just watching a parade of Black actors, the young mixed with the old, was enough to make this one of my favorite movies.

There are a number of stars for whom this was their last feature film, and to see them here together is reason enough to love this movie. This was Redd Foxx's last feature film. He went on to star in a sitcom with Della Reese that was inspired by their interaction in this movie. Also a few years after this movie came out, Richard Pryor was struck with multiple sclerosis and had to stop acting.

THE DIRECTIVE

Grab a group of friends and watch *Harlem Nights*. Everyone will find something or someone to love in this film.

GREEN LIGHT

Bams Hollywood Shuffle
(1987)

RATED R; running time 81 minutes

GENRE: Comedy

WRITTEN BY: Robert Townsend, Keenen Ivory Wayans, Dom Irrera

DIRECTED BY: Robert Townsend

CAST: Robert Townsend, Anne-Marie Johnson, Craigus R. Johnson, Helen Martin, Brad Sanders, Keenen Ivory Wayans, Ludie Washington, Eugene R. Glazer, Lisa Mende, Dom Irrera, Sena Ayn Black, Grand L. Bush, Roy Fegan, David McKnight, Nancy Cheryll Davis, Damon Wayans, Richard Cummings Jr.

THE STORY

Hollywood Shuffle, a self-financed, semi-autobiographical film by writer and director Robert Townsend, tells the story of Bobby Taylor (Townsend), an aspiring actor struggling to make it in show business while maintaining his dignity and self-respect. This is hard to do, as he's surrounded by crab-in-a-barrel coworkers (Keenen Ivory Wayans, Ludie Washington) to the left of him, and exploitative idiot TV executives (Eugene R. Glazer, Lisa Mende, Dom Irrera), to the right. Bobby is stuck in the middle, with a strong support system, including girlfriend Lydia (Anne-Marie Johnson), younger brother Stevie (Craigus R. Johnson), their grandmother (the late Helen Martin)—and a healthy imagination. One in which he sees himself not as a jive-talkin' knucklehead or a thug, as the rest of Hollywood sees him—but as a film noir detective, or Shakespearean thesp, or action hero. You know: just like any old actor.

THE UPSHOT

I love this film, for many reasons. I admire Robert Townsend for having the fortitude to do the film in the first place, mostly on his own dime, enlisting a huge group of fellow actors, comedians, and other struggling artists to help him make *Hollywood Shuffle* a reality. I remember watching interviews in which he talked about financing *HS* on maxed-out credit cards—back in the days when that kind of thing was fairly rare—and thought it was the coolest thing in the world to believe in something so strongly that you would put yourself in potential debt to keep it going.

But mostly, I love *Hollywood Shuffle* because, even after 14 years and a bit of progress on the Black Folk In Hollywood front, I find it still relevant and, more important, still *funny*. As with another old favorite of mine, *Blazing Saddles* (see page 263), there are certain lines that never fail to take me back as soon as I hear them:

"He killeded my brotha! I *loveded* my brotha!"

"I'm making Winky Dinky Dog ho'cakes . . . 'cause ho's gotta eat, too!"

"We need you to be a little more 'Black.' You know: stick your ass out, buck your eyes . . . you know how they do."

But Townsend and his writers don't rely on one-liners to carry the day, no sirree: Intermixed with the "serious" moral theme that drives the story, Townsend sprinkled daydream sketches throughout *Hollywood Shuffle*, skits in which cast members played multiple parts. I compare these rough skits to *Saturday Night Live* when it was still funny, or *Monty Python's Flying Circus N The Hood*.

I want to point out two sketches in particular: "Noir Detective," which leads to the funniest bit I've ever seen this particular Wayans brother do, in the person of Jerry Curl Johnson; and obviously "Speed & Tyrone: Sneakin' In the Movies." Once you see the latter skit, you'll have a taste of 3BC Flava.

BAMMER'S BOTTOM LINE

Hollywood Shuffle isn't the kind of movie everyone will get. If it seems dated, I think that's because some people are convinced that We *have* overcome, and should get on with it. I'm not quite there yet. From the looks of things, We may have just traded jive-talkin' superfly pimps and ho's, for trash-talkin' gangstas and baby mamas. Yeah, progress.

GREEN LIGHT

 **In Too Deep**
(1999)

RATED R; running time 99 minutes
GENRE: Police drama
WRITTEN BY: Paul Aaron and Michael Henry Brown
DIRECTED BY: Michael Rymer
CAST: Omar Epps, LL Cool J, Stanley Tucci, Nia Long, Hill Harper, Pam Grier

THE DIGEST

The movie starts off with Officer Jeff Coles (Omar Epps) lecturing to a group of rookies about going undercover. Through flashbacks, we learn what his life had been like while he was undercover as "Jay Reid." Jay Reid was trying to infiltrate the biggest "drug empire" in the state. This drug empire is run by "God," (LL Cool J) a ruthless, vicious, and foul-mouthed gangster. "God" rules with an iron fist, but he takes care of "his people" by feeding, employing, and supporting them. He'll pay their bills and rent as long as they let him use their apartment as an "office." You cross him, and the punishment will be swift and fierce. No one has ever been able to infiltrate his empire until Jeff/Jay came along.

THE DISH

The movie has plot holes (what movie doesn't?) and draaaags at certain points. But it was very interesting to watch Jeff get so completely consumed by Jay that at some point he loses himself altogether. He goes from a respectful young cop to a foul-mouthed, misogynistic, violent thug.

I had a few issues with this movie. For one, it didn't know which way it wanted to go. One minute they are showing "God" cutting out a tongue, the next minute he is feeding the entire neighborhood for Thanksgiving. I see that they were trying to show that "God" could be human too. But in doing so, they didn't allow the movie to flow. Nia Long is the obligatory girl next door/back home who keeps Jeff sane, but they never allowed her character to develop, so it's almost as if she was spliced in as an afterthought. Pam Grier didn't need to be there either. It's almost as if the writer or director owed her a favor, so they wrote her in at the last minute. Of course almost every other word is the "n" word, which bothers me to no end.

Still, and to my own surprise, I liked this movie. It is not Oscar-worthy, but it's good. And it was particularly satisfying that I didn't figure out what was going to happen to the characters. These gangster movies are usually so predictable. If nothing else, this movie gives you a lot of food for thought.

THE DIRECTIVE

Not a "must-see," but *In Too Deep* isn't a movie you'll want to avoid like the plague either. Be forewarned, there is a lot of violence.

YELLOW LIGHT

Bams Let's Do It Again
(1975)

RATED PG; running time 110 minutes
GENRE: Comedy
WRITTEN BY: Timothy March, Richard Wesley
DIRECTED BY: Sidney Poitier
MUSIC BY: Curtis Mayfield
CAST: Sidney Poitier, Bill Cosby, John Amos, Calvin Lockhart, Jimmie Walker, Ossie Davis, Denise Nicholas, Lee Chamberlin, Rodolphus Lee Hayden, Julius Harris, Val Avery, Billy Eckstine

THE STORY

Though *Let's Do It Again* has the same underlying premise as a "buddy flick," and much of the same cast as its Bill Cosby–Sidney Poitier predecessor, *Uptown Saturday Night*, *Let's Do It Again* isn't at all a sequel in the traditional sense of the term, sharing none of the characters or plotlines.

Here, Clyde Williams (Sidney Poitier) and Billy Foster (Bill Cosby) are blue-collar workers in Hotlanta, where they are also officials in the Brothers And Sisters Of Shaka fraternal order. Needing to raise a lot of money to keep the order going, Clyde and Billy, along with their wives Dee Dee Williams (Lee Chamberlin) and Beth Foster (Denise Nicholas), go to New Orleans. There, the men scheme to somehow make the impossible happen: to help the painfully scrawny boxer Bootney Farnsworth (Jimmie Walker) beat his much stronger opponent, 40th Street Black, in their heavily wagered title fight. One more problem, though: to do so, Clyde and Billy would have to also con rival gambling bosses Kansas City

Mack (John Amos) and Biggie Smalls (Calvin Lockhart). And they are not the type of gentlemen who like to be played.

THE UPSHOT

Let's Do It Again most def worked better for me than did *Uptown Saturday Night*. Why? Maybe it was the slammin' Curtis Mayfield soundtrack with music performed by The Staples Singers (miss ya, Pop Staples), or the addition of writer Timothy March, or Poitier's smoother direction—or maybe it was just inherently funnier. All I can say is, I enjoyed it much more.

Let's Do It Again has a very *Sting*-like feel to it, which was probably no accident; I could just hear it being hailed as "The Black *Sting*" back in the day. Aside from the obvious differences, though, where Newman and Redford concentrated on a noir groove, Cosby and Poitier's emphasis was on out-and-out humor. In the annals of timelessly good flicks, of course, there's no comparison; still, both approaches worked to great effect for their respective movies.

The supporting cast has a greater impact in *Let's Do It Again*, too. From John Amos and the returning Calvin Lockhart as bitter gangster enemies, to Lee Chamberlain (also a repeat player) and Denise Nicholas as perhaps accidental examples of the Proper Negro versus Unreserved Black cultural genotype (check out my "Black Factor" note below), *Let's Do It Again* had a more natural feel to its story and character development than did *Uptown Saturday Night*. As much as I love Ossie Davis, that whole "Shaka" subplot, and his part as Elder Johnson, had me flummoxed. Characterwise, the real weak link for me, though, was Jimmie Walker, the caricature. I'll admit that my distaste for him is completely superficial, based more on his *Good Times* character than on his (hard-to-fathom) boxer Bootney; but let me use my Bully Pulpit to say this: how *Good Times* could try to make America believe that thousands of young Black girls the country over could swoon for his "Kid Dy-No-Mite" buffoon, is *way* beyond me. Then again, I grooved on his brother militant Michael, so whadda I know?

The thing about *Let's Do It Again* that struck me as a sign of the times: I can't remember the last time that I saw a modern-day movie chase scene where there were no cars nor bullets involved. Yes, the '70s were a long time ago.

THE BLACK FACTOR

Maybe it's just me, and I'm reading something more into these characters than what director Sidney Poitier intended—after all, this *is* first and foremost a comedy. But there's something very deep about the studied character contrast between Kansas City Mack (whom Biggie saw as an "Old School Country Buck") and Biggie Smalls (an "Edjucated Fool," in Mack's eyes). Just as interesting a contrast, as I mentioned above, between the uptight ("Good Girl") Dee Dee and the gregarious ("Hoochie Mama") Beth. What does the way these characters saw themselves and each other say about Black Folk as a group then—and now?

BAMMER'S BOTTOM LINE

The best—or at least, funniest—of the Cosby-Poitier trilogy (with *Uptown Saturday Night* and *Let's Do It Again*).

And if there are any Hip hop-loving rug rats in your neighborhood, watch this flick with them, if only to see their reaction when they hear the name of Calvin Lockhart's character . . .

GREEN LIGHT

Bams Light It Up

(1999)

RATED R; running time 100 minutes
GENRE: Drama
WRITTEN BY: Craig Bolotin
DIRECTED BY: Craig Bolotin
CAST: Usher Raymond, Rosario Dawson, Robert Ri'chard, Fredro Starr, Forrest Whittaker, Vanessa L. Williams, Sara Gilbert, Clifton Collins, Judd Nelson, Glynn Turman

Have you ever seen an Usher music video in which he *didn't* remove his shirt?

THE STORY

Light It Up takes place in Lincoln High School, a run-down mess of a school in the inner city; many of its windows are broken or completely gone ("It's so cold in here," one of the students says, "you can see the sentences!"), water drips from the nasty ceilings, and the rooms are so overcrowded that some of the students have to stand along the wall space. The movie tells the story of six students: Rodney (Starr), a thug who may have more going for him on the inside than he lets on; Rivers (Collins), a quick-witted hustler with a heart; Lynn (Gilbert), a loner who gets some bad news early on; Stephanie (Dawson), an honor student who is seen as uppity because she's trying to get out of "the 'hood"; and Ziggy (Ri'chard), a sensitive artist and narrator of the story, who, along with his friend Lester (Raymond), sets off a confrontation with the authority figures at Lincoln. These include Principal Armstrong (Turman), who's overworked, underpaid, and too busy to hear about the deplorable classroom, and school cop Officer Jackson (Whittaker), "a $5 cop with a $50 attitude." Things come to a head after Jackson is accidentally shot and the students take matters into their own hands.

THE UPSHOT

The problem with this movie is that there was too much second-rate writing, thin subplots, sloppy execution, and excess baggage—namely, Williams as Audrey the Negotiator. Edit the movie a bit, and you'd have the makings of a good televised afterschool special, or, better yet, an HBO movie. But this flick had its heart in the right place. There was enough of a balance of decent actors across the age spectrum (though, truth to tell, except for Raymond and Ri'chard, the "kids" looked a wee bit long in the tooth) that it seemed neither a teen flick, nor an overly preachy morality play. Raymond (who, as an Urban Contemporary singer, really needs to keep his shirt on more) and Fredo Starr (a rap artist in his other life) were surprisingly good, though one-dimensional. The rest of the cast amiably went through their paces to the mildly surprising ending.

My biggest problem with this movie is that, like the kids, it didn't have any real depth of focus; it didn't know what it wanted to say. Its under-use of any of the adults—other than Whittaker—and the inexplicable addition of Williams, put the onus on Raymond et al to carry the load. Unfortunately, with the script they were given to work with, they weren't up to the task. More soapy than authentic, it managed to strum the violin strings without adding the rest of the band to provide a complete orchestration.

THE BLACK FACTOR

This one's more an "Inner-City Factor" than just a "Black Factor":

I often say that today's younger generation is, in a way, soft—specifically, the kids who are wannabe thugs by day but come home at night to a warm meal, an allowance, and, heck, a *house*, for that matter. Most children of working- and middle-class parents have been raised in a time when they always knew what a Nintendo is; when their gym shoes (and I'm aging myself by calling them gym shoes) often cost more than all the rest of the clothes on their bodies; when they didn't have to use wire pliers as a makeshift tuner for their (black-and-white) TV; when they didn't have to depend on condiments to fill their stomachs if mama's cabinet was bare—which was most of the time (all y'all former sugar- or mayonnaise-sandwich eaters, can I get an Amen?)

But even these kids, wannabes or not, are just like we were: confused, trying to make their way in life the best they can, wanting a good life, and, given guidance by authority figures that give a damn, willing to work for it. And *unlike* us, they have to deal with the true bangers on a daily basis, as well as a society that, like Jackson and Armstrong, has already made up its mind about them before they even had a chance to prove otherwise.

All I know is, I wouldn't be a kid again if you paid me.

BAMMER'S BOTTOM LINE

Though *Light It Up* loses ratings points for being thick with plot holes and soap-opera clichés, this reviewer heard what they were saying about how we all need to take the time to listen to each other—students and teachers, parents and children alike. If nothing else, it may lead to a post-movie discussion with your kids. Can't beat that with a stick, eh?

YELLOW LIGHT

Bams **Love and Basketball**
(2000)

RATED PG-13; running time 118 minutes
GENRE: Drama
WRITTEN BY: Gina Prince
DIRECTED BY: Gina Prince
CAST: Sanaa Lathan, Omar Epps, Alfre
Woodard, Dennis Haysbert, Debbi Morgan,
Harry J. Lennix, Gabrielle Union, Kyla Pratt,
Glenndon Chatman, Monica Calhoun, Tyra
Banks

> Sanaa is the daughter of director Stan
> Lathan. You might recognize his name
> from *Martin*, *The Steve Harvey Show*, *San-*
> *ford and Son*, and *Moesha*.

THE STORY

Love and Basketball is a tale of two friends who
share the same hoop dreams: Monica Wright
(Sanaa Lathan), a "plain girl" who wants to become the first woman in the NBA and sets aside
everything in her personal life to achieve that
goal; and Quincy McCall (Omar Epps), a popular
star on his high school and college teams, whose
climb to the top is less blocked than is Monica's.
Or is it?

Monica's banker father, Nathan (Harry J.
Lennix), supports her efforts, but her mother
Camille (Alfre Woodard), doesn't understand
Monica's "tomboy" ways. Quincy finds himself
situated between his bougie mother, Mona
(Debbi Morgan), and father, Zeke (Dennis Hays-
bert). A pro player himself, Zeke tries to keep
Quincy focused on becoming an educated man,

while trying to hide a few skeletons in his own
closet. As a struggling point guard freshman,
Monica quickly bumps heads with her coach, as
well as with Sidra (Gabrielle Union), an upper-
classman who is also a point guard. And as
Quincy and Monica's friendship turns into
something deeper, they also have to face the fact
that pro basketball may be neither obtainable nor
what either of them expected.

THE UPSHOT

In watching movies like *Soul Food* and *The Wood*,
I saw myself—as in, the larger Black community
in which I came up—as I rarely have on the silver
screen: everyday folk with dreams, aspirations,
trials and tribulations, existing within a rich culture having little or nothing to do with the
stereotypes of Black life put forth by far too many
White—and Black—filmmakers too eager to
compromise Our reality for a paycheck. But in
Love and Basketball, and in its protagonist, Monica Wright, I saw shades of myself that were star-
tlingly refreshing, and in a sense, cathartic, to
see.

To say "I loved this movie" would be an understatement. Omar Epps's capable turn as
Quincy was to be expected; Epps has long been a
solid actor, and his performance here was no exception. A bit more surprising was Dennis Haysbert's outstanding performance; he and Epps
played well off each other, and his Zeke character
provided a welcome spark to this film (as well as
an important message to the aspiring pro-ballers
in the audience). Haysbert has definitely come a
long way from his *Major League* days. The exception to the "strong males" rule was Harry J.
Lennix; Nathan was pretty much mute, though
Monica clearly identified more with him than she

did with her mother, Camille. It is unfortunate that his character wasn't given much to do.

But the women were, for me, what made this movie. Sanaa Lathan was nothing less than excellent as Monica; her passion for the game and her passion for Quincy were drawn out beautifully. Equally believable as a young woman experiencing her "first time," and a more mature, sensual woman playing "strip basketball," Lathan in her all-too-brief love scenes with Epps brought Black sexuality back to the mainstream movie audience as it hasn't been shown since *Jason's Lyric* way back in 1994. Alfre Woodard tears it up as a mother grossly underestimated by her daughter, especially near the end; Woodard is simply *powerful*, even in "small" roles. Debbi Morgan, whose movies as of late (especially *Eve's Bayou*) have made audiences all but forget her turn on daytime soaps, was somewhat overwrought as the done-wrong wife; it's too bad that some of the time spent on her character wasn't devoted to Nathan and his role in Monica's life instead.

And the Chick at the helm, writer-director Gina Prince, was strongest of all. Her performance here is reminiscent of John Singleton's strong entry into feature filmmaking (*Boys N the Hood*), but only in the sense that they put out such good works in their rookie year. That, and the fact that both are Black directors, is where the comparison ends; life in Singleton's *Hood* was vastly different from Prince's vision of Hoop Life.

And speaking of her vision, it was realized in innovative ways. Prince takes advantage of the basketball theme by breaking the movie into "quarters" ("First Quarter: 1981," "Second Quarter: 1988," and so on). She also uses background music well (starting with Al Green's "Love And Happiness"). It's generally historically accurate, but more important, the music plays a real role in the movie, as if it were a character. This contrasts greatly with most modern hiphop-flavored flicks, where the music only provides a means of selling the soundtrack (and it's usually "music *inspired by* the movie"). Prince's use of "first person" shots during one of Monica's games, provided a unique perspective on that character's situation. And as a writer, Prince put mostly believable words in her character's mouths; the actors made those words come to life, and the collaboration between writer-director and cast was wonderful to witness.

My one big issue was the turning point in Quincy and Monica's relationship. I had a very hard time believing that the thing that changed their relationship (trying to avoid spoilers here) would've really done so. While not a big enough issue for me to downgrade the movie's rating, it's a flaw that could've been easily addressed by Prince giving the characters a different conflict to stress over.

BAMMER'S BOTTOM LINE

Nothin' but net. It's lovely when a film starring and made by Black folk can be held up as an example of good moviemaking, without the " . . . for a Black film" addendum. That *Love and Basketball* could also tell a love story without resorting to "Booty Call"-ism, is icing on a tasty chocolate cake.

GREEN LIGHT

Shaft 2000

(2000)

RATED R; running time 97 minutes

GENRE: Action

WRITTEN BY: Richard Price; story by John Singleton & Shane Salerno and Richard Price, based on character created by Ernest Tidyman

DIRECTED BY: John Singleton

CAST: Samuel L. Jackson, Vanessa L. Williams, Jeffrey Wright, Christian Bale, Dan Hedaya, Busta Rhymes, Toni Collette, Richard Roundtree

THE DIGEST

Police Detective John Shaft (Samuel L. Jackson), named after his infamous uncle, John Shaft (Richard Roundtree), is investigating the assault on a Black college student. It appears that the young Black man was being taunted by an ultra-rich, ultraspoiled young white man Walter Wade (Christian Bale). The young Black man handles business by teasing him back. Because he got the better of Wade and Wade can't handle that, Wade clocks him upside the head with a metal bar. The young man dies on the stretcher, so what was once assault is now murder. Wade's father owns half the city and his pockets are deep. After two corrupt bail hearings, it becomes clear to Shaft that he is going to have to quit the force in order to get this guy and get him good. John, now a vigilante, sets out to nab Wade and find the one eyewitness to the crime.

Shaft is not alone in his quest. His former partner, Carmen Vasquez (Vanessa Williams), has his back. She is worried about him going over

the edge, so she risks her job in order to protect him from himself. He also has Rasaan (Busta Rhymes), who is Shaft's right-hand man. And, of course, all the ladies that just love Shaft to death. Shaft isn't the only one who has help. Wade has become friends with a Dominican drug lord named Peoples Hernandez (Jeffrey Wright). Peoples helps Wade out, hoping to gain access to the exclusive country club scene.

THE DISH

I adore Samuel Jackson. I adore him even though he almost always plays someone who is screaming and hollering or fussing and cussing, all of which can get a bit tiresome. In *Shaft* he was no different *except* he had a sense of humor about it and he had a more subdued and controlled rage, which really worked for me.

All in all, I dug the movie, its violence notwithstanding. What surprised me was that I finally "got it." I've been concerned that women were being portrayed as nothing more than sex objects in the *Shaft* movies, and that Uncle John Shaft and John Shaft were two of the biggest pigs on earth. But they're not. They just love women. They'll beat down a man for hitting a woman faster than they'll sleep with a woman. And because they worship women they'll sleep with as many as they can. The women who jump when one of the Shafts tells them to, aren't doing it because they have low self-esteem, but because they know that Shaft has their back, and the least they can do is ask, "How high?" Now that I get it, I'm down with *Shaft*.

THE DIRECTIVE

I think any fan of Richard Roundtree's Shaft will be happy with this one. Sam Jackson really does *Shaft* justice.

GREEN LIGHT

Cass Sweet Sweetback's Baad Asssss Song
(1971)

RATED R; running time 97 minutes
GENRE: Drama
WRITTEN BY: Melvin Van Peebles
DIRECTED BY: Melvin Van Peebles
CAST: Melvin Van Peebles, Mario Van Peebles, John Amos, Simon Chuckster, Hubert Seales, John Dullaghan, West Gale, Niva Rochelle, Rhetta Hughes

CASS'S CLIP

Sweet Sweetback's Baad Asssss Song opens with several Black women staring at a young Sweetback (Mario Van Peebles) stuffing food down his mouth, while another woman piles food onto his plate. This "will work for food" is how Sweetback gets paid doing odd jobs at a sex theater/house of prostitution. Sweetback evolves into a man when one of the women forces him to have sex with her.

Sweetback becomes a porn star and performs live sex shows for Beetle, a back alley theater owner. Two White cops familiar with Beetle's joint, drop by and ask Beetle for one of his boys to take down to the police station to make them look good "official-wise" and pretend they're working on a murder case. Beetle tells Sweetback about the deal and the cops tell Sweetback that they will not handcuff him until they get to the station.

These cops then receive a call to investigate a possible community disturbance. They arrest one of the troublemakers, and handcuff this dude and Sweetback together. On the way to the police station they take a slight detour so they can rough up this brotha. When they realize Sweetback is still handcuffed to this brotha, they uncuff Sweetback and continue beating this other brotha's ass. Witnessing the brutalization of his fellow brotha's rights disturbs Sweetback and he kills these racist pigs with his handcuffs. Sweetback is now on the run from Da Man.

DA 411

I commend anybody who writes, directs, and finances the production of a movie. That's where my praise for Melvin Van Peebles STOPS. If *Sweet Sweetback's Baad Asssss Song* was supposed to depict the realities of how Blacks were mistreated by a racist White society, that's not what I saw. Instead, what I saw was Van Peebles exploiting his young son, and pornography. I was sick to my stomach when I saw a naked young Mario Van Peebles being molested for the sake of his father's artistic vision. The moment this movie opened, Melvin Van Peebles should have been arrested and charged with child endangerment.

Van Peebles stated at the beginning of *SSBAS* that he was called the "Godfather of Black cinema." (People, this Emperor-Godfather is

WEARING NO CLOTHES!!!) He also said that he made *SSBAS* because he "got tired of seeing us portrayed that other way," and that he wanted a movie "where we won." He said he used the following criteria when he wrote *SSBAS:*

1. "The film was not going to be a copout." *SSBAS* did more than copout: it crapped out.
2. "I wanted it to look as good as anything The Man had ever done." Alex, I'll take-*Who Failed Cinematography* for $100 please.
3. "Entertainment-wise, I wanted it to be a muth-da-f#$* because I wanted something we didn't have to be ashamed of." If you consider cursing at the screen, saying, "Whadda f#$* am I looking at?" entertainment, then yeah.

CASS'S CONCLUSION

Sweet Sweetback's Baad Asssss Song starred the "Black Community" and was dedicated to all of the brothas and sistahs who had enough of The Man. Problem is, it just might not appeal to everyone's sense of community.

RED LIGHT ●

the Diva Turn It Up
(2000)

RATED R; running time 83 minutes
GENRE: Wednesday Night Ghetto
WRITTEN BY: Ray "Cory" Daniels, Chris Hudson, Kelly Hilaire, Robert Adetuyi
DIRECTED BY: Robert Adetuyi
CAST: Pras, Ja-Rule, Tamala Jones, Vondie Curtis-Hall

THE DIGEST

Diamond (Pras) is a struggling rap artist. He has a producer who is a coke fiend, a girlfriend who is pregnant, and his studio time will be cut short unless he can start paying full price. What's a brotha to do? To top it off, his manager, Gage (Ja-Rule), makes his money by running for the local Australian crime lord. Gage is a hothead and his temper keeps him in trouble. Diamond is the brains of the outfit and is always saving Gage from himself.

Despite his troubles, Diamond must cut his album so he can get off the streets and take care of himself and his pregnant girlfriend, Nia (Tamala Jones). His absent father (Vondie Curtis-Hall) shows up out of the blue, which upsets Diamond. But his father provides him with the courage and musical knowledge to make his album come together and it's 10 times better than it was. Gage comes through with enough money for them to cut the record and everything is once again happy in the Ghetto—then all hell breaks loose when it is discovered to whom the money really belongs.

THE DISH

Children, sometimes you walk away from a movie and you just want to start cussin'. I know everyone gave it their best efforts and the filmmakers had a small budget. But damn it, *Turn It Up* was a mess. I'm going to ignore the fact the "N" word was spoken about every 20 seconds right along with the "F" word. I'm going to ignore that the plot was bad and the dialogue was corny. Hell, I'm even going to ignore all the violence and the fact that Diamond didn't get off his lazy ass and get a job to finance his record. What I cannot in good faith ignore is this poor attempt to rip off *Purple Rain. That* burned.

What were those people thinking? Obviously, they weren't. This was the most uninteresting movie I've seen in a long time, and at 88 minutes, it was 88 minutes of nothing. I was asked to feel sympathetic to Diamond, but I couldn't even muster that. At the very least, they could have laid some hard tracks throughout the movie. And Gage? Gage was a straight-up punk thug. Ain't nothing cute about pulling guns on people for no reason and mistreating women.

In case you missed it, this movie was originally titled *Ghetto Superstar*. Ghetto Superstar, my behind. If he was a superstar, I missed it.

THE DIRECTIVE

Turn It Up was one long and very bad music video. Just tune into 12 hours of BET and MTV instead.

RED LIGHT

Bams Uptown Saturday Night
(1974)

RATED PG; running time 104 minutes
GENRE: Comedy
WRITTEN BY: Richard Wesley
DIRECTED BY: Sidney Poitier
MUSIC BY: Tom Scott
CAST: Sidney Poitier, Bill Cosby, Harry Belafonte, Calvin Lockhart, Rosalind Cash, Paula Kelly, Richard Pryor, Roscoe Lee Brown, Lee Chamberlin, Harold Nicholas, Ketty Lester, Flip Wilson

THE STORY

Steve Jackson (Sidney Poitier) and Wardell Franklin (Bill Cosby) are two working stiffs looking to have a good time uptown. They tip out on wives Sarah Jackson (Rosalind Cash) and Irma Franklin (Ketty Lester) and go to Zenobia's, a joint—named after Madame Zenobia (Lee Chamberlin)—where the high falutin' high rollers hang out for a little casino action. Unfortunately, thugs hit Zenobia's and not only take all the patrons' money and jewels but also Steve's wallet, which he later discovers held something more valuable than he ever imagined. Steve and Wardell seek the help of numerous neighborhood characters—including "Don" Geechie Dan Beauford (Harry Belafonte), the Don's rival Silky Slim (Calvin Lockhart), local hood Little Seymour (Harold Nicholas), inept private investigator Sharp Eye Washington (Richard Pryor), and a corrupt Congresscritter (Roscoe Lee Browne)—in retrieving the wallet.

THE UPSHOT

Let me be frank. By today's more jaded standards, *Uptown*'s humor just doesn't seem all that—how shall I put this?—sophisticated, anymore. I know, I know; my bourgie slip is showing again. But I just couldn't stay with the humor in this movie long enough to laugh out loud much, probably because the story itself seemed rather weak. Far too many plot holes and basic BS Meter—tweakers (c'mon now; Steve talked about having multiple jobs, but could afford to take a two-week vacation? Yeah. Right), caused my disbelief to lose altitude rather quickly. The rather lame ending didn't help matters much.

Still, the quality of individual lead performances is worth noting. As comedic costar, Sidney Poitier looked to be out of his field, especially compared to Bill "Shave And A Haircut?" Cosby. Much of the time, Poitier seemed to be barely hanging in there, trying to keep up with Cosby's antics, with a look of terror in his eyes whenever Cosby tore loose (though, admittedly, that may have been Director Poitier, panicking over losing control of Cosby). But even Cosby himself took a back seat to Paula Kelly, Richard Pryor, and Roscoe Lee Browne. Kelly, whom I loved in *Sweet Charity*, was Large as Leggy Peggy without being unnecessarily loud; Pryor was understated (for him), and had one of the best, spot-on, lines in the movie; and Browne wore his two-faced African (when it suited him)-American (when it didn't) politician role like a shining coat of armor.

And I must admit, it was nice to go back and see a time when there were *Men N the Hood* depicted on-screen in Black movies. Man, the '70s were a long time ago.

BAMMER'S BOTTOM LINE

My fellow children of the '70s, Bill Cosby/Sidney Poitier fans, or anyone looking for a decent classic Black movie to watch, rent *Uptown Saturday Night* for nostalgia's sake. It wasn't bust-a-gut funny, but the moments featuring Paula "Ruff And Stuff With Her Afro Puff" Kelly, Roscoe Lee Browne, and Richard Pryor, might bring a smile or two.

FLASHING YELLOW LIGHT

The Wood
(1999)

RATED R; running time 105 minutes
GENRE: Drama
WRITTEN BY: Rick Famuyiwa and Todd Boyd
DIRECTED BY: Rick Famuyiwa
CAST: Omar Epps, Sean Nelson; Richard T. Jones, Duane Finley; Taye Diggs, Trent Cameron; Malinda Williams, De'aundre Bonds, Tamala Jones, Lisaraye

THE DIGEST

The Wood above all is about true-blue friendship. It starts with everyone trying to find Roland, (Taye Diggs) who is getting married in three hours. Slim (played by that *FOINE* brotha, Richard T. Jones) is cussing and fussing while Mike (Omar Epps) is trying to remain calm and think with a level head. The phone rings and it's Roland's ex-girlfriend telling them that he is there and drunk. They go to collect him.

Once they get to him, they start to reminisce about the old days, and here is where the movie picks up speed and gets very interesting. We are treated to a look at some very normal teenagers—smart kids who know the value of an education but at the same time are consumed by their hormones.

THE DISH

"The Wood" is the nickname for Inglewood, California, a middle-class area of Los Angeles. Often when a movie is made about Black folks living in L.A., we see someone who tries to get out of the Ghetto on a sports scholarship but gets killed before the "big game." We'll see someone with a mouth full of gold sucking on a 40-ounce. We'll see some "common" woman in the street yelling and cursing and smacking on gum. This is not to say that the above does not exist or does not happen, *but* surprise, surprise. We are not a monolith.

As I watched *The Wood*, I saw my life up there. The movie opens up in 1985. I was 15 at that time and living in a middle-class Black neighborhood in Southern California. As in the movie, we had "sets" but no one worried about it. We didn't gang bang. We didn't spend every waking moment worrying about drive-bys and shootings. They happened, but we weren't consumed by it. We were more concerned with school, dating, sports, just like kids all over America, and *The Wood* illustrates this perfectly. Here are three Black men who became successful through hard work and not through "ballin'." For anyone of my generation, this movie is an endearing walk down memory lane. The music was "fresh" (Run DMC's "Peter Piper" was my *cut*), the clothes were outrageous (I saw one of my outfits in the movie—that horrid little two-layer dress from TJ Maxx, with red, black, and green flowers on it that I could *not* stay out of), and the hairstyles were something else (Jheri Curls everywhere. I wonder where the braids with coins glued to the tips were).

THE DIRECTIVE

Take notice, America, *The Wood* was exactly like the "Hood" I grew up in—normal, everyday, hardworking Americans with dreams, aspirations, and JOBS. What are you waiting on? Rent this one!

GREEN LIGHT

7

LIP SMACKERS
A.k.a. Date Flicks

So, you've gotten him to the point where he'll let you have his phone number, eh? Why not invite him over to watch something we Chicks think you'll both enjoy? And who knows—it may lead to chapter 8 and a booty call . . .

the Diva

A Knight's Tale
(2001)

RATED PG-13; running time 132 minutes
GENRE: Action/Adventure
WRITTEN BY: Brian Helgeland
DIRECTED BY: Brian Helgeland
CAST: Heath Ledger, Rufus Sewell, Shanynn Sossamon, Paul Bettany, Laura Fraser, Mark Addy, Alan Tudyk, Nick Brimble, Leagh Conwell

THE DIGEST

14th-century Europe, and Sir Ector is dragging his faithful squires from tournament to tournament. Sir Ector is a poor knight who is doing horribly in the tourney. So bad that his squires haven't eaten in three days. Then the unthinkable happens. Sir Ector dies. One minute he is on his horse, the next, he is under a tree drawing flies.

Starving, the squires make a decision that could end their lives. Desperate, William (Heath Ledger), Roland (Mark Addy), and Wat (Alan Tudyk) decide that William should finish out the tourney in Sir Ector's place. To their surprise, William wins. Once this happens, he knows that he can be what he has always felt he was born to be: a knight. Even though it is illegal for anyone not of noble birth to participate in the tourney, William wants to pursue his dream. He then convinces Wat and Roland to pose as his squires.

On the way to their first tourney, they come across a naked man traveling down the road. This man turns out to be Geoffrey Chaucer (Paul Bettany). In exchange for food, clothes, and a por-

tion of the winnings, Chaucer agrees to write William's much needed royal pedigree as well as serve as his herald. Soon, William (now known as Sir Ulric von Lichtenstein of Gelderland) is winning event after event. Over the course of his travels, he finds love and makes enemies. How long can his past remain a secret, and will it matter?

THE DISH

I'm *still* giggling. First of all, the movie is set in 14th-century Europe and the peasants are rocking out and singing "We Will Rock You" and "Golden Years." Second, Chaucer announces Sir Ulric for each competition like Ulric is Hulk Hogan, and says stuff like, "I'd like to send a shout out to Sir William, show him some love!" See, now that had me rolling. Though Paul Bettany as Chaucer completely stole the show, everyone turned in a solid performance. This is not to say there weren't flaws: It was predictable and, at times, slow—but I enjoyed it nonetheless.

THE DIRECTIVE

A Knight's Tale is a funny and enjoyable tale, indeed.

GREEN LIGHT

Almost Famous
(2000)

RATED R; running time 120 minutes
GENRE: Comedy/Drama
WRITTEN BY: Cameron Crowe
DIRECTED BY: Cameron Crowe
CAST: Billy Crudup, Frances McDormand, Jason Lee, Kate Hudson, Patrick Fugit, Fairuza Balk, Philip Seymour Hoffman, Michael Angarano

> Cameron Crowe is married to one of the Wilson sisters from the '70s rock band *Heart*.

THE DIGEST

It's 1969, and young William Miller (Michael Angarano) is digging life as a 12-year-old. The only things that trouble him are the combative relationship between his mother and his sister, and the fact that all of his male classmates have facial hair. He tries to play the peacemaker between his sister, whom he adores, and his mother (Frances McDormand), whom he loves, but who freaks him out. Fast-forward to 1973, and William has inherited an amazing record collection. Rock is in full swing with bands like The Allman Brothers, Black Sabbath, Jethro Tull, and the fictional band Stillwater. William (Patrick Fugit) is now a 15-year-old senior in high school. When he's not studying, he's writing articles on rock music and sending them into various music magazines. He first catches the eye of Lester Bangs (Philip Seymour Hoffman) the editor of *Creem* magazine. He serves as a mentor and guide for William, helping him to stay focused and teaching him the ropes.

While trying to get an interview with the band Stillwater, he meets a group of girls who call themselves Band-Aids. These girls stress that they are not groupies. They are fans of the music, as opposed to groupies who wantonly sleep with anyone in the band. (Of course, any one of those little hussies could be found in various band members' bedrooms at any given time, but that's another story.) The so-called leader of the Band-Aids is Penny Lane (Kate Hudson). She seems to be the only one who keeps her wits about her. She is smart, funny, and unfazed by all the glitz and glamour. She claims to only love the music and not the band members.

The story follows William as *he* follows the band from city to city trying to get an interview so he can write an article for *Rolling Stone*. Along the way he meets several challenges and leaves his boyhood behind. In fact, everyone in this film is on the road to discovery, each in their own little way trying to find themselves.

THE DISH

Well, I gotta tell ya. I really enjoyed this movie. I'm not a *huge* fan of '70s rock, I prefer R&B, but I can get down with Elton John, Fleetwood Mac, and Heart like nobody's business. If you are a fan of '70s rock then you will absolutely adore this film. There was some really good music in it. But the music is just the backdrop. It's really a coming-of-age story, one of the better told ones at that.

Philip Seymour Hoffman was divine, as nearly always. The endearing and extremely comical Frances McDormand cracked me up as

William's insane mother. Insane isn't the right word. Unorthodox is better. Billy Crudup (when did he get so cute?) as Russell Hammond, the lead guitarist of Stillwater, turns in a strong performance as well. Kate Hudson (Goldie Hawn's baby girl) proves that she can hold her own. She's strong, yet vulnerable. I'm sure her mama is proud.

I have to be honest here, though. It was hard for me to connect 100 percent with this movie. I was born in 1970. Does that make me a child of the '70s or a child of the '80s? I never understood the free love, drugs, and music scene. My '80s mentality finds that kind of behavior not free but debasing. At the risk of parroting the talk-show psychobabble of the '90s, "Those girls have low self-esteem." Or perhaps that was just how things were before the age of AIDS? Or is that just a copout, too? I don't know. However, you'll love this cute little movie with a wonderful cast.

THE DIRECTIVE

If you don't like rock 'n' roll, you might experience a cultural gap, but *Almost Famous* is still a good movie and a great date-flick.

GREEN LIGHT

 Behind Enemy Lines
(2001)

RATED PG-13; running time 113 minutes
GENRE: Action/Thriller
WRITTEN BY: David Veloz and Zak Penn
DIRECTED BY: John Moore
CAST: Owen Wilson, Gene Hackman, Joaquim de Almeida, David Keith, Olek Krupa, Gabriel Macht, Vladimir Mashkov

THE DIGEST

Lt. Chris Burnett (Owen Wilson) is attached to the USS *Carl Vinson*, which is working under a NATO detail patrolling Bosnia. Increasingly disillusioned with the constant fire drills and lack of excitement, he finally throws in the towel and submits a request for a transfer to his no-nonsense boss, Admiral Reigart (Gene Hackman). Admiral Reigart accepts his request, but first he must go on a reconnaissance mission over Bosnia, serving as navigator to pilot Lt. Michael Stackhouse. They appear to be best of friends, but Stackhouse isn't as tightly wound as Burnett. He is content to just go with the flow and follow the rules. Chris likes to break the rules every now and again. While manning the surveillance camera, Chris spots some activity, including military vehicles and equipment below, which, given the ceasefire, is a big no-no. The "bad guys" on the ground know this and promptly start firing missiles that down the plane. While Chris is moving to higher ground to radio for help, Stackhouse is executed and now Chris is on the run.

While on the run, he manages to get in touch with the ship and is assured that he will be picked up. What he doesn't know is that NATO Admiral Piquet (Joaquim de Almeida) has pretty much squashed the rescue attempt because he is afraid that it will hurt the tenuous relationship that NATO has with the Serbs. While waiting for rescue, Chris must keep his wits about him and survive in a situation that seems impossible. Can he get to the safe zone before the "Bad Guys" get him?

THE DISH

I was on the edge of my seat most of the movie. Philosophical and witty, Owen Wilson has perfected his on-screen persona. Gene Hackman was wonderful as the hard-nosed and gruff Admiral Reigart. It's hard to believe he's 71. Ya know, so is Clint Eastwood for that matter. Seventy ain't what it used to be. Olek Krupa and Vladimir Mashkov were the big surprises as the military leader and his assassin, both pursuing Chris from different angles. One quietly following and outsmarting him, the other loudly and obnoxiously letting him know that he is after him.

There were some hokey moments with this film. I was mildly irritated with the Matrix-esque attempts to make the film grittier. And the movie was sappy with patriotism, which can be annoying for some. Not to dis the Armed Forces, because I am grateful to them, but the "rah-rah let's get our boy back" tone was overdone. And I have to say this . . . the makeup artist needs to retire. Do you know how unnerving it was, watching a bunch of soldiers running around with perfectly arched eyebrows, eyeliner, rouge, and mascara? It was a crime. Every man who had more than three seconds of face time had arched eyebrows. Even the poor rebel teenager with the Ice-Cube T-shirt. Speaking of which, while nothing was said or im-

plied by the fact that the rebel teenager loved NWA and Cube, I think it should be explored. Did the teenage rebel see Cube and rap music as a rebellion against American society? Hmm . . .

THE DIRECTIVE

A bit violent, and the language was rough in spots, but *Behind Enemy Lines* was well worth the hour and 43 minutes.

GREEN LIGHT

 **Bridget Jones's Diary**
(2001)

RATED R; running time 92 minutes
GENRE: Romantic comedy
WRITTEN BY: Richard Curtis (based on the novel by Helen Fielding)
DIRECTED BY: Sharon Maguire
CAST: Renée Zellweger, Hugh Grant, Colin Firth, Jim Broadbent, Gemma Jones, James Callis, Shirley Henderson, Sally Phillips, Embeth Davidtz, Honor Blackman

Renée Zellweger gained a reported 25 pounds to play Bridget Jones.

THE STORY

When her mother, Pamela (Gemma Jones), steers Bridget Jones (Renée Zellweger) toward yet another disastrous hookup—this time with barrister and mama's boy Mark Darcy (Colin Firth), to whom Bridget takes an immediate dislike (and vice versa)—Bridget decides to take action to change her life. She starts by keeping a diary in which she honestly notes all of her bad habits and life-affectations, including her weight, her smoking jones, her tendency to drink, and, most of all, her potentially hazardous fantasy life. The object of her fantasy? Daniel Cleaver (Hugh Grant), Bridget's boss at the publishing firm in which they both work (it'd never happen here in the States. Can you spell "s-e-x-u-a-l h-a-r-a-s-s-m-e-n-t l-a-w-s-u-i-t"? I knew you could!)

Bridget's circle of friends includes her girlfriends Jude and Shazzer, and gay friend Tom, all of whom Bridget can count on for sisterly support, especially when she gets caught up in a triangle involving Daniel, Mark, and Mark's pseudo-girlfriend Natasha. Meanwhile, Bridget's mum, Pam, has a little surprise of her own for her husband, Colin. And, as often happens at times like this . . . wackiness ensues.

THE UPSHOT

Four quick things about *Bridget Jones's Diary*, which'll pretty much wrap up this brief-for-me review in a shiny little bow:

#1.   I don't get these kinds of movies, primarily because I've never been a Bridget Jones kinda Chick—having married, and stayed with, the first man who swept me off my feet at 18. Tell me true: Do womyn like this *really* exist? If so, remind me to never be one.

#2.   For all the hype about said diary, where the hell was it for most of the movie? It peeked out in an early Zellweger-Grant scene, but was soon tossed aside like a red-haired stepchild, until the crucial climactic mo-

ment. With little else of note going on, I might've been more interested in *reading* it than in watching it in absentia.

#3.   Here's a racial generality—White Girls kill me with their definition of "overweight." Ditto, "spinster."

#4.   That Huge . . . er, Hugh Grant was tolerable for once, was about the biggest shock and the most entertainment value that I got from *Bridget Jones's Diary*. Mebbe because he wasn't spending all his screen time playing the Fish Out Of English Water buffoon that he usually plays in American flicks.

As for the rest, I spent most of the movie going, "huh"? There wasn't a single believable bit of character development to be found in this flick's reels, though as the wife of a James Bond nut, I did appreciate the pun involving actress Honor Blackman. But for what it's worth, Texas's own Renée Zellweger (for whom I have a grudging admiration), did okay with that English accent. And what's up with Brits being upset with her for that, anyway? We gave them Michael Caine in *Cider House Rules* (see page 175), did we not?

BAMMER'S BOTTOM LINE

Bridget is what you get when grown women spend too much time writing diaries, and not enough time living outside of them. Me, I just don't get the hype. Oh, and for all you Bridget Jones' types who'll want to crucify me for my cavalier attitude about your Plight? Bah; just go out and get laid.

YELLOW LIGHT

Bams For Love of the Game
(1999)

RATED PG-13; running time 120 minutes

GENRE: Drama

WRITTEN BY: Dana Stevens (based on the novel by Michael Shaara)

DIRECTED BY: Sam Raimi

CAST: Kevin Costner, Kelly Preston, John C. Reilly, Jena Malone, Bill E. Rogers, Greer Barnes

> Kevin Costner played baseball, football, and basketball in high school.

THE STORY

Ever since he was a wee lad, Billy Chapel lived for the game of baseball. After spending his whole professional career as a pitcher for the Detroit Tigers, in the last game of what a teammate describes as "the end of a shitty season," he reaches down deep and lives in "the zone," potentially pitching a perfect game. He finds himself at a crossroads when the love of his life threatens to leave him. The question is, who is that love: his girlfriend Jane Aubrey, or baseball itself?

THE UPSHOT

I have no deep abiding love for baseball. Truth to tell, it bores me silly, as do most sports. And let me go 'head and get my rant out of the way: for a movie that proclaims the glory of being a Tiger, why the hell was Detroit so totally shunned in this flick? Bad enough that e-v-e-r-y friggin' game they played was an away game; they couldn't do Detroit the honor of mentioning its name more than once or twice, even just in passing? This aspect of the movie dulled its authenticity; had Chapel been made a Yankee instead of a Tiger, I could've dug it, but there was no real Tiger Pride as far as I could see.

Okay, now that *that's* out of the way, I'll surprise you a wee bit: I liked this flick, and, strangely, I don't quite know why. To be sure, it seemed to do everything it could to ensure that I *wouldn't* like it, from the Detroit-less Tigers, to being a baseball movie to begin with—and especially because of Kelly Preston. Man, that chick was hard to deal with. Initially, she seemed *way* too young for Chapel, and was also out-classed in the acting department even by Costner (who doesn't deserve all the flack he gets. Some, but not all). However, my major issue with her was that she looked and acted more like a Valley Girl than a Noo Yawka. She seemed too flighty at first, and her character began as unsympathetic for me, but as the movie progressed, she seems to "grow up" in fits and starts, though some of the crap she takes from Billy throughout had me wanting to shake her and wake her dumb butt up. In the end, though there could've been better choices of actresses for her role, she acquits herself adequately enough.

And Costner, the man himself; what of him? I'll put it like this: he wears his uniforms well. And that's no backhanded compliment. Though he looked too old for the part, I could believe him as a ballplayer. The shots of him (and his double) on the diamond were beautifully done by the cinematographer, especially the "clear the mechanism" scenes. And even when the pseudo-philosopher that's apparently inherent in all baseball players, came to the fore, I didn't run yelling and screaming from the theater. Costner's Billy Chapel seemed real to me.

As for the story itself, I was, surprisingly, interested in it. There was very little actual conflict, and what there was, seemed contrived. The baseball game itself was just a set-up for the flashbacks that told the story. I loved the character of Gus ("the ugliest wife in the league"; played by Reilly), and I found myself rooting for Billy's every pitch, straining to hear his "conversations" with the stadium crowd, his "worthy opponents" on the other team, and, most of all, with himself. Then there was the simultaneous love story which was rather bizarre, too; there was nothing there at all to grab onto, until the appearance of one of Jane's family members—Heather, who I found quite charming, in spite of my reservations about that kind of character being added to "save the day" (perhaps because Heather was played nicely by Malone). And, strangely enough, that whole plot took on a different feel from there; it became softer, sweeter; it became *interesting*. It threatened to lose my interest when Preston's lack of acting skills got in the way again, but the whole timbre of the movie changed with that one scene.

mix? Should we trip all over ourselves to include a Black or White friend? Oh how do we get the Black Dollar in to see this one?!?"

Fortunately, that postulation in this case would be wrong. That mindset, and the slippery slope it begets, didn't seem to be at the forefront in this movie, for the most part. The Black players clearly had a relationship with Billy, but so did the rest of the team. Billy respected Davis Birche (Rogers) a former teammate who happened to be Black (and whose wife Keisha—played by Sheila Lussier—also had an effect on Jane). And though the little time they spent on their personal relationship felt a little clumsy, it wasn't focused on long enough to make the problematic part of modern entertainment—showing White and Black folks together in nonworkplace settings—an issue. There was no big deal made of the fact that either Davis or Mickey Hart (Barnes), a current teammate whom he gave some sound advice to, in the role of Old Schooler, were Black. And that, in this instance, *was* A Good Thing.

THE BLACK FACTOR

It's much easier depicting an integrated workplace than it is to show folks of different races hangin' out after hours—but what if that workplace is the sports arena, as it is in this flick? I'd postulate that in those cases, there'd be the usual hand-wringing by The Powers That Be over how to handle The Race Issue: "Well," I hear The Powers thinking; "Should we show the team lineup as a reflection of what we actually see in real-life sports, or should we add a White or Black guy in the

BAMMER'S BOTTOM LINE

For Love of the Game was no *The Natural*, but at least it was no *Waterworld* either. If you need a feel-good movie right about now, you could do much worse.

FLASHING YELLOW LIGHT

His Girl Friday
(1940)

RATED G; running time 92 minutes

GENRE: Comedy

WRITTEN BY: Ben Hecht and Charles MacArthur
(play *The Front Page*) and Charles Lederer

DIRECTED BY: Howard Hawkes

CAST: Cary Grant, Rosalind Russell, Ralph Bellamy, Gene Lockhart, Porter Hall, John Qualen, Helen Mack

> You young'uns out there will remember Ralph Bellamy as Randolph Duke from *Trading Places* (one of the funniest movies Eddie Murphy has ever made).

THE DIGEST

The reporter Hildy Johnson (Rosalind Russell) has found the love of her life in Bruce Baldwin (Ralph Bellamy), a quiet and supportive insurance salesman who worships the ground Hildy walks on. Hildy doesn't know how to act; her ex-husband, editor Walter (Cary Grant), dragged her from one end of the country to the other. Always in search of a scoop for his Chicago newspaper, for their honeymoon.

Hildy eventually came to realize that the paper would always come first, and she wanted more in life, even more than being a reporter for Walter's paper. So she goes to the paper to tender her resignation. Walter is shocked but he keeps his wits about him. What is he going to do without Hildy? He hatches this elaborate scheme to keep Hildy, and it all centers around Earl Williams (John Qualen). According to Walter, Earl has been wrongly accused of murder and they must expose the truth before he is put to death.

Of course Hildy can't turn Walter down; a man's life is at stake. She and Walter uncover the story and, in the process, Walter shows Hildy that they were meant to be together. The real question is does she love him enough to give up her dreams of a normal life, one that includes children and a house with a white picket fence.

THE DISH

This movie is very funny! You have to pay very close attention or you will miss half the jokes. Cary Grant (with his fine self) is brilliantly witty. Rosalind Russell, probably the most underrated comediennes in history, is on top of her game. The chemistry and timing between these two is dizzying.

THE DOSE OF REALITY

Hildy was apparently a damned good journalist. She was the only woman in the "old boys" club, and for that she should be commended. But she went from wanting a man—Bruce—to *needing* a man—Walter. While I recognize *Friday* was written over sixty years ago, for my modern-day sensibilities, it was disappointing to see this groundbreaking independent character reduced to a woman who just had to have a man, not to mention that a "girl Friday" is a secretary-assistant. She was hardly that.

THE DIRECTIVE

Perfect for any day of the week, not just Friday. If you can't find *His Girl Friday* on TV, spend three bucks and rent it.

GREEN LIGHT

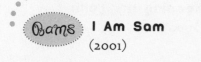 **I Am Sam**

(2001)

RATED PG-13; running time 132 minutes
GENRE: Drama
WRITTEN BY: Kristine Johnson, Jessie Nelson
DIRECTED BY: Jessie Nelson
CAST: Sean Penn, Michelle Pfeiffer, Dakota Fanning, Dianne Wiest, Doug Hutchison, Stanley DeSantis, Brad Allan Silverman, Joseph Rosenberg, Richard Schiff, Laura Dern, Loretta Devine

THE STORY

Sam (Sean Penn), a mentally disabled man and father of seven-year-old Lucy, has to fight to keep her when she grows to be more mentally developed than he is. Sam's friends—including Annie (Dianne Wiest), an agoraphobic and Lucy's godmother; Ifty (Doug Hutchison), who has attention deficit disorder; and Brad (Brad Allan Silverman), a bona fide ladies' man—try to help Sam fight against the System that tries to take Lucy away from him. The System includes Margaret the Social Worker (Loretta Devine) and Randy (Laura Dern) the foster mother the courts assign to Lucy's case.

But Sam can't just get by with a little help from his friends. He finds Rita (Michelle Pfeiffer), a lawyer with a sugar jones, who takes Sam's case pro bono almost as a dare from her coworkers. But Rita's got issues of her own, including an absent husband and a son who she thinks hates her for her own estrangement from him.

THE UPSHOT

I've often said that the average moviegoer is a lot less concerned with the technical aspects of a film than the nitty-gritty of it: "Is the movie good?" and "Is it worth damn near having to take out a second mortgage to take my family out to this movie?"are the primary concerns. But we're not stupid. We know when somebody has gotten a new toy and wants to try it out on an unsuspecting public. In *I Am Sam*, that somebody was director Jessie Nelson, and that toy was her nauseating use of ShakyCam, that filming technique used with a lot more finesse in TV shows like *Homicide: Life on the Street, NYPD Blue*, and the short-lived *Wonderland*. In those shows, ShakyCam usually didn't make your eyes cross; by contrast, the *I Am Sam* camera crew must've been suffering from a bad case of the DTs. If only for this reason alone, this movie earned my yellow-light rating.

But wait, that's not all! Nelson's cowriter Kristine Johnson made a bad situation worse by contributing to a TV movie–quality script. I'd expect to see this caliber of writing in an afternoon special made for television, not a feature film. The overtly melodramatic, syrupy thread that extended throughout this movie, capped by an ending that made me want to scream epithets, did a serious injustice to the actors and the tale they were trying to tell.

To be fair, some of those actors, and the characters they portrayed, worked for me. Sean Penn and Dakota Fanning had great chemistry together; Penn stayed just this side of Rainmanisms (though his constant Beatles references worked my nerves), and Fanning never resorted to the cute waif act that so many of her contemporaries employ. Though I thought Dianne Wiest's character was overkill, she once again rose above her material and added a needed touch of professional showmanship to this production. Richard Schiff's prosecutor was subtler than I would've expected. And of Sam's crew, I particularly enjoyed Stanley DeSantis as the paranoid Robert, and especially Brad Allan Silverman—who actually happens to be mentally disabled—as Playa Playa Brad. Silverman in particular is noteworthy, because he seemed to be the most natural actor of the bunch.

As for the rest, blech; Doug Hutchison, Laura Dern, and Loretta Devine were totally expendable. And as for Michelle Pfeiffer, I usually find her at least charming, and sometimes even good, in her films. But I desperately wanted her to just shut up here; I found her to be anti-sympathetic to the point of pain, and her characterization of Rita to be completely incredible. Every word, every syllable from her Rita rang completely untrue to me. Maybe I'm mistaken, but I don't think that was the intended effect.

BAMMER'S BOTTOM LINE

If there was a heartstring to be tugged, or a tear to be jerked, director Jessie Nelson and cowriter Kristine Johnson tugged and jerked as hard as

they could. Down, girls; you don't have to hit us so hard with the Whiffle Bat Of Melodrama.

And get a tripod next time, 'kay?

YELLOW LIGHT

ⓑⓐⓜⓢ Keeping the Faith

(2000)

RATED PG-13; running time 129 minutes
GENRE: Romantic comedy
WRITTEN BY: Stuart Blumberg
DIRECTED BY: Edward Norton
CAST: Edward Norton, Ben Stiller, Jenna Elfman, Eli Wallach, Anne Bancroft, Ron Rifkin, Brian George, Ken Leung

> Actress Jenna Elfman is married to the nephew of Danny Elfman, a composer who scores most of Tim Burton's movies. Danny also scored *Dead Presidents*.

THE STORY

Brian (Edward Norton), Jake (Ben Stiller), and Anna (Jenna Elfman) were inseparable friends as kids. But Anna moved to California with her family, leaving Brian and Jake behind in New York. Brian grew up to be a priest, Jake became a rabbi, and both were determined to "kick the dust off faith," bringing it into the 21st century, by staying in touch with their community. This is made somewhat difficult by the resistance of the elder rabbis (Eli Wallach, Ron Rifkin) who want to maintain long-standing tradition. Jake's life is further complicated by the matchmaking service his mother (Anne Bancroft) wants to perform for him—against his will.

Now all grown up and kinda sparkly, Anna reenters their lives when her business ("she's analyzing synergies, or synergizing analogies . . .") brings her back to New York. And suddenly, the "cloth" that both men wear, fits a little too snugly for comfort.

THE UPSHOT

I have to be careful not to gush here, lest I go into every single specific detail of what I liked about this movie. Though there's nothing particularly "new" in this movie—boy and boy meet girl; boy and boy fall for girl; girl moves away; girl comes back; boy and boy vie for her attention—the *way* it was told, and the sincerity with which it came across, was very refreshing.

As a director, Edward Norton brings a fresh view to the screen. For a first-time feature-film director, he did an amazing job of getting good camera shots, without going overboard. I especially liked his shots in and around the bar (uh, no pun intended). Perhaps it's because even though the barroom banter was funny, it wasn't forced humor—and even further, because it felt intimate in a way, instead of in-your-face. We've all heard the clichés about bartender-as-confessor; Norton somehow avoided the cliché and achieved a genuine sense of that reality, without making the humor maudlin. Scenes like this exist throughout the movie; you get the feeling that there's a real and important story being told, rather than a mass of images moving swiftly to a conclusion.

But as enjoyable as director Norton's work was to me, actor Norton's performance as Father Brian Finn was even more fun to watch. Whether he's sharing the scene with Jenna Elfman (with whom he had this incredible chemistry; Anna and Brian's relationship was much more convincing than was hers with Jake), with Ben Stiller, or with the "minor" supporting characters like the bartender (Brian George) and Karaoke Tong (Ken Leung), Norton's skill as an actor made me easily forget that this was the same man who played a skinhead in *American History X* and an airhead in *Fight Club* (see page 78). Norton is truly an underrated actor.

As I alluded to above, Elfman's best work was with Norton; she impressed me most when she was dealing with Brian's "crisis of faith." But to my pleasant surprise, I enjoyed Stiller's performance almost as much as I did Norton's, especially in their interactions. Ben Stiller is generally an acquired taste, one that I haven't picked up to date. But in *Faith*, he seemed less concerned about being "raw and edgy" than he has been in past performances (like his roles in *Mystery Men* and *Black and White*, for instance). Here, Stiller seems to sense how important it was that his rabbi came across as sincerely concerned about his "flock," and it shows in his performance. This is not to say that the good rabbi was all serious. What really made me sit up and take notice, though, is that Stiller didn't allow his comedy bits to overshadow Jake's struggles with being a needful human on the one hand, and feeling obligated to serve his congregation in the way he thought they needed him most, on the other.

Just as I said to myself, "there's nothing about this movie I don't like!" the end started to slow down, to almost crawl. The flaws in it, however, made me appreciate it all the more, from the efforts of the main cast, to the importance of the "minor" characters (that bartender had me in absolute stitches, as did Tong), to the curiosity I've developed about Judaism. Even at its worst, it was better than most.

THE BLACK FACTOR
Actually, let's dish on "The Church Factor" today.

As the daughter of a fiery Baptist mother, I connected to this flick on so many levels, especially when the rabbi and the priest attempted to get their respective members to participate more in the services. The most obvious connection came when Jake brought the Black choir in to the synagogue, to liven up the services. I was immediately taken back to the time when I was the drummer (hence, "Bammer," dig?) for a campus choir. The experience was definitely memorable. Though the scene was played for laughs on-screen, I have a feeling Jake's bunch had as good a time as we all did. The church scenes also reminded me of the time when my Holy Ghost–shoutin' mother went to a service at the Catholic Church. Needless to say, St. Cecilia's was never quite the same after Mama was in tha' house...

But beyond those connections, I related easily to Jake and Brian's message itself, that of trying to reach their members on a personal level: not through the recanting of years and years of traditional rites, but by appealing to their sense of community.

Thus endeth the sermon.

BAMMER'S BOTTOM LINE
Hallelujah! *Keeping the Faith* is an unadulteratedly, unequivocally good movie. I would say "Bless me, Father, for I have laughed," but that'd be too corny.

GREEN LIGHT

 Music of the Heart
(1999)

RATED PG; running time 124 minutes
GENRE: Drama
WRITTEN BY: Pamela Gray
DIRECTED BY: Wes Craven
CAST: Meryl Streep, Aidan Quinn, Angela Bassett, Cloris Leachman, Gloria Estefan, Charlie Hofheimer, Kieran Culkin, Michael Angarano, Henry Dinhofer, Jane Leeves. As themselves: Karen Briggs, Jonathan Feldman, Jean-Luke Figueroa, Ramon Diane Monroe, Mark O'Connor, Sandra Park, Itzhak Perlman, Arnold Steinhardt, Isaac Stern, Michael Tree, Charles Veal Jr.

THE STORY
Music of the Heart is the true story of Roberta Guaspari (Streep), a violinist and former Navy wife freshly divorced from her philandering husband, who is pressed to find a job. She doesn't have a lot of prospects in her suburban environment, where she lives with her mother (Leachman) and

sons Nick (Hofheimer) and Lexi (Culkin, 15-years-old), until Brian Sinclair (Quinn), tells her about a teaching job that may be available—in East Harlem. Principal Janet Williams (Bassett) is skeptical at first, but soon she is convinced to let her work as an elementary-school substitute music teacher in her school, where Roberta meets Isabel Vasquez (Estefan), an assorted batch of students, and, later, Dorothea Van Hauften (Leeves), who may be able to open doors for Roberta and her violin students as time goes on.

THE UPSHOT

Remember the old Mickey Rooney movies where, when the gang needs to raise funds for a project, they just "put on a show"? Well, with *Music*, it's 1990s, meet the 1940s.

I'll be frank: most of the back story of this movie was kinda dull; I can't say that I cared much about Roberta's story as it pertained to her husband, her kids, her mother, or even the strange relationship with Brian (and boy, did Quinn look weird). Neither the normally strong Streep, nor the equally powerful Bassett, could quite pull the first half of this movie out of the doldrums; and though Estefan was refreshingly natural in her big-screen acting debut, she wasn't really all that integral to this flick. The young actors made it worth watching, but it was a task otherwise.

But I gave it the green light for three reasons: First, the story picked up the pace in the second half. Second, Wes Craven, predominantly known for his "Freddy Kruger" slasher flicks, played a soft hand here, only giving in to his horror-flick trickery once. And, most important, the kids were allowed to be genuine elementary-age kids, not

ruffneck hooligans from da' hood, read'ta buss' up a be'ouch, nor insufferably cute Projects projects, waiting for Missy Roberta to deliver them up from out of bondage.

Otherwise, there were no real surprises in this one. The usual tour-de-force that is Meryl Streep was more subdued (though I loved the way she handled the kids, with a strong hand), and Angela Bassett seemed almost an afterthought. But not every movie needs to be the next big thing, after all. *Music of the Heart* ends as a feel-good movie that left me feeling good—and that's just what the doctor ordered.

THE BLACK FACTOR

"Black people don't play the violin."

If you've ever said, or thought, something like that, try to imagine what it's like hearing it directed at you, violin-in-hand. And imagine it coming from a Black person. Stupid, right? And, unfortunately, all too common (substitute "skydive" or "go hang gliding"—or any number of pleasures of which I partake—for "play the violin," and you feel me). We are, far too often, Our own worst enemies when it comes to life-choices; We (rightfully) fight tooth and nail for the ability to gain access to "common areas," then We deride others of Us who go through doors that aren't usually painted Black. So you probably won't be surprised to know that I took great pleasure in seeing so many Black and Latino faces in Roberta's classes. Almost made me want to take up the fiddle.

On that ubiquitous other hand, in one scene, Naim's mother, a Black woman, pulls him out of Roberta's class, saying that she would not let her son be treated as an object that needed to be "rescued" by Roberta. The character's concern is one that's shared by this reviewer, when it comes to movies such as this. The assumption is that the parents can't, or won't, make any effort to try to make a better life for their children, and therefore need the paternalistic rescue attempts of people who otherwise have no stake in the neighborhood. However, the vibe in this movie is that the teacher just wanted to open up a window that none of the kids had opened to them before; the extent to which this has been achieved, should be able to be seen via the real-life students.

BAMMER'S BOTTOM LINE

With *Music of the Heart*, Wes Craven proves he's good for more than just hack-n-slash. And there was even a public service announcement giving the phone number to make donations to Roberta's group, Opus 118: 212-831-4455.

GREEN LIGHT

Bams **Price of Glory**
(2000)

RATED PG-13; running time 117 minutes
GENRE: Drama
WRITTEN BY: Phil Berger
DIRECTED BY: Carlos Avila
CAST: Jimmy Smits, Jon Seda, Clifton Collins Jr., Maria del Mar, Sal Lopez, Louis Mandylor, Danielle Camastra, Ernesto Hernández, Paul Rodriguez, Ron Perlman

THE STORY

Arizona-based Arturo Ortega (Jimmy Smits) coulda been a contenda—until his opponent opened up a can of whupass on him in a 1977 boxing match.

Thirteen years later, Arturo starts to live out his dream of boxing glory through his young sons Sonny and Jimmy, both of whom he trains in a Mariposa, Arizona, gym. Sonny is the more skilled of the two brothers—something that Arturo never lets Jimmy forget—but when Sonny and Jimmy do relatively badly at a Silver Gloves tournament, their youngest brother Johnny surprises the whole Ortega crew by announcing that he's ready to give up street football to become a boxer, saying "them two stunk!"

Ten years later...17-year-old Johnny (Ernesto Hernández) intensely prepares for his Golden Gloves tournament and catches the eye of boxing scout Pepe (Paul Rodriguez) and promoter Nick Everson (Ron Perlman). Everson approaches Arturo with the offer to "relieve" him of his managing duties for Sonny (Jon Seda) and Jimmy (Clifton Collins Jr.), "throwing in" Johnny for good measure. But Arturo has his eyes on the prize—the glory days he sees ahead. The question is, is it glory for them—or for him?

THE UPSHOT

This movie went from being enjoyable in its look at family dynamics from a Latino point of view not usually seen in mainstream Hollywood to being a candidate for TV Movie of the Week. I can't quite pinpoint when *Price of Glory* lost its slight edge, but it did. Maybe I blinked. Or maybe I was just thrilled to see so many Mexican-Americans portrayed on the Silver Screen *without* the stereotypically scripted behavior we've come to expect, that I didn't notice the lack of depth all along. Either way, this movie left me wanting more than it was prepared to deliver.

Early on, though, there were winning performances; Seda, in particular, surprised me with his relatively muted turn as Sonny (if you've ever watched him chewing the scenery in *Homicide*, you'll know why I was surprised). His acting here was aided, no doubt, by the fact that he once was a Golden Gloves boxer himself; he definitely looked comfortable on the body bag. Equally good in the early stages were Clifton Collins as the put-upon Jimmy, and Maria del Mar as Arturo's wife, Rita. I cheered when I saw the interaction between Arturo and his wife, as they looked genuinely attracted to each other, and dedicated (in different ways) to their sons. And in his feature-film debut, Ernesto Hernandez as Johnny Ortega didn't quite give an Oscar-worthy performance but he had his intense-scowl look down pat.

On the other side of the ring, Ron Perlman was never convincing as a boxing promoter;

about the only thing he could've promoted was a bout of sleep. I never did figure out what purpose Danielle Camastra's character, Mariella, served; a throwaway role if I ever saw one, and maybe it was just me, but Louis Mandylor did not look like he belonged in a boxing ring, though his turn as the rather mean-spirited Davey Lane did seem to serve as a needed bit of conflict and tension that was missing from most of the movie. After all, what's a title bout without someone talking trash?

Above all, Jimmy Smits gives a winning performance as patriarch Arturo Ortega. At times funny, and at other times pensive and sad, Smits showed a side of his acting abilities that wasn't allowed to come to the fore nearly enough during his *NYPD Blue* days.

So why did *Price of Glory* fall so flat? Beats me. Maybe it developed wobbly knees from going a round or two too long, and collapsed under the weight of delivering a Message. The editor could have easily excised a half-hour or so with no ill effects, giving it a tighter focus and less repetition on the theme. Certainly, they could've lost the irritating Paul Rodriguez in a pile of film in the trash dump; he used up his fifteen minutes a lifetime ago.

In the end, there just didn't seem enough there to rally around; by the time the obligatory title match came around, enough of the outcome had been telegraphed beforehand. And though the movie seemed authentic on the boxing front, from both the writer's standpoint as well as the cinematographer's great shots of the pugilistic action—one in particular, with young Arturo hitting the canvas, tore right through me—the spirit seemed to drain out of the movie as it rolled on. What had started out as a fun flick, with great Latin sounds and interesting characters, wound up as worthy of being a TV after-school special.

BAMMER'S BOTTOM LINE

More a glancing blow than a knockout, *Price of Glory* still gets props for what it *didn't* show: stereotypical Latinos, Hollywood-style. That's worth at least an extra point or two on my score-card.

FLASHING YELLOW LIGHT

Proof of Life

(2000)

RATED R; running time 135 minutes

GENRE: Drama

WRITTEN BY: Tony Gilroy (based on an article by William Prochnau)

DIRECTED BY: Taylor Hackford

CAST: Meg Ryan, Russell Crowe, David Morse, David Caruso, Pamela Reed, Wolframio Benavides, Michael Kitchen, Daniel Lugo, Mario Sanchez, Pietro Sibille

> *Proof of Life* tanked at the box office. It had a budget just over 65 million dollars and only made around 36 million in its theatrical run.

THE STORY

Peter Bowman (David Morse), an engineer for a multinational oil company trying to build a well—as cover for their ultimate goal: to build an oil pipeline, which just happens to be on the same lines as a drug field—is kidnapped by the ELT, a South American Rebel Faction that is more interested in "earning" money than in political gain. After the company, which sent Peter to that country, fails to support Peter in his time of need, international kidnap-and-ransom agent Terry Thorne (Russell Crowe), Terry's friend and partner, Dino (David Caruso), and Peter's wife, Alice (Meg Ryan), work closely together to try and bring Peter safely home. So closely together, in fact, that Terry starts developing feelings for Alice.

THE UPSHOT

With David Morse, *Proof of Life* had one of the best character actors working today. In the limited screen time he had, David Morse as the kidnappee far outclassed the rest of the field; his was the only character of the bunch that I gave two figs about coming out alive.

Meg Ryan's damsel in distress, in the person of Alice Bowman, at least had the good grace to not be the same air-headed so-and-so Ryan seemed so eager to play as a young Hollywood actress. Indeed, her Alice was reminiscent of one of Ryan's strongest characters yet, the tough-as-nails military chick in *Courage Under Fire*; Alice even *cries* like Ryan's *Courage* character. Which is to say, Alice has a very been-there-done-that feel to her. And though Crowe must have been still riding high from the success of *Gladiator*, he apparently decided to play it safe in a minimally defined role that might've been much more interesting had it been more fully fleshed out.

Of the supporters, Wolframio Benavides (as Juaco, the hot-headed rebel) and Morse shared a few interesting moments as a captor and his willful captive; unfortunately, those moments weren't allowed enough room to breathe and grow into a full-fledged defining event for either of the actors or their characters. Of the remaining main supporters, Pamela Reed was far too screechy as Peter's older sister; and Caruso—whom I so dearly loved as Detective Kelly in his infamous *NYPD Blue* role—*very* quickly wore out his wildly overacting welcome in a questionably humorous supporting part.

The direction and writing was as unremarkable as the South American scenery was beautiful; drop Stallone's *Rambo* in that jungle, maybe you'd have a more thrilling (if not meaningful) story. The most irritating thing about *Proof* is that it took forever to get to an easily anticipated point that could've been more quickly achieved with more than half of the movie edited out.

THE BLACK FACTOR

Even though this movie is set in a fictional South American country, I don't know if I'm qualified to address Latino issues, especially those concerning South American drug trafficking problem. But I'd like to know if it's just me, or is anyone else tired of the brunt of the blame for the consequences of America's War On (Some) Drugs, being laid entirely at the feet of South America with no blame being assigned to the War On (Some) Drugs itself?

BAMMER'S BOTTOM LINE

Proof of Life committed the unforgivable act of boring me to death.

YELLOW LIGHT

The Replacements
(2000)

RATED PG-13; running time 114 minutes
GENRE: Comedy
WRITTEN BY: Vince McKewin
DIRECTED BY: Howard Deutch
CAST: Keanu Reeves, Gene Hackman, Brooke Langton, Orlando Jones, Jon Favreau, Rhys Ifans, Faizon Love, Michael "Bear" Taliferro, Ace Yonamine, Troy Winbush, David Denman, Michael Jace, Jack Warden, Brett Cullen, John Madden, Pat Summerall, Mark Ellis

THE STORY

It's 1987, and the Washington Sentinels, spearheaded by spoiled wimp quarterback Eddie Martel and his teammates, go on strike. It seems their millions are not enough to cover the necessities of life, such as insurance on a Mercedes and the like. Team owner Edward O'Neil (Jack Warden) calls on former coach Jimmy McGinty (Gene Hackman) to recruit and lead a replacement team of players to a possible playoff spot. McGinty, whom O'Neil earlier fired under suspicious circumstances, agrees to this only if he can have complete control over the short-lived team of ragtag unknowns, coulda-beens, and never-weres.

Keanu Reeves plays guitar for the band Dogstar. Whoa.

The replacement team McGinty puts together includes QB Shane "Footsteps" Falco (Keanu Reeves), currently a plankton-remover best known for his disastrous Sugar Bowl game; wide receiver Clifford Franklin (Orlando Jones), fleet-of-foot but slow-of-hand comic relief; defensive lineman Daniel Bateman (Jon Favreau), an ex-Navy SEAL and current SWAT cop who loves smashing things—and people; kicker Nigel "The Leg" Gruff, loveable Welsh drunk and footballer on both sides of the Pond; offensive linemen Jamal Jackson and Andre Jackson, brothers and bodyguards for rap stars; offensive lineman Jumbo Fumiko, so huge he has to be a sumo wrestler, of course; running back Walter Cochran, with a Bible in one hand and a drink in the other;

Add a few others and an obligatory love story between Shane and head cheerleader Annabelle Farrell (Brooke Langton), and you've got yourself a football flick! Blech.

THE UPSHOT

Okay, let's bring the penalty flags out for unnecessary stupidity: *The Replacements* is unoriginal, transparent, hackneyed, clichéd, poorly written and directed, but still very funny in spots, particularly when Jon Favreau as Daniel "SWAT" Bateman was on the screen. Try as I might, I couldn't help but laugh at the big lug as he proceeded to rip up every scene he was in, with an all-out as-

sault on every character that came into his field of vision. There's something weird about laughing at an abusive cop-cum-footballer, I know; but dammit, Bateman was *funny*—as was John Madden, either parodying himself or just playing Madden straight. The other good funny bits came from uncredited players: the hilarious (at first) cheerleading squad, especially the ditzy blonde who couldn't spell; and Mark Ellis as coach of the San Diego team. I damn near busted a gut when he asked the referee to make the lap-dancing cheerleaders "stop shaking their asses" so his team could concentrate on the game.

But the fun was interrupted by long stretches of dumbness. Gene Hackman, bless his talented heart, truly gave it a shot, but the writer saddled him with nothing but clichés. Orlando Jones made me want to spit(!) every time I saw his bug eyes on the screen; his big scene (where he preens to Gloria Gaynor's "I Will Survive") was cute for the first few minutes but lasted way too long (the writer and director repeated this pattern throughout the movie), and his character's sudden bout of Bob Doleism (calling himself "Clifford Franklin" over and over again) seemed a desperate attempt to make sense out of a generally senseless character. As the warm place to put It, Brooke "Sandra Bullock Jr." Langton didn't seem to add much warmth, though the fault is again mostly attributable to Vince McKewin's poisoned pen. And, of course, Keanu "whoa" Reeves brings his own special brand of dumb to most every movie he occupies. This isn't always a bad thing—it did wonders for him in *The Matrix* (see page 18)—but here, he looked like he was sleepwalking through the flick, waiting for *The Matrix 2* to start filming.

The heaviest penalties should be assessed to writer Vince McKewin and director Howard Deutch; if it were up to me, neither of these hacks would be let anywhere *near* a motion picture set ever again, especially not Deutch. Deutch is apparently from the *Frasier's* "if less is more, then think of how much more more would be!" school of directing. Blech.

THE BLACK FACTOR

Let's look at that starting lineup again, shall we?

On defense, we have:

An intense SWAT guy who pounds people for a living, but it's all good because he's on the Right Side Of The Law (White guy);

A fun-loving Welshman who boozes and gambles a wee bit too much, but daggonit, he's "weeierry" (White guy);

A sumo wrestler who's main "fault" is that he's big, but he balances that out by being fun, hip, and otherwise nonstereotypically Asian (Japanese guy);

A player who is deaf, Not That There's Anything Wrong With That (White guy).

And the offending line?

A swishy, cowardly, bug-eyed clown (Black guy);

A (and I'm sure I'll be roasted for this one) Jesus Freak (Black guy);

Two brothers (no doubt *Me, Myself & Irene* rejects) who are as thuggish as you can get without wearing Prison Blues (Black guys);

Someone who actually wears Prison Blues (Black guy).

Gotcha.

BAMMER'S BOTTOM LINE

There's absolutely nothing new in *The Replacements* that would make its lameness worth sitting through, other than a few hilarious moments—and in my book, a few moments do not a movie make. As sports flicks go, you'd be better off renting *Mystery, Alaska* (see page 83) or *The Natural* (just to name two). Or, if you like more humor in your sports, check out the original *Major League*.

YELLOW LIGHT

 Romeo Must Die

(2000)

RATED R; running time 120 minutes
GENRE: Action
WRITTEN BY: Eric Bernt (based on the story by Mitchell Kapner)
DIRECTED BY: Andrzej Bartkowiak
CAST: Jet Li, Aaliyah, Delroy Lindo, Isaiah Washington, Russell Wong, Henry O, Anthony Anderson, Edoardo Ballerini, Jon Kit Lee, D. B. Woodside, DMX

> If you enjoy Jet Li, make sure you rent *Fong Sai Yuk* (pronounced "fong sigh yook"), part 1 and part 2. These are two of his Hong Kong films. You may have to settle for a subtitled version. Whatever you manage to find, you won't regret it.

THE STORY

The Sings and the O'Days are not your typical American family: they are the Hatfields and The McCoys, the Jets and the Sharks, the Montagues and the Capulets, of the Oakland California riverfront, slugging it out over property rights that are meaningful only to a greedy few.

Isaak O'Day (Delroy Lindo) wants to get out of the gangster racket and become a legitimate businessman, and take his daughter Trish (Aaliyah), son Colin (D. B. Woodside), and right-hand man Mac (Isaiah Washington), with him. Standing in his way is one last deal, securing riverfront property to sell to NFL development broker Roth (Edoardo Ballerini) who is also dealing to O'Day's rival overlord, Chu Sing (Henry O) and his family.

THE UPSHOT

Romeo Must Die was a must-see movie for me. Sure, I knew it was another in a long line of "chop sockey" action flicks that was probably high on flash and low on substance. Sure, I knew that Aaliyah and DMX would probably not be burning up the screen, thespianly. Sure, I knew that *Romeo* was delegated to the Unspoken Ghetto of release days for "Black" films—Wednesday nights—most likely because of its "violence quotient" (more on this in the "Black Factor" below and in introduction, page xvi). But heck, it had Jet Li—the *only* good thing about *Lethal Weapon 4*—so it couldn't be half bad, could it? "Half bad," actually, is a good description here.

Just like guys don't really read *Playboy* for the articles, few people go to action adventures expecting to see, well, *Shakespeare*. In that sense, *Romeo* didn't disappoint too much; the audience was asked to swallow some pretty far-fetched stuff (in-

cluding stunts that would've made the folks behind *The Matrix* proud), and, to a great extent, we played along, *some* of us whilst rolling our eyes, but that's to be expected when one can spot the obligatory turncoat only a few minutes into the movie, and see the unsurprising developments unfold from a mile away. No, the story in and of itself didn't bother me—but the three card monte–like misdirection of its underlying premise did.

What do I mean by that? Given the title, *Romeo* should have the slightest of love story issues, no? But, in fact, there was no genuine "love story" between Aaliyah's Trish and Jet's Han. Whoever came up with the breathless "tags" for the movie—"A young Chinese businessman in New York is asked to broker peace between two mobs . . ." "Han soon takes his brother's place in the war and becomes entangled in the violence, until he falls in love with the daughter of the rival gang's leader . . ."—must've seen a *much* different movie than did I. Flirt, they did; but if that's what they call "love," I don't want any.

Good thing, then, that my main interest wasn't in seeing Jet Li and Aaliyah lock lips. What I *did* go to see was Jet kick butt and take names—and he, along with Russell Wong, obliged in high fashion. I would do them both an injustice in trying to describe their martial artistry as performed on screen; "poetry in motion" is as close as I can get. Jet Li especially impressed me in this, his second American film. Given the skills of Bruce Lee and the charm and humor of Jackie Chan, Li's quiet, yet powerful presence should lead the way for more (and hopefully, better) American movie roles in the near future.

All else blended into the background. Lindo and Washington gamely gave their gruff Black

Gang Overlords roles their best shot, but far out-distancing them were Henry O and Wong. Even in his scenes sans martial arts, Wong was quite enjoyable to watch, as was O, especially when playing against Li. As casino owner Silk, rap artist DMX barely registered on the radar; but on a positive note, Anthony Anderson's comic-relief bit as Maurice, one of O'Day's bodyguards, was funny enough to elicit a laugh or two along the way.

All in all, not earth shaking, but not too shabby for a Wednesday night at the movies. Hold up: a Wednesday night? Hmmm...

THE BLACK FACTOR

"If it's Wednesday, a Black film must be opening."

So says "Media Circus" columnist James Surowiecki in his *Salon* article on the subject of seemingly obligatory releases of many "Black" (Surowiecki calls them "urban") movies on Wednesday instead of Friday. Though it is not officially acknowledged by the folks who decide when releases will occur, the pattern of a great deal of "Black" movies being released on Wednesdays can be traced back to 1993's *New Jack City* and *Boyz N the Hood*—not coincidentally, the same time that some knuckleheads of the Black persuasion decided to ruin it for the rest of Us by opening fire at and around a few theaters showing the movies.

Watch carefully for the trend yourself. As long as there are shortsighted planners in Hollywood—and ignorant knuckleheads amongst Us—there is no doubt in my mind that segregation For The Greater Good shall continue to exist.

BAMMER'S BOTTOM LINE

Green light for *Romeo Must Die's* kick-butt action and stunts, the soundtrack by Stanley Clarke (and Timbaland, if you like hip hop), and for its light humor—but . . . Yellow for everything else.

FLASHING YELLOW LIGHT

 **The Rookie**
(2002)

RATED G: running time 129 minutes
GENRE: Sports/Drama
WRITTEN BY: Mike Rich
DIRECTED BY: John Lee Hancock
CAST: Dennis Quaid, Rachel Griffiths, Brian Cox, Angus T. Jones, Beth Grant, Jay Hernandez, Chad Lindberg, Rick Gonzalez, Angelo Spizzirri, Royce D. Applegate, David Blackwell, Rebecca Spicher

THE STORY

Young Jimmy Morris, a baseball aficionado, had the misfortune of being the son of a travelin' Navy man; as a kid, his father, Jim Morris Sr., moved him and his mother Olline from place to place, never settling down for long. This played havoc on Jim's abilities to stick with one baseball team . . . and affected even the adult Jim (Dennis Quaid). Even after getting out from under his stern father's wing, Jim's dream of making the majors were dashed early on, when he blew out his pitching arm in the minors.

Fast-forward a decade: Jim Morris, now a high school chemistry teacher, also coaches the school's baseball team in a Texas town where football, not baseball, is king. Morris—fighting apathy in kids such as team captain Joaquin Campos, catcher Joel Delagarza, fielder Joe David Werst, and pitcher Rudy Bonilla—accepts a motivational challenge from his boys: they'd go from "worst to first" and make it to the District Championship, if Morris promises to let his fastball fly once again by trying out for a major league team. They make the championships, keeping their promise. Will Jim?

It's funny, all the things that gave me pause about *The Rookie* seemed to work in its favor. Its G rating apparently made the cast and crew work harder to recreate a true story that was neither overly melodramatic nor simplistic. The kids were beyond cute—they were adorable, especially Hunter (Angus T. Jones)—but not annoyingly so. As a sports movie, it had more in common with *The Natural* than *Field of Dreams*, but felt more genuine than either of them.

The Rookie is pleasing on many levels: writer Mike Rich scribes just enough down-home folksiness to make its inhabitants interesting, but not so much as to make them look silly. Director John Lee Hancock exhibits an eye for the epic, without making it look as if he's trying too hard. Cast members Rachel Griffiths and Brian Cox (as Morris's wife and father), provide solid support, as do Jay Hernandez, Chad Lindberg, Rick Gonzalez, and Angelo Spizzirri as Morris's high school students. Along with young Mr. Jones, his cuddly co-star, Rebecca Spicher as Jessica, and Royce D. Applegate and David Blackwell as townsfolk Henry and Cal,

the supporting cast give the stalwart Dennis Quaid a firm foundation upon which to build his leading character. The older Quaid gets, the more interesting he becomes; and though he looks older than even the Oldest Rookie he portrayed, his skills as an actor make him seem ageless.

BAMMER'S BOTTOM LINE
It's a rarity to see a G movie done so well, without the smarminess one comes to expect in a family film. Disney, it seems, has done it again; mad props to ya, "Walt." *The Rookie* is the feel-good move of the year.

GREEN LIGHT

Bams **Serendipity**
(2001)

RATED PG-13; running time 85 minutes

GENRE: Romantic comedy
WRITTEN BY: Marc Klein
DIRECTED BY: Peter Chelsom
CAST: John Cusack, Kate Beckinsale, Jeremy Piven, Molly Shannon, John Corbett, Bridget Moynahan, Eugene Levy

John Cusack and Jeremy Piven really are best friends...

THE STORY

By sheer random chance—or was it fate?—Jonathan (John Cusack) and Sara (Kate Beckinsale) meet in a New York department store. Instantly attracted to each other, though they are each involved with other people, Jonathan and Sara coyly try to make a connection. Sara is a big believer in fate; she comes up with a test of fate, which they both fail. Their connection is broken, and they go their separate ways. End of story . . . or is it?

A few years later, Jonathan is engaged to his girlfriend Halleh (Bridget Moynahan), and Sara is with her boyfriend Lars (John Corbett). But Jonathan and Sara's chance meeting still weighs heavy on both their minds. Jonathan enlists his best friend, Dean (Jeremy Piven), to help him find Sara—and Sara does the same with her best friend, Eve (Molly Shannon).

But really—what's the chance they'll ever see each other again?

THE UPSHOT

It's been a long time since I came away from a movie feeling so pleased across the board. I was very much taken in by the crisp writing by Marc Klein, director Peter Chelsom's keen eye for time passages and for New York (though I wish that the City By The Bay had been as lovingly caressed by Chelsom as was NYC), the soundtrack, and especially the acting by the four main players.

John Cusack gives another solid performance. Likewise, Jeremy Piven's turn as Jonathan's friend Dean is indicative of Piven's long history of providing strong character support in whatever project he's cast. Together, Cusack and Piven took a situation that could've been easily played for straight yuks, and endowed it with a humorous but quiet dignity that made me smile.

But it was the fine work by Kate Beckinsale, and especially Molly Shannon, that truly surprised me. That's not to say there weren't a few disappointments. Eugene Levy's anal salesclerk shtick threatened to take this movie to a place I really didn't want it to go. And the unsurprising ending was just that—unsurprising—though I was grateful that Chelsom and Klein didn't take the totally easy way out by making Halleh and Lars unlikable cretins whom Jonathan and Sara just *had* to dump. In the end, my fortunate accidental discovery of *Serendipity* was that it made a cool afternoon a bit more pleasant. And that's good enough for me.

BAMMER'S BOTTOM LINE

Serendipity is an unabashed Chick flick and a fun date movie. What I liked most about *Serendipity* was its maturity in the face of an implausible story; these characters were speaking in adult tones in spite of the ridiculous nature of this movie's concept. The best of the dialogue scripted for them might not be words you or I would use in daily language, but for me, they were words I *wish* I were clever enough to come up with. In this, *Serendipity* was light romantic fare at its best.

GREEN LIGHT

Shane
(1953)

RATED G; running time 118 minutes

GENRE: Western

WRITTEN BY: Jack Schaefer (story), A. B. Guthrie Jr.

DIRECTED BY: George Stevens

CAST: Alan Ladd, Jean Arthur, Van Heflin, Brandon De Wilde, Walter "Jack" Palance, Emile Meyer

> Cheryl Ladd (Chris from the TV series *Charlie's Angels*) was married to David Ladd—one of Alan Ladd's sons. Their daughter, Jordan, is an up-and-coming actress.

THE DIGEST

Little Joey (Brandon De Wilde) is outside, pretending to shoot at range animals. As he is taking aim at a deer, a man appears on the horizon. As the stranger gets closer, Joey notices that the stranger is obviously a gunslinger, a fact that resonates with Joey because he loves the idea of being a gun fighter. The stranger, we find out, is called Shane. Shane decides to take a break from riding and plays with Joey for a while.

Meanwhile, Joe Sr. (Van Heflin) is visited by a man who shows up with a gang. This man, "Ole Man" Ryker, forcefully requests that Joe leave the area. Joe tells Ryker that he is not leaving, and if Ryker wants the land, he'll have to take it from him. Well, Ryker doesn't want to hear this. He was one of the first settlers in the area, and be-

cause of that, he feels that he should be given leeway to drag his cattle wherever he wants, new settlers be damned. Joe, on the other hand, works like a dog to provide for his family, and he doesn't scare easy. What neither of them knows is that Shane is not just an out-of-work field hand.

Once their paths cross, Joe encourages Shane to leave the fighting to him; after all, he doesn't want to drag him into something that might harm him. Shane agrees with Joe, but, unbeknownst to Joe, Shane has made a pact with Marian: Joe's wife. He has promised Marian that he will look after Joe and he intends to keep his word.

THE DISH

I'm not a big fan of westerns. I grew up in the '80s and, as far as I'm concerned, it's not a western unless Clint Eastwood is in it, you know what I mean? But I have to tell you, this movie was wonderful. I was on the edge of my seat.

On its shallowest level, it's just a story about a weary gunslinger coming to town to rescue everyone. But if you dig a little deeper, you'll see that it really is about so much more. It's about the nonsycophantic adoration of a child who idolizes a complete stranger as if this stranger has always been in his life. It's about a man fighting to keep everything he holds dear, most of all the land he has struggled to maintain. And finally, it's about a man trying to outrun his shady past but is forced to embrace it in the unluckiest of circumstances.

Look for a very young Jack Palance as the enforcer of the cattle rancher. My favorite lines in the entire movie—Cattle Rancher: "I don't care! I'll kill him if I have to!" Enforcer: "You mean, *I'll* kill him if you have to." And since this is in the lip-smacker chapter, of course, there's sexual tension.

THE DIRECTIVE

If this were the 1800s, I'd want a "Shane" too. Make a special trip to the video store and pick this one up.

GREEN LIGHT

The Straight Story
the Diva

(1999)

RATED G; running time 111 minutes

GENRE: Dramedy

WRITTEN BY: John Roach & Mary Sweeney

DIRECTED BY: David Lynch (yes, *the* David Lynch. I half expected to see a dwarf and a dead girl)

CAST: Richard Farnsworth, Sissy Spacek, Jennifer Edwards, Barbara E. Robertson, John Farley, Harry Dean Stanton

> Richard Farnsworth was a stuntman for 40 years before moving into acting.

THE DIGEST

Alvin Straight is 73. He lives in a small Iowa town with one of his daughters, Rose (Sissy Spacek). Life in Laurens, Iowa, is slow. Wheat fields and grain mills surround it. You get the impression that everyone there is content to live life at a very slow pace. The highlight of Alvin's day is playing cards and gossiping with the other older men in town.

Alvin, an ornery old cuss, is diagnosed with emphysema and *still* smokes. He has his schedule and his habits and he refuses to deviate from either. That is until his daughter receives a disturbing phone call. It seems that Alvin's only brother, Lyle, has had a stroke. Alvin and Lyle had a fight 10 years earlier and refuse to speak to one another. He decides that he is going to get himself together and go visit his brother who is 255 miles away. But how is he going to get there? He can't drive. His daughter Rose is very mildly retarded and she can't drive either.

Well, Alvin is resourceful. He starts to build this huge trailer, sends his daughter to buy hot dogs, and heads off to the hardware store. At the store, he buys some very interesting goods. Once he gets back home, it becomes apparent that he plans to hitch the trailer to the back of his riding lawnmower. And thus begins Alvin's trip.

THE DISH

Okay, I'm a sentimental sucker. But I just love movies that my grandmother and I would have been able to sit through together. *The Straight Story* is one of them. I hope I didn't just put a nail in its coffin. I don't want to scare you off, but it's the truth. This movie is aimed at our elders. They didn't even market it to demographics under 40 (not that 40 is old).

There is no cursing or bloodshed; no immature or silly little jokes. Surprisingly, David Lynch is the director and this movie is a clear departure from his previous works. My life is enriched because of it, even though I'm not in the correct demographic.

And what great acting; Sissy Spacek should've been nominated for Best Supporting Actress.

THE DIRECTIVE

Spend a nice Sunday with grandma. Take her out to brunch and then check out *The Straight Story*. This movie tugs straight at your heartstrings.

GREEN LIGHT

the Diva Three Kings
(1999)

RATED R; running time 114 minutes
GENRE: War/Comedy/Drama/Action
WRITTEN BY: John Ridley and David O. Russell
DIRECTED BY: David O. Russell
CAST: George Clooney, Mark Wahlberg, Ice Cube, Spike Jonze, Cliff Curtis, Nora Dunn, Jamie Kennedy, Saïd Taghmaoui, Mykelti Williamson

> Spike Jonze is married to Sofia Coppola. Sofia is the daughter of Francis Ford Coppola, the niece of Talia Shire, and the cousin of Nicolas Cage (who changed his name from Coppola). Not to mention, Spike is a director in his own right, of music videos as well as feature films.

THE DIGEST

The movie begins in March of 1991, the end of the Gulf War. Archie Gates (George Clooney) has a few months to go until retirement and is on the verge of getting kicked out of the army. Troy Barlow (Mark Wahlberg) joined up because his wife was pregnant and his salary as a copy-machine repairman wasn't cutting it. Conrad Vig (Spike Jonze) is a backwoods country boy with a junior high school education and he's in because he had nothing better to do, and finally, Chief Elgin (Ice Cube) is a Muslim who is escaping a dead-end job as a baggage handler for the Detroit airport.

With the war being over, the American army is given the task of rounding up Saddam's soldiers. Each prisoner has to remove his clothes so the army can make sure that the soldier is not hiding any weapons. During a standard check, Troy and Conrad come across a soldier who has a piece of rolled-up paper stuck in his butt. They *carefully* remove the paper. Upon further inspection, it is determined that it is a map of one of Saddam's bunkers, a bunker full of gold bullion. And so the quest begins.

The bunker is in a small village, "100 kliks" north of the base. Since they are on an unauthorized mission, they sneak out at dawn and head toward the town. Once they get there, they meet no resistance. In fact, they are surprised that the civilians are actually glad to see them. They raid the bunker and force the soldiers to help them carry the loot. End of story, right? Wrong.

What they soon realize is that Saddam doesn't care about the material goods; he wants to control the rebels and the citizens. The American soldiers are shocked when they witness civilians being tortured and murdered. They decide to help the civilians. Because of this, a few Iraqi soldiers are killed, breaking the cease-fire agreement and allowing Iraqi soldiers to kill American soldiers.

THE DISH

In what is a fairly political movie, American foreign policy is called into question and examined, and it's this aspect of the film that separates *Three Kings* from all other war movies. It boldly takes a stance against gun violence and the American tendency to be self-absorbed. It also showed a very human side of the people involved in this war. It dealt with the negative stereotypes of the Iraqi people. There were a lot of Iraqi people fighting against Saddam and they were promised help by George Bush Sr. and never got it. This movie also tackled the mental oppression of Black folks in America, using Michael Jackson "who keeps carving up his face" as an example of Eurocentric oppression and thinking. It was pretty tight.

I *really* enjoyed this movie. I was very impressed with Ice Cube. Somewhere between *Friday* and *Player's Club* he learned how to act. After this movie, I no longer view him as a rapper. D'shay Jackson (Ice Cube's real name) is an actor who just happens to know how to rap. Same with Mark Wahlberg (although it can be argued that he can't rap), somewhere between Calvin Klein ads and *Boogie Nights*, he picked up some acting skills. Each and every character in this movie was memorable from the dingbat reporter to the little Iraqi girl. Even the camera work was fresh and new.

THE DIRECTIVE

A crown jewel of a movie, *Three Kings* is one of the better war-themed movies I've watched. Do yourself a favor and check it out. Amen!

GREEN LIGHT

the Diva   What Women Want
(2000)

RATED PG-13; running time 123 minutes
GENRE: Comedy
WRITTEN BY: Josh Goldsmith (story), Cathy Yuspa
DIRECTED BY: Nancy Meyers
CAST: Mel Gibson, Helen Hunt, Ashley Johnson, Marisa Tomei, Lauren Holly, Mark Feuerstein

Mel Gibson and his wife of 21 years have seven children.

THE DIGEST

Nick Marshall is a cad. A rounder. A tramp. (Can you tell that I've seen *Lady and the Tramp* recently?) But given the fact that he is so nice, women excuse him for being a chauvinistic jerk. Women let him use them and the men give him "hi-fives" for getting all the "chicks."

All is right in his world until he loses a promotion to a woman. The ad agency he works for is losing market share because they don't know how to appeal to women. In an attempt to capture a piece of the pie, Nick's boss (Alan Alda) hires the brilliant Darcy Maguire (Helen Hunt) as creative director. Darcy implores everyone to get inside the head of a woman. Nick decides to give it a try. During his exploration, he accidentally electrocutes himself. When he wakes up, he can hear what women are privately thinking. Nick has been so self-absorbed that he didn't know how much the women in his life dislike him. Even his daughter thinks he's a jerk.

How does Nick deal with this golden knowledge? Does he use his new gift to take advantage of women or does he use his gift to right some of the wrongs?

THE DISH

An extremely uneven movie, it was funny for about 15 minutes, and they weren't even consecutive. There were times I giggled my behind off, and others when nothing but crickets could be heard.

But the lack of laughs wasn't the only problem. I was also bothered that not one woman had a redeeming quality. They were all plagued with self-doubt or self-pity. They were bright and capable women, yet the *minute* a man walked into their lives, they became blithering idiots. This is not to say that these types of women don't exist. I know a few myself, but *every* woman in this movie had some issues and most of those issues were tied to some man.

To make matters worse, the characters played by Delta Burke and Valerie Perrine were confusing. It's clear they were aging showgirls, perhaps friends of Nick's mother's. What isn't clear is if he is the only one that could see them; if not, what was their purpose other than to fuss over him? And if someone else can see them, why didn't they mention that?

On a positive note, Mel Gibson's dance routine was cute.

THE DIRECTIVE

This woman wants to have a long talk with the writer of *What Women Want*.

YELLOW LIGHT

kay, you've looked at the list of movies in this chapter and decided that we 3 Chicks are on crack. Come on, who in their right mind would put *The Green Mile* in chapter called "Booty Call"? Well, work with us for a minute. Say you're checking some cool dude or fine mama out. You've managed to get him/her over to the pad a few times, but they always leave after the 90-minute movie is over. Check this out: *The Green Mile* is a 3-plus-hour movie, right? Figure in a 1-hour dinner and about 20 minutes of discussion after the movie, the two bathroom breaks . . . that's five hours. *Somebody* is spending the night after all that!

We felt that this chapter should include movies that spark discussion, such as *The Green Mile*; movies with Nekkid-Bumpin' Uglies scenes and adult content, such as *The Thomas Crown Affair, Whipped,* or *Any Given Sunday,* and movies that bring forth a waterfall of tears, such as *Pay It Forward* (this, of course, gives her the opportunity to say "hold me" and him the opportunity to show how sensitive he is). You can thank us later for the sheer brilliance of our *Green Mile–Booty Call* idea.

Any Given Sunday
(1999)

RATED R; running time 165 minutes

GENRE: Drama

WRITTEN BY: John Logan (based on the novel by Rob Huizenga)

DIRECTED BY: Oliver Stone

CAST: Al Pacino, Jamie Foxx, Cameron Diaz, Dennis Quaid, James Woods, LL Cool J, Matthew Modine, Ann-Margret, Aaron Eckhart, John C. McGinley, Jim Brown, Bill Bellamy, Lawrence Taylor, Lauren Holly, Lela Rochon, Clifton Davis, Charlton Heston

THE STORY

"On any given Sunday, any team can win or lose." Such is the type of platitude spouted by Tony D'Amato (Al Pacino), the tired, worn-out coach of the Sharks pro football team. The Sharks are a so-so team whose glory days are behind it, and their chances of making it to the playoffs are threatened by the injury of aging veteran quarterback Jack "Cap" Rooney (Dennis Quaid)—who, along with Luther "Shark" Lavay (former real-life football player Lawrence Taylor), was already considered to be expendable by owner Christina Pagniacci (Cameron Diaz in a tour-de-force role), a no-nonsense hard-hitter who inherited the team from her late father, a compatriot of Tony. But Pagniacci is the least of D'Amato's worries: he also has to contend with idiot sports reporter Jack Rose (John C. McGinley); hungry assistant coach Nick Crozier (Aaron Eckhart); slimy team doctor Harvey Mandrake (James Woods); showboat running back Julian Wash-

ington (LL Cool J); and third-string young-gun quarterback Willie Beamon (the outstanding Jamie Foxx), a wild player (on and off the field) who has a strange projectile ritual.

THE UPSHOT

This flick opens with a quote by legendary football coach Vince Lombardi, who compares football players to warriors—and this theme is advanced throughout the movie by D'Amato and others. Fortunately, I was distracted from that ridiculous comparison by the movie's opening images of the Sharks and their opponents. Director Oliver Stone (who, casting himself as a football announcer, might have found a new calling) and his cinematographer grab the viewer immediately with the MTV-like cuts from the field to the stands to overhead shots of the stadium; similar photography is shot throughout a great deal of the movie. In the hands of a lesser (younger?) cast and director, this camerawork might've shown the emptiness under the window dressing; but here, it emphasizes the storyline—to the deficit of the traditionally shot, slower parts of the story. The slow parts, however, were few and far between.

The story pitted Old School versus New Jack in a standard parable: Owners are greedy fat cats who only care about the bottom line. Older players are grizzled rich men who Do It For The Gipper. Younger players are spoiled rich boys who do it for the Benjamins—and the adoring fans, who keep giving them the Benjamins. Team doctors just wanna pump you up. But the story is told in a fresh way that keeps the audience's attention for the most part; and though most of the characters' lines are drawn early on, few if any of the characters have a surplus of redeeming qualities; indeed, the best part of the telling of *Sunday* lies in the "badness" of the characters: D'Amato is a frightened has-been with narrow vision; Pagniacci has no heart; Washington can't hold on to the ball in his anxiousness to get to the next page in the record books; Shark has more brawn than brains when it comes to his health; Beamon gets the big head and disses his teammates and his girlfriend, Vanessa Struthers (Lela Rochon); Mayor Tyrone Smalls (Clifton Davis), a Black man, is shown as questionably dirty as any White politician might be; assistant coach Montezuma Monroe (Jim Brown, in another standout role) doesn't pamper his players one iota, calling their manhood into question at the drop of a hat; Cap's wife, Cindy (Lauren Holly), shocks us with her bitchitude; and so on. Not many totally redeeming qualities in *this* bunch. And up to the point where Pagniacci and Beamon see the light, I grooved on their badness.

Though the photography and direction were great, the members of this large cast were just as important to this flick. As noted above, Foxx, Diaz, and Brown were superb. Pacino and Quaid, though solid, played as "old" as they looked. Quaid seemed to want to just pass Go and Collect $200 (plus a percentage of the receipts). If I hadn't seen the execrable *True Crime*, I might've given Woods some play here; but since he's playing the same one-note character here that he did in that movie, his just-short-of-over-the-top acting gets no love from this reviewer; Bill Bellamy (as wide receiver Jimmy Sanderson) made me smile with his pep talk to himself, though he was far overshadowed by Foxx and LL Cool J. But on

a sour note, as the constantly soused Margaret Pagniacci (Christina's wacky mother), Ann-Margaret was just irritating.

If you're like me, the players (on and off the field) in *Any Given Sunday* won't elicit any sympathy—and neither will their counterparts in real life. But the story here was told well enough to let me leave my cynicism on the sidelines for three hours (and, by the way, is it a coincidence that this movie lasted damn near as long as a real pro game would? Hmmm . . .).

THE BLACK FACTOR

I can't speak highly enough of Jamie Foxx in his role in this flick. Though I knew he was funny and talented from his *In Living Color* days (nota bene, Hollywood: Jim Carrey wasn't the only one in that cast. But they don' hear me doe . . .), the depth of his acting here really made me sit up and take notice. Funny in the right spots ("My Name Is Willie" had me rollin') but serious in others, he smoked Pacino in their breakfast scene together, and had some good stuff to say about the role of Black athletes—something that's been a long time in coming. But is anyone listening?

BAMMER'S BOTTOM LINE

Any Given Sunday could've stood a more careful snip or two in the editing box (and a little less ham-handedness during Beamon's and Christina's Obligatory awakenings). But the excellent cinematography, tight cast, great ending scene, and good soundtrack (which offers more than just the usual "urban contemporary" songs), made the time watching this flick, time well spent. And did I mention bru-man in the locker room? Woo Lawd!

GREEN LIGHT

The Cell
(2000)

the Diva

RATED R; running time 115 minutes
GENRE: Thriller/Horror
WRITTEN BY: Mark Protosevich
DIRECTED BY: Tarsem Singh
CAST: Jennifer Lopez, Vince Vaughn, Vincent
    D'Onofrio, Marianne Jean-Baptiste, Jake
    Weber, Dylan Baker

THE DIGEST
Catherine Deane (Jennifer Lopez) is a world-renowned child psychologist. For the past 18 months she has been working with an experimental procedure that allows one to enter the mind of another. She has been using this technique to try and bring a little boy out of a coma. She has not been successful. Meanwhile, serial killer Carl Stargher (Vincent D'Onofrio) is finally caught, but he has a catastrophic schizophrenic episode that causes him to fall into a coma before the FBI can determine where his last victim is. The FBI takes him to Catherine's facility and convinces her to enter his mind and figure out where the last victim is.

THE DISH
Disjointed, bumpy, and wholly manipulative, this movie sucked. When Catherine enters Carl's mind, she finds him as he was when he was a child—very abused. The movie then seeks to make us feel sorry for Carl because he had a horrendous childhood. Yes, he did. His childhood blew, but he should not use that as an excuse for his current bad behavior.

The plot, what little of it there was, was bad and hard to follow. The special effects were pretty decent, but weren't good enough to carry the film. It was like watching someone's bad acid trip. The movie never decided in which direction it wanted to go, and when it picked a direction, it took too long to get there. In addition, there is some shocking and grotesque material in this film and I'm sorry that I witnessed it. We, the audience, were forced to puff on the same crack pipe that whoever made this movie was hitting, and I, for one, was not pleased.

THE DIRECTIVE
Don't even bother with this one. It's pointlessly gross.

RED LIGHT

Bams The Cider House Rules
(1999)

RATED PG-13; running time 129 minutes
GENRE: Drama
WRITTEN BY: John Irving (based on his novel)
DIRECTED BY: Lasse Hallström
CAST: Tobey Maguire, Michael Caine, Charlize Theron, Delroy Lindo, Paul Rudd, Jane Alexander, Kathy Baker, Erykah Badu, Kieran Culkin, Kate Nelligan, Heavy D, K. Todd Freeman, Paz de la Huerta, Sean Andrew, Spencer Diamond, Skye McCole Bartusiak, Erik Per Sullivan

THE STORY

Dr. Wilbur Larch (Michael Caine) is an unusual man in an unusual place during an unusual time: along with Nurse Angela (Kathy Baker) and Nurse Edna (Jane Alexander), Larch oversees a home for unwanted children—born and yet-to-be born—in St. Cloud, Maine, on the brink of World War II. The abortions he performs are illegal, but in his eyes, they are necessary, considering the alternative—terribly unsafe back-alley hatchet jobs. This, though, is little comfort to young Homer Wells (Tobey Maguire); along with housemates Buster, Mary Agnes, Copperfield, Hazel, Fuzzy, and the adorable Curly, Homer grows up as an orphan under the care of Larch and the nurses, and becomes almost as skilled as the good doctor himself. The difference, though, is that Homer objects to Larch's actions, and has no intentions of being an abortionist.

Homer's life takes a drastic change when Wally Worthington, an Air Force pilot, brings his girlfriend, Candy Kendall (Charlize Theron), to St. Cloud for an abortion. When they leave, Homer goes with them to Wally's family's cider mill, and experiences life as an apple picker. There, he meets Wally's mother, Olive (Kate Nelligan), and a band of migrant workers led by Mr. Rose (Delroy Lindo), his daughter Rose Rose (Erykah Badu, in her acting debut), Peaches (Heavy D), and Muddy (K. Todd Freeman). But Homer's former life isn't quite behind him; not yet . . .

THE UPSHOT

I went into *The Cider House Rules* fully prepared to be either disappointed or put to sleep by yet another art flick. I need to get rid of my jadedness; it would've done this film a disservice had I let it win out. *Cider* was like a breath of fresh air.

It was told almost as a bedtime story; I could easily hear the nurses reading it to the kids as a lullaby; not for sleepy-time, but instead to soothe them from the reality that not many people were interested in adopting them once they were no longer babies. Of course, not every aspect of the film was as peaceful as all this; the harsh reality of choosing to end a life was a heavy burden to bear by mother and doctor alike. That the movie didn't get bogged down with the heaviness is indicative of the quality of the writing and the script.

One would think that a flick that dealt with such a big issue as abortion, from both sides of the fence, would come off as overly strident. But there was no heavy-handed pro-choice or pro-life message involved; the real message addressed the humanity of the characters.

And oh, the humanity. The characters and actors felt as natural as those you might meet in a small town in 1940s Maine. Other than the horrible go at an American accent, I could easily believe Caine's Dr. Larch, and the compassion he had for orphans and pregnant mothers alike; the way he and the nurses made the orphans feel special without patronizing them warmed my jaded heart. Maguire, as the eagerly naive Homer, was charming and engaging, and I look forward to seeing him in more movies. Ditto Charlize Theron; my estimation of her acting skills shot way up after this flick. In fact, I can't remember a missed note from *any* of the actors or characters—including the children. Heck, *especially* the children; after the sour taste that *Stuart Little* (see page 317) left in my mouth for Cutesy Orphan Kids, I was pleasantly surprised by the easygoing performances of the young actors (and I fell in love with Spencer Diamond; I'd adopt him in a heartbeat!).

The movie took a weird turn when Homer left the orphanage for the cider mill; it wasn't exactly *difficult* to follow, but the motivations (so to speak) for the actions of the characters involved, weren't as clear during this part of the movie as they were in the orphanage. That said, Delroy Lindo once again knocked my socks off; I find it hard to believe that, considering what his Mr. Rose character went through, I could feel as . . . attached . . . to his character *after* the movie ended, as I did going in. Though Erykah Badu's movie debut drew my attention (too much, in spots; was she wearing contacts?), Lindo's powerful performance *kept* it.

THE BLACK FACTOR

I sometimes have to remind myself that, especially in period pieces like this, expressions of "strength" (so to speak) by Black folk are of necessity more muted than I'd hope they'd be in modern-day movies. I should not have expected, for example, Rose Rose (a Black Woman) to take issue at Candy Worthington's (a White Woman) charitable efforts to give her hand-me-downs, not because hand-me-downs are a sign of poverty, but because she was never invited to sup with the Worthington family, while Homer, whom the Worthingtons have just met, is immediately invited to share a repast. White Privilege once again rears its ugly head!

BAMMER'S BOTTOM LINE

A sweet story with characters that felt real, one could almost forgive Michael Caine for his awful American accent—which gave way to his otherwise brilliantly understated performance. An additional tip o' the hat to Delroy Lindo for pulling off the seemingly impossible. *Cider House Rules* is a simple story with a heart.

GREEN LIGHT

 **Dogma**
(1999)

RATED R; running time 128 minutes
GENRE: Comedy
WRITTEN BY: Kevin Smith
DIRECTED BY: Kevin Smith
CAST: Ben Affleck, Matt Damon, Linda Fiorentino, Alan Rickman, Chris Rock, Salma Hayek, Jason Mewes, Kevin Smith, Jason Lee, George Carlin, Barret Hackney, Jared Pfennigwerth, Kitao Sakurai

> Kevin Smith produced an extremely short-lived TV series on ABC, *Clerks: The Animated Series*, based on characters from many of his movies. What possibly could've possessed him to take his act to the boob tube, we'll never know.

THE STORY

In this dark comedy, Matt Damon and Ben Affleck (respectively) play Loki and Bartleby, AWA (Angels With Attitudes). They have issues with the Big G because, as Old Testament angels, they were cast out of heaven for going against God's will (Loki was the Angel of Death, and Bartleby tried to get him to chill one day. Big no-no, it seems. The Old Testament God wasn't havin' it.). Banished to Wisconsin until the end of the world, they hear about a loophole: in an effort to get parishioners back into church, Cardinal Glick (George Carlin) invokes a dogmatic rule that would wipe the slate clean for any and all sinners who pass through the arch of his New Jersey church. Loki and Bartleby reason that what's good for mortals is good for angels, too.

Meanwhile, on the other side of town . . . Metatron, the embodiment of the Voice of God (Alan Rickman) contacts Bethany (Linda Fiorentino), an abortion-clinic worker with religious issues of her own, and enlists her to stop the angels from going through the arch. In classic road-movie form, she meets a series of folks on the way: Jay and Silent Bob (Jason Mewes and Kevin Smith), whom she sees as the Prophets Metatron predicted, but who see her as a potentially great lay; Rufus (Chris Rock), the 13th Disciple who insists that he was left out of the Bible because he was the only Black Disciple; Serendipity (Salma Hayek), a muse who somehow ended up in a strip club; and on the side of Evil, Azrael and the Stygian Triplets (Jason Lee; Barret Hackney, Jared Pfennigwerth, and Kitao Sakurai), Lucifer's henchmen and doers of bad deeds. Wackiness ensues.

THE UPSHOT

Dogma, to my understanding of the meaning of the word, is blasphemous. But here's the kicker: the blasphemy is directed not at religion (that is, the faith of the believer) but at Religion (that is, the organization known as "The Church"). Specifically, Religion in the form of the Catholic Church (which, in my youth, I called "stand-up-sit-down-stand-up-kneel"). And as someone who's had issues with the Church (specifically, the Baptist Church, a.k.a. "The Fashion Show," but that's another rant for another time), I diggit.

That aside, my feelings about the movie as a movie—versus the movie as a statement—are a lot less forgiving. I was irritated at the movie far too often to recommend it unconditionally. For starters, you'd have to totally assume that God wouldn't be hip to what Loki and Bartleby were up to, and worse was the "explanation" of why that was (which, like a Greek tragedy's deus ex machina, magically made itself known at the end of the flick). Not helping matters any were some of the actors who seem to have called in their parts. Amongst the sinners are Carlin's cardinal (which, given his HBO special where he totally trashes the Church, makes this particular sin unforgivable), Rickman (the actor must've imbibed the tequila that his Metatron character kept spitting out), Lee (a hammy devilette with horns . . . gimme a break. What, they couldn't get Jim Carrey?), and especially Fiorentino, totally unbelievable in what should've been a key role; she damn near put me to sleep with her bored-stiff acting. And let's not forget the (Smith's words, not mine, folks) "Shit Demon." Actually, let's.

But by far, the brunt of the blame goes to Damon and Affleck (and, of course, Smith's pen). Damon's Loki was just *way* too out there, cussin' for cussin's sake. I had to remind myself that Loki *was*, after all, the Angel of Death. Affleck played Bartleby rather nicely to begin with; his Good Cop to Loki's Bad Cop worked for a while. But it all came tumbling down after the train scene; suddenly, they both got an epiphany and inexplicably switched characterizations—and ruined any chances of redeeming the movie from there forward. And to top it off, the closing scene was corny and hokey, as if Smith ran out of shock-value material to toss at the viewer, yielding to conventionality at the end.

There were, however, bright spots in the most unexpected of places. Chris Rock, as usual, was the funniest thing in the movie; Salma Hayek was pretty durn good here, certainly measurably better than Fiorentino; Kevin Smith was amusingly expressive; and Jason Mewes . . . man. His whacked-out Jay was simply a trip. Once I got over the shock of his behavior, I kinda dug him.

In the end, I had a love-hate relationship with *Dogma;* I was mad at it for not being what it could've been, but appreciated it for what it was. Even if I didn't always agree with it.

BAMMER'S BOTTOM LINE

In all their eagerness to be Bold And Controversial!—while at the same time stay user-friendly (read: not alienating the target box-office demographic) by going for the funny bone (and missing), the filmmakers left something to be desired in the execution. Still, you gotta give Smith & Crew an attaboy for having the nads to at least give it ye olde college try. The bottom Bottom Line? *Dogma* gets my green-light rating because I feel compelled to see it again, flaws n' all.

GREEN LIGHT

The Family Man
(2000)

RATED PG-13; running time 125 minutes
GENRE: Dramedy
WRITTEN BY: David Diamond & David Weissman
DIRECTED BY: Brett Ratner
CAST: Nicolas Cage, Téa Leoni, Jeremy Piven, Don Cheadle

THE DIGEST

Jack Campbell has it all. He is president of a company that is on the verge of a 130 billion-dollar deal, lives in a posh Manhattan apartment, drives a Ferrari, and has women at his beck and call. Jack is so content that he doesn't think twice about throwing away the telephone number of his ex-girlfriend Kate (Téa Leoni), the woman who was the love of his life. They haven't spoken in 13 years, so why should they now? Besides, all is right with the world. Well, his world, anyway. All that changes when Jack gets a craving for eggnog.

Jack walks into a corner liquor store to buy some eggnog; while he is there, he hears a commotion. Another customer is attempting to cash in a lotto ticket, and the clerk won't take it. The clerk believes that the customer is trying to run a scam. The situation gets heated and the customer pulls out a gun. Jack steps in and tries to defuse the situation. Jack's solution means that he must leave with the customer. Jack gets the customer outside and learns that his name is Cash. He immediately begins intervention on Cash (Don Cheadle). He tells Cash that whatever the problem is, committing a crime won't solve it. Cash tells him that he doesn't need any help, to which Jack replies, "everyone needs something." Cash asks Jack what he needs and Jack tells him he has everything and needs nothing. Cash then tells Jack that whatever happens to him, he brought it on himself. A puzzled Jack goes home and falls asleep.

Jack wakes up bright and early the next morning and finds himself in a bed that isn't his, and Kate is sleeping next to him. In the distance, he can hear screaming kids and a dog barking. Jack is getting a "glimpse" at his life as it would be had he not left Kate 13 years ago. He can't go back to his normal life until he figures out what he needs. Does he choose love and family or a high-powered career?

THE DISH

We've all seen *It's a Wonderful Life*. If not, catch it next Christmas, it's on every year. It's much better than its blatant rip-off—*The Family Man*.

There was ZERO chemistry between Nicolas Cage and Téa Leoni. I mean ZERO. That made watching it all the more painful. On the other hand, young actress Makenzie Vega sparkled as their daughter, Annie. Her interactions with Nicholas were wonderful and accounted for the best parts of the movie.

THE BLACK FACTOR

And I had a big problem with Don Cheadle's character. Did they need to make him a thug? Couldn't he have accomplished what he needed to over a business dinner? Two colleagues discussing their lives over dinner maybe? They could even have met at a health club. If the point was to see what he would do in a life-threatening situation, why not stage a car accident?

THE DIRECTIVE

At times, I wish I had fallen asleep and woke up elsewhere, too.

FLASHING YELLOW LIGHT

the Diva **15 Minutes**
(2001)

RATED R; running time 110 minutes
GENRE: Action/Thriller
WRITTEN BY: John Herzfeld
DIRECTED BY: John Herzfeld
CAST: Robert De Niro, Edward Burns, Melina Kanakaredes, Avery Brooks, Karel Roden, Oleg Taktarov, Vera Farmiga

THE DIGEST

Emil (Karel Roden) and Oleg (Oleg Taktarov) have traveled to New York all the way from somewhere in Eastern Europe. Oleg declares that he has come to this country to visit for a few weeks and watch movies, especially his favorite, *It's a Wonderful Life.* He intends to make a movie while he is in New York. The truth of the matter is, however, they have come to this country to meet up with their old partner in crime and get their

cut of the money from a bank robbery they all committed.

When they arrive at the friend's apartment, they find out that he has spent all of the money. In a fit of rage, Emil kills him and his wife. Oleg, obsessed with the thought of making a movie, decides to film the whole thing. A few hours later, New York's finest—Eddie Fleming (Robert De Niro)—is called to an apartment fire. He and his detectives assume that the couple died because of the fire. But fire marshall Jordy Warsaw (Edward Burns) determines within two minutes that it's a fire designed to cover up a murder.

Meanwhile, Emil and Oleg are learning a lot about American society by watching talk shows and news shows. They've convinced themselves that they can get their money by committing a series of horrible crimes, filming them, and selling them for one million dollars to tabloid television, then finally pleading insanity while they are on trial. The sad thing is, their plan just might work.

THE DISH

This movie offers up a scathing look at the media. You want to feel contempt for the tabloid television show, but you can't when the police and the fire department use the media themselves. The fire chief berates Jordy for not being a camera whore like Eddie, because the more visibility the fire department has, the more money they can secure for the next budget.

The writer, John Herzfeld, also hit the jackpot in using humor to desensitize his audience to the gore. The movie was intentionally witty during some of its vilest scenes. Consequently, the violence was easier to digest, so I found myself laughing at that goofball Oleg pretending to be Frank Capra. That concept is brilliant.

Edward Burns was simultaneously a bit underused and a victim or his overacting. This movie belonged to De Niro, who was brilliant, Roden, Taktarov, and Farmiga (who plays a vulnerable witness to their crimes).

THE DIRECTIVE

Deserving of more than 15 minutes of fame.

GREEN LIGHT

Frequency
(2000)

RATED PG-13; running time 124 minutes
GENRE: Drama/Science fiction
WRITTEN BY: Toby Emmerich
DIRECTED BY: Gregory Hoblit
CAST: Dennis Quaid, Jim Caviezel, Elizabeth Mitchell, Andre Braugher, Noah Emmerich, Shawn Doyle, Daniel Henson, Stephen Joffe, Michael Cera

THE STORY

The pretty lights in the sky—the storm known as the aurora borealis—have a surprise in store for John Sullivan (Jim Caviezel), a Queens cop who still mourns the death of his father, Frank (Dennis Quaid), 30 years past. As the movie opens, John, his best friend Gordo, and Gordo's son

Gordy Jr. discover a chest belonging to Frank, a firefighter in 1969; the chest—which contains a shotgun, pictures of his father, and a ham radio ("so this is what people used before the Net, huh?")—will link him to his father in ways he never believed could happen.

The radio allows John to reach out to his past and change it, affecting not only his own life, but also that of his family, and his father's best friend, Satch DeLeon (Andre Braugher). But changes made in the past have a direct effect on the future—John's present time—and because of these changes, a serial killer may have been allowed another chance to kill again.

THE UPSHOT

Issues, Issues everywhere . . .

Issue #1: The movie's treatment of the concept of time travel, through what writer Toby Emmerich (brother of Noah, who plays Gordo) calls "multiverses." If you can't get past this concept and suspend your disbelief from the start, you will likely not be able to enjoy this flick. I got past it, though I still have questions about how "multiverses" affect some parts of the characters' lives, but not others.

Issue #2: The way director Gregory Hoblit chose to let the viewer know that something important was about to happen. Hoblit all too often hit the audience with the dreaded Whiffle Bat of exposition, by way of using close-ups on things that would be of great import later on in the story. There's an aurora borealis storm out tonight . . . wham! And look! at that dead cop's name . . . wham! But even with that Whiffle Bat hitting me upside the head as often as it did, I *still* found a couple of key sequences baffling.

Issue #3: Call me picky, but if you're gonna begin with one premise—that using a ham radio requires you to hold down the talk button ("keying") to transmit—you damn well should stick with that premise. I'd rather be asked to believe that you *don't* key the mike to talk, than to have characters start keying at first, but later have radio conversations *from clear across the room* with no microphone in sight.

With all those issues in the way, you might think I didn't like the movie, but actually I did. Though it wasn't great, it was good enough to keep me interested in what was going on; and the sense of sincerity that came across from the actors—especially Dennis Quaid and Jim Caviezel—made it convincing, however farfetched. Given the nature of the parts they're playing—a father and son caught up in what seems like an implausible situation—Quaid and Caviezel go beyond the gimmickry in science fantasy, making the viewer believe that they have genuine affection for one another. It borders on saccharine at times, but the movie rarely suffers for the melodrama inherent in such a tale.

The supporting players, especially Noah Emmerich as the humorous yet never buffoonish Gordo, and Shawn Doyle in a particularly slimy but pivotal role, did well in their parts; and the younger versions of John and Gordo (Daniel Henson and Stephen Joffe) never came off as typical bratty movie kids. The special effects and opening titles were well done, and the attention paid to continuity, except with regards to one character (noted below), was noteworthy. And if nothing else, *Frequency* succeeds because it *does* leave the viewer pondering the question at its base: "What if . . . ?"

THE BLACK FACTOR

Issue #4: One of the best actors You've Never Seen—Andre Braugher as Satch DeLeon cum "Frank Pembleton." You've never seen this actor play to his full potential, until you've seen him on stage, or even in *Homicide*, or in the Spike Lee joint *Get on the Bus*. More's the pity—because Braugher's one baaad mutha (shut yo' mouf) when he's allowed to cut loose. Forget the conditional "Black"; he's one of the best *actors* out there, period. Here's to Braugher, Being Seen.

That having been said, Braugher did not "age well" in this movie. Given that there were 30 years between the time that he knew both Sullivan men, Satch should have looked a lot older than he did in his scenes with Caviezel. Except for a few bags under his eyes and a gray hair or two, there was hardly any noticeable change in Satch. I know, "Black don't crack," but whoever dropped the ball in makeup needs to be whupped.

BAMMER'S BOTTOM LINE

Frequency isn't great, and the science (fiction) is iffy, but the special effects were very well done, and the audience was cheering and crying in all the right spots. It's certainly worth a look-see. But stop me before I say something corny like "received transmission loud and clear."

GREEN LIGHT

The Green Mile
(1999)

RATED R; running time 187 minutes

GENRE: Drama

WRITTEN BY: Frank Darabont, from a novel by Stephen King

DIRECTED BY: Frank Darabont

CAST: Tom Hanks, David Morse, Bonnie Hunt, Michael Clarke Duncan, James Cromwell, Michael Jeter, Graham Greene, Doug Hutchison, Sam Rockwell, Barry Pepper, Jeffrey DeMunn

Magical Negro Alert!!

THE DIGEST

The story in *The Green Mile* is being told some 60 years later by Paul Edgecomb (Dabbs Greer) to a friend. While watching a Fred Astaire movie at the home for the elderly where he now resides, Paul is overcome with grief and needs to cleanse his soul. He recalls a time in his life when he was 44 years old and the head prison guard on "The Green Mile," the name of the death row at the state prison. It's named for the fact that floors are green and you feel as if you are walking a mile when heading to the electric chair. Younger Paul (Tom Hanks) rules The Mile with kid gloves. His philosophy is that you must treat the men on The Mile with dignity and respect. These men are under enough strain as it is, and if you heap more on them, they are likely to snap. They have nothing to lose, so they will be more apt to really hurt someone.

One day, Paul is informed that The Green Mile will be getting a new prisoner. Measuring 7 feet and 350 lbs., John Coffey (Michael Clarke Duncan) is a big man. Another guard, Brutus (David Morse), who is an imposing man himself, is stunned when he sees Coffey and asks Paul to come and take a look. Paul is floored, but, instinctively, not scared at all. He leads John to his cell and removes the shackles and cuffs. He asks John if there will be any problems, and John, with tears in his eyes, says, "Naw, Boss, but do you leave the lights on at night? I'm scared of the dark in places I don't know too well." All of the guards are speechless. Here is this man that can crush all of them, and he is soft-spoken and scared of the dark. Paul immediately gets the case file and reads up on why John is there.

John has been convicted of the rape and murder of two little White girls. He is found holding their broken and bloody bodies and crying. His first statement was: "I tried to stop it but it was too late. I couldn't take it back." He is immediately tried and sent to "The Mile" under the care of Paul.

Paul is confused. How can a man who is afraid of the dark have committed this crime? It just doesn't wash with him. But he isn't moved to do anything about it. Then miracles begin to happen. John just knows things. He feels things. He doesn't know why God smiled on him, but He did. He has given John the ability to feel the soul of a person; a gift that has the potential to destroy everything around him or make everything better. His decisions change the lives of everyone on The Mile.

THE DISH

Phenomenal. Superb. Outstanding.

There will be people who hate this movie. It's three hours long and the story drags a bit. There are going to be people who complain about the racial issue (see "The Black Factor"). I strongly encourage you to set that aside and just watch the film. Applaud Michael Clarke Duncan for his treatment of John Coffey. Duncan was able to understand that God touched John, and as such he should not beat us over the head with his portrayal. John needed to be mellow, shy, sensitive, and sad. Coffey knew that he had to be meek despite his enormous size, and, lastly, he knew he had to show John as a man whose soul was in pain.

There wasn't one flawed performance in the entire movie. A lot of the credit for this should go to writer-director Frank Darabont. This is the second time he has tackled a Stephen King novel, the first time being *The Shawshank Redemption.* Complex and multilayered, Stephen King's books are very difficult to adapt to the screen without taking many liberties and cutting lots of corners. The end result is usually a movie that tanks at the box office—*Christine, Firestarter, Maximum Overdrive,* and *Sleepwalkers,* just to name a few. Darabont has managed to keep creative control in order to uphold the integrity of the original story. If that means a three-hour movie, then so be it.

There are many memorable characters and scenes. I will never forget John, his eyes filled with tears, as he holds a mouse in his giant hands. I'll never forget the determination in the eyes of Brutus when he chooses to risk his job. Nor will I forget the sadness in the eyes of Paul

Edgecomb when he abides by John's wish, a wish that he thinks will be an abomination before God.

THE BLACK FACTOR

Now some Black folks are going to be *pissed.* At the onset, it appears as if this is yet another movie about a White savior of a Black man. I saw it as the exact opposite. I saw this movie as one where the Black man is the savior of the White men. Nonetheless, it is hard to listen to some of the Whites refer to Big John as "nigger" and "negra." Thankfully, this doesn't happen very often.

THE DIRECTIVE

Don't just rent *The Green Mile;* add it to your video collection. They don't get much better than this.

GREEN LIGHT

High Fidelity
(2000)

RATED PG; running time 113 minutes
GENRE: Comedy
WRITTEN BY: D. V. DeVincentis & Steve Pink & John Cusack and Scott Michael Rosenberg, based on the novel by Nick Hornby
DIRECTED BY: Stephen Frears
CAST: John Cusack, Jack Black, Lisa Bonet, Joan Cusack, Iben Hjejle, Todd Louiso, Tim Robbins, Lili Taylor, Natasha Wagner

THE DIGEST
Rob Gordon (John Cusack) is a normal, if not a bit extreme guy. He owns a record shop that specializes in actual records. Y'all remember what records are, right? He and his two employees, Barry (Jack Black) and Dick (Todd Louiso), spend the day making Top 5 list. The movie opens with Rob making the ultimate Top 5 list. His girlfriend of the past few years has left and he is going over his Top 5 all-time break-ups. At some point, Rob decides to contact the women in the Top 5 to get some closure. At the same time, he is trying to win back his latest girlfriend, Laura (Iben Hjejle).

The more he tries to get Laura back, the more she pushes him away and this causes his meltdown, a meltdown that Barry and Dick get the brunt of. They take it in stride, providing the funniest scenes in the movie.

THE DISH
What is it about John Cusack that makes me run out and see his movies? Is it the fact that I was a teenager in the '80s, raised on John Hughes? Is it that every eclectic character John plays is memorable and well portrayed? Is it because he is such a damn good actor? Or is it because he, along with his sister, Jan, and actors such as Andre Braugher, Sean Penn, Tim Robbins, Susan Sarandon, and Alfre Woodard have carved out a special niche in Hollywood? a niche that keeps pushing the limits and producing quality cinema.

But Cusack wasn't the only delight. Jack Black as Barry, is an absolute hoot in this movie. Other smart casting decisions made the movie enjoyable. Lisa Bonet puts in an appearance as a folk singer. Who knew she could sing? It was also nice seeing "Denise Huxtable" on screen. Between the story and the cast, there are a few surprises and an uncredited cameo. The movie is worth seeing. But as much as I liked this film, I do have to point out that it is slow in parts and has some very large plot holes, which, when I wasn't laughing at Jack Black (who can "sang," y'all), I spent a fair amount of energy trying to figure out.

THE DIRECTIVE
Check it out for 113 minutes of fun and laughs—and if you're a Cusack fan, then it's a must-see.

FLASHING YELLOW LIGHT

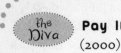

Pay It Forward
(2000)

RATED PG-13; running time 122 minutes
GENRE: Dramedy
WRITTEN BY: Catherine Ryan Hyde (book) and
   Leslie Dixon
DIRECTED BY: Mimi Leder
CAST: Haley Joel Osment, Kevin Spacey, Helen
   Hunt, Jon Bon Jovi, Angie Dickinson, Jay
   Mohr

THE DIGEST

It's the first day of school for seventh grader
Trevor McKinney (Haley Joel Osment). It's also
the first day at a new school for Eugene Simonet
(Kevin Spacey), Trevor's social science teacher.
Eugene has severe burn scars, and he uses the
awkward silence among the students to inspire
them with his extra credit assignment. He challenges the kids to find something they don't like
about the world and change it. Most of the kids
pick tasks that are easy to accomplish. Starting
a recycling program, writing to the president,
painting over graffiti, etc. Trevor takes it a step
further. He wants to start what he calls "Pay It
Forward." Trevor decides that he must help three
people who cannot help themselves. In return,
instead of repaying him, those three people must
each help three people, and it goes on exponentially.

Trevor's first task is to help a homeless man
get back on his feet. Much to the chagrin of his
mother, Arlene (Helen Hunt), he brings the man
into their home. This upsets Arlene to the point
where she rushes to the school and confronts Eugene. He explains to her what the assignment is.
He just wants the boy to try. The meeting leaves
an impression on both of them, and Trevor then
decides that it's his duty to help his mother and
his teacher get together.

Meanwhile, unbeknownst to him, "Pay It Forward" is slowly making its way across the country. A reporter becomes a recipient and starts to
track down the story. No one can believe that it
was a young 11-year-old and a class assignment
that has got people all across the country doing
random acts of kindness for strangers.

THE DISH

Grab a Kleenex. We were all crying. Even the men
who were trying to play it off.

Stellar performances from everyone. On the
screen everyone displayed raw emotion. I was impressed with Spacey as Lester Burnham in *American Beauty*, but Eugene Simonet was also superb.
I've never seen Helen Hunt in such a vulnerable
role. What can I say about Haley? This young
man has something.

THE BLACK FACTOR

As astounded as I was by the movie, you know
I had a few issues, right? I'm less than thrilled
with the portrayal of the people of color in this
film. There was one jackass in this movie.
ONE. He was a brotha. He paid it forward like
he was supposed to. No problem. In fact, he
plans to pay it forward while he is in jail. My
issue? The only significant Black person in
this movie spends time in the slammer and he
has a foul mouth. Everything was "Nigga"
this, "Nigga" that. Was he keeping it real? Per-

haps. Could he have been a workaholic instead of a gangster? Sure, why not? Why not break some stereotypes? There was a brief moment when I saw his intelligence: It was almost as if he was acting hardcore to cover up the fact that he was smart and had a good heart. *Sigh*. I guess I can't have my cake and eat it too. My other issue? The thugs at school were Hispanic. Also, a 3BC fan pointed out that in the book upon which the movie is based, the teacher is a Black Vietnam vet. My colleague wrote, "When I read the book I was thinking they'd maybe cast Denzel Washington and perhaps Michelle Pfeiffer. I am not Black but it does seem unfair that when there are so few good roles for good actors like Denzel, they'd go and deliberately take one away (even though Kevin Spacey is great too, but . . .)"

Now I've got even more issues.

THE DIRECTIVE

This is a gut-wrenching story that manipulates the heartstrings. Even with all of my issues, the performances were so dynamic that *Pay It Forward* is worth renting.

GREEN LIGHT

The Royal Tenenbaums
(2001)

Bams

RATED R; running time 108 minutes
GENRE: Dramedy
WRITTEN BY: Wes Anderson, Owen Wilson
DIRECTED BY: Wes Anderson
CAST: Gene Hackman, Anjelica Huston, Ben Stiller, Gwyneth Paltrow, Luke Wilson, Owen Wilson, Danny Glover, Bill Murray, Kumar Pallana, Grant Rosenmeyer, Jonah Meyerson, Alec Baldwin (narrator)

THE STORY
Let's tell this Dysfunctional Folks 'R' Us story *Magnolia*-style, shall we?

Royal Tenenbaum (Gene Hackman), estranged and strange patriarch, wants to push his way back into his family's life; he uses their housekeeper Pagoda (Kumar Pallana) as a spy.

Etheline Tenenbaum (Anjelica Huston), who has finally put Royal behind her after raising their genius offspring on her own, is writing a book about them—*Family of Geniuses*—and is falling in love with accountant Henry Sherman (Danny Glover) along the way.

Chas Tenenbaum (Ben Stiller), is a financial tycoon who has issues with the cold way his father treated him as a child. Still grieving over his dead wife, Chas overprotects his sons Ari and Uzi.

Margot Tenenbaum (Gwyneth Paltrow), is a prize-winning playwright whom Royal never let forget that she was adopted. Married to Raleigh St. Claire (Bill Murray), a brilliant author and researcher in his own right, Margot leads a secretive, and very unhappy, life.

Richie Tenenbaum (Luke Wilson), a pro tennis player who has sympathy for Royal, deep feelings for his sister, and issues with her husband.

Richie's best friend is Eli Cash (Owen Wilson), also an author; Eli wanted to be one of the Tenenbaums.

THE UPSHOT

Despite what you may have heard, this movie is *not* a straight-up comedy. It has comedic elements, some of which will likely catch you off-guard. But don't think that writers Wes Anderson and Owen Wilson (Eli) were aiming strictly for your funny bone; at least, not without a side trip to your thinking cap. This movie deals with the dysfunctions rampant in a somewhat-loveless family. But is it really loveless? True, of the many characters in this ensemble film, only Royal and Chas seemed to display anything resembling an emotion; but I got the distinct feeling that in spite of their dysfunctions, they loved each other very deeply. If not for love, who would stick with such wack people?

The casting seemed a bit off. It should've been a no-brainer for real-life, look-alike brothers Luke and Owen Wilson to play the brothers here, with Ben Stiller instead playing the wacky friend. Gene Hackman seemed right in his element as the gregarious Royal; Stiller did anal quite well (hmm . . . maybe that's not the right choice of words); Owen Wilson again played his type right on the money; and if Gwyneth Paltrow was going for disaffected waif, she nailed it. But I'm at a loss as to what Bill Murray's whole deal was. The same can be said of Anjelica Huston—

who never seemed to be about much—and Danny Glover, who seemed to serve more as a plot point than a realized character, at least until the end.

Finally, I kept searching for hidden meaning in every frame. Beyond the glorious attention to detail by director Anderson and this movie's art department (somebody get that group a raise; those weird paintings alone are worth the price of admission), I tried rooting out all parables, because, surely, the costumes they wore throughout the movie, those trashed gypsy cabs, and the Green Line buses *had* to mean something, right? Or I could be totally wrong; *The Royal Tenenbaums* could just be yet another weird-ass movie about people whose lives are totally outside my ability to fathom. Only they aren't. I've known an absent father; I understand a widowed son; I totally get a distant daughter, a neglected husband, a bewildered mother. The package these people were presented in might look different from the outside, but the contents inside are quite familiar. Well, except for the incestuous bit. That I don't get.

BAMMER'S BOTTOM LINE

Bammer sez watch this movie. Your madness may vary from my own, but at least you will have had the opportunity to judge whether *The Royal Tenenbaums* is bloody brilliant, or bloody awful, for yourself.

GREEN LIGHT

The Score
(2001)

RATED R; running time 123 minutes
GENRE: Thriller
WRITTEN BY: Daniel E. Taylor and Kario Salem
(story) Kario Salem, Lem Dobbs and Scott
Marshall Smith (screenplay)
DIRECTED BY: Frank Oz
CAST: Robert De Niro, Edward Norton, Angela
Bassett, Marlon Brando, Jamie Harrold

> Mr. Oz is also the voice of Kermit the Frog
> and Yoda.

THE DIGEST

Nick Wells (Robert De Niro) has been living a full life for some years now. On most days, he is the owner of an upscale jazz club in Montreal. On other days, he is a safe cracker. Nick is ready to give it all up and just concentrate on his club and work on his relationship with his longtime girlfriend, Diane (Angela Bassett). Well, his best friend and "fence" for the last 25 years, Max (Marlon Brando), has other plans. Max has come across a scepter that belonged to King Louis XIV, worth about 30 million dollars. Max has mounting debts and has set his eyes on that prize. First, he must convince Nick to take the gig. Max has a contact in the customs office where the scepter is being held—an arrogant upstart named Jackie (Edward Norton) who has zero respect for Nick. That's only part of the problem. Nick prefers to work alone. He likes to be in control of the situation, and with Jackie, he has no control whatsoever.

The cut that Max offers proves to be too much for Nick to pass on. He convinces himself that with this final gig, he will have enough money to give up his life of crime and settle down with Diane. He'll be home free as long as Jackie doesn't blow it with his constant second-guessing and immature mistakes.

THE DISH

Good movie, but that the filmmakers underutilized Angela Bassett was very disappointing. There was really no point in her being in the movie. There was no point in having *any* female interest in the movie, for that matter, because the character was not fleshed out enough. Diane appeared about every 30 minutes, swapped spit with Nick, and then she was gone.

I loved Marlon Brando, though his voice, which sounded like Minnie Mouse, was annoying. Another surprise was Jamie Harrold playing a twentysomething superhacker. The 10 minutes of screen time he had, had me cracking up. He was a stereotypical hacker: living in his parents' basement, surviving on pizza and Jolt, and working on the computer 20 hours a day. Even though I was laughing at him, I have to tell you that he would not have been my child. The way he spoke to his mother was horrible! Nevertheless, a techie myself, I'm glad he was in the movie.

It is very difficult to match De Niro on screen. He chews up every scene and spits it out, and whomever he is working with is left in the dust. Not so this time. I think De Niro really toned things down and let "Nick" be mellow, laid back, and a little vulnerable. Also, I think that Edward Norton is one of the most underrated actors around (check out *Primal Fear*). He really has begun to master his craft. I've even begun to forgive him for *Fight Club* (see page 78).

Not everything was perfect, mind you. The plot started to wind down in the middle of the heist, so the ending was a bit anti-climactic. But despite this, I really enjoyed myself. It was wonderful to watch a movie for adults.

THE DIRECTIVE

The Score is a great date movie for the singles in the house. And for the married with children, grab a dinner and a movie.

GREEN LIGHT

The Thomas Crown Affair
(1999)

RATED R; running time 109 minutes

GENRE: Action/Thriller

WRITTEN BY: Leslie Dixon & Kurt Wimmer, based on the 1968 screenplay by Alan R. Trustman

DIRECTED BY: John McTiernan

CAST: Pierce Brosnan, Rene Russo, Denis Leary, Ben Gazzara, Frankie Faison, Fritz Weaver, Charles Keating, Mark Margolis, Faye Dunaway

THE DIGEST

Thomas Crown (Pierce Brosnan) owns an acquisition firm and is a very rich man. His passions are swallowing up other companies and fine art. Thomas decides to steal a painting worth $100 million. It's never clear why he does it, because clearly he can afford to buy it. Nor are we privy to how he sets up the heist. We just know he steals it. Katherine Banning (Rene Russo) is a bounty hunter who is hired by the insurance company to investigate the theft. She sniffs out Thomas Crown as the culprit immediately, something the New York Police Department was unable to do. The movie takes off as they begin to play a game of cat and mouse. They constantly try to "one up" each other, each one meeting the challenge and taking it a step further.

You sense that they both are having fun and you, the audience, are having fun right along with them. I found myself torn between wanting her to catch him and wanting him to get away. Trying to guess what the next move was going to be, it was like watching a chess game evolve on the screen.

THE DISH

There was definite chemistry between Brosnan and Russo. They left us, the audience, on the edge of our seats with anticipation. It was refreshing to see two very sexy 40+-year-olds interact with each other on this level. I'm so sick of seeing men playing opposite women young enough to be their daughters when there are plenty of qualified actresses who are closer to their age. This movie was funny, smart, intriguing, and well written, acted, and directed. It was a breath of fresh air. And, as a woman, I enjoyed seeing Katherine Banning stay a step ahead of the seasoned detectives played by Frankie Faison and Dennis Leary.

THE DIRECTIVE

If the only affair with Thomas Crown you'll get is a vicarious one, thanks to a trip to the local video store, it'll be worth the trip.

GREEN LIGHT

Bams Vanilla Sky
(2001)

RATED R; running time 145 minutes

GENRE: Drama/Thriller

WRITTEN BY: Cameron Crowe (based on the film by Alejandro Amenabar and Mateo Gil)

DIRECTED BY: Cameron Crowe

CAST: Tom Cruise, Penélope Cruz, Cameron Diaz, Kurt Russell, Jason Lee, Timothy Spall

THE STORY

David Aames (Tom Cruise) is a man who has everything: fast cars, hot chicks, and a publishing firm left to him by his well-respected, famous father. But perhaps everything is not as it seems. It appears that David's life, in many aspects, is but a dream. The car he owns is a Mustang, not a Ferrari. His publishing firm is only tenuously his, with the board members he unaffectionately calls "The Seven Dwarfs" waiting anxiously to wrest control away from him. And his bedmate, Julie Gianni (Cameron Diaz)? Let's just say our boy Dave doesn't spend his time checking for birds to appear every time she is near.

Still and all, David has a good life. But things change for him rather quickly when Julie rips a page out of the *Alex Forrest Manual Of F**k Buddies* (their words, not mine), sending David tumbling painfully down that rabbit hole. David tries to cling to some semblance of normality, desperately wanting to pursue Sofia Serrano (Penélope Cruz), the almost-girlfriend of his friend Brian Shelby (Jason Lee). But a murder, a reanimated dog, and a psychologist Dr. Curtis McCabe (Kurt Russell), who tries to unscramble David's brain, get in the way.

THE UPSHOT

I freely admit, Tom Cruise makes my skin crawl. He may be cute and all, but I'd love to forcefully wipe that ever-present smirk off his face. More important, I just don't think he's that good an actor. All these things, of course, inform my admittedly biased view of his performance.

But even if I liked, or at least could tolerate Cruise, the story in *Vanilla Sky* is told in such a drawn-out, tedious, unfocused way that this movie would've been one I'd have easily walked out of, á la *Face/Off*, back in my pre–3 Black Chicks days. For me, it was a done deal when I saw Steven "A.I." Spielberg in a cameo. This was within the first 30 minutes of this flick. I'm not even sure this movie would've improved with a radical edit.

No one escaped here: Cruise, of course, is a given; Penélope Cruz, whom I actually like, seemed to be in another movie entirely; Cameron Diaz suffered from having to play not only a pathetic role, but one in a movie that used her character as a means to drive the plot forward instead of as a character in her own right; and Jason Lee just didn't have enough screen time to make his presence known (as opposed to Kurt Russell, whose psychologist character was just more flotsam added to the overloaded pile of jetsam). Actually, I would've preferred to see more of Thomas Tipp (Timothy Spall) and the Dwarfs rather than the glamorous rich trio of David, Sophia, and Julie; there's something about lumpy old guys that appeals to me.

The sole, higher-than-red-light saving grace of this bland concoction was that, past its desperation to be Lynchianly Trippy, *Vanilla Sky* did at least accomplish its otherworldliness without resorting to Kewl Future tricks. I give Crowe props for reining it in in that sense; controlling the environment of *Vanilla Sky* to look no different than any Lifestyles of the Sick and Shameless background. Not that that's something to aim for. I'm just sayin'.

BAMMER'S BOTTOM LINE

Vanilla Sky proves again that a bunch of mumbo-jumbo nonsense muddled together in a long-running package does not a deep thriller make. What a misnomer: even vanilla has more flavor than what this flick serves up. Blech.

YELLOW LIGHT

Bams **Whipped**
(1999)

RATED R; running time 85 minutes
GENRE: Comedy
WRITTEN BY: Peter M. Cohen
DIRECTED BY: Peter M. Cohen
CAST: Amanda Peet, Brian Van Holt, Zorie Barber, Jonathan Abrahams, Judah Domke, Callie Thorne

THE STORY

Brad, Zeke, and Jonathan are three wild-and-crazy guys who get together for weekly Sunday brunches, along with their married (and thus, no longer wild or crazy), completely whipped friend, Eric, to compare notes on their female conquests over the past week. All's well in their individual worlds—studly stockbroker Brad, horndog beatnik Zeke, and sensitive, onanistic Jonathan imagine themselves quite the ladies' men, and have the raunchy stories to prove it—until they each find a woman who completes them; someone who is more than their match. Who knew Mia (Amanda Peet) would be the perfect fit for *each* of them?

THE UPSHOT

I can enjoy a raucous film every now and then. I can groove on comedies in which the humor is derived from base situations (the basest of which, some might say, is Gettin' Some)—as long as the premise or the characters don't insult my intelligence. And for me, *Whipped* fit that bill nicely.

There's nothing very deep about it, no truth

that would forever alter the viewer. And the moral at the end—that the way (some) men troll for chicks is muy lame—is likewise nothing new. I was appreciative that *Whipped* avoided the patronizingly typical way most flicks of this nature try to depict the boy-likes-girl-likes-other-boy-likes-same-girl-likes-other-boy.

The "feel" of the film was quite appealing. Multiple elements—from the nicely done opening credits, to the "weekly" titles (I admit, I'm a sucker for inside-joke titles), and even the overdone-on-TV breaking of the fourth wall (where the characters talk directly to the camera as if they are being interviewed)—took this movie to a different place than its subject matter would suggest it belonged. And indeed, the feel of the movie helped it overcome some glaring flaws that might have otherwise been deal-breakers, including the incredibly immature way the male characters (especially Brad) spoke, as if the actors (or writer) thought they were in a high-school flick, and the fact that at least two of the characters (Zeke and Jonathan) were anything but the God's Gift To Women that they thought themselves to be. In fact, I'd be shocked to find that New York women were *really* that hard up; those two guys were by no means All That. The point being, my Disbelief had a hard time staying Suspended when it came to taking this motley trio at face value as being Playas. That aside, *Whipped* moved along at a good pace, though I was disappointed that Amanda Peet as Mia didn't have a much bigger speaking part. I would've walked away completely disappointed if it hadn't been for her ending scenes. Even with that, her Mia was more a concept than a fully developed character.

The trio of bachelors, and the obligatory married guy friend against whom the trio measured themselves, were the true stars of this show. Actors Van Holt, Barber, Domke, and Abrahams (respectively), performed their jobs quite well.

And the biggest kick of all, for me? Seeing Callie "gag" Thorne play the kind of inconsequential sleazy slut, for which her acting abilities were obviously ho'd . . . oops, I mean, honed. Talk about your perfect casting.

THE BLACK FACTOR

Often, when I watch a "White" movie (which begs the question of what constitutes a "White" or a "Black" movie, but that's another topic for another time), I wonder to myself, "Self, could you imagine this as a 'Black' movie?" And in the case of *Whipped*, the answer was easily "yes." But I can't help but wonder: had it been a "Black" film, could the creative folks behind it have avoided playing it along the lines of *Booty Call* or *The Players Club?*

Whipped earned my admiration precisely because, though much of the posturing was there, it had the foresight to avoid the clichés inherent in the situations it depicts and tackle the questions it asked in a somewhat more mature fashion.

Now, before anyone gets all upset, note that I am *not* saying White "Booty Call" flicks are better than Black "Booty Call" flicks by default. What I *am* saying is, in this specific case, the makers of *Whipped* overcame its predecessors' faults by making the *way* they told the story much more interesting and much less pathetically and stereotypically obvious (though to some degree, just as titillating) in the end. Ka peech?

So, what does this say about *Black* flicks within this genre? Maybe nothing. But it does say something about the audience for such films. Folks like me could tolerate the "Booty Call" flicks more if they had some substance behind their empty-calories style. I don't see nuttin' wrong with a little bump-n-grind. But surely We can do better than yet another long-form BET video, right? Uh, right?

BAMMER'S BOTTOM LINE

While it's nowhere near gut-bustin' funny, *Whipped* does provide an entertaining and refreshingly different look at the oldest war in the book: the war of the sexes. Take note, fellas: those wack lines y'all use are *transparent*.

GREEN LIGHT

9

Not too long ago, the mere mention of "Chick Flick" easily brought images of sniffling women to mind. You could just see a group of women crowded into a theater and watching a movie about "How he done her wrong!", all the while passing tissues back and forth. Or you could picture a group of women sitting in the theater fuming while watching a movie about the best girlfriend sleeping with the husband.

Well, those days are long gone (we hope). Yes, we still have so-called tearjerkers, but we also have chicks out there kicking some serious booty. Along with the tears (*Girl, Interrupted*), the ass-kicking (*The Long Kiss Goodnight*), and the damsel in distress (*The Contender*), we have some laughter (*Charlie's Angels*), too.

African Queen
(1951)

UNRATED; running time 104 minutes

GENRE: War drama

WRITTEN BY: C. S. Forrester (novel); adapted
for the screen by James Agee and John Huston

DIRECTED BY: John Huston

CAST: Humphrey Bogart, Katharine Hepburn,
Robert Morley, Peter Bull, Theodore Bikel

> Bette Davis was supposed to play Rose,
> but Bette got pregnant and had to bow
> out.

THE DIGEST

It's 1914 in German-occupied Africa, and Rose
Sayer (Katharine Hepburn) is a missionary with
her brother, Reverend Sam Sayer (Robert Morley), in a small African village. The two Britons
have taken on the seemingly arduous task (heavy
sarcasm) of converting the local savages to Chris-
tianity (end sarcasm).

All of their work seems for naught, because,
they are informed by the local river trader and
captain of the *African Queen*, Charlie Allnut
(Humphrey Bogart), that World War I has begun
and there is a good possibility that the Germans
might come by and bother them. Sure enough,
the Germans come through and burn their village to the ground just because they are royal
British subjects. All this proves to be too much
for the Reverend, which leaves his sister to completely fend for herself. Thankfully, Charlie decides to take Rose with him down the river to
safety.

Can a sinner and a missionary manage to stay
together for weeks, without going at each other's
throats? Rose and Charlie sure put that query to
test and they almost fail.

THE DISH

This was a great movie, but not a great movie for
me. At the beginning of the movie, Charlie
throws his cigar on the ground in front of the locals like one would throw meat at a pack of dogs.
This really upset me. But with these types of situations, you have to take it in context. The movie
was set in 1914 and made in 1951, not exactly the
times of racial sensitivity. Such insensitivity has
made it very hard for me to objectively look at
some of Hollywood's "classics," many of which
were filmed or set in a time when there was zero
respect for minorities. Not that they respect Us
all that much now, but it's a lot better than it was.

Apart from the above, I did enjoy this movie.
The witty repartee between Humphrey and Hepburn rivaled the exchanges between them and
their usual partners, Lauren Bacall and Spencer
Tracy. For 90 minutes it's just those two, and I
found myself not even caring. In fact, I was disappointed when it was no longer just them floating down the river in the *Queen*.

THE DIRECTIVE

African Queen is well worth renting. Just remember to take everything in context.

GREEN LIGHT

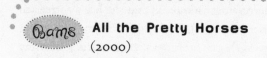

Bams All the Pretty Horses
(2000)

RATED PG-13; running time 132 minutes

GENRE: Drama

WRITTEN BY: Ted Tally (based on the book by Cormac McCarthy)

DIRECTED BY: Billy Bob Thornton

CAST: Matt Damon, Henry Thomas, Penélope Cruz, Lucas Black, Rubén Blades, Miriam Colon, Robert Patrick, Bruce Dern, Sam Shepard

> All though he is known primarily as an actor, this is not the first time Billy Bob Thornton has directed a movie. That honor goes to *Sling Blade* (1996).

THE STORY

Texas, circa 1940. John Grady Cole (Matt Damon) is the last in a long line of Texas cowboys; "last," because after his beloved grandfather's death, Cole's shortsighted mother decides to sell the ranch, breaking John's heart. A cowboy through and through, Cole heads off on horseback for Mexico with his friend and sidekick, Lacey Rawlins (Henry Thomas).

Not long after they set out, they come across young upstart Jimmy Blevins (Lucas Black) whom they let tag along with them toward their destination. They eventually reach the ranch of Don Hector de la Rocha (Rubén Blades), whose family, like John's, has owned their ranch for generations. John takes comfort in this, and feels that he's found his new home. He also takes comfort in the company of de la Rocha's beautiful daughter, Alejandra (Penélope Cruz), much to the consternation of Alejandra's aunt Alfonsa; soon, all hell breaks loose.

THE UPSHOT

Director Billy Bob Thornton once lamented that people in this Video Age have the attention span of a gnat and those people might not have an appreciation for *All the Pretty Horses*. Apparently, this isn't the kind of film a heathen gnat like me is interested in. Me, or the snoring gentleman in the row behind me. At least I managed to stay awake the whole time. Maybe not quite *alert*, but awake.

True, the amazing Lucas Black helped keep me awake; the young man has a talent far beyond his years, and I hope that as long as he stays in the business, he remains an actor and doesn't become a Macaulay Culkin–like Star. Writer Ted Tally's adaptation from the best-selling novel wasn't too strange, though hearing Matt Damon's affected drawl and euphemisms did draw a chuckle or two out of me. Penélope Cruz was sufficient as "the beautiful and pouty" love interest as was the Mexican scenery around her, but Rubén Blades was criminally underused, and the balance of the Mexican cast seemed to be there more as props than as characters. Stars Damon and Henry Thomas were fine, within reason.

BAMMER'S BOTTOM LINE

In all fairness, *All the Pretty Horses* isn't *bad*, per se; it's just a film you have to be in the right mood to see. Deliberately slow-paced, it's not for the faint-hearted. Or the sleepy. Or those unimpressed by repetitious slow-motion cuts and me-

andering storytelling. Other than that . . .
zzzzzzzzzzzzzz

YELLOW LIGHT

---

the Diva   Angel Eyes
(2001)

RATED R; running time 101 minutes
GENRE: Romance/Drama
WRITTEN BY: Gerald Dipego
DIRECTED BY: Luis Mandoki
CAST: Jennifer Lopez, Jim Caviezel, Sonia Braga,
   Terrence Howard, Jeremy Sisto, Shirley Knight

> J. Lo is the highest paid Latina actress *ever*. She commands at least 10 million a picture. Go on, girl! Now if you could just keep the "man" drama out of your life . .

THE DIGEST

Sharon Pogue (Jennifer Lopez) is a hardened yet dedicated Chicago police officer. She spends her nights patrolling the mean and cold streets of the city, while her days are spent in solitude. She's lonely and yearns for companionship, but she can't seem to find the right guy. Lack of a personal life begins to creep into her professional life. Her partner, Robby (Terrence Howard), notices that she's becoming more and more aggressive on the job and tells her about it. She just shuts down and becomes even more bitter. What

Sharon doesn't know is that she has a secret admirer. Catch (Jim Caviezel) roams the same streets that Sharon does, yet he spends his time doing good deeds. Turning off car lights that a driver has left on; letting a neighbor know that they left their keys in the door.

One day, Catch is at the right place at the right time and he crosses paths with Sharon. Now it's her turn to be intrigued. Are these two people meant to be soul mates or are they flirting with disaster? Can they help heal each other's wounds?

THE DISH

Angel Eyes had a lot of potential, but, sadly, it failed, and the main reason it failed was Jennifer Lopez. I have nothing against "J. Lo," but she just didn't capture the vulnerability that Sharon needed. I also felt that there wasn't very much electricity between her and Jim Caviezel. Jim Caviezel, on the other hand, was wonderful. You could look into his eyes and see the pain in his heart. Perhaps that's the problem; Jim was so good that he made J. Lo look mediocre.

My other problems with the movie stem from the writing; as a police officer, Sharon did some pretty idiotic stuff. In addition, the movie periodically lost steam and I found myself looking at my watch.

THE DIRECTIVE

Though promoted as a thriller or scary movie, *Angel Eyes* is a romantic drama. Whatever the genre, you may need to pray that you don't die from boredom.

YELLOW LIGHT

Charlie's Angels
(2000)

RATED PG-13; running time 98 minutes
GENRE: Action/Comedy
WRITTEN BY: Ryan Rowe, Ed Solomon and
John August
DIRECTED BY: McG
CAST: Drew Barrymore, Cameron Diaz, Lucy
Liu, Bill Murray, Tim Curry, Sam Rockwell

> All of the original Angels were offered
> parts, which they turned down.

THE DIGEST

Charlie (voiced by John Forsyth) is back and he
has a new set of Angels. This time around, we
have Dylan (Drew Barrymore), Natalie (Cameron
Diaz), and Alex (Lucy Liu). These three ladies are
very different from Angels of the past. For
starters, they are well versed in martial arts and
electronics (their only weapons). Dylan is the resident bad girl—sexpot. She dreams of having a father figure in her life. Natalie dreams of being a
dancer. And Alex dreams of putting her privileged
life behind her and becoming a family woman.

The three Angels are called upon to solve a
case involving a geeky software developer who
has been kidnapped along with his software. If
the software "gets into the wrong hands," it will
affect global privacy, the wrong hands being
those of Roger Corwin (Tim Curry). The Angels
must use all of their cunning and smarts to re-
claim both the software and the software developer, Knox (Sam Rockwell).

THE DISH

I loved *Charlie's Angels*. Yes, I know it's basically a
T&A action film, but how is that different from
the TV show, which was pretty stupid? People
tuned in to watch hair flipping and boobs flop-
ping. It certainly wasn't for the dialogue or the
plot. Drew Barrymore (she is also the producer)
and the writers understood this. They didn't try
to make the movie serious or change the concept.
And that's why I loved this movie. The cast was
having fun parodying themselves.

The special effects were cool if a bit unbelievable. My favorite scenes were the ones that had
the Angels kicking butt, and "The Soul Train"
scene. When Diaz broke out and started doing
the Robot, I died. And I loved how they used music throughout the film.

THE DIRECTIVE

Charlie's Angels is a nice diversion. Just dumb
down, stare at the screen, and set your expectations low.

GREEN LIGHT

 **The Contender**
(2000)

RATED R; running time 126 minutes
GENRE: Political drama
WRITTEN BY: Rod Lurie
DIRECTED BY: Rod Lurie
CAST: Joan Allen, Gary Oldman, Jeff Bridges, Sam Elliott, Christian Slater, William L. Petersen, Saul Rubinek, Robin Thomas, Mike Binder, Philip Baker Hall, Mariel Hemingway, Kathryn Morris, Kristen Shaw

> Joan Allen was nominated for Best Actress for this role.

THE STORY

The Clinton era is over, yet there's another Democratic White House with yet another sex scandal on its hands: this time, involving an ex-Republican of the female persuasion.

The vice president of the United States has died, and President Jackson Evans (Jeff Bridges) searches for a replacement amongst his Democratic party. A candidate, Governor Jack Hathaway (William L. Petersen), is proposed after he heroically tries to rescue a woman whose car crashes into the river in which he's fishing. But the shadow of Ted Kennedy is cast much too wide for Hathaway to escape, and Evans and his chief of staff, Kermit Newman (Sam Elliott), reject Hathaway on the basis of possible misperception and potential innuendo.

Wanting someone who looks good above all, Evans decides on naming Senator Laine Hanson

(Joan Allen) as his new VP. Insisting that the reason for not wanting Hanson in the Number Two spot has nothing to do with her gender, but that she certainly wouldn't be appointed "just because" she's a woman, young Democratic Senator Reginald Webster (Christian Slater) seeks out Shelly Runyon (Gary Oldman), the Republican chairman running the VP confirmation committee, asking if he could be part of Runyon's committee. Before the confirmation hearings begin (using tactics that "even the FBI wouldn't touch"), Runyon and Webster discover that Hanson may have had a scandalous sexual past. They then set out to destroy any chance of Hanson ever seeing the White House from the seat of power.

THE UPSHOT

My jaded snarkasm is, I think, my biggest moviewatching handicap. Let *one* teeny bit of nonsense be shown on screen like, say, the portrayal of an Honest Politician and WHOOSH! the air just squirts right outta my Disbelief's suspension, sending it tumbling . . .

The Contender was chock-full of good performances leading to a dead end. Joan Allen was excellent as the downtrodden, too-good-to-be-true Senator Hanson. Gary Oldman, as the sleazy, slimy Shelly Runyon, immersed himself fully into a role in which he acts and looks completely different from his previous roles; why his name isn't brought up when his contemporaries like Streep and De Niro are mentioned, is beyond me. In two strong supporting roles, Christian Slater as naive junior senator, and especially Sam Elliott as Kermit Newman, often own their scenes. And even though Jeff Bridges' food-obsessed version of the president was too comical for me to get behind, he was Clintonesque enough to be believable throughout the first 100 or so minutes of this flick.

So why'd *The Contender* fail to get the 3BC equivalent of two thumbs up? This movie was like the best passage in a dancehall tune: the passage itself may be great, but in the end, the song just repeats one phrase over and over.

The "one phrase" in *The Contender* split itself in two: on the low octave, it's "Republicans Are Bad, Mean / And Ugly Too"; and in the high register, it's "Look At The Honest Politician Done Wrong / And Taking It Up The Wazoo." And both notes, hit repeatedly and loudly, were enough to deaden my eardrums.

THE BLACK FACTOR

Setting aside the fact that, unless I misremember, the only speaking part a Black actor got in *The Contender* was that of a White House waiter (how's *that* for a rosy outlook of Our role in the Democratic future?), let's focus on The Female Factor and how it comes back to The Black Factor, shall we?

What piqued my curiosity most is that, in some ways, the words "female" and "Black" could be used interchangeably in this movie; couldn't you just hear those senators saying "I don't mind that he's *Black,* but I won't vote for him simply because of that!" or even better, "This is what comes of Affirmative Action!" Terms being somewhat interchangeable or not, though, I doubt that a political movie that *did* interchange them would ever be made. Unless it was a Black movie. Make that a Black comedy. Starring the Wayans Brothers as Stepin and Fetchit.

BAMMER'S BOTTOM LINE

Since my lack of respect for the whole of American politicians informed my suspension of disbelief, I just couldn't take this movie at face value. "The Pretender" is a *much* better title for a portrayal of an Honest Politician, eh?

FLASHING YELLOW LIGHT

Cass Corrina, Corrina
(1994)

RATED PG; running time 115 minutes
GENRE: Comedy/Drama/Romance
WRITTEN BY: Jessie Nelson
DIRECTED BY: Jessie Nelson
CAST: Whoopi Goldberg, Ray Liotta, Tina Majorino, Joan Cusack, Jenifer Lewis

Corrina, Corrina is based on writer/director Jessie Nelson's real life.

CASS'S CLIP

Corrina, Corrina takes place in 1959. Manny Singer is grief-stricken due to the recent death of his beloved wife. Now a single parent, Manny is overwhelmed with the responsibility of raising his seven-year-old daughter, Molly. Manny's job, as a jingles writer, becomes more stressful because Molly has chosen not to speak since the death of her mother. Manny needs a maid to help with household chores as well as a nanny to act as a surrogate mother. *Of course* all the applicants are unacceptable until Manny meets Corrina Washington. Corrina reluctantly interviews for the job because it seems this recent college graduate is only qualified to be a nanny. *Of course* Manny hires Corrina, and therein lays the seemingly heartwarming story of Manny, Molly, and Corrina, and their lives together during this difficult transition.

DA 411

I really wanted to enjoy *Corrina, Corrina* because I'm a big fan of both Ray Liotta and Whoopi Goldberg. But the pairing of these two stars as lovers was as believable as Whoopi and Ted Danson's love affair. On the other hand, Tina Majorino played a realistic seven-year-old Molly. She convinced me that she was motherless, and I felt her sense of loss.

Once the plot was revealed, I couldn't get past one of my major pet peeves: another movie where a Black woman takes care of a White child. Yeah, we all know how much White children love their Black nannies and/or mammies, at least according to the movie industry. In an era of so-called political correctness, why do studio execs continue to depict Black women as subservient workers? Following that logic, since thousands of Black nannies have raised a nation of Caucasians, why do so many bigots and racists *still* exist?

CASS'S CONCLUSION

Whoopi has played this role far too many times that it's not a stretch for this sistah to act.

YELLOW LIGHT

Bams **Coyote Ugly**
(2000)

RATED PG-13; running time 94 minutes
GENRE: Drama (I guess . . .)
WRITTEN BY: Gina Wendkos, Jeff Nathanson
DIRECTED BY: David McNally
CAST: Piper Perabo, Maria Bello, Adam Garcia, Izabella Miko, John Goodman, Tyra Banks, Bridget Moynahan, Melanie Lynskey, Adam Alexi-Malle

> One of the characters states that they are from Piedmont, North Dakota. That's great, except for Piedmont is in South Dakota . . .

THE STORY

Fame! I wanna live forev— . . . oops, wrong flick.

Violet Sandford (Piper Perabo), is a semi-orphaned songwriter who loves her dad (John Goodman) but needs to prove that she can make it in the Big Apple. Violet strikes out on her own. With the naiveté that surely comes from living a mere 42 miles away from New York. Of course, she soon learns that in the mean streets, it's a dog-eat-dog world and if she is indeed going to make it, she'll have to develop a fiercer bite and stop being so gullible: a trait that made her fall for the oldest trick in the "new girl in the Big City" book when she's led to believe that smooth-talking busboy Kevin O'Donnell is a music club owner. Though even *that* connection might not have done her much good: see, she has this big stage fright issue. Seems like Violet just can't get a break.

Enter the women of Coyote Ugly, a "bar" that sells more funky diva attitude than it does booze. When Violet overhears Coyote Divas Zoe (Tyra Banks), Cammie (Isabella Miko), and Rachel (Bridget Moynahan) talking about how well they're paid for doing their combination bartender-dancer-funky-diva routine, Violet convinces bar owner Lil (Maria Bello) to let her become a Coyote, which might be the avenue for her break into Show Bidness.

And on tomorrow's episode of *All My Young and Restless Children* . . .

THE UPSHOT

Yawn! Sorry, fellas. I know that many of y'all were chompin' at the bit to find a nonviolent antidote to the ubiquitous Chick Flicks that you seem to think dominate movie screens. But to those who think that some anorexic-looking, Victoria's Secret–wearing übermodels shaking their booties on a bar provides that long-needed salvo, I ask you: Is that really the best you can do? Nope, I ain't hatin' on those übermodels because they're beautiful. If I could be said to be hatin' on them at all, it's because *Coyote*'s characters and their issues were downright *boring*. Snooze-worthy, *ABC Afterschool Special*–boring.

The actors, confined within the limitations of the script and direction ("Okay girls, shake your booties! Okay—Cut! Okay, Piper, you and Adam do something mushy and romantic here! Okay, Cut!), perform their dubious tasks adequately, though Piper Perabo just does nothing for me. She played naive as just plain dumb, and the results of each of her actions were telegraphed a mile away. John Goodman's big-lug Dad was amusing at first, but eventually wore as thin as

Violet's walls. Bridget Moynahan showed some gusto as Scary Spice . . . er, Rachel, but it all really amounted to lame setups to show how well Violet could "overcome." Only Maria Bello showed up with any semblance of subtlety; her Lil was understated at first, and I had high hopes for her. Until the writers dashed my hopes upon the Wall Of Happy Endings. Bah.

Hey, I don't see nuttin' wrong with a little bump-n-grind. But *too* little, in a movie that's played up to be about strong chicks owning their sexuality just grinds my gizzard. Forget the Britney Spears angle and the dialogue even a porno writer would eschew; let's have more "tittielation," Mr. Hollywood!

THE BLACK FACTOR

I have to give the filmmakers some credit in their adding a new twist on the "Brotha Rule" (see page xv) in the form of Tyra Banks's character Zoe (though I reckon that should really be the "Sistah Rule," eh?). And you can get "Spot the Spot" points. There is a Black guest in the wedding scene who dances with one of the White guests (and trust me: it was mere background noise. If those two characters were dating one another, I'm Barbara Bush).

BAMMER'S BOTTOM LINE

Take away the tits-n-ass in *Coyote Ugly*, and you have the makings of a TV Movie-of-the-Week.

FLASHING RED LIGHT

Girl, Interrupted
(1999)

RATED R; running time 127 minutes
GENRE: Drama
WRITTEN BY: James Mangold (based on the
    book by Susanna Kaysen)
DIRECTED BY: James Mangold
CAST: Winona Ryder, Angelina Jolie, Clea Du-
    Vall, Vanessa Redgrave, Whoopi Goldberg,
    Brittany Murphy, Elizabeth Moss, Jared Leto,
    Jeffrey Tambor, Travis Fine

> Whoopi Goldberg is the only woman to
> have received the prestigious Mark Twain
> Award for Humor.

THE DIGEST

Set in 1967, and based on a true story, *Girl, Inter-rupted* is about Susanna Kaysen, a confused and lost young woman who doesn't know what she wants to do with her life other than write. She doesn't want to get a job. Nor does she want to go to college. To make matters more confusing, she's exploring her sexuality.

The patients at The Claymoore House are a motley crew, from a young lady suffering from anorexia to one who is a sociopath. At first, Susanna is overwhelmed. But after a week, she fits right in. She takes her cues from Lisa (Angelina Jolie), staying on her good side so as not to raise her ire. The facility's head nurse, Valerie (Whoopi Goldberg), also befriends her. Along the way she discovers that she doesn't need Lisa to survive, and it is this that awakens her mind and heart.

THE DISH

The themes from *The Wizard of Oz* run blatantly and predictably throughout this movie. It makes it almost corny. We would have been better served if we could figure that out for ourselves rather than having had it spoonfed to us.

THE BLACK FACTOR

Yet again Whoopi's cast in a role where she is saving a White child: See also *Clara's Heart, Corrina, Corrina* (page 201), *Bogus, The Long Walk Home.* This is not to say that these are bad films; in fact, I enjoyed a few of them. I also maintain that the roles she chooses are not entirely her fault. It's hard enough for a 24-year-old Black woman to get decent roles, let alone a Black woman in her 40s, and I'm also extremely happy that she's at least work-ing. I just wish they gave her more to choose from. She's either the comedic best friend or the savior of all broken White children.

THE DIRECTIVE

A bit predictable but, despite my issues with the movie, I did enjoy it, because it offered a very chilling look into our mental-health system 30 years ago. Thank goodness things have changed.

YELLOW LIGHT

Hanging Up
(2000)

RATED PG-13; running time 92 minutes
GENRE: Comedy/Drama
WRITTEN BY: Nora Ephron (based on the story by Delia Ephron)
DIRECTED BY: Diane Keaton
CAST: Meg Ryan, Diane Keaton, Lisa Kudrow, Walter Matthau, Adam Arkin, Cloris Leachman, Jesse James

> This was Walter Matthau's last picture. He passed away in July of 2000. His best friend of nearly 40 years, Jack Lemmon, followed him 11 months later—passing away in June of 2001.

THE STORY

In what probably sounded better on paper than what was actually realized, Eve (Meg Ryan), Georgia (Diane Keaton), and Maddy (Lisa Kudrow) are sisters who really strain to have issues with each other, with their dying father (Walter Matthau), with their estranged mother (Cloris Leachman), and with the phones that seem to rule their lives.

THE UPSHOT

As the middle of seven sisters, I had been anticipating seeing *Hanging Up* for weeks. Surely, I thought, they'd be addressing issues like the ones I've had with my younger and older siblings for thirtysomething years now. Surely, I thought, I'd leave the theater with a better understanding of the mystique that is sisterhood—or at least, pleased at having been able to identify with the chicks on screen ("yeah girl, my sister tried to play that sh . . . tuff too!")

Boy, was I wrong. This movie can be summed up in a single phrase: the Ephron sisters (Nora and Delia, cowriters of this dud) need to keep their boring issues to themselves.

I tried, Lord knows I did, to find *something* to write about. The storyline just bored me to tears, being linear and obvious as it was; the acting was tedious; the dog was as unnecessary as the unfortunate inclusion of Adam Arkin as Eve's husband, Joe, and Jesse James as their son, Jesse (not that they did anything wrong, per se, only that they were just so much dead wood in a forest full of logs); Diane Keaton's direction was uninspiring; and the whole phone gimmick was too through after the first or second time it was crammed down the viewers' throats. Except for Leachman's somewhat interesting role as the mother who didn't want to be a mother, nothing else about this movie justified it taking up 92 minutes of my life.

I won't take up more minutes of *your* life trying to make more out of this by-the-numbers movie than needed. You won't laugh, you won't cry, you won't feel moved to tell your sisters you love them.

BAMMER'S BOTTOM LINE

If you've seen the trailers for this flick, you've seen the movie. No, not just the best parts, I mean that you've seen the *movie*; the other 90 or so minutes are just filler. Boring, trite filler at that. Guess I'll have to wait for the Black *Hanging*

Up to see my sisters and me on the big screen, after all.

RED LIGHT

The Long Kiss Goodnight

the Diva

(1996)

RATED R; running time 120 minutes
GENRE: Action/Thriller
WRITTEN BY: Shane Black
DIRECTED BY: Renny Harlin
CAST: Geena Davis, Samuel L. Jackson, Yvonne
    Zima, Craig Bierko, Tom Amandes, Brian Cox,
    Patrick Malahide, David Morse

Geena Davis was married to the director Renny Harlin. They separated in 1997 and divorced sometime after that. She also placed 24th out of 28 semifinalists for the U.S. Women's Olympic Archery Team.

THE DIGEST

Samantha Caine (Geena Davis) leads a fairly normal life. She is a mother with an adorable daughter whom she loves; she has a great boyfriend, a great job, wonderful friends, and a nice home. The town loves her. They've made her Mrs. Claus for the annual parade. The only problem is she has amnesia and doesn't know anything about her life prior to eight years ago. She's got old knife scars and bullet wounds. Maybe she was a cop? Her only clue to her past is a filed-down key. Desperate to find out about her past, she always keeps private investigators working. She's stopped using the expensive ones and just hopes one of the "low-rent" investigators will find something. She prays that one day her memory will come back. It does, with a little help. During a car accident, she receives a blow to the head. While she is in the hospital, a version of herself appears in her mind's eye. This version has chopped-off blond hair, smokes, curses, and calls herself Charly Baltimore.

Meanwhile, some criminal is watching TV and sees Samantha on the Christmas float. He starts going berserk and yells at the screen that he wants his eye back. A closer look at his face shows that one of his sockets has been sewn shut. Hmmm, maybe Samantha wasn't a cop. Her latest detective, Mitch Hennesy (Samuel L. Jackson), has found out something about her past.

As they travel, her memory slowly comes back, and we find out that she was actually an ass-whupping spy working for the government, and they prefer her dead. Well, they're in for a big surprise.

THE DISH

This is one of my favorite movies. I don't know why. It's superviolent. The plot has a zillion holes in it. But damned if I haven't seen it 8 or 9 times. Maybe it's the fact that she whups everyone. Maybe it's the whole maternal thing of saving your child. Maybe it's all the stuff that gets blown up. Maybe it's the fact that Samuel Jackson cracks me up in the movie. Perhaps it's a combination of all of the above.

THE DIRECTIVE

This *Kiss* wasn't long enough. I want a sequel! Get some popcorn and a pillow and just hang out.

GREEN LIGHT

---

the Diva Nurse Betty
(2000)

RATED R; running time 90 minutes
GENRE: Comedy
WRITTEN BY: John Richards
DIRECTED BY: Neil LaBute
CAST: Morgan Freeman, Renée Zellweger, Chris Rock, Greg Kinnear, Aaron Eckhart, Tia Texada, Allison Janney

THE DIGEST

Betty (Renée Zellweger) has spent all of her life in Kansas. She married a local car dealer, works at the local diner, and went to the local high school. You get the picture. Her dream was to become a nurse, but that dream was squashed by her philandering jerk of a husband, Dell. Betty doesn't hold a grudge. She just goes through life working and religiously watching her favorite soap opera, *A Reason to Love*, starring the man of her dreams, Dr. David Ravell as portrayed by George McCord (Greg Kinnear). As far as Betty is concerned, all is right with the world as long as she can watch her soap.

One night, when her husband thinks that she's gone out, he brings home two men to discuss some shady business. Betty turns up the sound on the TV soap and drowns out the conversation. Eventually she hears some roughhousing going on and peeks outside. What she sees is too violent for her. She shuts the door and turns back to the soap, and her mind immediately checks out.

From that moment on, Betty mixes reality and fiction. She believes that Dr. Ravell really does exist and that she is his former fiancée. She decides to leave her husband (whose "accident" she has blocked out of her mind) and go find Dr. David and make everything right.

What follows is her hilarious trip to Los Angeles. What she doesn't know is that the car that she's using is full of stolen dope. So now the men who were after her husband, Charlie (Morgan Freeman) and Wesley (Chris Rock), are following her.

THE DISH

Chris Rock, along with Allison Janney and Tia Texada, made this movie for me. Chris cracked me up. "I'll kill that bitch like she scratched my car." See, I know that's a horrible statement, but coming out of his mouth? I was on the floor. I spent the entire movie laughing at him.

Morgan Freeman really surprised me. I don't think I've ever seen him in a comedy or with a pottymouth, for that matter. It was refreshing. He took his job as a hit man *very* seriously, as if he were working a regular 9–5 job. That in itself was enough to make me giggle. All of the other actors were wonderful. The movie was perfectly cast.

THE DIRECTIVE

Nurse Betty is a great date movie, in a nontraditional sense. Check it out.

GREEN LIGHT

 Random Hearts
(1999)

RATED R; running time 133 minutes

GENRE: Romance/Drama

WRITTEN BY: Darryl Ponicsan, based on the novel by Warren Adler

DIRECTED BY: Sydney Pollack

CAST: Harrison Ford, Kristin Scott Thomas, Charles Dutton, Bonnie Hunt, Dennis Haysbert, Susanna Thompson, Peter Coyote, Bill Cobbs, Sydney Pollack

> Harrison Ford is a trained carpenter and licensed helicopter pilot.

THE STORY

Internal Affairs Sgt. "Dutch" Van Den Broeck (Harrison Ford) thinks he's in a perfect marriage; so does Kay Chandler (Kristin Scott Thomas), a candidate for Congress from the fine state of New Hampshire. But as they both find out after their respective spouses were killed in an airplane crash, they're sadly mistaken. After some investigation into the crash, Dutch finds out that his wife was cheating on him with Chandler's husband. Even with this knowledge, Dutch feels driven to find out Why! Oh! Why!, enlisting his wife's reluctant-to-tell coworkers (Bonnie Hunt as Wendy Judd, among them) to solve the "mystery," and proceeds to make his and Chandler's lives miserable—until they fall for each other. An underlying subplot runs throughout, with Dutch and Alcee (Dutton) investigating dirty detective George Beaufort (Haysbert), who's extorting funds from barkeep Marvin (Cobbs).

THE UPSHOT

I'm about to say something I don't ever recall saying in response to a Harrison Ford flick: what-the-hell was that? This movie was a mess; a bore and a half! And that's putting it mildly.

I went into the theater wondering to myself, "Self, what are they going to say in this movie in two hours and 11 minutes? 'My wife/husband was cheating on me, and I'm pissed about it!'?" And sure enough, that's exactly what was said. Honestly, that's it in a nutshell. Harrison Ford whom I've loved in almost everything else he's done (including *Regarding Henry*, which shares a few elements of this flick, except it actually was worth seeing) primarily scowled and growled. Thomas bravely forged on, trying to make something out of nothing, and almost convinced me that she'd make it all the way through the flick without forgetting to use her American Accent (funny, the things you notice when you're being bored to tears). And as for the cheating slimette Peyton Van Den Broeck and her partner in crime, cheating slime Cullen Chandler, Susanna Thompson and Peter Coyote's better scenes were obviously left on the cutting floor by director Sydney Pollack, who inexplicably decided to insert himself into the role of campaign TV director Carl Broman instead of making way for all of the actors who could've done a much better job of making this movie watchable. Pollack needs his ass whupped for this one; and Harrison Ford shouldn't walk away too quickly, 'cuz he has a belt waiting with his name on it, too.

Part of the problem is the sheer dearth of plausible storyline. I mean, come on, it's a *Titanic* setup: they screwed, they crashed, they died. Where's the mystery in that?

THE BLACK FACTOR

After seeing Charles Dutton so badly ignored in this flick, I wanted to cry, really I did. Bill Cobbs and Dennis Haysbert (who looks much better here than he did as Kenneth in *Waiting to Exhale* but has a ways to go until he looks as good as he did as Pedro Cerrano in *Major League*) didn't fare much better. It occurs to me, though, that this movie would've been served better if they'd have just concentrated on the bad-cop subplot, and dropped the god-awful main plot here. Better yet, let's just whup Sydney Pollack's ass and be done with it.

BAMMER'S BOTTOM LINE

I feel used, Harrison. Why! Oh! Why! did you bother with this one? Indiana Jones, we hardly knew ye. Point blank: *Random Hearts* is proof positive that not every novel can, or should, be made into a movie. They shoulda called it *Random Scenes.*

RED LIGHT

Bams   Saving Grace
(2000)

RATED R; running time 93 minutes
GENRE: Comedy
WRITTEN BY: Mark Crowdy, Craig Ferguson
DIRECTED BY: Nigel Cole
CAST: Brenda Blethyn, Craig Ferguson, Martin Clunes, Valerie Edmond, Tcheky Karyo, Phyllida Law, Jamie Forman, Bill Bailey, Tristan Sturrock, Clive Merrison, Leslie Phillips, Diana Quick, Linda Kerr Scott, Ken Campbell

> Brenda Blethyn changed her name from Brenda Bottle.

THE STORY

In a small coastal town in Merrie Olde England, Grace Trevethen (Brenda Blethyn), a recent widow and avid horticulturist, discovers to her horror that not only was her philandering husband screwing around behind her back with another woman, he also had some shady dealings that left her in serious debt. With the threat of her home being taken away from her, Grace turns to her former Scottish yardsman Matthew (Craig Ferguson) for advice. Matthew, who partakes of demon weed on a regular basis with local doc, Dr. Bamford (Martin Clunes), helps Grace hatch the idea to take some of Matthew's dying marijuana plants and sell them. That's right: sweet middle-aged Grace will become a (gasp) drug dealer!

With Grace now reduced to "having" to sling dope to make ends meet, can hilarity still ensue?

THE UPSHOT

When one speaks of The War On (Some) Drugs, at least here in the Untied States, pictures of burned-out crack houses, doped-up kids, Ghetto drive-bys, and dealers dripping in gold (stereo) typically come to mind. Rarely does one conjure up a picture of a quaint little old lady "doing what she has to" to get by.

Saving Grace paints that very picture, in its veddy British way. And as a lifetime Uhmerkin gal who grew up in an Uhmerkin Inner City (Detroit), I had quite a time reconciling its images with those images we're shown every night on the news on this side of the Pond.

The first thing you should know about *Saving Grace* is that, at least by American standards, it's fairly absurd. Maybe I live a sheltered life, but within *my* circles, at least, had the whole town known what Matthew and Grace were doing, I dare say they wouldn't have been doing it for long; between a cop taking them in, or the neighbors stealing their brightly lit stash, I have no doubt that here in near-suburban Podunkville, the chances that there would be a Grace in our backyard are slim to none.

That caveat aside, the folks involved with *Saving Grace* looked like they were having a bowl . . . er, a ball. Though this movie stretched the limits of my disbelief at times, the major players involved with it were quite pleasing to watch and root for. Which raises yet another interesting question: is it kosher to root for these—let's call a spade a spade, shall we?—for these drug dealers? Is it okay to do so as long as the person slinging the dope isn't your everyday Ghetto dweller (and only doing it because she "has to," unlike those Ghetto dwellers who must so obviously

enjoy the fringe benefits of living a life of crime that they don't follow their true calling in life)? See, maybe it's just me, but I can't quite get around the hypocrisy of the whole situation.

The performances in *Grace* were all solid, even though near the end the story started to get less credible. The scenery was beautiful, the actors comfortable in their roles, and the writing was fairly tight. As Grace, Brenda Blethyn mixed humor and pathos quite well, and presented the audience with a performance that puts some of our best and brightest young movie stars to shame; given her storyline, she could've easily stunk up the screen, and it is to her credit that she was able to cultivate what might have been a pathetic character into what ended up as a beautiful blossom. The same could be said about much of the rest of the cast, especially Martin Clunes as the dopey doc; and when his character uttered the line (paraphrased) "Why is marijuana illegal, yet the drug alcohol is not?" I wanted to shout "preach, brudda!"

On the whole, the movie was enjoyable enough, and in a perfect world, that would be all that needed to be said. My problem is that the ongoing War On (Some) Drugs here in the New World made *Saving Grace* lose a little something in the translation.

THE BLACK FACTOR

Yes, it's just jokes, I know. Yes, British humor is an acquired taste. And yes, everything doesn't have to be about race and the assumptions one makes based upon who is holding the joint at the time. But my mind keeps jumping back to this question, which I'd like to hear an honest answer to: in America, at least, given our attitudes about The War On (Some) Drugs, and our (mis)perceptions and prejudices about who is a criminal and who isn't, how different a movie would this have been if the little old lady in question, wasn't a little old *White* lady?

BAMMER'S BOTTOM LINE

You don't have to be high to enjoy *Saving Grace*. But being English might help.

FLASHING YELLOW LIGHT

 **What Lies Beneath**

(2000)

RATED PG-13; running time 130 minutes
GENRE: Thriller
WRITTEN BY: Clark Gregg (based on the story by Sarah Kernochan)
DIRECTED BY: Robert Zemeckis
CAST: Harrison Ford, Michelle Pfeiffer, Diana Scarwid, Miranda Otto, James Remar, Katherine Towne, Joe Morton, Amber Valletta

THE STORY

Unbeknownst to genetics scientist Norman Spencer's wife, Claire (Michelle Pfeiffer), Norman (Harrison Ford) had an affair with a student of his (Amber Valletta) a year ago. The consequences of this dalliance may be coming back to haunt Norman and Claire after their daughter, Caitlin, moves away to college. Without her daughter, Claire has a great deal of time alone in a house that may be haunted by the spirit of Norman's father, who committed suicide there before Norman and Claire moved in. At least, that's one version of the story. It may also be the ghost of Mary Feur, a new neighbor who, Claire suspects, met with foul play when her husband, Warren, left mysterious tire tracks in the yard after one of their many fights. Or it may be Claire's friend Jody, a flake who, even in all her flakiness, doesn't quite believe that Claire is seeing ghosts, yet gives her a conjuring book to go along with her spooky O-u-i-j-a board (and while I'm at it, how'd they get "weegee" out of "O-u-i-j-a"?). *Or* it may be her psychiatrist, Dr. Drayton (Joe Morton), who tries to ply her with his fireballs.

Or it may be something completely different . . .

THE UPSHOT

Psycho taught me not to take showers.

What Lies Beneath has ruined baths for me.

I hope they don't make *Attack Of The Killer Bath Sponge* anytime too soon.

It is no accident that *What Lies Beneath* put me in mind of Alfred Hitchcock's *Psycho;* indeed, many of Hitchcock's films have been mentioned by some pundits in the same breath as *Lies,* and even the director himself admits to stylizing the film with a Hitchcockian feeling in mind. To a degree, it is a successful attempt, though it didn't *start* that way.

What Lies Beneath had one of the slowest-paced opening acts I've ever seen in a thriller, to the point where I thought I was witnessing another of Harrison Ford's rare failures, and that Michelle Pfeiffer was turning about as ditzy as Meg Ryan. Thankfully, that didn't last.

It is difficult to say anything about the movie that doesn't wind up as spoilage; the twists and turns are all an important part of what's going on, and I don't want to untwist a single twist for anyone still reading, so I'll just stick with the performances in this space. Harrison Ford took a huge chance in roaming away from his general nice guy roles. He was very effective playing a part that put me in mind of *Ghost Story*, one of my absolute favorite scary flicks. But as good as Ford was, Michelle Pfeiffer was even better, and in the end, she stole the show. Her portrait of Claire, pushed to the brink of insanity by conditions that become clearer to her as the film progresses, was one of her finest performances to date, especially within the last half hour or so of the film, and most especially in her (shudder) bathtub scene.

THE BLACK FACTOR
I ty not to blow up any time any Joe Schmo Black actor or actress is lost in the shuffle of a given movie. However, when a talented actor like Joe Morton (headshrinker Dr. Drayton) is grossly underused, I must take umbrage. I'll just assume that his better stuff was left lying on the editor's floor, for time and space considerations. Hey, leave me alone with my fantasies.

BAMMER'S BOTTOM LINE
What Lies Beneath is a decent nod to the master, Hitchcock, by the student, Zemeckis.

And 'scuse me a sec, y'all. This one goes out to My People: *"GET . . . OUT!!!"*

(Big ups, Eddie Murphy, for that eternally perfect line.)

GREEN LIGHT

Bams   Woman on Top
(2000)

RATED R; running time 83 minutes
GENRE: Romantic comedy
WRITTEN BY: Vera Blasi
DIRECTED BY: Fina Torres
CAST: Penélope Cruz, Murilo Benício, Harold Perrineau Jr., Mark Feuerstein, John de Lancie

THE STORY
Brazilian-born Isabella Oliveira (Penélope Cruz) has two great qualities: she's extremely beautiful and she's a great cook—and one strike against her: debilitating motion sickness. It affects her to the point where she can't move at all unless *she* controls her movement; she has to drive, she has to dance lead, and, during sex, she has to be the one on top.

This creates a problem with her equally beautiful husband, restaurateur and balladeer Toninho Oliveira (Murilo Benício); a man's man who takes the credit for his successful restaurant while his chef wife does all the work in the background, Toninho just can't hack not being in control of every facet of Isabella's life, and rebels in the best way he knows how: he has a quickie with one of their neighbors.

Isabella, outraged, leaves Toninho. She flies despite terrible motion sickness, to San Francisco, where she hooks up with her childhood friend Monica Jones (Harold Perrineau Jr.). Monica happens to be a transvestite (and, thankfully, not a "tragic" one; Perrineau looked *good* as a woman, day-am!) After a wee struggle in looking for a job, Isabella gets a teaching gig in a local culinary school, which leads to her discovery by TV producer Cliff Lloyd (Mark Feuerstein). He is as awestruck as nearly every other man—and woman—by Isabella's beauty as well as her cooking talents, as is Lloyd's boss, Alex Reeves (John de Lancie). But even as things go well for Isabella, she still finds herself missing one important thing: control.

THE UPSHOT

Let's go back to "The Story" for a minute, to the part where I said "Toninho just can't hack not being in control of every facet of Isabella's life," because that's where my first problem with the beautifully filmed *Woman on Top* begins: I didn't get that impression right off. Yes, the script *did* mention it here and there; but precious little in the early bits of the movie convinced me that it was such a problem that it became unbearable to Isabella. In fact, I was surprised that events played themselves out as quickly as they did in this short (timewise; long, storywise) film; the audience was treated to many romantic scenes of the two beautiful lovers doing what comes natu-

rally to them, a couple quick glances of Isabella's control issues, then *BAM!* her control issues (and his sudden need to be On Top himself) break them up. Uh … huh? Where'd *that* come from all of a sudden?

Problem two: we switch quickly to San Francisco, where we meet Monica "RuPaul With Better Makeup" Jones and swiftly learn, in the space of a sentence or two from Monica and Isabella, of their long-standing childhood friendship. These quick snippets and the similarly speedy introduction of TV producer Cliff Lloyd seemed an afterthought, a way of identifying the characters without giving the audience a solid look at what they were made of. It felt rushed, as if the filmmaker was hurrying to get to a certain point in the movie, only to repeat that point over and over again. Which leads me to …

Problem three: the sense of deja vu. That is, the feeling that the movie constantly repeated itself; how irritating, then, that the film switched gears from being too little, too quickly, to being too much, too often. Hard to believe that in the space of only 83 minutes, a movie can say what it had to say, and still have, oh, a good 40 minutes of filler added. Isabella and Toninho lovingly gaze at each other, they have a misunderstanding; Lather, Rinse, Repeat. Isabella tastes something that reminds her of Toninho, she remembers making love to him; Lather, Rinse, Repeat. This happens ad nauseam throughout the movie, enough to give *me* motion sickness.

Three things that *Woman on Top* did have going for it, and that elevate it from the mundane straight-yellow-light rating, were the strong attractiveness of, and chemistry between, Cruz and Benício; the funkiness of Perrineau's Monica

Jones; and the best, most noncommercial sound-track I've heard in ages. Alas, these strengths were not enough to make this one-note film work its magic in the end; while there were pleasant moments scattered throughout, the moments didn't congeal into a satisfying whole.

THE BLACK FACTOR

(Or, to be more precise, for this movie, the "Ethnic Factor.")

I'm not sure whether it was reasonable for me to expect to gain Cultural Understanding from a comedy about people who happen to be Brazilian simply because I'd never seen a comedy about Brazilians before. But I was bothered by feeling that the only thing I learned about Brazilians is that they make great music and great food.

The most ironic thing about Isabella's Issue with the network TV Suits' insistence on

her show not being "so ethnic," is that the only thing that seemed at all ethnic about *Passion Food*, was Monica's dress and Toninho's backup band. "Sexy as all get up"? Sure. But "ethnic"? Hmmm.

BAMMER'S BOTTOM LINE

I wavered on rating this film: part of me wanted to give *Woman on Top* an unabashed green light for its beautiful Brazilian music and its even more beautiful stars, Penélope Cruz and Murilo Benício. My green light, though, generally indicates that I'd pay to see the movie again and I just don't think that's the case here. Still, it's worth seeing once, if only to see Harold Perrineau Jr. outdo RuPaul's shtick. Man, whadda woman . . .

FLASHING YELLOW LIGHT

ow it's time to take a little break and have some fun.

A few of these questions have been answered within the reviews you've been reading. Others you may have to do a little research on. The answers are in the appendix (see page 359).

NOTE: *A few of these movies are still in the theaters as of May 2002, and because of this, their totals change daily. For the purpose of this book, we're using the information that is available to us as of late May, 2002, and we are not adjusting the movies for inflation.*

Unless otherwise noted, the "Total Gross" refers to money made during its theatrical run(s) and not home rentals and purchases.

1. How many nominations did *The Color Purple* receive?
   a. Was one of these nods for Best Director?
   b. Bonus: Name 5 of the nominations.
   c. How many did it win?
2. True or False: No Black man has ever won the Best Actor Academy Award.
3. Name the 8 African-Americans who have won Oscars.
4. How old was Laurence Fishburne when he was in *Apocalypse Now*?
5. What now-famous director wrote *The Wiz, Sparkle, Car Wash*?
6. How much did Halle Berry make for *Swordfish*?
7. Who was the first Black film director and producer?
8. Who was the first Black actress to be nominated for Best Actress?
9. How many Academy Awards has Paul Newman won?
10. What actresses have won all 4 major awards—Oscar, Grammy, Tony, and Emmy?
11. Name 2 of the top 5 actors whose movies have grossed the most ever.
12. Name 5 of the top 20 highest-grossing films of all time.
13. What movie had the biggest opening weekend ever?

14. What very popular '80s sitcom actor had bit parts in 2 separate trilogies *and* was in (actually his voice was in) high-grossing movies that hit the theaters in the following years: 2001, 1999, 1998, and 1995?
    a. Name the actor.
    b. Name the sitcom.
    c. Name the trilogies.
    d. Name the recent movies.
15. What was the first movie that De Niro and Pacino worked together on screen?
16. Who was the only person to ever have won Oscar, Tony, and Emmy Awards in the same year?
17. What Mississippi attorney-author wrote six books, that were eventually adapted to movies?
18. Which actor has a Ph.D. in Literature from New York University?
    a. Denzel Washington
    b. Whoopi Goldberg
    c. Angela Bassett
    d. Samuel L. Jackson
19. Bernard Schwartz is the birth name of which actor?
    a. Jack Lemmon
    b. Tony Curtis
    c. Harrison Ford
    d. Kirk Douglas
20. Which actor had parents who were Mexican freedom fighters during the Mexican Revolution?
    a. Martin Sheen
    b. Penelope Cruz
    c. Anthony Quinn
    d. Rita Moreno
21. What actor is a descendant of a family known as The Royal Family of American Stage and Theater?
22. What actor, while attending Harvard, roomed with a currently famous politician?
23. In 1994, which actor became the first to win back-to-back Oscars for Best Actor in over 50 years?
24. African-American women have been nominated seven times for Best Actress Academy Awards. Name those actresses and the movies for which they received the nominations.
25. In which movie did Clint Eastwood utter, "Go ahead, make my day"?
    a. *Dirty Harry*
    b. *The Dead Pool*
    c. *Sudden Impact*
    d. *High Plains Drifter*

you probably don't own the CD for *West Side Story* or *Singin' in the Rain*, but we bet you know some of the songs. And we know y'all Old Hats are still boppin' to that Rose Royce *Car Wash* 8-track—don't even try to front!

An American in Paris
(1951)

UNRATED; running time 114 minutes
GENRE: Musical
WRITTEN BY: Alan Jay Lerner
DIRECTED BY: Vincent Minnelli
MUSIC BY: George Gershwin
LYRICS BY: Ira Gershwin
CHOREOGRAPHY BY: Gene Kelly
CAST: Gene Kelly, Leslie Caron, Oscar Levant,
Georges Guétary, Nina Foch

THE STORY

Ex-GI Jerry Mulligan (Gene Kelly) did what any red-blooded American boy would do after World War II came to a close: he stayed in Paris, to pursue a career in painting. His "career" consisted of starving, mostly. He shared such a fate with his best bud, Adam Cook (Oscar Levant, who I've come to adore almost as much as I love Kelly), a gifted curmudgeon of a concert pianist who just might be the world's oldest child prodigy. Adam, a self-effacing chain smoker, is also best buds with the somewhat more successful French music-hall star Henri Baurel (Georges Guétary), an older man who took in young Lise Bouvier (Leslie Caron) during the Resistance, fell in love with Lise and asked her to marry him.

One problem: once carefree bachelor Jerry lays eyes on Lise, he is hooked. Actually, *two* problems: Jerry's new arts patron, the worldly and jealous Milo (as in, "Venus de") Roberts (Nina Foch), wants Jerry for herself.

And on tomorrow's installment of *All My Bold and Beautiful Children* . . .

THE UPSHOT

An American in Paris has moments of absolute brilliance, and I'd easily put it up against most of the dreck passing for movies these days; but there was an . . . emptiness of plot here that just failed to reach the sustained high notes of *Singin' In the Rain* (see page 227) or *West Side Story* (see page 229), for instance. Maybe it was just the idealistic memory I had of that tight jumper Kelly wore out, but I certainly remembered *Paris* being a little brighter, a little more dazzling, in my youth.

On the other hand, there's still a lil' sum'n sum'n about *An American in Paris* that raises it above your standard boy-meets-girl-let's-dance musical plot; something a bit hard-edged that makes *Paris* more kin to the more socially relevant *West Side* than Kelly's fluffier *Rain*. That "something," I posit, is Oscar Levant. Yes, *Paris* has plenty of hokey numbers, like many of its predecessors. Yes, *Paris* has a musical-standard dame-in-waiting in the person of the smoky and underused Nina Foch, and a charming ingénue (well, to an extent) in the magnificent Leslie Caron. Yes, *Paris* has great Gershwin standards, and, in Minnelli, a director who knew how to make a musical just the way movie audiences used to want them to be made. And oh yes, *Paris* has Kelly showing off all his charms in that skintight leotard . . . ahem. But what *Paris* also has that few of the more lighthearted musicals haven't got, was Oscar the grouch, all-too-briefly snarking his way through *An American in Paris* like he owned the joint.

THE NUMBERS

Okay, so the plot's got issues; but what of the trademarks of any musical worthy of the name?

"Oom-pa-pa by Strauss"

Cringe moment #1. Georges Guétary started off rubbing me the wrong way (shouldn't it be illegal for a French guy to attempt German?) and never recovers. Next!

"I Got Rhythm"

Ahhh . . . much better. I've always loved this number; Gene Kelly seemed to work so well with those kids, as if he were a dancing version of *ER's* Dr. Ross. It's funny, though, that he used American to teach French kids English. Hooked on Ebonics, Jerry?

"Tra-La-La"

Cringe moment #2. I like an almost-shirtless Kelly like the next hot-blooded chick; but Lord, that man really couldn't sing, as he proved with that misbegotten high note at the end. Minnelli must've directed him to pretend that someone yanked his testicles at that moment.

"Our Love Is Here to Stay"

The most sensuous, romantic song-and-dance pairing I can ever recall seeing on film. Some swoon over Astaire and Rogers; but Kelly and Caron, in this beautiful scene, do it for me.

"Stairway to Paradise"

I love this number, if only because it always makes me want to do my impression of Henri Tha Playa President. I'll try to remember to do it for Oprah next time I see her.

"Third Movement: Concerto In F"

Adam's manifesto and a brief glimpse into the genius of serious pianist Oscar Levant. A few years ago, I remember seeing a PBS documentary on Levant that went into detail about what a tormented soul he was. I don't think I've ever been sadder about the life of a celebrity than I was after watching that documentary. But even in my sadness, I came away with a deeper appreciation for his work in *Paris*."

"S'swonderful"

Giving my boy Guétary a break for a minute, I liked this threesome piece with him, Kelly, and Levant. By this point, it seemed as if Kelly was repeating some taps, but Levant's humorous expressions help make this number a winner.

"An American in Paris"

This 17-minute ballet (which includes Kelly in the skintight leotard I keep drooling over) is what ultimately caused me to go ga-ga over all things Gene Kelly. Hey, sue me for having a rich fantasy life.

BAMMER'S BOTTOM LINE

Some of the background "noise" may have been a wee bit disheartening to see, but the heart of a Gene Kelly musical—the singing and dancing—still stand the test of time in *An American in Paris*.

GREEN LIGHT

Anchors Aweigh
(1945)

UNRATED; running time 143 minutes

GENRE: Musical

WRITTEN BY: Isobel Lennart (based on the
story by Natalie Marcin)

DIRECTED BY: George Sidney

MUSIC BY: Georgie Stoll, Jule Styne

LYRICS BY: Sammy Cahn

CHOREOGRAPHY BY: Gene Kelly

CAST: Frank Sinatra, Kathryn Grayson, Gene
Kelly, José Iturbi, Dean Stockwell, Pamela
Britton

THE STORY

Joseph Brady (Gene Kelly) and Clarence "Brook-lyn" Doolittle (Frank Sinatra) are two navy boys out on the town in Hollywood. Joe's a man of the world, and wants to push up on his honey, Lola; but bookworm Clarence stops Joe by tagging along. Clarence finally wears Joe down and promises to stop bugging him if Joe will hook him up with a girlie girl.

On a collision course with Joe and Clarence is sweet little Donald Martin (Dean Stockwell), an orphaned boy living with his aunt Susan (Kathryn Grayson). The cops pick Donald up when he runs away from home to join the navy. When the navy "volunteers" Joe and Clarence to help them convince Donald to go home, light-ning strikes twice: Donald is instantly attached to Sailor Joe, and Clarence goes gaga for Susan. Thing is, Joe and Susan grudgingly fall for each other. Oops.

THE UPSHOT

Strangely enough, Kelly seemed to fit perfectly into his third-billed status. His Joe seemed much more a springboard character than did Clarence, though I beg to differ on Kathryn Grayson hav-ing been second-billed. She grated my cheese from the moment she appeared, as stiff as card-board, and only made things worse when she sang. Oh my sweet Lord, did I ever leap for the MUTE button whenever she opened her mouth. Sorry, but I didn't see any chemistry there; I can't for the life of me see what Joe could've possibly been attracted to in Aunt Susie.

Usually, kids in movies (or adults voicing kid-types, á la Michael J. Fox in *Stuart Little*, see page 317), give me heartburn. Young Dean Stockwell (later, of *Quantum Leap* fame, no less!) had no such effect in *Anchors Aweigh*. Little Stockwell succeeded not with smart-alecky behavior, but with what appeared to be sincerity, charm, and natural wit. And when he and Kelly smiled at each other . . . oooweee.

The icing on the *Anchors Aweigh* cake was Frank Sinatra, especially when he *wasn't* the focal point. What a kick it was to watch that skinny fella fidget in the background, unconsciously stealing the limelight from Kelly with a nervous tic, an outburst of laughter (watch what he does in the police station scene, partially blocked by Kelly), and especially his famous voice. And therein is the key to the magic of *Anchors Aweigh* for me; given a big dose of Sinatra's singing, Kelly's dancing, and Stockwell's cute little self, I was one happy Chick.

The Numbers

Though none of the numbers here worked as well as in other Kelly musicals, there were a couple of charming numbers of note:

"Brahms's Lullaby," "Donkey Serenade," and "Hungarian Rhapsody"

Sinatra brought the familiar "Lullaby" and "Serenade" to life. The "Hungarian Rhapsody" scene, though, weirded me out.

"I Begged Her"

Cute song, one that threatens to bring out the Latent Femi-Nazi in me, but it's the Kelly-Sinatra dancing that I grooved to more here. Much as I loved Kelly, Sinatra was a much better dancer than Kelly was a singer.

BAMMER'S BOTTOM LINE

Anchors Aweigh is a movie you're not likely to forget—despite my grumbling about Gene Kelly's female costar.

GREEN LIGHT

Bams Guys and Dolls

(1951)

UNRATED; running time 150 minutes

GENRE: Musical

WRITTEN BY: Joseph L. Mankiewicz (based on the play by Abe Burrows)

DIRECTED BY: Joseph L. Mankiewicz

MUSIC BY: Jay Blackton

LYRICS BY: Frank Loeser

CHOREOGRAPHY BY: Michael Kidd

CAST: Marlon Brando, Frank Sinatra, Jean Simmons, Vivian Blaine, Robert Keith, Stubby Kaye, B. S. Pully, Johnny Silver, Sheldon Leonard

THE STORY

Nathan Detroit (Frank Sinatra) has been engaged to his doll, Adelaide (Vivian Blaine), for 14 years and running, but he just can't seem to commit. But his biggest problem is that as proprietor of the oldest established permanent floating craps game in New York, he is expected, by his sidekicks Nicely Nicely (Stubby Kaye) and Benny Southstreet (Johnny Silver), as well as big-shot mobsters like Harry the Horse, Angie the Ox, and Society Max, to actually have a *game* floating. This would be no problem if it were not for the heat, in the form of Lieutenant Brannigan (Robert Keith), who keeps Nathan from running his establishment in established places. About the only place left for Nathan to take care of his . . . friends . . . is a local garage that wants $1,000 "insurance." Nathan and his cohorts don't have that kinda dough; what's a respectable racketeer to do?

Enter Sky Masterson (Marlon Brando), a slick rick who, Nathan knows, will bet on anything. Nathan comes up with the perfect sucker bet: he wagers Sky $1,000 that Sky could never seduce straight-laced missionary Sarah Brown (Jean Simmons), a bet which Sky, who thinks all dames are the same, eagerly takes. Sky just didn't figure he'd fall for the kooky chick.

THE UPSHOT

I tried to get my *Guys and Dolls* groove on. But try as I might, I never got into the *G&D* Experience. It wasn't the lighthearted misogyny; in a lot of ways, those "broads" and "dolls" and whatever the guys called them, were treated more genteelly than some of us thoroughly modern chicks. It wasn't the superbright colors, the staged feeling, or even the let's-dance-at-the-drop-of-a-dime; I got all of that in spades with *An American in Paris* and *West Side Story*, and I was quite jiggy with it. And it wasn't even the exaggerated movie gangsta-speak; I've been exposed to it plenty on ABC's *NYPD Blue*, though, admittedly, *Guys and Dolls* does it *much* better.

Whatever the problem was, it most def was *not* Marlon Brando. I found him, and his Sky, totally pleasing. Who knew the man who coulda been a contenda, could be so charming as a song-and-dance man? Besides Sky, I liked the secondary characters much more than the other leads. I found myself wishing that Jean Simmons would let her Sarah Brown character fade away in the background, especially when she broke out in a song; I didn't find Frank Sinatra nearly as enjoyable here as Nathan Detroit, as I did when he was a few years younger in *On the Town* (see page 226) with Gene Kelly; and if I had to

listen to what Vivian Blaine offered as Miss Adelaide *one more second*, I think I might've bitten somebody. But for every irritating lead, there was a sweet Nicely Nicely, or a funny Harry the Horse, or a cool Big Jule. So, what was up with my discontent?

I've come to the realization that my issues with *Guys and Dolls* are firmly rooted in the music. And for a musical, that is most def not a good thing.

BAMMER'S BOTTOM LINE

I know I'm walking a fine line just this side of blasphemy against classic musicals, but I couldn't get with *Guys and Dolls*. One thing's for sure, though: Marlon Brando was most def a charmer. I did keep waiting for him to yell "Stellaaaa!" though.

FLASHING YELLOW LIGHT

---

the Diva **Josie and the Pussycats**
(2001)

RATED PG; running time 98 minutes
GENRE: Comedy
WRITTEN BY: Deborah Kaplan & Harry Elfont
DIRECTED BY: Harry Elfont, Deborah Kaplan
CAST: Rachel Leigh Cook, Tara Reid, Rosario Dawson, Alan Cumming, Parker Posey, Gabriel Mann

THE DIGEST

Josie McCoy (Rachel Leigh Cook), Melody Valentine (Tara Reid), and Valerie Brown (Rosario Dawson) are struggling musicians known as The Pussycats. The lifelong friends are determined to take their band from the garage to the mainstream. Unfortunately, they can only get gigs at the local bowling alley in Riverdale where they have to play on a bowling lane and pay for shoe rental. Despite all of this, they press on.

A twist of fate changes their world. The airplane of DuJour, (the boy band of the day . . . literally), crashes in Riverdale. DuJour's record company immediately starts looking for another band and comes across The Pussycats. Wyatt Frame (Alan Cumming), the record company executive, signs them immediately and, within two days, they are on top of the world and the charts. Little do the Pussycats know, Wyatt Frame and his boss, the evil Fiona (Parker Posey), are behind a plot to rule the world by putting subliminal messages in the Pussycats' songs. They have teamed up with the government and companies around the world to plant marketing messages within the songs. Suddenly, for no apparent reason, the nation's teens decide that they must wear orange and drink Pepsi. The Pussycats must struggle to stay together and at the same time save the kids of America from product placement.

THE DISH

This plot was as stupid as a plot from the cartoon (which I love, by the way). The difference is that the cartoon is 20 minutes long and the cartoon doesn't try to be clever. The satire behind the marketing ploys and product placement was a brilliant idea, but it was so over-the-top that it was too much. Halfway through the movie, I kept saying, "Okay, I get it already."

The music was pretty good, which comes as no surprise, since Babyface was involved. And as an impressive bonus, the actresses actually learned how to play the instruments and most times it's really them you are hearing play. As far as the acting goes, the only character I liked was Melody.

THE DIRECTIVE

Purr-fectly awful . . .

FLASHING RED LIGHT

Moulin Rouge!
(2001)

the Diva

RATED PG-13; running time 126 minutes
GENRE: Musical
WRITTEN BY: Baz Luhrmann and Craig Pearce
DIRECTED BY: Baz Luhrmann
CAST: Nicole Kidman, Ewan McGregor, John Leguizamo, Jim Broadbent, Richard Roxburgh, Jacek Koman, Matthew Whittet

THE DIGEST

"This story is about truth, beauty, freedom, but above all, love." This is how Christian (Ewan McGregor) begins his autobiographical story of love found and love lost. Christian is a young, impressionable writer-poet when he sets foot in Paris in

1899. His father has told him that he is entering into a city of debauchery and sin, and should be ashamed of himself, but Christian craves the artistic freedom he will have in Paris. He doesn't know just how much freedom until he spies the famous Moulin Rouge, a glamorous and gaudy nightclub. Here you can see the infamous CanCan being danced and, if you have enough money, the beautiful Satine (Nicole Kidman), the most famous courtesan in all of Paris, will favor you.

Through a twist of fate and mistaken identity, Satine sets upon Christian. Christian is hoping to entice her with his poetry, so she will agree to support a play he and his friends wish to produce. Satine, on the other hand, thinks that Christian is the rich Duke of Worcester (Richard Roxburgh) who will invest in the club if he can spend the night with Satine.

Christian is instantly in awe of the beautiful Satine, but he thinks that she will never fall for a poor poet. Satine does fall for Christian, even after she finds out he is not the Duke but the entire club is depending on her to get the money from the Duke. Satine and Christian find a way to express their love for one another while Satine maintains a relationship with the Duke, who is completely clueless until jealousy tears at the fabric of Christian and Satine's love and the whole charade threatens to come crashing down upon their heads.

THE DISH

I was dumbstruck after watching *Moulin Rouge!* It was intoxicating almost like a drug, and I immediately wanted to see it again. The music took some getting used to. *A Knight's Tale* (see page 143) did a better job of blending contemporary music in a movie set in an era before the songs came out, however, Nicole Kidman and Ewan McGregor did outstanding jobs in their singing, *especially* since they aren't singers.

Whoever decided to design the sets as if this were a play and not a movie gets kudos from me. This brilliant idea only added to the ambience of the movie. And the costumes were breathtaking. Nicole can wear some clothes. John Leguizamo was wonderful as Toulouse-Lautrec, the voice of reason for the characters in the movie.

THE DIRECTIVE

"The greatest thing you'll ever learn is to love and be loved in return"—a great line from a great movie, *Moulin Rouge!*

GREEN LIGHT

Bams O Brother, Where Art Thou?

(2000)

RATED PG-13; running time 103 minutes
GENRE: Adventure-Comedy
WRITTEN BY: Ethan Coen, Joel Coen (based on Homer's *The Odyssey*)
DIRECTED BY: Joel Coen
CAST: George Clooney, John Turturro, Tim Blake Nelson, Charles Durning, John Goodman, Michael Badalucco, Chris Thomas King, Holly Hunter, Stephen Root, Wayne Duvall, Ed Gale, Ray McKinnon, Quinn Gasaway, Lee

Weaver, Mia Tate, Christy Taylor, Musetta Vander

THE STORY

O Brother, Where Art Thou? is a down-home, no-place-like-home, road story, in the vein of one of the first, and best, of them: Homer's epic poem, *The Odyssey*.

In Depression-era Mississippi, three convicts, Everett Ulysses McGill (George Clooney), Pete Hogwallop (John Turturro), and Delmar O'Donnell (Tim Blake Nelson) bust out of the chain gang they're on in search of the $1.2 mil treasure Everett had stolen and stashed away. Everett, a self-made leader who is as concerned with his hair and the pomade that keeps it slicked back as he is with the treasure they're after, doesn't inspire much confidence in the hot-headed Pete or the somewhat dimwitted Del; but since he's the best they've got, they reluctantly follow his lead. The threesome are cautioned by an old soothsayer (Lee Weaver) that their way would be fraught with dangers, but our three heroes are determined to see their odyssey through.

Along their journey, they come across some situations epic and not-so-epic, involving Pete's back-country cousin Wash and his son Bog; Tommy Johnson, a guitarist at a crossroads in his life; a radio announcer whose "can" allows a surprising outlet for the trio plus one; Homer Stokes, a reform candidate for governor who really means it when he says he represents the Little Man; a trio of sweet siren temptresses; and many more creatures, great and small. The threesome are searching for many things, including redemption and divine intervention, but, like the Ulysses of centuries ago, what they want most is to find their way home.

THE UPSHOT

Do me a favor: the next person that tells you George Clooney is a talentless, pretty-boy hack, pop 'em in the mouth. Better yet, take them to see *O Brother, Where Art Thou?* If they ain't convinced by his magic therein, there just ain't no convincing 'em. In the Odyssey-inspired *O Brother, Where Art Thou?* Clooney more than holds his own against the likes of actors' actors John Turturro, Charles Durning, and Holly Hunter.

In fact, it's Hunter that set in mind the movie that *O Brother* reminded me most of: the Coens' equally quirky (though somewhat better) *Raising Arizona*, in which she costarred with John Goodman. *O Brother* survives the comparison. Though it's not quite as "groundbreaking" as *Arizona* was, for my money, *O Brother, Where Art Thou?* is just as much fun.

The treats in *O Brother* came from all sides: for one, while each actor was given a chance to shine—Clooney and the hilariously deadpan Tim Blake Nelson especially—the ensemble effort that the Coen Boys seem to inspire was evident. Within this large cast, from John Goodman's broad portrayal of conman Big Dan Teague, to Michael Badalucco as George Nelson, the gangsta who wouldn't accept the name society would deem him fit to hold, to the multiple *Odyssey*-esque characters in between, the players built each segment of *O Brother* onto the next, layering its rich tones along the way. Second, behind the scenes, the Coen Brothers worked their magic in a way I haven't seen from them since *Fargo*.

If anyone involved with this dynamite production could be said to be flat, it would have to be Charles Durning; I've seen his Governor Pappy act one too many times in similar good ol' boy roles, and it quickly wore a nerve for me. And besides, Paul Newman portrayed the guv'ner from Louisiana much more memorably in *Blaze* a few years back.

THE BLACK FACTOR

And speaking of "Magical Negroes" . . .

Soothsaying *is* magical, no two ways about it. So I'm not sweatin' Lee Weaver's role as the Black at all; it is as it was *supposed* to be, so I suggest that anyone who wants to get up in arms about it, should take a pill.

I *do*, however, have a bit of a bone to pick with Chris Thomas King's rather dull portrayal of Tommy Johnson, a role apparently inspired by the fabled story of blues guitarist Robert Johnson. But my quibble with King, I reckon, is one that he could never overcome, because for the life of me, I can't imagine anyone ever doing a better job at playing "Robert Johnson" than the incomparable Joe Seneca, as he did in *Crossroads*. Sorry, Chris; you never had a chance.

BAMMER'S BOTTOM LINE

The real test of a green-lighter, for me, is whether I'd want to see the movie again, if only eventually. *O Brother, Where Art Thou?* passed that test and then some, because I was ready to rewatch this flick immediately. If only to hear the "Soggy Bottom Boys" work it again.

GREEN LIGHT

 **On the Town**
(1949)

UNRATED; running time 98 minutes
GENRE: Musical
WRITTEN BY: Adolph Green & Betty Comden (based on their Broadway play)
DIRECTED BY: Stanley Donen, Gene Kelly
MUSIC BY: Leonard Bernstein, Roger Edens
CHOREOGRAPHY BY: Gene Kelly
CAST: Gene Kelly, Frank Sinatra, Betty Garrett, Ann Miller, Jules Munshin, Vera-Ellen, Alice Pearce, Bern Hoffman

THE STORY

Small-town navy boys Gabey (Gene Kelly), Chip (Frank Sinatra), and Ozzie (Jules Munshin) have a 24-hour pass in New York, and are out to see the sights. Sights like Ivy Smith (Vera-Ellen), Hilde Esterhazy (Betty Garrett), and Claire Huddesen (Ann Miller) will do just fine, thank-yew-verra-much. When the boys see a poster for Miss Turnstiles, a.k.a. Ivy Smith, Gabey is enchanted and sets out to meet the famous (or so he thinks) Miss Turnstiles to ask her out on a date that night. "In a city of four million women," he actually does find Ivy, then loses her, then finds her again, then . . . well, you get the picture. Chip and Ozzie have their hands full, too: Ozzie pursues Claire, an anthropologist who'd like to study his bones, and Chip finds himself being pursued by Mae West's little sister, Hildy.

THE UPSHOT

On the surface, *On the Town* doesn't seem all that deep; just another Boy Gets Shore Leave—Boy Looks For A Hookup—Boy Meets Girl—Boy Falls

For Girl—The End kinda flick but there's more to *OTT* than meets the eye. Besides its Oscar-winning musical score, *OTT* broke new ground as the first musical to be filmed partially on location, and the difference shows. The opening scenes establish a great, realistic look at New York from a tourist's eyes. I also liked the use of the "clock" to countdown the hours left for the navy boys, a technique used better, and more sparingly, here than in some modern-day films.

But for me, the kicker in this movie was Betty Garrett as the lusty Brunhilde Esterhazy. To be sure, Gene Kelly and Frank Sinatra continued their charming *Anchors Aweigh* (see page 220) ways, and for the first time since *An American in Paris* (see page 218), I haven't wanted to pop Gene Kelly's girl upside the head; I found Vera-Ellen quite pleasing here, and I loved her voice. The comic relief Jules Munshin as fifth-wheel Ozzie, Ann Miller as his girl Claire, and especially Alice Pearce as Hilde's lonely-hearts roommate Lucy Shmeeler, were also good in their supporting roles. But Garrett added some sho'nuff serious spice to this tale, to the point where I was wondering if they'd have a scene with Hilde and Chip crawling out of a Navy locker á la *Stripes*. Woo laud.

I suppose I could overanalyze many of the plot points of this and other typical '40s musicals, from a '00s point of view. I could discuss the Peter Pan syndrome many of Kelly's characters seem to exhibit, dish on how Sinatra's skinny-boy guys often got smacked around by dolls, cogitate on the whys and wherefores of all the various and sundry floozies that inundated these musicals, yada yada blah blah blah. But where's the fun in that?

THE NUMBERS

A few of the numbers in *On the Town* rank up there with my all-time musical favorites, including "New York, New York," "Come Up to My Place," and "On the Town."

BAMMER'S BOTTOM LINE

If nothing else, *On the Town* finally convinced me that sex existed in the movies long before they had a rating for it (and an MPAA against it). Back then, they were just more subtle about it than the current batch of cinema artistes. I can diggit.

GREEN LIGHT

Bams Singin' in the Rain
(1952)

RATED G; running time 103 minutes
GENRE: Musical
WRITTEN BY: Betty Comden, Adolph Green
DIRECTED BY: Stanley Donen, Gene Kelly
MUSIC BY: Nacio Herb Brown, Lennie Hayton
CHOREOGRAPHY BY: Gene Kelly
CAST: Gene Kelly, Donald O'Connor, Debbie Reynolds, Jean Hagen, Millard Mitchell, Cyd Charisse, Rita Moreno

THE STORY

The 1920s were a time of flappers, and the Charleston, and silent movies. And Don Lockwood (Gene Kelly) and his leading lady, Lina Lamont (Jean Hagen), were huge silent-movie stars. Don, along with his buddy Cosmo Brown (Donald O'Connor), enjoyed the benefits of stardom even when his adoring fans got to be a bit too much for him, and when Lina foolishly believed the media hype that she and Don had a lil' sum'n sum'n goin' on. Luckily for him, he met and fell for Kathy Selden (Debbie Reynolds), a feisty chorus girl with big dreams of the New York stage.

The '20s were also a time of tremendous upheaval: for the movies, it was a time when "The talkies" came along to change the world. Producer R. F. Simpson (Millard Mitchell) initially played off the importance of the newfangled technology, thinking it was just a passing fad. Soon, though, the brass at Monumental Pictures realized that they'd best jump on the bandwagon, and remake their latest flick, *The Dueling Cavalier*, into a musical talkie of their own. Only one problem: contrary to her beliefs, Lina can't sing, can't dance, and when she talks, her voice could curdle milk.

THE UPSHOT

Yes, I *know* everyone loves *Singin'*. Yes, I *know* it sits high on the American Film Institute's ranking of Really Good Flicks. And yes, I most def have lots of respect and admiration for the makers of *Singin' in the Rain;* my torrid love for Gene Kelly is a torch I carry to this day. But I still call this one second-best to *An American in Paris*, for two nitpicky but irritating reasons: the relative weakness of Debbie Reynolds as Kelly's paramour—as my girl Lina might've said, "I kaaaan't staaan' 'er!"—and the lack of much to do for Kelly's sidekick, Donald O'Connor.

Believe me when I say that those two flaws hardly marred the excellent work that is *Singin'*.

My minor dislike for Reynolds and her Kathy Selden character is not a real showstopping disdain. Except for Kathy's original spunk when first confronted with movie star Don Lockwood, there just didn't seem to be much there worthy of Don's pursuit.

I have nothing but praise for the rest of the cast, however. Gene Kelly, of course, can do no wrong by me (well, he didn't have the best singing voice, but oh, that body.) Here, as usual, he danced divinely, and though his acting wouldn't be called Shakespearean, he had a charm that more than made up for any thespian shortcomings he might've had. Jean Hagen was Ghettofabulous as the screechy but fun Lina Lamont; a true diva if ever I saw one. Also excellent in supporting roles were Millard Mitchell as the marvelously henpecked R. F. Simpson, and Cyd "Legs" Charisse as the femme fatale dancer who spoke volumes without saying a word. And in only her fourth feature film, living legend (and deserving of a Latina Factor all her own) Rita Moreno's bit part as Lina's bud Zelda is a small taste of what was to come for her.

THE NUMBERS

The heart of any musical, especially one made during the '40s and '50s, is its musical numbers (duh!). And *Singin' in the Rain* is chock-full o' good ones, including "Make 'Em Laugh" which made my jaw drop the first time I saw it.

"Singin' in the Rain," the classic title song. Anything I say about this magnificent, classic number will be woefully insufficient. Suffice it to say that that's one lucky umbrella. And the struttin' fella ain't half bad.

"Broadway Melody." Clocked in at 14 minutes, this number is the great capper "*Singin*'" deserves. A story-within-the-story, I can't decide what I liked most about this number: Kelly, of course, the very leggy Cyd Charisse, or the coin-flipping mobsters. Ah, who'm I kiddin'; I liked it all. As my Brit friends would say, bloody brilliant!

BAMMER'S BOTTOM LINE

Betty Comden and Adolph Green's screenplay may have been the backbone of *Singin' in the Rain*, but Nacio Herb Brown and Lennie Hayton's music, and Gene Kelly's fantastic choreography were its heart and soul.

GREEN LIGHT

The Guinness Book of World Records lists Rita Moreno as the first person to win the Big Four awards—Emmy, Grammy, Oscar, and Tony.

This is disputed by many. Some claim that even though Barbra Streisand's Tony was a noncompetitive one, she was the first. Others argue that Helen Hayes reached this goal in 1976—a year before Moreno.

Bams West Side Story
(1961)

UNRATED; running time 151 minutes

GENRE: Musical

WRITTEN BY: Jerome Robbins, Ernest Lehman (based on the play by Arthur Laurents and *Romeo and Juliet* by Shakespeare)

DIRECTED BY: Jerome Robbins, Robert Wise

MUSIC BY: Leonard Bernstein

LYRICS BY: Stephen Sondheim

CHOREOGRAPHY BY: Jerome Robbins

CAST: Natalie Wood, Richard Beymer, Russ Tamblyn, Rita Moreno, George Chakiris, Tucker Smith, Tony Mordente, David Winters, Eliot Feld, Susan Oakes, Simon Oakland, Jose De Vega, Ned Glass

THE STORY

The place: New York. The time: the 1950s. Whites hang out on one side of the 'hood, Puerto Ricans on the other; and never the twain should meet. But someone forgot to tell that to Tony (Richard Beymer) and Maria (Natalie Wood). Tony, a good White boy, and Maria, a good Puerto Rican girl, defy tradition by falling in love, much to the chagrin of their families, their friends, and their respective homies in the rival gangs, the White Jets and the Puerto Rican Sharks. The Jets, led by Riff (Russ Tamblyn), and the Sharks, led by Maria's brother Bernardo, try to talk "sense" to Tony and Maria, to no avail. All hell breaks loose when Bernardo's girlfriend Anita (Rita Moreno, who is as good as it gets) tries to deliver a message from Maria to Tony via the hardheaded and hardhearted Jets; and dire consequences follow.

THE UPSHOT

Forget that the late Natalie Wood was no more Puerto Rican than I am, that she wouldn't know a Puerto Rican accent if it bit her on the butt, and that Wood, Rita Moreno, and Richard Beymer actually had singing doubles (Marni Nixon, Betty Wand, and Jimmy Bryant, respectively). Forget that of all the males cast for *West Side Story*, Richard Beymer seemed the most out-of-place. And forget that one doesn't usually perceive singing and dancing gangbangers as a menace (not in these days of drive-by shooting, anyway. I prefer the cop-rock types myself . . . but I digress).

Forget about all that, because it simply does not matter. The strength of *West Side Story* lies in its earnestness and in the way it conveyed the immediacy of its tale without compromising its obvious roots as a stage play. In spite of their shortcomings, I *believed* in Wood's Maria and in Beymer's Tony. And because of the powerful performances of the supporting cast (chief among them the fiery Moreno, George Chakiris, and Russ Tamblin as fated gangleaders, Simon Oakland as the soul-dead Lieutenant Schrank, and my favorite chick of 'em all, Susan Oakes as the ruffneck Anybodys), *West Side Story* will always be much more than just another musical for me.

Not to discount the musical portion of the program; not in the least. Even without its message, *WSS* could still stand on its musical merits alone. Composer Leonard Bernstein and Lyricist Stephen Sondheim whipped up a masterful score; choreographer Jerome Robbins created memorable dance sequences (who could ever forget "America"? or "Cool"? or . . .); and though Ernest Lehman's script seems a bit dated by today's standards, director Robert Wise beautifully put it all together in a film that truly deserves to be hailed by a term that's so often abused these days: a classic.

BAMMER'S BOTTOM LINE

I could note, I reckon, that *West Side Story* tore up the Academy Awards in 1961, with 10 total Oscars, including Best Picture, Best Supporting Actor (George Chakiris), and Best Supporting Actress (Rita Moreno). But it hardly matters. Y'all already know that *WSS* was da bomb, right? If ya don't know, now ya know.

GREEN LIGHT

the Diva   **The Wiz**
(1978)

RATED G; running time 133 minutes
GENRE: Comedy/Musical
WRITTEN BY: L. Frank Baum (novel), William F. Brown (play), Joel Schumacher (D'OH)
DIRECTED BY: Sidney Lumet
CAST: Diana Ross, Michael Jackson, Nipsey Russell, Ted Ross, Mabel King, Theresa Merritt, Lena Horne, Thelma Carpenter, Richard Pryor

Have you ever listened to how funky "You Can't Win"—a song I personally wore out on my vinyl album as a child—really is? This is what Bams and I mean by when "Michael wuz Black"—not only does he party on this song; if you listen to the soundtrack close enough, you hear both him and the cowardly lion (original cast member Ted Ross) "tear up" some of these songs by ad libbing.

THE DIGEST

The Wiz is a coming-of-age story. Dorothy is a grown woman who has lived under her aunt and uncle's roof all her life and has had no desire to leave. "She's 24 years old and never been west of 125th Street." She tells her aunt that she is quite content teaching kindergarten and living at home. With that, she picks up the trash to take it outside. Toto runs ahead of her and, as she gives chase, a snow funnel cloud sweeps her and Toto up and drops them in Oz, where Dorothy blossoms. She meets many new friends and takes charge of her life. She learns the importance of love, family, and friendship.

First, she is met by the Munchkins who tell her that when she landed in Oz, she landed on the Wicked Witch of the East, "Ever Mean," and killed her. The munchkins are ecstatic, as is Miss One, the Witch of the South. She is a numbers runner and her speeches are cleverly peppered with numerical references (written-produced by the musical cast behind the scenes: Quincy Jones, Ashford and Simpson, Charlie Smalls, and Luther Vandross). Miss One sends her off to meet the Wiz who can help her get home. At first, she meets the Scarecrow (Michael Jackson). He is being mistreated by the crows who have him believing that he has no brain, and that it's his life's mission to be up there for their enjoyment. Dorothy saves him from the nasty crows and convinces him to travel with her. Together they find the Yellow Brick Road that takes them to the Wiz. Dorothy and the Scarecrow dance and "Ease on Down" the road and next find their way to the Tin Man (Nipsey Russell) who is trapped underneath his 400-lb. tin wife. After they "Slide Some Oil" on him, they find out that he doesn't

have a heart. So they invite him to "Ease on Down" to see the Wiz.

As they progress, they run into the Lion (Ted Ross). He shows them that he is "A Mean Ole Lion" and has them scared witless until Toto bites him. We then learn that he is really a coward. Well, the Wiz can fix that too.

Together they make their way to the Emerald City. The group meets several challenges along the way, challenges (including getting out of an opium den, which went over my head as a child) that require courage, heart, and intelligence, even though each one thinks they are lacking these attributes. Once they get to the fabled Emerald City, we are treated to an elaborate musical number with Quincy Jones as the focal point. After they are finished being awestruck, they request to see the Wiz (Richard Pryor).

But there is one small problem. *The Wiz* is just a normal man and he's lost, too. They are devastated. Dorothy, however, reminds them of all the times they used their hearts, brains, and courage to help them succeed. Everyone had what they were looking for all along, except Dorothy. She still has no way of getting home—or so she thinks. Glinda the Good Witch of the North (Lena Horne) appears and tells Dorothy that she had the power to go "Home" all along. With that, Dorothy clicks her heels three times and, before she knows it, she's back home, more mature and ready to meet all the challenges that await her.

THE DISH

Every single time I watch *The Wiz*, I fall for it anew, and am struck by how multilayered it is, and by how I catch something different with each viewing. Joel Schumacher, who directed *Batman*

& *Robin*, *8MM*, and *A Time to Kill*, wrote the screenplay. He also wrote the screenplays for *Sparkle* and *Car Wash*. Who knew? Another little fact about *The Wiz*: Sidney Lumet, the director, was married to one of Lena Horne's daughters.

As for the cast, Diana Ross's voice is as strong as I've ever heard it, but she had no business playing this part. She was a bit too old for it. We all knew Michael Jackson could sing, but he surprised me with his acting. It's no Oscar-winning performance, but given his lack of experience, he did very well. Lena Horne steals the show with her appearance. She sends chills up and down my spine every single time she belts out that finale. No one, and I mean *no one*, could have done that better.

THE DIRECTIVE

Every child should have the pleasure of seeing *The Wiz*. And adults shouldn't pass it up either.

GREEN LIGHT

throughout the history of cinema, White folks have found themselves in trouble on many occasions. Someone is always being attacked by an alien; swallowed up in a natural disaster; dogged by the "gubmint"; chased by a ghost or evil spirit; tied to a railroad track; left to die in the elements by their platoon leader . . . you get the picture. The movies reviewed in this chapter all fit this theme.

WHEN BAD THINGS HAPPEN TO WHITE FOLKS

A Beautiful Mind
(2001)

RATED PG-13; running time 135 minutes
GENRE: Drama
WRITTEN BY: Akiva Goldsman (based on the
   book by Sylvia Nasar)
DIRECTED BY: Ron Howard
CAST: Russell Crowe, Ed Harris, Jennifer Con-
   nelly, Paul Bettany, Adam Goldberg, Josh Lu-
   cas, Anthony Rapp, Christopher Plummer

THE STORY

John Forbes Nash Jr. (Russell Crowe) was a brilliant mathematician, to the point of arrogance;
aloof in social situations, to the point of being
slapped by the women he clumsily pursued; and
the winner of a Major Prize late in life. John
Forbes Nash Jr. was also quite . . . disturbed.

A Beautiful Mind takes the audience on a journey through Nash's life, from his early years at
grad school with fellow students and scientists,
to his courtship of Alicia (Jennifer Connelly) and
his secret project for the Department of Defense,
by William Parcher (Ed Harris). It is this secret
project—decoding information from the Rus-
sians in the "Commie scare" days in America—
that leads Nash to the breaking point. The closer
Nash gets to cracking the code, the more paranoid he gets about being discovered by the Rus-
sians. And throughout it all, his college
roommate Charles (Paul Bettany) is there to encourage Nash. Or perhaps not. Things aren't always as they appear, and Nash's version of reality,
at times, isn't reality at all.

THE UPSHOT

The good thing about not knowing the true story
that a film is based on is that you don't have expectations going in to see the movie.

The bad thing about not knowing the true
story is, now that I've read an article pointing out
the discrepancies between the book this movie is
based on, the movie, and real life, I'm completely
confused about what is and is not real regarding
John Forbes Nash Jr. And worse—now I'm questioning how that makes me feel about A Beautiful
Mind itself. And that, my friends, is most def not
a good thing.

I was all set to write up my review of this
movie until I read a USA Today article by Andy
Seiler, titled "It's 'Beautiful,' But Not Factual." As
the title suggests, the story told in A Beautiful
Mind might be based on truth, but the question
is, how loosely? Now why'd I have to go and read
that before I wrote my screed?

If Seiler's article is correct, then A Beautiful
Mind is less "based on a true story" than it is an
outright fable. But all that said, does that make A
Beautiful Mind any less good? Mostly, no. In spite
of director Ron Howard's bent toward white-
washing subjects of his movies to make them
more palatable to a general audience, and Crowe's
Rainman-like portrayal of Nash, I found A Beautiful Mind to be an interesting, fascinating film to
watch. The visuals in Beautiful are as important as
the story itself. Maybe even more so, because they
effectively show the inner workings of a beautiful
and twisted mind in a multifaceted way, a way
that verbalizations never could. I commend
Howard for his use of show-not-tell in this way.

I'm sure Crowe's performance will be talked
about in certain circles, but for me, it's Jennifer

Connelly who deserves the most kudos. Her Alicia is the one who bridges the gap between John's inner world and the reality around him. She forces this movie and its characters to make sense—even if her life on film distorts facts. But still, I'm left to wonder if, like John Nash's own, this movie's version of reality isn't all it's cracked up to be.

BAMMER'S BOTTOM LINE

A Beautiful Mind is one of the top 10 movies of 2001, despite concerns about its authenticity.

GREEN LIGHT

---

the Diva **Bless the Child**
(2000)

RATED R; running time 87 minutes
GENRE: Thriller
WRITTEN BY: Tom Rickman and Clifford Green & Ellen Green
DIRECTED BY: Chuck Russell
CAST: Kim Basinger, Jimmy Smits, Rufus Sewell, Ian Holm, Angela Bettis, Christina Ricci, Yan Birch, Lumi Cavazos, Holliston Coleman

> Christina Ricci gets the "See, You Can Eat and Still Have a Cute Body" Award from The Diva.

THE DIGEST

The Star of Jacob is shining for the first time since the birth of Christ. Christians and Satan worshippers believe that this is the sign that the next Messiah has been born. Maggie O'Connor (Kim Basinger) is surprised by an unexpected visit from her heroin-addict sister. Said sister has brought Cody, her 9-day-old daughter (played by a 4-month-old), drops her off, then jets, leaving Maggie to raise the child.

Early on the child shows signs of slight autism. Maggie is inclined to put her in a special Catholic day school. By the time she is six, she starts to exhibit the ability to do strange things: resurrect the dead, make things spin, hear voices, and see angels. Around this same time, there is a rash of child murders: each child born on 12/16/99, the same day as Cody.

We come to find out that Eric Stark (Rufus Sewell), the leader of a sect of Satan worshippers, is looking for the Messiah with plans to turn him/her evil. If he's not successful, he'll kill him/her. Once he gets a hold of Cody, Maggie must find her and save her before Easter Eve, or mankind is lost.

THE DISH

Have you ever gotten angry after watching a movie because it comes "this close" to being worthy . . . and it's not? Or, better yet, the movie is filled with stupid behavior to the point where you almost shout at the screen? Well, that's how I felt while watching *Bless the Child*. The following stuff had me wishing for some popcorn to throw at the screen.

• Maggie knows she is going up against evil, so she promptly goes home and puts on a skirt and two-inch heels.

When the special Catholic school is recommended to Maggie, our brainiac utters what has got to be one of the worse lines in cinematic history, "As long as it's not too religious." It's CATHOLIC.

When Maggie is getting ready to shoot Stark, he says, "Feel the evil. Feel the hatred. Let it run through you. It feels good, doesn't it?" Ummm, anyone remember Darth Vader? Hello? Let's be original.

THE DIRECTIVE

Anyone who sits through *Bless the Child* deserves to be blessed. Though I will say this: the minor special effects were quite good; otherwise this movie would get a straight red light.

FLASHING RED LIGHT

Blair Witch 2: Book of Shadows
(2000)

RATED R; running time 80 minutes
GENRE: Horror/Horrible
WRITTEN BY: Joe Berlinger & Dick Beebe
DIRECTED BY: Joe Berlinger
CAST: Kim Director, Jeffrey Donovan, Erica Leerhsen, Tristen Skylar, Stephen Barker Turner

THE DIGEST
Lawd, where do I begin?

Stephen and Tristen are a couple of students who are researching the Blair Witch, as well as all the hysteria that was caused by the release of the film. Trying to prove the "group hysteria theory," they hire Jeffrey to take them on a tour of the forest. Jeffrey lives in Burkittsville, home of the Witch, and capitalizes on the popularity of the last film by selling T-shirts and twigs.

He invites Erica (who is a Wiccan) and Kim (who is this Goth chick) to come along for the ride. Erica wants to point out that Wiccans are misunderstood, and Kim just thinks the whole thing is cool. They all get drunk over a campfire and when they awaken, the camp is trashed. But that's just the first of the "scary" things they encounter. (If you didn't see the first film, see page 3 for a synopsis.)

THE DISH

One of the reasons I loved the first *Blair Witch* was that it was very original. It allowed you to use your imagination. This one was boring and hit you over the head with everything and wasn't scary at all. I almost fell asleep.

The film was only 80 minutes long but I was through after 30. Among the many things that irritated me was the sheriff. He was a jackass. If he treated me the way he was treating them, I'd be placing a call to the ACLU.

It was a waste of my flippin' time and it will be a waste of yours. I wouldn't even rent this mess.

THE DIRECTIVE

I wanted to cast a few spells myself on the writers . . . evil spells.

RED LIGHT

Castaway
(2000)

RATED PG-13; running time 143 minutes
GENRE: Adventure/Drama
WRITTEN BY: William Broyles Jr.
DIRECTED BY: Robert Zemeckis
CAST: Tom Hanks, Helen Hunt, Nick Searcy, Lari White, Chris Noth

> Production of *Castaway* was shut down for six months while Tom Hanks shed 50 lbs.

THE DIGEST
It's the holiday season of 1995 and Chuck Noland (Tom Hanks), a systems engineer for FedEx, is flying all over the world trying to keep things running smoothly. His girlfriend, Kelly (Helen Hunt), is understanding, but she is starting to grow a little tired of their lives being run by FedEx. This doesn't seem to bother Chuck, because he takes his job so seriously that when he was a FedEx driver, he borrowed a bike to finish delivering his packages when his van broke down. That's dedication.

For once, Kelly and Chuck seem to be having a normal Christmas, when Chuck gets paged. He has to catch a flight overseas to solve a problem. He and Kelly get out their calendars and plan to be together on New Year's. He promises to come home on time without fail. Or so he thinks.

Chuck is flying on a cargo plane when they encounter a storm. They fly off course to avoid the storm, but they don't quite get out of the way. The plane crashes in the middle of the ocean and Chuck washes up on shore. All Chuck has is a few FedEx packages and the clothes on his back. He is not a survivalist; he's a FedEx guy. How is he going to make it? It becomes a challenge to stay alive, not only *physically* but *mentally* as well.

THE DISH
One of my main concerns about this movie was the thought of watching Tom Hanks by himself for 90 minutes. My fears were unfounded. Hanks was great. It was very interesting to watch him hold on to a tiny string of sanity. When he is alone on the island, he is always *this* close to completely losing it, but pulls back each time.

What I ended up disliking about the movie is that it didn't show us anything new. We've seen a dozen movies about someone being stranded on an island. I want to see what happens when that person comes home. *Castaway* touched on this, but very briefly. There was a hint that it might have gone on further, but this part was edited out. I understand that the movie would have been three hours long had they explored this aspect, but I wanted to see it nonetheless. Think about it, you are gone from civilization for "x" amount of years, how do you deal with things that are now considered basic amenities? Like cable modems (is my geek showing)? Okay, a cable modem isn't a basic amenity, but you get my drift.

I also had trouble dealing with the occasional flouting of reality. For example, when he knew the plane was having trouble, he went into the bathroom and washed his face. Ummmm . . . why? You're gonna crash, sit your behind in a chair and buckle up! Despite my issues, it was a fairly solid movie.

THE DIRECTIVE

I felt like the *real* ending had been Castaway, but it's worth seeing. Unless, that is, you don't care for Tom Hanks. You won't see anyone but him for most of the movie.

FLASHING YELLOW LIGHT

Days of Wine and Roses

(1962)

RATED R; running time 117 minutes
GENRE: Drama
WRITTEN BY: J. P. Miller
DIRECTED BY: Blake Edwards
CAST: Jack Lemmon, Lee Remick, Charles Bickford

> All we can say is "Damn." That's some serious addiction.

CASS'S CLIP

Joe Clay (Jack Lemmon) is a seemingly happy public relations executive, and finding gorgeous women to "entertain" businessmen at social gatherings is part of his job duties. Kirsten Clay (Lee Remick) is an executive secretary and aspiring actress. Their paths cross when Joe mistakenly assumes that Kirsten is one of the "entertainers." Joe, already tittering on the brink of alcoholism, convinces nondrinker Kirsten to try a brandy Alexander. Joe and Kirsten fall in love somewhere in between countless happy hour binges and discussions about morality.

Fast forward. Joe and Kirsten are now married, and are five-packs-a-day cigarette-smoking, full-blown alcoholics. Jobless, Joe and Kirsten have to get cleaned up. Joe believes that in order for them to get sober they must leave their environment. The problem is, how does one run away from one's self? Arnesen (Charles Bickford), a nursery owner and Kirsten's father, allows them to move in with him. Now, after a month of sobriety, Joe is the perfect employee. He helps Arnesen move plants, shrubs, and trees around in the greenhouse. Kirsten refuses to help out until Joe shows her the two bottles of booze strapped to his legs and tells her about the bottle of bubbly stashed in one of the pots in the nursery. Kirsten can't say "no!"

Even after our happy-hour couple guzzles down the two bottles, it's still not enough. One of the most disturbing scenes in *Days of Wine and Roses* occurs when Joe goes on a destructive rampage of the greenhouse in search of the stashed bottle. Other poignant scenes include the scene in which Joe is put into a padded room to detox, and the unsettling scene in which Kirsten, in her drunken stupor, tries to seduce her father.

The ending is sad and inevitable.

DA 411

Long before I saw the movie, my mother and I used to sing *Days of Wine and Roses* while my father played it on the piano. Then, when I saw the movie, I felt tricked because I couldn't understand how this seemingly beautiful love song had such a haunting meaning. (I didn't learn the meaning of the metaphors until the sixth grade.) An incredible performance is given by Jack Lemmon. He was so convincing, he was hard to watch because we all know someone like the character he portrayed. Lee Remick's performance was also sound.

Considering the era this movie was made in, *Days of Wine and Roses* tackled many issues about addiction and alcoholism still relevant today.

CASS'S CONCLUSION

Days of Wine and Roses is a must-see movie for enablers, as well as children raised by alcoholics.

GREEN LIGHT

the Diva   Don't Say a Word
(2001)

RATED R; running time 113 minutes
GENRE: Thriller
WRITTEN BY: Patrick Smith Kelly and Anthony Peckham, based on the novel by Andrew Klavan
DIRECTED BY: Gary Fleder
CAST: Michael Douglas, Sean Bean, Brittany Murphy, Famke Janssen, Oliver Platt, Jennifer Esposito, Skye McCole Bartusiak

THE DIGEST

Dr. Nathan Conrad (Michael Douglas) has an excellent reputation as a child psychologist. He is able to reach children that no one else can reach, so it is not unusual when he is called to try to deal with Elisabeth Burrows (Brittany Murphy).

18-year-old Elisabeth has been in mental hospitals for the past 10 years. She has had 20 different diagnoses from 20 different doctors and hospitals. Her current doctor is concerned, because for the first time ever, she's tried to kill someone.

Within 5 minutes of talking to Elisabeth, Dr. Conrad realizes that she has been more or less pretending. When her doctors pinpoint her ailment, she mimics another patient. Nathan theorizes that she is doing this to stay institutionalized. He turns the case back over to Dr. Sachs (Oliver Platt). When he returns home, he is greeted by his bedridden (thanks to a skiing accident) wife, Aggie (Famke Janssen), and his 8-year-old daughter, Jessie (Skye McCole Bartusiak). He tucks Jessie in bed and promises to take her to the Macy's Parade the following day. When he wakes up the next morning, he makes breakfast for the family only to find Jessie gone. When he sees that the chain on the door has been cut, he fears the worst. Before he can do anything about it, his phone rings. He is instructed not to involve the police or his daughter will be dead. He is ordered to unearth a secret from Elisabeth's brain by 5 P.M. or his daughter will be killed.

Nathan is tasked with the hardest case in his life. He's got 7 hours to open the mind of a very disturbed young lady. Can he save her and his daughter?

THE DISH

There were quite a few "ummm, whatever" moments. For instance, the bad guys managed to get cameras throughout Nathan's house, even in the bedroom. Now how in the hell did they get that many cameras in that bedroom with the wife being stuck in bed? And I was not surprised to see that *somebody* got offed at 79 minutes. 19 minutes late, but I think we can still call this the Brotha Rule. (See page xv for an explanation of the Brotha Rule.)

Famke Janssen and her character were just a waste of space. They should have fleshed her character out more or not used her at all. The bad guy played by Sean Bean (doesn't his name just make you giggle?) wasn't that menacing. I would have lied and told him that I had the number then kicked his ass when we met face to face for the exchange.

What a waste of time. Just hold her upside down over a roof ledge. She'll talk then.

THE DIRECTIVE

Shhh, *Don't Say a Word*... it's not that good. This is a decent date movie, but not a must-see.

YELLOW LIGHT

Bams Flawless
(1999)

RATED R; running time 110 minutes
GENRE: Drama
WRITTEN BY: Joel Schumacher
DIRECTED BY: Joel Schumacher
CAST: Robert De Niro, Philip Seymour Hoffman, Barry Miller, Wanda De Jesus, Skipp Sudduth, Daphne Rubin Vega, Wilson Jermaine Heredia, Nashom Benjamin

THE STORY

Walt Koontz (Robert De Niro) is a heroic, retired cop, liked and respected in his 'hood, and missed by his pal and former cop Tommy Walsh (Skip Sudduth). Walt likes to spend his time at "Private Dancer," doing the tango—vertical and horizontal—with the sultry (and greedy) Karen, much to the consternation of the not-so-sultry (to his narrow-minded eyes), Tia.

"Busty" Rusty Zimmerman (Philip Seymour Hoffman) is, in his words, "an artist; not a drag queen, but a female impersonator . . . a woman trapped in a man's body"; he and his friends Cha Cha and Amazing Grace are constantly taunted by Walt, who is about as homophobic as they come.

Their worlds collide when Walt has a stroke after trying to take a bite out of local neighborhood crime. His physical therapist recommends singing lessons to Walt, to help him to speak better, and since Rusty "sings" with his friends as part of their drag show, *Femme Fatale* . . . wackiness ensues.

THE UPSHOT

One would think that a film starring the normally superb Robert De Niro and "new" (to some, but he's been around for quite some time) show stealer Philip Seymour Hoffman, would be a sure thing. One would be wrong.

I felt betrayed. To be fair, it wasn't *bad*, exactly; it just wasn't *good*; certainly, not up to the potential of the talent involved (including director Joel Schumacher). Besides wondering why in the world the flaming gay stereotype was resurrected for the umpteenth time on film, I felt little connection with anything going on in this flick. I simply didn't care, because there was precious little to care about. Walt was an Archie Bunker wannabe; so what? We've been there, done that before. Rusty and his friends were Gay And Proud Of It, and will dress down anyone who doesn't accept them—big deal. Yes, homophobia's bad, we know. Now tell us something we don't.

By means of providing further contrasts in secondary characters deserving of our sympathy or pity, Leonard Wilcox as a snitching hotel manager served as a mere distraction, a quick chuckle or two; and while Tia was sweet, I had to wonder what in the world she saw in Walt. The whole "Gay Republicans" shtick was cute while it lasted; but besides some cheap laughs about how dumb homophobes are, not much was accomplished by all the little parts that made up the whole of *Flawless*.

Overall, Hoffman put on a good show; in fact, in his grandiose style, he carried even De Niro, who had to tone down his usually punchy performance to be believable as a victim of a stroke, but one man doth not a movie make. Maybe next time, fellas. Maybe next time.

THE BLACK FACTOR

Robert De Niro is known for his . . . affinity . . . for Black chicks (Not That There's Anything Wrong With That . . .), so it wasn't too surprising that his character would also be down with other ethnicities; namely, Wanda De Jesus's Karen (who, I daresay, is attractive to even this stalwart heterosexual Chick). Oh, nothing; just an observation.

And though this is a bit of a stretch for the Black Factor, I can't help but think of the controversy that arises any time gay groups seek to equate their struggle for rights with that of Blacks; there are some Blacks who deny that there's equity in the situations, and some gays who insist that there is (and, of course, since there are many gay Blacks, many of *them* say that they are affected twice over). Say what you will about all that, but it occurs to me that, as is true with many such squabbles between "minority" groups, the best way for those who are in power to *remain* in power is to make sure that those who are not in power remain so, and what better way to keep the powerless powerless, than by provoking separation between like groups?

Think on that for a bit.

BAMMER'S BOTTOM LINE

"Flawless"? I think not. "Irredeemably, Inexplicably Flawed," now that's more like it.

I have no idea what the folks behind *Flawless* were trying to say with this flick. Whatever the hell they were trying to say, it sure didn't make the transition from the screen to the audience very well, no matter how dressed up it tried to be.

YELLOW LIGHT

Hannibal
(2001)

RATED R; running time 130 minutes

GENRE: Thriller/Horror

WRITTEN BY: Tom Harris (novel), David Mamet (screenplay)

DIRECTED BY: Ridley Scott

CAST: Anthony Hopkins, Julianne Moore, Giancarlo Giannini, Frankie Faison, Hazelle Goodman, Zeljko Ivanek, Ray Liotta, Gary Oldman

> Had we been in this movie, we'd still be having BBQ pork ribs.
> Y'all feel us?

THE DIGEST

Dr. Hannibal Lecter (Anthony Hopkins) has been gone for 10 years now. Dr. Lecter has planted himself in Florence, Italy, serving as curator for a museum. To his credit, he has been very good, hasn't eaten one person in a good 12 years. Meanwhile, Clarice (Julianne Moore) has built a solid reputation within the FBI. She has been placed in charge of several big cases, most notably the capture of Evelda Drumgo, a local drug Kingpin (she's a woman, does that make her a Queenpin?).

Because of a burning desire for revenge on Dr. Lecter, Clarice is about to cross paths with Dr. Lecter again. Mason Verger is the only victim of Dr. Lecter's to survive. I'm not completely sure what happened, I closed my eyes, but it would seem that Mason took to molesting children and was sent to Lecter for psychotherapy. At some point, Mason invited Dr. Lecter over and Dr. Lecter offered him some drugs and then convinced Verger to hang himself up and slice his face off, the pieces of which Hannibal feeds to the dogs.

Verger is *very* pissed and has been searching for Hannibal in order to get him back. He finds him with the help of the Florence police department. Meanwhile, back in D.C., Clarice is in hot water over a bust that went wrong. She has been forced by this jerk from the Justice Department, Paul Krendler (Ray Liotta), to go on leave until everything is straightened out. Verger has taken advantage of this and has decided to use Clarice as bait. He knows Lecter won't be able to resist a Clarice in distress, even if it's not physical distress.

THE DISH

Um. Eewww. This one was much grosser than the first. How gross was it? I won't spoil it, but I will tell you this much, I'm giving up pork. Blech. This is *not* for the squeamish. I'm not squeamish and I had trouble.

Julianne Moore did a good job of portraying Clarice, but I missed Clarice's vulnerability. In the past, their relationship was such that Clarice was trying to be a "big girl"—a grown up—and Hannibal was always able to make her feel like she was nothing more than a scared child. The fact that this was missing was disappointing to me. Also gone was a good sense of a cat-and-mouse chase.

I found no use for Mason Verger (Gary Oldman). He was there for the creepy factor. While I would be angry about my appearance as well had

I sliced off part of my face, he did do it to himself. Hannibal pushed him toward it, but he was holding the cutting utensil.

THE BLACK FACTOR

I was disappointed by the portrayal of Black folks in here. All of them were drug thugs and the one who wasn't was making illegal profits on the name of Hannibal Lecter. Come on, Hollywood.

THE DIRECTIVE

This one was mediocre. It was nearly as bad as *Red Dragon/Manhunter* (another Hannibal movie) and it wasn't nearly as brilliant as *Silence of the Lambs*. It was so gross, I almost didn't make it to the end. I'm giving it a double rating. A green light for fans of the series; you'll want to make sure you don't miss it. A flashing yellow for those who have never read the books or seen the previous movies.

GREEN LIGHT
For Hannibal diehards.

FLASHING YELLOW LIGHT
For everyone else.

The Haunting
(1999)

the Diva

RATED PG-13; running time 112 minutes
GENRE: Thriller/Horror
WRITTEN BY: David Self (book by Shirley Jackson)
DIRECTED BY: Jan de Bont
CAST: Liam Neeson, Lili Taylor, Catherine Zeta-Jones, Owen Wilson

THE DIGEST

Eleanor "Nell" (Lili Taylor) has been taking care of her mother for the past 11 years. Her mother passes away and she feels a bit lost. Her sister and brother-in-law have told her that they are going to sell her mother's apartment, so too bad. She can come live with them and baby-sit her nephew. She is rightly insulted. Then again, that little boy needs a behind-kicking anyway, so maybe she should have taken them up on the offer. Instead of moving in with her sister, however she decides to apply for a research program on insomnia. Little does she and the other two participants know, the professor is really studying how people deal with fear, and that is how they end up in the haunted house.

A few things happen over the course of the night right off the bat, mostly to Nell, and no one believes her. After the initial "things that go bump in the night," the movie fails to pick up speed. I spent the last 90 minutes wondering when the good stuff was going to start happening. It didn't. The movie is just one bad special effect after the other. Further, the ending is corny and predictable.

THE DISH

Well, children, what can I say? Really, you can't sleep, so you and a bunch of strangers take up residence in an empty mansion. Is it just us, or is this one of the dumbest things you've ever heard of? There is no way in *Hell* the sun would have set on my behind in that haunted house after the first night. Period. Had I been in the film, it would have been over in 45 minutes. The second the walls begin calling my name . . . catch my smoke as I'm booking down the street. No discussion.

I had such high hopes for this film. Suave Liam Neeson. Gorgeous Catherine Zeta-Jones. A pissed-off house. But it was a complete let-down. People were actually laughing at scenes I don't think were intended to be funny.

THE DIRECTIVE

I wouldn't waste my time or money on *The Haunting*.

RED LIGHT

---

the Diva   **Hollow Man**
(2000)

RATED R; running time 125 minutes
GENRE: Thriller
WRITTEN BY: Gary Scott Thompson (story), Andrew W. Marlowe
DIRECTED BY: Paul Verhoeven
CAST: Elisabeth Shue, Kevin Bacon, Josh Brolin, Kim Dickens, Greg Grunberg, Mary Jo Randle, Joey Slotnick, William Devane

THE DIGEST

Sebastian Caine (Kevin Bacon) heads up a Super Secret Government Project and has managed to figure out how to make living things transparent. Fearing that he is about to lose funding, he wants to try it on a human and picks himself. The problem is that Caine was arrogant before, and now that he is invisible he's even worse. He's also very aggressive. It becomes harder and harder to control him. The team wants to end the project, so Caine sets out to kill them, especially his second-in-command and former girlfriend, Dr. Linda McKay (Elisabeth Shue) and her new undercover boyfriend, the lead medical doctor Matthew Kensington (Josh Brolin).

THE DISH

I rarely miss a Kevin Bacon movie. But this time he wasn't enough. The special effects were pretty cool. But even that wasn't enough for me either. The dialogue was so bad that I couldn't concentrate on the visuals. Not to mention all the just plain stupid stuff that had me ready to kick the chair in front of me. For instance, we all know that a gorilla can break you in half in like 10 seconds, right? So why do you put your face up to the cage when you can't see where the now-invisible gorilla is? Why are you begging to have your head smashed?

The director, Paul Verhoeven, owes me yet *another* apology. I'm still waiting on one for *Starship Troopers*—one of the worst movies of 1997. I should also mention his other gem, *Showgirls*. Paul doesn't write this mess, true enough, but he keeps attaching himself to these bad projects, seemingly giving them clout and raising our expectations. Well, no more. The Diva has learned her lesson. I'm going to his next movie anticipating a "Vertastrophy" (my word for another Paul Verhoeven catastrophe). I want to be surprised that it's good instead of upset that it's bad.

 **The Insider**
(1999)

RATED R; running time 152 minutes
GENRE: Drama
WRITTEN BY: Eric Roth (based on the article by Marie Brenner)
DIRECTED BY: Michael Mann
CAST: Al Pacino, Russell Crowe, Christopher Plummer, Diane Venora, Philip Baker Hall, Gina Gershon, Wings Hauser, Debi Mazar, Lindsay Crouse, Stephen Tobolowsky

THE BLACK FACTOR
There is one Black scientist in that group. Guess who is the first scientist to go? Follow me now: the Black one (Mary Randle). So it's a "she" instead of a "he," it's the Sistah Rule instead of the Brotha Rule (see page xv). The fact remains: the Black person was the first to go. We can say one thing, for the most part, Hollywood is consistent.

THE DIRECTIVE
At times, I wanted the whole film to be "hollow."

YELLOW LIGHT

THE STORY
After Jeffrey Wigand (Russell Crowe), a scientist and VP at tobacco giant Brown & Williamson (B&W) is fired, he is pursued by CBS's *60 Minutes* producer Lowell Bergman (Al Pacino) who has been given anonymous tips by an insider that tobacco companies knowingly and willfully put harmful chemicals in their cigarettes to get smokers hooked on them. Even though Wigand has been fired, he hesitates to talk to Bergman and reporter Mike Wallace (Christopher Plummer) about the company, due to a confidentiality clause he signed with B&W.

After Bergman convinces Wigand that he and a group of lawyers he has hired can protect him, Wigand agrees to be interviewed by Wallace; but that confidentiality clause comes back to haunt both men when Bergman, Wallace, and executive producer Don Hewitt (Phillip Baker Hall) are put under pressure by CBS's legal department, led by Helen Caperelli (Gina Gershon), to drop Wigand's interview from the *60 Minutes* story. Remarkably, the CBS executives do just that, leaving Wigand to suffer the smear campaign alone.

THE UPSHOT

Let me be perfectly frank: I didn't go to see *The Insider* because I'd heard it was da bomb. I didn't go because I had 2.5 hours of free time on a lonely Saturday night (trust me, I didn't), nor because I had a hankerin' to see a good-guy-vs.-bad-guy fable. I'll be straight-up with you: I went to see this flick for the same reason that tens of Johnny-come-lately critics and moviegoers went to see it after its re-release: because it was nominated for an Academy Award. I'll not put forth any illusions that I cared for the tone of this film, for its high moral stance about the trials and travails of the Little Whistleblower versus the Big Bad Tobacco Company in the one corner, and the Evil Media Empire in the other. Little Man Blow Whistle. Big Bad Tobacco Company Squash Little Whistleblower. Evil Media Empire Leave Little Whistleblower Twisting In Wind. Little Whistleblower Fight Back. Good Triumph Over Evil. End Of Movie. And, to an extent, that's how it's laid out for the viewer.

That extent, of course, doesn't do much justice to the powerhouse performances by Pacino, Crowe, and the underappreciated Plummer, an actor whose characters always have the same sly grin that a Rottweiler might just before he tears you a new one. Crowe garnered an Oscar nomination for his against-type performance, a nod that he richly deserved. And the aforementioned Pacino puts in a solid performance that makes me wonder why he, too, wasn't seriously considered for a nomination. Lack of character flaws aside (though it was a central issue for me that both

Bergman and Wigand were presented as Put-Upon Heroes with little culpability), they both did an outstanding job in keeping the noticeably longish movie going smoothly, for the most part.

Michael Mann's direction, on the other hand, tended to get in the way for me. Some people might find Mann's so-close-up-the-nose-you-wanna-grab-a-tissue close-ups to be the pinnacle of cinematic art; I found them as tedious as Wigand's hallucinations were laughable. Mann didn't totally screw the pooch—his artistic use of light and shadows and beautiful shots of the Mississippi coastline really worked for me, as did his general direction of the actors themselves. But those close-ups gave me a daggone headache.

As for the movie itself, in the end, it all boils down to this: the movie, as good as it may have been, failed to impart a sense of urgency, because of the times we live in in American society. Crooked politicians, slimy lawyers, opportunistic media outlets, morally bankrupt businesses: they're all part and parcel of "the System" in which we all are trapped; for all its chest-thumping, this movie isn't telling us something we don't already know.

BAMMER'S BOTTOM LINE

The good performances in *The Insider* are wasted on a "No sh*t, Sherlock" tale.

GREEN LIGHT

The Last Castle
(2001)

RATED R; running time 126 minutes

GENRE: Drama

WRITTEN BY: David Scarpa and Graham Yost, from a story by Scarpa

DIRECTED BY: Rod Lurie

CAST: Robert Redford, James Gandolfini, Mark Ruffalo, Steve Burton, Delroy Lindo, Clifton Collins Jr., Brian Goodman, Paul Calderon, Frank Military, Michael Irby, Samuel Ball, George W. Scott, Jeremy Childs

THE DIGEST

Eugene Irwin (Robert Redford) is a three-star army general who has pleaded guilty to disobeying orders (as a result of his disobedience, 8 people were killed). His sentence is 10 years in the Castle. The Castle is a military facility for army men who have committed crimes while serving the country. It is run by Colonel Winter (James Gandolfini) with an iron fist inside a cashmere glove. Colonel Winter is manipulative and controlling. He'll smile at you while he is giving a hand signal to the guards to kill you.

When General Irwin arrives, he finds out that Colonel Winter is one of his biggest fans. The colonel believes that they should be naming a prison after General Irwin, not sending him to one. But an off-handed remark by General Irwin mortally insults Colonel Winter, and even though the General didn't mean any harm, he considers him an enemy.

Because of General Irwin's illustrious career, the men in the Castle gravitate toward him. This sticks in Colonel Winter's craw. As the men get close to the general, they let on that there have been several deaths of inmates since Colonel Winter took over. Not just deaths, but murders. They want General Irwin to contact his friends at The Pentagon. At first, the general doesn't want to get involved. He wants to just do his time and get out. Soon he starts to see how the rules are subtly broken by Colonel Winter. When he decides to do something about the injustices, the men are right behind him 100 percent.

It becomes a battle not unlike a chess game between the two officers. Can Colonel Winter outfox an old fox? There can be only one king. Who will it be?

THE DISH

I almost felt sorry for Colonel Winter. James Gandolfini gave him a vulnerability that easily put us in his shoes. I felt his pain when he was insulted. It was like an 8-year-old boy being dissed by his favorite baseball player. Robert Redford was brilliant. He played the other inmates like pawns on a chessboard, but not in a malicious way. He let them make their own decisions while he unobtrusively guided them. Delroy Lindo was a breath of fresh air. His part as a two-star general and friend to General Irwin was small but significant.

If there was a flaw, it was in the insufficiently explored relationship between Irwin and his daughter, played by Robin Wright Penn. Penn's role gave us insight into Irwin's failure as a father, it was really not necessary. They didn't flesh out their relationship enough for it to be an integral part of the story and, therefore, it should have just been left out.

THE DIRECTIVE

If I had a castle, I'd want General Irwin on my side. *The Last Castle* is another one of those great "adult" movies. Make a date with your spouse. Take the kids to a friend's house and catch this flick.

GREEN LIGHT

Lost Souls

(2000)

RATED R; running time 97 minutes
GENRE: Horror
WRITTEN BY: Pierce Gardner and Betsy Stahl
DIRECTED BY: Janusz Kaminski
CAST: Winona Ryder, Ben Chaplin, John Hurt, Alfre Woodard, Elias Koteas, Sarah Wynter

THE DIGEST

Maya Larkin (Winona Ryder) has a dubious distinction—she has survived an exorcism. As a result, she is called upon to help with the exorcism of a man in a mental ward. The exorcism fails, but she takes some books and writings that she found there, nonetheless.

The papers contain a series of numerical codes that she manages to decipher. It states that Satan is coming to earth and taking over a human form. The human is Peter Kelson (Ben Chaplin), an author of books about serial killers, including a book about the man on whom they had tried to perform the exorcism.

She contacts Peter and, upon doing some research, they find out how he fits the criteria for the satanic transformation. You must be a child born of incest and you must never have been baptized, among other things. Peter fits everything to a T. They also find out that the transformation will take place on his 33rd birthday, so they are running out of time and must stop the devil from walking among mankind.

THE DISH

Baptize Peter's ass. End of story. It's really that simple. Since you must meet every single criterion, why not pick one thing and change it. The simplest would be to baptize him. But NOOOOOOOO. They have to run around the city and waste time. Is it just me or does that not make sense?

The movie was engaging for about 45 minutes. After that I was just like, "Baptize him, kill him, or leave him be, but do something so I can go."

Nothing else stood out. Nobody's acting was horrible, but nobody's was exceptional either.

THE DIRECTIVE

Rosemary's Baby, 30 years later, only not as good.

RED LIGHT

Bams **Play It to the Bone**
(1999)

RATED R; running time 124 minutes
GENRE: Comedy
WRITTEN BY: Ron Shelton
DIRECTED BY: Ron Shelton
CAST: Woody Harrelson, Antonio Banderas,
Lolita Davidovich, Lucy Liu, Tom Sizemore,
Robert Wagner, Richard Masur

THE STORY

Since the inception of 3BC, I've grown much more tolerant about movies; setting aside outright ig'nant crap like *Supernova*, I've learned to roll with the cinematic punches, suspend my disbelief, and give a movie the benefit of the doubt, even those I give the red light. But I have a line that cannot be crossed: Bammer's First Commandment of Flicks is: "Thou shalt not be filled to the brink with pointlessness."

Vince Boudreau (Woody Harrelson) and Cesar Dominguez (Antonio Banderas) are best pals and professional boxers with a past; on their last legs, they're given a final chance at redemption. But this comes at a price: they have to fight each other. Called as a last-minute undercard match, by sleazy promoters Hank Goody (Robert Wagner), Joe Domino (Tom Sizemore), and Artie (Richard Masur), they head for Las Vegas in a Badass car (I'm not exaggerating; it should've been billed as such in the closing credits). Taking them on this inexplicable road trip from Los Angeles to Las Vegas is the Badass car's owner with whom they've both had "past experience," Grace Pasic (Lolita Davidovich); and joining them after

a pit stop is Lia (Lucy Liu), a "free spirit" who never met a drug or a penis she didn't like.

THE UPSHOT

Play It to the Bone is billed as a comedy, but it had me asking "why?" and "how?" so many times, it shoulda been classified a mystery.

The biggest "why?" by far was the completely unrealistic road trip itself. Work with me here: Vince and Cesar have the fight of their professional lives thrust upon them. Given the opportunity by the boxing promoters to take a flight from Los Angeles to Vegas, they instead go pick up Grace (more weird than the badass the film tries to make her out to be) so she could drive them there? WHY? Of course, it didn't help that, at what Grace called the "halfway point to Vegas," she went on to say they were still five hours out. Even going down the "scenic route," the *whole trip* between L.A. and L.V. wouldn't take that long. Folks, the BS meter worked overtime on this one.

Another "why" I mostly know the answer to already: Why pad the movie with pointless cameos from the likes of Kevin Costner, Steve Lawrence, and, of all people, Rod Stewart? The HBO boxing commentators (Larry Merchant, Jim Lampley, and George Foreman), I could understand; but what with all those pointless cameos by animate and inanimate objects alike, two words came swiftly to mind: "product placement." Some would say that my dwelling on such things only set me up to not like this flick; thinking too long and hard about a comedy, they say, often leads to disaster. To those "some," I say this: I hate having my intelligence insulted.

Director Shelton earned my disdain for taking such outlandish shortcuts just to get to the sole salvation of the movie—the big fight; and though the big fight made sitting through everything else almost worth it, I don't think I could trust a movie bearing the credit "Written and Directed by Ron Shelton" ever again.

All that said, the big fight was a doozy; almost enough to make me want to forgive the entire movie. Shelton et al did a bang-up job in those scenes (no pun intended). I'll say this much: if you dig Antonio Banderas or Woody Harrelson for their looks, you won't want to see what happens to them in the process of their fight. Though I was more impressed with Denzel Washington's physicality during his turn in the ring in *The Hurricane* (see page 45), Harrelson and Banderas were no slouches in the squared circle. In a word, that fight was *intense*.

THE BLACK FACTOR

A few weeks back, a 3BC reader asked me why I don't have a "Female Factor" as well as a "Black Factor," my "Chickness" being as important, so the thought goes, as my "Blackness." I've been looking for an "in" for an FF ever since. Looks like I've found one.

I don't watch FOX TV's *Ally McBeal*, but I've seen enough snippets of it to know that costar Lucy Liu is supposed to be the resident badass chick there. Having played a similar role in Mel Gibson's *Payback*, Liu is likely seen by casting directors as the innocent-looking young thing with a heart of stone, a challenge to men and women alike. I have absolutely no doubt that that's why she was cast in this movie. And I have absolutely no doubt that it

was about the dumbest move of all, second only to the illogical road trip itself. The entire part of Lia in this flick could've been excised from the film and scattered to the wind, with nary a skipped beat. Of course, it would've put the sole onus of being Femme Fatale square in Davidovich's lap, and with the bizarre way *her* part was written, that might have been one blow too many.

Why, Shelton; why?

BAMMER'S BOTTOM LINE

Play It to the Bone rates a conditional yellow for its sheer pointlessness; everything up to and after the big fight had me rolling my eyes, but man, that fight was *brutal*. I haven't been so repulsed, yet so fascinated, by anything in a long time. If you can stomach it (and the "comedy" that precedes it), it's probably the movie for you.

YELLOW LIGHT

The 6th Day

(2000)

RATED PG-13; running time 124 minutes
GENRE: Thriller
WRITTEN BY: Cormac Wibberley and Marianne Wibberley
DIRECTED BY: Roger Spottiswoode
CAST: Arnold Schwarzenegger, Michael Rapaport, Tony Goldwyn, Michael Rooker, Sarah Wynter

THE DIGEST

It's the near future and cloning is all the rage. You clone just about anything except humans. Cloning a human is a violation of the "6th Day Law." This law refers to the biblical passage "and God created man on the sixth day." The penalties for breaking this law are fines and imprisonment, but when has that ever stopped anybody?

Adam Gibson (Arnold Schwarzenegger) is your everyday family man. He has a wife and daughter who adore him. He runs his own helicopter charting service and has a philosophical problem with the idea of cloning. He doesn't want to get the family pet cloned when it dies from a "mysterious dog virus," even though the dog's death will break his daughter's heart.

He believes in the natural progression of life. But Adam decides that he should investigate the idea of pet cloning one more time before he makes a final decision.

After going to the pet store, Adam heads home to celebrate his surprise birthday party, only to discover that he, or rather his clone, is already home and someone is trying to kill the *real*

Adam, so the cloned one can take his place for good. He can't figure out why he has been cloned, so he must now try to find some answers and take his life back.

THE DISH

I didn't know if I was coming or going, and I'm not sure the writers knew either. In fact, I think they lost their train of thought. "A mysterious dog virus"? What kind of crap is that? They could have at least made up a disease.

The Sixth Day was slow and laborious. The acting was mediocre at best and plot had more holes in it than I could keep up with. Though I like Arnold and I like his movies, I did not like this. I was pretty disappointed.

THE DIRECTIVE

The writers should have to spend 6 days in the theater watching this movie 24-7.

RED LIGHT

The Sixth Sense

(1999)

RATED PG-13; running time 105 minutes
GENRE: Thriller
WRITTEN BY: M. Night Shyamalan
DIRECTED BY: M. Night Shyamalan
CAST: Bruce Willis, Haley Joel Osment, Toni Collette, Olivia Williams, Donnie Wahlberg

THE DIGEST

At the beginning of the movie, we are introduced to Dr. Malcolm Crowe (Bruce Willis), a psychologist who has just received an award for his work with children. His celebration is rudely interrupted by a former patient (Donny Wahlberg who has lost so much weight he looks like he has been hitting the pipe) who has broken into his home to tell him that he misdiagnosed him 10 years earlier. This causes Dr. Crowe to revisit a current patient, Cole Sear (Haley Joel Osment), and rediagnose him. Cole has been having behavioral problems in school and at home. Dr. Crowe thinks the boy is acting out because his parents recently divorced.

Dr. Crowe follows Cole to a church where the child is hiding out and playing with action figures. After he talks to Cole, it becomes clear that he is in the church for sanctuary. Why would a child need to seek protection? He is seeking protection from "them." When Cole is asked why he won't open up to his mother, he says, "When my mom looks at me, she doesn't see me as a freak like everyone else. I don't want her to look at me like they do."

Cole "knows" things. Like the unwritten history of a building that was actually a slaughterhouse; the nickname of a teacher; how to speak Latin. Everyone is completely puzzled, most of all Dr. Crowe. Cole's mother doesn't understand what is going on with her child, but she supports him nonetheless, taking him at face value when he tells her that he has no idea why all the cabinet doors are open again. Finally, after a particularly brutal episode with a ghost, Cole tells Dr. Crowe that he can see dead people. The people don't realize that they are dead and they are walking around like everyday people.

Dr. Crowe doesn't believe Cole, but he has problems of his own. He has been so consumed by Cole, his marriage has suffered tremendously. In light of his marital problems, he ends his sessions with Cole. But he still can't quite let ago. After going over his notes about the patient that broke into his home, he comes across something that gives Cole's story credibility. And now he seeks to "cure" Cole.

THE DISH

Children, what can I say? I'm a sucker for Bruce Willis. I'll see anything with him in it. Well, you can imagine that I was waiting with bated breath for *The Sixth Sense* and was I pleasantly surprised! This was not a Bruce Willis film. This was a Haley Joel Osment film. I've never seen a child act so well. Twenty minutes into the film, I had forgotten about Bruce. This child was riveting.

One Caveat: This is a Thriller/Drama. Don't watch this movie expecting cool effects and on-the-edge-of-your-seat action. But the plot twist at the end of the movie is *very interesting*. It will make you view the movie in a completely different light and appreciate it for its originality. Also, I really liked Cole's mother played by Toni Collette. The mother-son relationship in this movie was endearing.

THE DIRECTIVE

One of the most original paranormal films I've ever seen, *The Sixth Sense* is a movie that you have to see.

GREEN LIGHT

Sleepy Hollow
(1999)

RATED R; running time 105 minutes

GENRE: Thriller

WRITTEN BY: Andrew Kevin Walker, based on the short story "The Legend of Sleepy Hollow" by Washington Irving

DIRECTED BY: Tim Burton

CAST: Johnny Depp, Christina Ricci, Michael Gambon, Miranda Richardson, Casper Van Dien, Mark Pickering, Michael Gough, Jeffrey Jones, Ian McDiarmid, Christopher Walken

THE DIGEST

It's 1799, and Ichabod Crane is a New York City constable. He fancies himself a forensics specialist but is met with opposition from the local judges. They don't feel the need to give autopsies. Ichabod is adamant about the need to have more thorough investigations of crimes. The elder judges, tired of hearing him argue, give Ichabod a break. They tell him that he must prove himself and his outlandish ideas by completing a task in the small Upstate New York town of Sleepy Hollow. It seems that some fool is killing people by chopping their heads off, and it's up to Ichabod to find the killer and solve the murders.

He travels to the small yet prosperous farming community of Sleepy Hollow. He is welcomed by all of the town's elders. They are relieved that someone has come to help them rid the town of "The Headless Horseman." And Ichabod is mildly amused that the townspeople are insistent that the killer is really a ghost. He is less amused to find out that the killer steals the victims' heads.

THE DISH

First things first. I understand dedication to one's job, but if I see clear evidence that something without a head is killing people, I'd have to tender my resignation.

This was not Disney's version of *Sleepy Hollow*, that's for dang sure. It was Tim Burton's, and he can be a bit too weird for those who don't quite understand his style. And this might make it difficult for some of y'all to appreciate this take on *The Legend of Sleepy Hollow*, but I happen to dig Tim Burton. His version of the classic was entertaining and funny. It had a few rough spots where it dragged, and, as I mentioned earlier, it's kinda gory and gross at times. But Christopher Walken plays the Headless Horseman, and that alone is enough to see this enjoyable film, plus Christina Ricci is back in her element.

THE DIRECTIVE

Sleepy Hollow is a murder mystery with a little romance in the background. It's also pretty gory. If you have a weak stomach, you might want to pass this one up.

GREEN LIGHT

Stigmata
(1999)

RATED R; running time 142 minutes
GENRE: Thriller/Horror
WRITTEN BY: Tom Lazarus
DIRECTED BY: Rupert Wainwright
CAST: Patricia Arquette, Gabriel Byrne, Jonathan
Pryce, Nia Long, Dick Latessa, Portia de
Rossi, Patrick Muldoon, Rade Sherbedgia

THE DIGEST

Patricia Arquette is Frankie Paige, a young hairdresser in Philly who likes to party. She receives a
package from her mother that contains a rosary.
Her mother is traveling in Brazil and bought it off
of a little street urchin. What Moms doesn't
know is that the rosary belonged to the town
priest who just died. She also doesn't know that
there has been some weird stuff going on in that
priest's church, like doves showing up in huge
numbers, water dripping in reverse, and the
statue of the Virgin Mary weeping blood.

Meanwhile, the instant Frankie opens the
package, she begins to feel weird. Next thing you
know, she gets these wounds on her wrists. After
other wounds appear, it is determined that she
has the stigmata, or the 5 wounds of Christ. No
one believes it at first because she is an atheist
and stigmata afflict only the devout. The Vatican
sends chief investigator, Father Andrew (Gabriel
Byrne), to see what's going on. He is ready to
write Frankie off, until he actually sees the
wounds for himself. He becomes determined to
unravel the mystery and save Frankie before she
gets the fifth wound, which will kill her.

Here is where the scope of the movie changes.
We find out that it's not really about the stigmata, but something that will hold dire consequences for the church.

THE DISH

If you want to spend two hours of your life
watching a social commentary on the ills of the
Catholic Church, then *Stigmata* is the movie you
cannot afford to miss. And even then your two
hours will feel like twelve. And why is the pope always sending the grunts to do the dirty work? Let
him get his behind whupped by possessed people
once in a while. I don't drink alcohol, but maybe
I should have taken a few swigs of Night Train or
Mad Dog 2020 to dull the pain of having had to
sit through this movie.

Truthfully, it's not the worst movie I've seen,
the anticlimactic and lackluster ending notwithstanding. I guess I was disappointed because I was
expecting to see the '90s version of *The Exorcist*.

Nia Long's character isn't essential. But at
least they didn't kill her off. And can I be catty
for a second? Patricia girl, you are married to
Nicholas Cage, I know you can afford it . . . get
your grill fixed. Nothing wrong with wearing
braces in your 30s. You are too cute to have jacked
up "teef."

THE DIRECTIVE

Well, I'll get right to it. If you are expecting *The
Exorcist*, then keep your little chump change and
get your nails done.

YELLOW LIGHT

Bams Stir of Echoes
(1999)

RATED R; running time 93 minutes

GENRE: Thriller

WRITTEN BY: David Koepp (based on the novel by Richard Matheson)

DIRECTED BY: David Koepp

CAST: Kevin Bacon, Kathryn Erbe, Illeana Douglas, Kevin Dunn, Conor O'Farrell, Zachary David Cope, Eddie Bo Smith Jr.

> Have you ever played the Kevin Bacon game? It's really fun. Look it up on the Internet and see if you can find less than six degrees of separation between Kevin Bacon and Bob Hope.

THE STORY

Tom Witzky (Kevin Bacon), his wife Maggie (Kathryn Erbe), and son Jake (Zachary David Cope), all lead a mostly happy life in a not-quite ethnic but very neighborly neighborhood in Chicago. After Maggie's sister Lisa (Illeana Douglas), hypnotizes a skeptical Tom at a house party, Tom has pretty nasty recurring visions and remembers some deep, dark secrets—secrets that somehow involve Jake. Spooky.

THE UPSHOT

Bammer doesn't do horror flicks; whether they're properly called "thrillers," "suspense," "slasher pics," whatever, I don't do them. So why was I there? Beats me. Did I enjoy it? Well . . . partially.

When a reviewer's very first notes are "where in the hell did Bacon pick up that wack accent?" and "and what in the hell is that raggedy shtuff doing hanging on his chin?" there's something kinda wrong with that movie. But surprisingly, the first half of this flick was kinda good. Once the heart of the thing was established, and Bacon dropped his weak attempt at Chitownspeak, this movie was trippy. Scary in all the "right" parts, almost funny in others, *Echoes* really came to life after the hypnosis scene. The sex scene immediately following was even affected by it.

The movie kept going strong until nearabout the midway point, when more and more characters were introduced, including the neighborhood, a character unto itself. We're shown that this 'hood is as tight as any in Compton, Da Bronx, or Your Town, USA—and just about as liable to break out in a block party, or a fight. And as time goes by, Tom's visions get weirder and more intense, to the point where he and Maggie stop seeing eye to eye. Too bad it's at this point that the movie starts dipping into the Goofy Juice.

As the secrets are revealed, and things are shown to not be what they seem, the veil is lifted and Bacon and Co. are called on to act weird. They do that, in spades, but probably not in the way they'd hope it'd turn out. The less the special effects were used, the less effective the story was. Only near the end, when the gimmick was played out in full, did the original "magic" and scariness come back. But by then it was too late. Combined with a tell-all scene (they should've remembered Exposition Rule #1: leaving it to the audience's imagination works *much* better than telling all) and a blink-and-you'll-miss-it climax, the end scene had me wondering, "Why the hell did I just watch this?"

And I *still* don't know what the title was all about. Ya find out, lemme know.

Still, I'll give *Echoes* credit for one thing: it was rich with characters; the actors, on the other hand, were a mixed bag. Kevin Bacon was on again (he's one of those on again/off again actors that drive me crazy, because you can't call it with him); Kathryn Erbe was a waste but she played well off young Zachary; Illeana Douglas does a mean pothead; and Kevin Dunn and Conor O'Farrell had the protective-father-of-teenage-boys bit down pat. Would that that were enough to have made this movie work all the way through.

BAMMER'S BOTTOM LINE

If you're gonna only be halfway spooked, as is the case with *Stir of Echoes*, the "spooked" part should come at the end, not at the beginning.

FLASHING YELLOW LIGHT

Lara Croft: Tomb Raider
(2001)

RATED PG-13; running time 101 minutes
GENRE: Action
WRITTEN BY: Patrick Masset and John Zinman (plus about 9 other folks)
DIRECTED BY: Simon West
CAST: Angelina Jolie, Jon Voight, Iain Glen, Daniel Craig, Noah Taylor, Chris Barrie

> Angelina Jolie is the daughter of Jon Voight and the wife of Billy Bob Thornton. Her lips are the black sheep of the family . . . oops, did we just say that?

THE DIGEST

Lady Lara Croft (Angelina Jolie), daughter of famed archeologist Sir Richard Croft (Jon Voight), must save the world. Lara herself is an archeologist, or a "tomb raider." This time the artifact in question is one that will give someone the power to control time. With help from her father, from beyond the grave, Lara races against time to collect all the pieces of the artifact before all the planets align in an event that happens every 5,000 years.

While she jumps from continent to continent, she meets up with her former lover and rival Alex West (Daniel Craig); he is working for Manfred Powell, a self-made lawyer (Iain Glen). Manfred also covets the artifact. He intends to give it to the evil cartel, the Illuminati.

Lara must use her wits, charm, talent (or breastesses, whatever you want to call 'em), not to mention her war chest of gadgets, to save the world from the evil doings of men.

THE DISH

Folks, have you ever stared at the movie screen and begun to cry? Not because it's a sad scene and not because you are laughing, but rather because you are looking at something so awful that your eyeballs hurt? You stare at the screen managing to blink every few seconds, all the while asking yourself what you have done to make God punish you so.

Welcome to my world. I knew I was doomed after the first 10 minutes. I've never played the Tomb Raider video game, so I came to it with fresh eyes and innocent expectations. Never again shall I make that mistake. I spent the last 30 minutes of the movie praying that I could somehow be sucked into the screen and throw myself into the Icelandic waters surrounding the movie set.

The performances were pretty forgettable. But I feel most sorry for Angelina. I understand that she went through a lot during the making of it. What I really want to know is how she was able to run around the Arctic without a sports bra and not get nipply. And how did they get her to walk around in those thin clothes in Iceland? You couldn't pay me enough.

I have nothing interesting to report about the other actors.

THE DIRECTIVE

Tomb Raider should have been buried never to be found.

RED LIGHT

 Vertical Limit
(2000)

RATED PG-13; running time 126 minutes
GENRE: Action
WRITTEN BY: Robert King, Terry Hayes
DIRECTED BY: Martin Campbell
CAST: Chris O'Donnell, Bill Paxton, Scott Glenn, Robin Tunney, Izabella Scorupco, Nicholas Lea, Alexander Siddig

THE STORY

Our earnest young hero, mountain-climber Peter Garrett (Chris O'Donnell), is estranged from his fellow mountain-climbing sister, Annie (Robin Tunney), after a tragic accident involving their father (Stuart Wilson). Consequently, Peter never wants to climb again. Peter learns that Annie has joined the climbing crew of megabillionaire Elliot Vaughn (Bill Paxton), an eccentric adventurer who's using the planned climb up the really big mountain called "K2" as a publicity stunt coinciding with the inaugural flight of his Majestic Airlines (Richard Branson . . . calling Virgin Airlines' Richard Branson . . .)

Of course, Vaughn, an evil megalomaniac in disguise, has a secret, one which involves the wizened mystic climber Montgomery Wick (Scott Glenn), who has plans of his own for the evil megalomaniac once he finds out that Vaughn plans to go up K2 with a climbing team, led by the best damn climber Tom McLare (Nicholas Lea).

But when something goes terribly wrong with the climb, earnest Peter insists on rescuing his now-damsel-in-distress sister, enlisting the aide of wizened mystic Wick, comic relief Aussie dude Malcolm (Ben Mendelsohn), sensitive and prayerful guide Kareem (Alexander Siddig), and medic climber Monique Aubertine (Izabella Scorupco).

Don't be fooled, though: despite what the credits say, Chris O'Donnell isn't really the star of this show. No, the *real* focal point of this flick is the mountain itself. K2, in all its treacherous glory, was far and away the big kahuna here.

THE UPSHOT

By all rights, I shouldn't have liked *Vertical Limit*. After all, action flicks usually aren't my thing, especially mindless (or, in the case of this movie, overly, implausibly earnest) action flicks. So it came as a shock to me when I realized that not only did I *like* this movie, I was thrilled, and even *surprised*, by it.

The audience never had *time* to fret over the relatively transparent storyline, because whenever there was a moment to sit there and think "hey, waaaait a minute . . . ," BOOM! we were hit with something new comin' 'round the mountain.

Vertical Limit is one of those rare Action Flicks that overcomes (if not transcends) the genre in which it resides; it maintains its high excitement level throughout, keeps the viewer guessing about what comes next, and even lets its supporting characters have more interesting bits than the so-called stars have.

BAMMER'S BOTTOM LINE

"Story? We don' need no steenkin' story!" Seriously, though, *Vertical Limit* was a helluva roller-coaster ride, from beginning to end, a thrill a minute. If you don't mind a see-through plot and story resolution you can predict from a mile away, *Vertical Limit* is the Action Flick to catch.

GREEN LIGHT

yes, it's true; us Chicks aren't always looking to scowl about what White Folks are doing at the movies. Even we Chicks like to laugh every now and then. Check out our reviews of movies that cracked us up—some quite unintentionally, others on purpose. See if you can tell which is which.

A Christmas Story
(1983)

RATED PG; running time 94 minutes

GENRE: Comedy

WRITTEN BY: Jean Shepherd, Leigh Brown, Bob Clark (based on the novel by Jean Shepherd)

DIRECTED BY: Bob Clark

CAST: Melinda Dillon, Darren McGavin, Peter Billingsley, Ian Petrella, Scott Schwartz, R. D. Robb, Zack Ward, Yano Anaya, Tedde Moore, Jeff Gillen, Patty Johnson, Drew Hocevar, John Wong, Jean Shepherd (narrator as adult Ralphie)

THE STORY

In 1940s Indiana, all the hyper-imaginative Ralphie (Peter Billingsley) wanted for Christmas was a genuine Red Ryder 200-shot Carbine Action Air Rifle. Not much to ask for, right?

Not if you ask Ralphie's mom (Melinda Dillon), who firmly believes that he'd shoot his eye out. Ralphie's dad (Darren McGavin) doesn't have much to say on the subject; he's too busy fending off the dreaded Bumpus Hounds. Ralphie's little brother is no help either; he has his hands full making a mountain out of a molehill of mashed potatoes. And on top of all that, Ralphie, his brother, and his friends Flick and Schwartz find themselves under the tyranny of neighborhood bully Scut Farcus and his diminutive friend Yano Anaya. If only Ralphie had his trusty old blue BB gun, he'd save the day!

His English teacher, Miss Shields, might've just provided Ralphie a save-the-day chance when she assigns his class a normally dreaded themed essay to write. And this year's theme? "What I Want for Christmas."

THE UPSHOT

A Christmas Story is a rare combination of solid, unwhitewashed family fare and down-home humor, wrapped up with a pretty bow by a stellar cast, a surprisingly good director, and a brilliant storyteller ("writer," I've always thought, is too small a word for those talented few who can tell stories that are as meaningful when spoken aloud as they are on paper).

The 1940s never seemed as much fun as it did in *Christmas*. Previous depictions of the Good Old Days were downright *boring*. Not so with this re-telling. Though *A Christmas Story* was an '80s flick, it had none of the earmarks of that bizarre period in history.

Ralphie's friends, family, and neighborhood resonated with me because they reminded me of the close-knit, but slightly warped, neighborhood of my youth. Much of the credit for the genuine atmosphere of the last-name-less family certainly goes to the actors playing them. In the no-cutesy roles of the imaginative Ralphie and his goofy younger brother Randy, Peter Billingsley and Ian Petrella, respectively, have a freshness untainted by the smart-aleckyness of a Macauley Culkin in the irritating *Home Alone* series. I Felt Melinda Dillon's (humorous) pain as Mom when she tried and failed to eat a hot meal for want of satisfying her family's need for a second helping. But while her stay-at-home Mom was certainly a product of her times, she had a spark in her eye and a strength in her voice that let the audience know that her time would surely come. Supporting players Scott Schwartz as Flick, Tedde Moore as the put-upon teacher, Zack Ward and Yano Anaya as big bully Scut Farkus and his short-stuff toady Grover Dill, round out a brilliantly realized cast.

But for me, *Christmas* was delivered on the talents of actor Darren McGavin as the turkey-lovin', furnace-fightin', hound-dog-hatin', cussin'-up-a-storm Dad. I kid you not: tears *roll* whenever I watch the histrionics Dad goes through when he's tackling any of life's tough problems. McGavin, for me, was nothing less than perfect playing a role with as much versatility as a Robert De Niro would come to possess.

And just color me floored when I found out that Bob Clark, director of that cinematic wonder called *Porky's*, helmed *Christmas*. It's like night and day: *A Christmas Story* is about as far away from *Porky's* as *Supernova* is from being a real movie. (Of course, Clark went on later in his career to direct the horrid *Baby Geniuses*. Go figure.) In any case, I tip my hat to Clark for his excellent eye and ear for what was needed to let the fabulous Jean Shepherd's lovingly told tale, come to pass.

BAMMER'S BOTTOM LINE

A Christmas Story is the kind of genuinely heartwarming yet sincerely funny family flick that you wouldn't mind watching at any time of the year. DVD thingies or no, it's a worthy addition to your movie shelf. This movie should become a family Xmas tradition. It is, hands down, the best Christmas-themed movie out there.

GREEN LIGHT

Bedazzled
(2000)

RATED R; running time 93 minutes
GENRE: Comedy
WRITTEN BY: Peter Cook and Dudley Moore (original 1961 screenplay)
DIRECTED BY: Harold Ramis
CAST: Brendan Fraser, Elizabeth Hurley, Frances O'Connor, Orlando Jones

THE DIGEST

Elliot Richards (Brendan Fraser) is working a dead-end job, lacks the social skills to keep his coworkers from avoiding him, has no friends, and the girl of his dreams doesn't even know that he is alive. All this makes him ripe for the picking when the Devil (Elizabeth Hurley) is looking for a soul to take.

The Devil overhears Elliot say that he would give anything to win Allison (Frances O'Connor) and offers to help him. The Devil grants Elliot seven wishes with which he can do whatever he wants. All of his wishes center around making Allison fall in love with him. The problem is that the Devil has a sense of humor. Elliot is never specific and things go haywire every time. With each subsequent wish, Elliot makes up for the mistake of the previous one, but of course leaves something else out. In the end, Elliot learns that he can only be happy by being himself.

THE DISH

It's a plot we've seen a dozen times, but I loved it anyway. It was obvious to me that the actors had a blast each playing six different people, especially Brendan Fraser. I tell you, when he was the basketball player who was as dumb as a post and had a physical shortcoming, I almost fell on the floor. It was so dumb it was funny.

If you've had a bad day at work and just want to watch something that doesn't require a lot of thought, then check it out. Sometimes we all need to just stare at a screen for a while.

THE DIRECTIVE
A cute movie that will leave you feeling bedazzled.

GREEN LIGHT

Bams Best in Show
(2000)

RATED PG-13; running time 90 minutes
GENRE: Comedy
WRITTEN BY: Christopher Guest, Eugene Levy
DIRECTED BY: Christopher Guest
CAST: Michael Hitchcock, Parker Posey, Catherine O'Hara, Eugene Levy, Christopher Guest, John Michael Higgins, Michael McKean, Jennifer Coolidge, Patrick Cranshaw, Jane Lynch, Larry Miller, Ed Begley Jr., Fred Willard, Jim Piddock, Bob Balaban

THE STORY
Conformation dog shows are competitions in which purebred dogs are judged against the physical standards of their breeds and vie for the ultimate "best of show" championship (as opposed to field trials, which test dogs for their obedience and similar abilities). But the target of this satirical "mockumentary" are the lengths that the human "owners" of the dogs go through to get the coveted Blue Ribbon.

Attending the Dog Show are the following dogs and their hilarious humans:

Beatrice the neurotic Weimaraner, whose humans are high-strung Illinois yuppies Hamilton Swan (Michael Hitchcock) and his wife, Meg (Parker Posey), most likely the cause of Beatrice's many issues;

Winky the scruffy Norwich Terrier, hailing from Fern City, Florida and bringing the man magnet Cookie Fleck (Catherine O'Hara) and her two-left-footed salesman husband, Gerry (Eugene Levy), along for the show;

Hubert, the laid-back Bloodhound, accompanied by Pinenut, North Carolina's, own Good Ol' Boy Harlan Pepper (Christopher Guest who is also the director), dog fancier and owner of The Fishin' Hole;

Tyrone, the pampered Shih Tzu, cohabitating along with his sister, Miss Thang (uh, Miss Agnes), with New York gay couple Scott "Ice Ice Baby" Donlan (John Michael Higgins) and Stefan Vanderhoof (Michael McKean);

And the prissy Poodle and two-time Mayflower winner, Butch, who lives at the Cabot Mansion with young, rich Anna Nicole-esque Sheri Ann Ward Cabot (Jennifer Coolidge) and her very old, very silent husband, Leslie Ward Cabot (Patrick Cranshaw), and is being shown at Mayflower by the rather butch in her own right Christy Cummings (Jane Lynch).

THE UPSHOT

Dag, this flick was *FUNNY*! I can't remember when I've laughed more at a satire. *Best in Show* did an excellent job of deflating the craziness surrounding the bizarre world of conformation dog shows.

The writing and directing were tight, and the humans' performances were spot-on wacky, though Michael McKean's Stefan was the most straight (*uh, no pun intended*) of the lot. Still, I hesitate to point out any of the actors here, they were *all* just that good; and the fact that they could play these caricatures with such straight faces, most déf earns my praise. Hmmm . . . actually, I should point out that in addition to the great bits from all the actors mentioned in "The Story" above, Larry Miller as Max Bergman, one of Cookie's *many* ex-boyfriends, Ed Begley Jr. as the manager of the Hotel Taft, and Fred Willard as Mayflower announcer Buck Laughlin, also had me in stitches.

Best in Show tickled my funny bone in the way that only a mockumentary about a subject I hold near and dear, could. Whether you're a dog or a cat person, you should see this flick, unless, that is, you can't laugh at yourself. Don't worry; the rest of us will laugh at you.

BAMMER'S BOTTOM LINE

Two paws up! Reminiscent in tone to *Raising Arizona*, with more than a passing resemblance to mockumentary *This Is Spinal Tap* cowritten by Guest and McKean, *Best in Show* certainly ranks as one of my favorite comedies. I don't think I'll ever be able to watch Westminster the same way again.

GREEN LIGHT

Blazing Saddles
(1974)
Bams

RATED PG; running time 93 minutes
GENRE: Comedy
WRITTEN BY: Andrew Bergman, Mel Brooks, Richard Pryor, Alan Uger, Norman Steinberg
DIRECTED BY: Mel Brooks
CAST: Cleavon Little, Gene Wilder, Harvey Korman, Madeline Kahn, Slim Pickens, Mel Brooks, Alex Karras, David Huddleston, Liam Dunn, John Hillerman, George Furth, Claude Ennis Starrett Jr., Richard Collier, Charles McGregor, Dom DeLuise, Burton Gilliam, Count Basie

THE STORY

The old western town of Rock Ridge stands in the way of progress by way of the railroad that Attorney General Hedley "Not Hedy, Hedley!" Lamarr (Harvey Korman) is trying to build on the backs of Chinese, Black, and Irish laborers. Lamarr wants the townsfolk to leave Rock Ridge, since land there will be worth much moolah when the railroad goes through town; but the townsfolk, all of whom are surnamed "Johnson," aren't ready to go. With the help of dimwitted Governor Lepetomane (Mel Brooks), Lamarr comes up with a plot to make the town so mad they'd be read'ta go . . . enter Sheriff Bart (Cleavon Little). Stage left.

THE UPSHOT

I like the tag on the back of the DVD box: "Mel Brooks's Comic Saga of Cowboys and Imbeciles." That pretty much covers it.

I'm amazed at how many *Blazing Saddles* lines have made their way into my everyday life. The husband wants me to do something that I don't really mind doing much, but I want to josh with him?—"Work work work work work"! Asked to do something incredibly stupid at the office, against my better judgment?—"Mongo only pawn . . . in game of life!"

Silly "merit" games being played at work?—"Badges? We don' need no steenkin' badges!" And many a bruthaman has gone for the double whammy—" 'Scuse me while I whip this out" and my all-time favorite, "Where the White wimmen at?"

I don't do those lines justice, I know. *Blazing Saddles* is as much about the delivery of great lines by its actors as it is about the writing and directing itself. I can't say there's a bad act in the lot, though it's the supporting cast that really worked this film into a froth: the Johnson Chorus—Olson Johnson (David Huddleston), Rev. Johnson (Liam Dunn), Howard Johnson (John Hillerman), Van Johnson (George Furth), Gabby Johnson (Claude Ennis Starrett Jr.), Dr. Sam Johnson (Richard Collier)—bring to mind Greek comedy. Am I warped, or what?

Stars Cleavon Little and Gene Wilder (Jim, the Waco Kid) were matched well, in a way that even Richard Pryor (one of the writers here) didn't quite capture in later pairings with Wilder; and Little riding into town, Gucci'd out with Count Basie providing the theme music, is but one classic moment the underrated actor provided in this film. However, it was Harvey Korman, Alex Karras as Mongo (that horse!), Slim Pickens as Taggart ("You use your tongue prettier'n a $20 whore"—I wish I could use that one

more often!), and the late, great Madeline Kahn as bon viveuse Lili Von Shtupp, who had me rolling on the floor. I'd do Kahn's amazing, Oscar-nominated performance an injustice if I didn't mention how much her show-stopping "I'm Tired" number almost made me bust a gut the first time I saw it. Man, I loved that woman. Mel Brooks's madness petered out near the end (though the very last scene was redeeming).

Watch out for double entendres and sight gags that fly across the screen; some so quickly or subtly, they're easy to miss.

THE BLACK FACTOR

I really shouldn't like this film. Forget about the slapstick humor; what with my general movie temperament, my stridency against racial slurs and misogyny, and my Black Factor bent, this is the type of film my militant side tells me I really shouldn't like. If *Blazing Saddles* had been made in today's climate, I probably wouldn't have liked it nearly as much. But to see it in such a light—to only notice the fart jokes, to only hear the "Niggers," the "Chinks," the "faggots," and the "rapes"—is to miss the point entirely.

And what is that point? For me, then and now, Mel Brooks's point is that racists and their ilk are the stupid ones, ripe to be ridiculed and ignored for the idiots they are. In *Blazing Saddles*, we don't laugh *with* these fools, we laugh *at* them. For me, that was truly the point. Well, that and fart jokes are funny as hell. In the hands of a master, that is.

BAMMER'S BOTTOM LINE
Along with *Blazing Saddles,* check out *Young Frankenstein* and *Spaceballs,* also by Mel Brooks.

GREEN LIGHT

the Diva **Bowfinger**
(1999)

RATED PG-13; running time 98 minutes
GENRE: Comedy
WRITTEN BY: Steve Martin
DIRECTED BY: Frank Oz
CAST: Steve Martin, Eddie Murphy, Heather Graham, Christine Baranski, Jamie Kennedy, Adam Alexi-Malle

> This is the 10th film Steve Martin has written. Other titles include *The Jerk, Dead Men Don't Wear Plaid,* and *L.A. Story.*

THE DIGEST
Steve Martin plays Bobby Bowfinger. He is a ne'er do well, wannabe director. He is given a script by a friend and is convinced that it is the best script he has ever read. The movie-to-be is called *Chubby Rain*—it's like *Invasion of the Body Snatchers* except the aliens enter your body through rain. Well, Bowfinger just has to make this movie. So he cons his way into a lunch meeting with a producer. The producer tells him that if he can get Kit Ramsey (Eddie Murphy) to play the lead role, he will make sure that the movie is distributed. And so begins the biggest con game ever perpetrated in Hollywood since somebody convinced that town that Kevin Costner could act.

Enter Kit Ramsey. Kit is the hottest action hero in Hollywood. He is also a huge prima donna. He is paranoid and bitter that he hasn't won an Oscar. In fact, according to him, the only way you can win an Oscar in Hollywood is if you are playing "someone White and retarded, or a slave" (close to the funniest line in the movie).

Bowfinger knows he'll never get Kit to star in this movie, so he decides to shoot the movie around him. He has his actors go walk up to Kit and speak their dialogue as Bowfinger films it from a distance. What Bowfinger doesn't know is that Kit has some serious mental issues. He already believes that aliens are out to get him, so with the actors walking up to him and talking "Juputian or Jupinese," he is going nuts.

THE DISH
Lost yet? If you are, I wouldn't blame you. This is the primary problem with the movie. It's a little hard to follow what's going on. Sometimes it moved *really* slowly and at other times it was almost madcap. Eddie Murphy as Kit Ramsey is annoyingly over-the-top. But Eddie Murphy as Kit's body double, "Jif," is hilarious. As Jif, he is a few fries short of a happy meal and extremely naive. Eddie and Steve both show their comedic genius with Jif, Murphy in his portrayal and Martin in his writing (he wrote the script). If Eddie had been able to play Jif the entire movie, I would have loved this film. As it were, I chuckled throughout most of the film when I should have

been on the floor, rolling. Although I'll tell you, the last three minutes of this movie had everyone, including this Diva, on the floor. It is hands-down one of the funniest scenes on celluloid I've ever seen.

I would *strongly* recommend this movie to anyone who loves Steve Martin and has been waiting for him to return to the days of *The Jerk*. As with any Steve Martin vehicle, you have to pay attention, because there are lots of little things you'll miss. Like the fact that both of Eddie Murphy's characters are named after peanut butter brands. Christine Baranski was excellent, as an "almost Diva," and Heather Graham was surprisingly funny.

THE DIRECTIVE

Steve Martin fans will get a kick out of *Bowfinger*! Eddie Murphy fans probably won't.

GREEN LIGHT

---

the Diva **Galaxy Quest**
(1999)

RATED PG; running time 102 minutes
GENRE: Comedy
WRITTEN BY: David Howard and Robert Gordon
DIRECTED BY: Dean Parisot
CAST: Tim Allen, Sigourney Weaver, Alan Rickman, Tony Shalhoub, Sam Rockwell, Daryl Mitchell, Enrico Colantoni, Robin Sachs

The "Ensign Rule" trumps the "Brotha Rule" (see page xv).
This time.

THE DIGEST

Galaxy Quest was a *Star Trekkish* TV show that aired in the '80s, and has a fierce following. There are *G.Q.* conventions where all of the fans dress up as their favorite characters.

Commander Peter Quincy Taggart is played by Jason Nesmith (Tim Allen) and he, having played the commander, is the most popular and has a huge ego. So huge that it is wearing on everyone's nerves. Lieutenant Tawny Madison (Sigourney Weaver) and her fellow thespians have been putting up with it for 18 years and the crew is tired of it. He is always late to the conventions, takes over the show, and is basically a jerk. Alexander (Alan Rickman) is irritated that he is defined by one famous line and the fact that he, as a Shakespearean-trained actor, has to wear an alien cranium. Everyone else good-naturedly deals with their popularity, but there is tension.

During one convention, Jason is in the restroom and overhears a few fans making fun of him. It sours his mood so much that he doesn't notice how different one group of fans that has approached him is. Those three fans somehow find his house and convince him to come help them. He thinks it's just another gig, but they are asking him to save their people. The fans are actually aliens who think that Jason and the others really have a spaceship and *really* travel the galaxy saving people. After they convince Jason to help them, he recruits his "crew," and they work to save the aliens from an evil enemy.

THE DISH

While I've never been into *Star Trek* or *Deep Space 9*, I'm still a geek. This is not something I readily admit, but I'm coming out of the geek closet. *The Matrix* is one of my favorite movies, and *Galaxy Quest* is not far behind. This movie had me *rolling*. *Galaxy Quest* is very kid-friendly. Any child can see it, but it will probably be better appreciated by the 11+ crowd.

THE DIRECTIVE

Rent this one—I'm still laughing.

GREEN LIGHT

THE DIGEST

Amanda (Monica Potter) is unlucky in love. Every single serious relationship she has had has ended in disaster. When she walks in on her boyfriend sleeping with someone else in *their* bed, she decides that she has had enough of men.

With the busting of her boyfriend, she needs to find a new place to live. She answers a room-for-rent ad. It's $500.00 a month, which is a *huge* bargain in New York City. There *has* to be a catch. The catch is that she will be living with four gorgeous models, and she'll be sleeping in the closet. Well, what normal people call a closet, anyway. To the models, the closet is actually a converted bedroom; Amanda is just renting a very tiny room.

Jade, Roxanna, Candi, and Holly have no concerns except for looking cute. They aren't the sharpest knives in the drawer, but sweet nonetheless, so Amanda gets along with them just fine. All is right with the world until Amanda, against her better judgment, realizes she's attracted to her neighbor, Jim (Freddie Prinze Jr.). By all accounts, he is perfect, yet Amanda tries her darnedest to find flaws with him. Eventually, she gives up and lets herself fall for him. As soon as she lets down her guard, she witnesses him murder someone. So much for being perfect, right? The police can find no evidence of a murder. Should Amanda trust her heart or her mind and eyes?

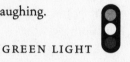

Head Over Heels
(2001)

RATED PG-13; running time 95 minutes
GENRE: Comedy
WRITTEN BY: Ron Burch (story), Ron Burch & David Kidd (screenplay)
DIRECTED BY: Mark Waters
CAST: Monica Potter, Freddie Prinze Jr., Shalom Harlow, Ivana Milicevic, Sarah O'Hare, Tomiko Fraser, Raoul Ganeev

Freddy Prinze Jr. is the only child of the late Freddy Prinze—star of the '70s sitcom *Chico and the Man*.

THE DISH

Lawd, I had to deal with a theater full of 14-year-old girls sighing, "Awww. He is so sweeeet," every single flippin' time Freddie Prinze Jr. said something. (Side note to my mother . . . please tell me that I wasn't like that. If I was, how did you stop yourself from killing me?) Beyond that, I haven't laughed this hard since I watched *Miss Congeniality* (see page 19). Those models had me on the floor. I have to admit that I don't particularly like bathroom humor, but this movie does it well. This is a solid comedy with great performances from all involved.

THE DIRECTIVE

Head Over Heels is worth seeing, but only if you go in with low expectations. If you enjoyed *Charlie's Angels* (see page 199) or *Miss Congeniality* (see page 19), you will love this movie.

GREEN LIGHT

 Heartbreakers
(2001)

RATED PG-13; running time 122 minutes
GENRE: Comedy
WRITTEN BY: Stephen Mazur, Paul Guay, Robert Dunn
DIRECTED BY: David Mirkin
CAST: Sigourney Weaver, Jennifer Love Hewitt, Gene Hackman, Ray Liotta, Jason Lee, Nora Dunn, Anne Bancroft, Jeffrey Jones

THE STORY

It's the old one-two con: Dear Old Mom Angela (Sigourney Weaver) left-hooks some poor fool into marrying her, then daughter Page (Jennifer Love Hewitt) sucker-punches the scheme by se-

ducing him into a compromising position, so that The Jilted Bride can collect on blackmail . . . er, I mean, alimony. All in the family, I reckon.

After snagging philandering chop-shop owner Dean Cumanno (Ray Liotta) this way, Page wants out of the mother-daughter con game to set up her own separate scams. Angela doesn't think Page can hack it, but reluctantly agrees to help out, until an IRS agent (Anne Bancroft) bursts their bubble. Needing some quick cash, Page agrees to one more big con; so the two set off for prime rich-White-guy hunting grounds: Palm Springs.

There, they pick out tobacco billionaire William B. Tensy (Gene Hackman) as their new mark; the constantly hacking Tensy seems an easy enough mark, though Page would rather go after younger game. But complicating things for them both are Tensy's stern, dedicated housekeeper (Nora Dunn) and Jack (Jason Lee), a bartender with the hots for Page's alter con-ego.

THE UPSHOT

Well, it's not *completely* mindless. Nope, that's *Monkeybone* territory. *Heartbreakers* was more like *Dirty Rotten Scoundrels* with tits. Oh boy, am I gonna hear it for *that* one.

Despite all the flailing about, the obligatory love story between Page and Jack was the least interesting thing about *Heartbreakers*, though I was shocked when I realized that I actually *liked* both characters, though. What *Heartbreakers* had going for it was more an ensemble groove, with each character actor adding their own zesty spice to the mix.

Sigourney Weaver, in one of her best comedic performances since *Working Girl*, and Ray Liotta, in one of *his* best performances in a lonnnnnng time, had great comedic timing together, as did, much to my shock, Weaver and Hewitt. As it stood, Hewitt was much more convincing as the put-upon con daughter than as the love interest; I could live with that, though, because the con was the thing. And though his was a one-trick pony, Gene Hackman's hacky cigarette baron character, William B. Tensy, kept me grinning for most of the movie. The cast seemed to giggle playing off each other; and in turn, the audience giggled right back.

There's not much depth to *Heartbreakers*, certainly nothing exciting and new!, despite the lame "I'm like this because I have male-abandonment Issues" subplot, but sometimes a good laugh is its own reward.

THE BLACK FACTOR

Um ... how about the "Chick Factor" instead?

I admit I don't have much firsthand experience at being a horny guy who has, apparently, never seen a pushup bra he didn't like, so somebody help me out here: what is it about a curvy chick flashing her tits that makes guys stoopid? Are fellas really so desperate that all it takes is a little whiff of femininity, to make y'all give away the farm? Well, *somebody* sure thinks y'all are, given all the curvy-busty-chicks-nags-and-idiots plots in comedies these days. But maybe I'm just play-hatin' because I know I won't look half as good as Ms. Weaver when I turn 50. Ms. Weaver, you look good ... Work it, girl.

BAMMER'S BOTTOM LINE

No, it's not *The Sting*, nowhere near it. But *Heartbreakers* was a funny, lighthearted comedy, and who doesn't like to laugh?

GREEN LIGHT

I'm the One That I Want (2000)

RATED R; running time 96 minutes
GENRE: Comedy
WRITTEN BY: Margaret Cho
DIRECTED BY: Lionel Coleman
CAST: Margaret Cho

THE DIGEST

I'm the One That I Want is a concert film featuring Margaret Cho that was filmed at the historic Warfield in San Francisco. This was a homecoming performance for Margaret, who grew up in San Francisco where her parents owned a bookstore that catered to a gay clientele. This, perhaps, is why she was very comfortable saying some of the things that made me most uncomfortable. She liberally uses the word "faggot," for one, which made me cringe every single time—cringe in the same way that I do when I hear the word "Nigga." Once I was able to get beyond that, her routine worked for me.

Margaret uses her comedy to thumb her nose at "The Powers That Be" (T.P.T.B.) in Hollywood. Or, better yet, to tell them to kiss her grits. These are the people who granted her a sitcom, *All-American Girl* (which I loved, by the way), the first sitcom to ever be predominately Asian. Then T.P.T.B. told her she wasn't skinny enough. This sent her on a quest to lose weight. So much so, she got sick. They told her she wasn't Asian enough, so they hired an Asian consultant. Some of the Asian community praised her and some condemned her. Then, after she changed everything about herself and her reality to fit their image, T.P.T.B. abruptly canceled the show. They left her broken and searching for her identity. Unfortunately, she turned to alcohol and drugs to try to rediscover herself.

THE DISH

Margaret gives us a look inside of her world, a world that, at times, was very painful. Some of those glances we should be all too familiar with—for example, always having an impossible-to-reach standard of beauty paraded before us. It's a shame what happened to her, but I'm glad she's here to tell us about it.

Aside from the horrors of Hollywood, Margaret shows us the joys of being Asian. Her routines about her mother are some of the funniest routines that I've ever heard. I felt a little guilty laughing at first. I wasn't sure how much of it really was her mother and how much of it was a caricature of Asian mothers as whole. I decided not to analyze it too deeply and take it at face value. When taken at face value, her interpretation of her mother is hilarious. If nothing else, it is very clear that Margaret loves her mother.

Margaret is brilliant. Comedically brilliant, along the same vein as Pryor and Murphy.

By the way, Margaret, you look good, girl, tell Hollywood to take an enema.

THE DIRECTIVE

The very funny *I'm the One That I Want* is for adult audiences only.

GREEN LIGHT

Just Visiting
the Diva
(2001)

RATED PG-13; running time 88 minutes
GENRE: Comedy
WRITTEN BY: Christian Clavier, Jean-Maire Poire, and John Hughes
DIRECTED BY: Jean-Marie Gaubert
CAST: Jean Reno, Christina Applegate, Christian Clavier, Matthew Ross, Malcolm McDowell, Tara Reid, Bridgette Wilson-Samaras

Jean Reno was a well-established movie star in France before we caught notice of him in the 1994 film *The Professional*.

THE DIGEST

Count Thibault the Sixth (Jean Reno) is traveling to England to marry his beloved Princess Rosalind (Christina Applegate), and he couldn't be happier. As he travels, he has ample opportunities to prove his fearlessness by rescuing many a damsel in distress, and he does so with ease. Not even his servant Andre (Christian Clavier), a man so funky that he even makes the French who are not known for the bathing habits faint, can displease him. All is right with the world until he gets to the fair Rosalind's castle.

Unbeknownst to Thibault and Rosalind, Rosalind has a secret admirer who will stop at nothing to get her. It is this man's jealousy that sets in motion a tragic event. An event so horrible, that Thibault must go back in time to correct it or he will lose Rosalind forever.

With the help of a local wizard (Malcolm McDowell), Thibault attempts to change history. There is one problem: the wizard forgets an ingredient, so instead of traveling to the past, Thibault and Andre are transported to the future. Chicago in the year 2000, to be exact. There, they come face to face with Juliet (Christina Applegate), who is the spitting image of Rosalind.

Thibault must somehow convince Juliet that they really are from the 12th century and that they must somehow get back. While they try to figure this out, he takes Juliet under his wing and empowers her and teaches her to stop being a doormat for her slimy boyfriend, Hunter (Matthew Ross).

Can he make things right, and, if not, can he adjust to living in Chicago 900 years after his birth?

THE DISH

With a perfect cast, this is an entertaining and hilarious movie. There were some plot holes and some dips when the movie seemed to drag on forever, but all in all I was very happy with it.

The casting was spot on. Jean Reno and Christian Clavier convinced me that they were not of this time. The little things we take for granted amazed them. Television, light switches, running water, and all the little gadgets and appliances. Malcolm McDowell had an "absent professor" quality about him that was hilarious.

THE DIRECTIVE

A pleasant diversion. No thinking is required. Just stare at the screen and giggle. *Just Visiting* is also a nice movie for the family to watch together.

GREEN LIGHT

 **Legally Blonde**

(2001)

RATED PG-13; running time 96 minutes
GENRE: Comedy
WRITTEN BY: Amanda Brown (novel), Karen McCullah Lutz and Kirsten Smith (screenplay)
DIRECTED BY: Robert Luketic
CAST: Reese Witherspoon, Selma Blair, Victor Garber, Holland Taylor, Jennifer Coolidge, Matthew Davis, Oz Perkins, Luke Wilson

> Oz Perkins is the son of the late Anthony Perkins—ya know—Norman Bates from the Hitchcock's classic *Psycho*.

THE DIGEST

Elle Woods (Reese Witherspoon) has it all. She is dating the most eligible frat brother, she's president of her sorority, she has a doggy that loves her, and she's graduating with a 4.0 in fashion merchandising. Then her world comes crashing to an end. She fully expects to one day be Mrs. Warner Huntington III, but Warner is going away to Harvard Law School and wants to be a senator by age 30. He reasons that Elle doesn't fit in those plans. Her blood isn't "blue" enough. She tries to reason with him by pointing out that she grew up across the street from Aaron Spelling, hoping this will make him change his mind. Well, it doesn't, of course. All seems lost when Elle gets it in her head to become the woman Warner wants, by going to Harvard Law School herself. Elle aces her LSAT, has a Coppola direct her admissions video, and soon finds herself on the East Coast at Harvard, fighting for her man and fighting against a system that discriminates against blondes.

THE DISH

Um. Hmm. Well, my first reaction was, "I'm going to be ill." Why should I feel sorry for this explosion of pink and blonde? She has everything at her fingertips anyway and now I'm supposed to sympathize with her because she can't keep her man? Elle's character was just like some of the blond sorority girls with whom I went to college, and I was irritated by. Not to mention all of the racial baggage that comes with me being asked to feel sorry for a Caucasian woman whose biggest struggle is trying to find a Gucci bag on sale and buy the correct red dress. But I got over it. She *is* my sister in "Divadom," and I know how hard it can be to match reds and find Gucci bags on a decent sale.

Even though I got over it, the movie was still a letdown. It failed where *Clueless* succeeded. The dialogue wasn't as witty or snappy, and it didn't flow as well. The help Elle provides on a murder case is extremely farfetched, even for a comedy. Except for her two dingbat best friends who were funny, no performance really stood out for me.

THE DIRECTIVE

Legally Blonde is a nice little weekend diversion, but nothing more.

YELLOW LIGHT

Bams **The Legend of Drunken Master**

(1994; dubbed in English 2000)

RATED R; running time 102 minutes
GENRE: Comedy/Action
WRITTEN BY: Edward Tang, Tong Man Ming, Yuen Chieh Chi
DIRECTED BY: Lau Ka Leung
CAST: Jackie Chan, Ti Lung, Anita Mui, Lau Ka Leung, Wing Fong Ho, Chin Kar Lok, Ken Lo, Ho Sung Pak, Felix Wong

> Make sure you watch Jackie Chan movies until the last credit rolls. He often has stunt outtakes.

THE STORY

The Legend of Drunken Master humorously tells the story of Chinese folk legend Wong Fei-Hung (Jackie Chan), young master of the "Drunken Boxing" kung fu style of martial arts.

In this almost plot-overloaded movie, Wong Fei-Hung and his hapless brother Cho travel by train with their father, Dr. Wong Kei-Ying, bringing medical supplies back to their home. Part of their supplies—some medicinal ginseng—gets mixed up in the baggage of the ambassador, leading to a struggle between Fei-Hung and a mysterious old man, Tsan, over the package. The struggle gets especially interesting when Fei-Hung tries to impress Tsan with his Drunken Boxing style of kung fu (which he doesn't do nearly as well when he's *not* drunk).

Wong also has comical misunderstandings with his father, who doesn't want Fei-Hung to either fight *or* drink, both of which, of course, Fei-Hung does in abundance with his mother, Madame Wong (Lucy Ricardo, reincarnated), and with his friendly rival, who spars with Fei-Hung for the attention of the lovely Fong (Wing-Fong Ho). Fei-Hung and his folks face epic battles with the ambassador (who has the fastest kicks I've ever seen), and his minion Henry, and a rather hot bed of coals. What follows are some of the outright funniest skits and amazing martial arts scenes I've ever seen in one movie.

THE UPSHOT

There comes a time in every chick's life when she has an epiphany so mind-blowing, it forever alters her life, causing her to grow up far quicker than she expected to.

My time came Sunday, when I realized that Bruce Lee *isn't* the greatest martial artist the movie world has ever seen.

Okay, so maybe I exaggerated a wee bit; maybe Chan didn't exactly rock my world, but he did shake the foundations a bit. It really was quite eye-opening to see just how bad the man is and in a relatively unpolished, six-year-old movie, no less!

To some, the plot of a martial arts movie is like the plot of a porn flick: most people don't bother paying attention to the words; they just want to get to the action (the same has been said about Black "booty call" comedies, so don't trip over the analogy). Which goes to show you how warped we Westerners can be sometimes, because the plot *was* well developed in *Legend.* Still, I won't lie; I got lost in the back story with the English overlord (I *think* that's what he was supposed to be), to the point where I totally dismissed him whenever he came onscreen. I imagine part of my confusion comes from the fact that I haven't seen the film *Legend* is a sequel to, 1978's *Drunken Master,* and thus don't fully know who's who within Fei-Hung's circle of friends and enemies. I'm fairly sure that I got some of the names mixed up in "The Story" above, unfortunately.

But the point remains: this movie was a lot more than the "chop socky" so often dismissed when we see a "karate flick." Sure, the kung fu was there at base, and rightly so (I'd pay to see those scenes by themselves, especially the final battle; it was *that* good). But the humor was *strong,* especially with Anita Mui; I swear I cracked a rib on her account! and I even found myself crying with sadness when Fei-Hung got chewed out by his father. Add some interesting cultural references on top of that, and you have yourself a well-rounded movie. Granted, it's no *Citizen Kane;* but could Kane drink like a fish and then kick serious butt? Thought not!

BAMMER'S BOTTOM LINE

I have never, ever, laughed harder, or damn near cried my eyes out, at "just a karate flick," the way I did during *Legend.* Bruce Lee was baaad, no doubt; but Jackie Chan is the Man. Chan has stood the test of time and *still* comes out swinging. Sit down, Steven Segal; take a hike, Jean-Claude Van Damme. Check out this older Jackie Chan flick, and see what legends truly are made of.

GREEN LIGHT

Meet the Parents
(2000)

RATED PG-13; running time 108 minutes
GENRE: Comedy
WRITTEN BY: James Herzfeld
DIRECTED BY: Jay Roach
CAST: Ben Stiller, Robert De Niro, Teri Polo, Blythe Danner, Owen Wilson, Nicole Debluff, Jon Abrahams, James Rebhorn, Phyllis George

> Director Jay Roach is married to Susanna Hoffs of the 80's group The Bangles. She sometimes provides music for his films.
> Also, Blythe Danner has another name—Gwyneth Paltrow's mommy.

THE STORY

Meet the Parents is a comedy of errors: most of which were made by Greg Focker (Ben Stiller).

Greg, a male nurse, is in love with elementary-school teacher Pam Byrnes, and wants to marry her; but just before he has a chance to propose, he finds out Pam's father, Jack (Robert De Niro), a "rare flowers dealer," expects any potential suitor of his daughter to ask him for her hand in marriage. Since Greg has yet to meet Pam's family, they set off to meet Jack and Pam's mother, Dina, during the weekend when Pam's sister, Debbie, is preparing to marry her doctor boyfriend.

Greg's suitcase, which didn't fit in the plane's overhead storage, is lost by the airline, and from there, a series of interconnected foibles befall Greg, affecting the whole Byrnes family, much to the consternation of Jack, who doesn't like or trust Greg even though Jack has a secret or two of his own. And yes: wackiness ensues.

THE UPSHOT

Whatever special water Robert De Niro drinks that makes him so talented, somebody oughta bottle it up and give it to Hollywood's 20 Million Dollar Club (you hear me, DiCaprio?). Serious or funny, De Niro runs big-time *circles* around those so-called *stars* earning beaucoup bucks.

Oh yeah: and Ben Stiller ain't so bad, either.

There were a bunch of folks in this cast—decent supporters, all—but make no mistake: this puppy was Robert De Niro's and Ben Stiller's to play with. And play with it they did.

That Ben Stiller could crack a rib or two, comes as no surprise; the man had me near tears as his weekend went swiftly to hell in a great big basket. But De Niro was like a treasure found for me. I won't waste my time or yours in recounting the dozens of serious movies in which he worked his acting magic; and though I've seen him crack a smile or two in flicks like *Midnight Run* and *We're No Angels* (and, of course, as an obligatory mobster type in *Analyze This* and similar fare), in

Parents, his mere facial twitch or "innocent" crack kept the audience roaring. I can't wait to see his next comedy showcase.

The weakness of this movie was that there were too many characters and situations that were left underused. Blythe Danner was game as Jack's ditzy wife, Dina, but De Niro could've almost as easily gone it alone without too much muss and fuss. The rest of the family seemed equally mere appendages. And it's a crying shame that the dysfunctional natures of both Pam's ex-boyfriend Kevin (Owen Wilson) and her brother, Denny (Jon Abrahams), weren't further explored; surely, those characters had much more to offer than being simple "straight men" for Greg and Jack.

Fun though *Meet the Parents* may have been, because it concentrated almost exclusively on two characters out of many, it wasn't as great as it could've been. Still, I noticed no shortage of grins, and had a good time remembering the first few meetings I had with my now-husband's family. At least *I* never had issues with raw sewage . . .

BAMMER'S BOTTOM LINE
At times laugh-out-loud hilarious, *Meet the Parents* reintroduces a different, funnier side of Robert De Niro to the world (or at least, to that part of the world that didn't bother with that *Rocky and Bullwinkle* mess).

GREEN LIGHT

the Diva Mystery Men
(1999)

RATED PG-13; running time 117 minutes
GENRE: Comedy
WRITTEN BY: Neil Cuthbert, based on the comic book created by Bob Burden
DIRECTED BY: Kinka Usher
CAST: Ben Stiller, William H. Macy, Hank Azaria, Geoffrey Rush, Janeane Garofalo, Greg Kinnear, Paul Reubens, Wes Studi, Kel Mitchell, Lena Olin, Claire Forlani

> Superheroes for the little man. Who needs them to fly when they can just smack their enemies upside the head with a shovel?

THE DIGEST
Welcome to Champion City, Home of Captain Amazing (Greg Kinnear). Captain Amazing has managed to keep the city safe from crime and evil villains, so safe that he doesn't have anyone to fight and is losing his endorsements. He helps secure the release of his old nemesis, Dr. Casanova Frankenstein (Geoffrey Rush), who has just spent the last 20 years in a prison for the insane. Casanova isn't out more than 10 minutes when he calls on his two sidekicks, "The Disco Boys," Tony P. and Tony C. (Pras from the Fugees wearing a big old Afro was worth the cost of admission).

Captain Amazing finds out that Casanova is up to his old tricks, and confronts him. Casanova promptly kidnaps him, and Champion City is in peril. Once it is clear that Captain Amazing is kidnapped, a group of ragtag superhero wannabes decide to save Captain Amazing and help him fight crime. "Mr. Furious" (Ben Stiller) has the "power" to get very angry, problem is, nothing ever happens after he loses his temper. "The Bowler" (Jeanine Garofalo) can strike out anything with her bowling ball. "The Shoveller" (William H. Macy) knows how to work a shovel like a set of nunchaku, and so on. Can these mishap-prone wannabes save Champion City and its hero, Captain Amazing?

THE DISH

Mystery Man is filled with dumb jokes and corny lines, but I found myself cracking up. If you liked *There's Something About Mary*, *The Nutty Professor*, or *Dr. Doolittle*, you'll like *Mystery Men*. It's light on plot but big on sight gags and sophomoric humor. The makers of the movie realized the majority of the people watching this flick would be kids. They took great care to make sure there was not an ounce of blood, not one curse word, and no real nudity (one of the superheroes loses his costume), and all the weapons were non-lethal. There was also a message that kids and adults alike could benefit from: "Believe in yourself." Once the superheroes believed in themselves and each other, nothing could stop them.

A friend of mine complained that the movie could have been much more. That may be true, but I didn't expect more. I wasn't looking for a solid plot. I was looking for laughs and special effects. I got both. The "look" of Champion City was astounding. It reminded me a lot of *The Fifth Element*. The special effects were campy, but there is only so much you can do when you decide to go low on the violence scale. Plus it got a few points

for having my favorite Diva, Jenifer Lewis, in it as "The Shoveller's" wife.

THE DIRECTIVE

Bottom line. If you like stupid jokes and aren't expecting much more than mind-numbing laughter, then rent *Mystery Man*. If you want substance, this is not the movie for you.

FLASHING YELLOW LIGHT

Bams **Notorious C.H.O.** (2002)

UNRATED; running time 95 minutes
GENRE: Comedy (concert)
WRITTEN BY: Margaret Cho
DIRECTED BY: Lorene Machado
PERFORMER: Margaret Cho

THE STORY

"Love yourself without reservation . . . love each other without restraint. Unless you're into leather." Words to live by. And speaking of "words," since *Notorious C.H.O.* is a concert for adults only, so too is this review. If Bad Words makes you want to reach for your Bible, stop reading now.

Notorious C.H.O. is comedian Margaret Cho's followup to her 2000 comedy concert *I'm the One That I Want* (see page 269), filmed on digital video in Seattle in early 2002. In addition to Cho's standup bit, the opening and closing sequences feature fan reaction, and, a treat for those who enjoyed Cho's very funny impersonation of her mother in her last film: Cho's mother and father, in the flesh.

And even more than she did in her last joint, Cho rocked the house.

THE UPSHOT

"Irreverent" is a phrase that's overused these days, too often without merit. But it's completely apropos in the case of *Notorious C.H.O.*, and of Margaret Cho herself. Starting with her warped twist on the September 11 tragedy—Yes, America, It's Okay to Laugh Again—Cho made it clear that she was taking no prisoners.

In reviewing her previous concert film, I was caught off guard by Cho; not having had much familiarity with her background and humor, it took me a while to warm up to her the first time around. But having seen *I'm the One* on film, then seeing her concert live in Seattle in 2000, as well as meeting her backstage afterwards, I knew what to expect in *Notorious C.H.O.*—at least, I thought I knew. Still, I was surprised at how long, and hard, and often, I laughed while watching this concert.

To call her comedy blue would be an understatement. There are few of her jokes and observations that I could repeat in this review that wouldn't be censored (if 3BC had a censor . . . and since we don't, here's my favorite line of the concert, regarding "the only gay bar in Scotland: That place should just be called 'Fuck Me In the Ass' Bar and Grill").

What sets Cho apart from the foul comedians that eventually ruined *Def Comedy Jam*, though, is that unlike their constant barrage of meaningless filth, there is a message behind Cho's sharp wit; one that softens the edges just a wee bit. If she riffs on gay men not wanting to hear of her troubles in climaxing during straight sex, she counters that riff with a tribute to the two drag queens who wouldn't let a doofus agent convince Cho that Asians had no place in show business. If she clowns on her mother and father, she balances that with the obvious love she has for them. If she takes straight men, and the issues they bring, to task . . . well, as she might put it, she likes dick, whaddya do?

And she doesn't give herself a break, either; without hesitation, she tells the audience about her varied and sundry self-esteem problems— and more important, how she overcame them and is now able to look her detractors in the eye with a hearty Fuck You Very Much. This is why I've claimed Cho to be 3BC's Adopted Sista. She seems so incredibly genuine, so true to herself, that even as a short Chick, she stands head-and-shoulders above so many of her opportunistic fellow celebrities (can you say "Rosie O'Donnell"?). As funny as she is, when Miz Cho brings The Message, you know it isn't just lip service.

Hmmm. Considering some of Cho's habits, maybe that's a bad choice of words . . .

BAMMER'S BOTTOM LINE

Not since Richard Pryor's searingly funny, introspective concerts, has a comedian made me laugh through the tears the way Margaret Cho has. As I said of her in *I'm the One That I Want:* Preach, sista!

GREEN LIGHT

The Original Kings of Comedy
(2000)

RATED R; running time 117 minutes
GENRE: Comedy (concert)
DIRECTED BY: Spike Lee
CAST: Steve Harvey, D. L. Hughley, Cedric the Entertainer, Bernie Mac

> As D. L. Hughley likes to say, "Y'all need Jesus."

THE STORY

Named after the long-running comedy tour that began in 1997 and ended on the same stage in 2000, *The Original Kings of Comedy* was filmed at the Charlotte Coliseum in North Carolina on February 26 and 27, 2000, and features stand-up comedians and actors Steve Harvey, D. L. Hughley, Cedric the Entertainer, and Bernie Mac. The four men are shown not only onstage but also in short, behind-the-scenes bits that give the audience a brief look at what motivates these Four Kings. Look and listen closely, and you might find that what you see onstage is not necessarily what you'd get in real life.

THE UPSHOT

Let's get one thing straight, from jump: if one is to speak of kings of comedy—especially filmed concert comedy, and most especially in terms of originality—any exclusion of Richard Pryor is suspect. So, are Messieurs Harvey, Hughley, Entertainer (yes, I know), and Mac heirs to Pryor's crown or just mere pretenders to the throne?

I think Pryor can rest easy. This foursome is good, no doubt, but it'll take a lot more than their approximately 30 minutes of stage time each, to wipe away any memories of *Richard Pryor: Live on the Sunset Strip* from my mind.

That said, past the "trash talk" title of this Spike Lee joint, the four "Kings" comedians do fit the bill for an audience that is used to their brand of comedy and, let's face it: that audience consists mostly of cultural Blacks, and Whites who are down.

Each of the four comics have had successes in similar venues: Harvey hosts *It's Showtime at the Apollo* and is the star of *The Steve Harvey Show* TV series; Hughley was the original host of BET's *Comic View* (back when it was funny) and, like Harvey, is also star of a self-titled TV series (*The Hughleys*); Cedric the Entertainer was the host of the second year of *Comic View* (back when it was still funny, though well on the way to becoming the unfunny joke that it is today) and costars on *The Steve Harvey Show;* and Bernie Mac, along with his ongoing role on *Moesha*, has appeared in movies like *Life*, and *Above the Rim*, and *Ocean's 11*, and now has his own hit show on Fox. But in this comedy concert, it was their skills as veteran stand-up comedians that came into play. With varying degrees of success.

Those "varying degrees" were strange, considering that each of the four had very similar routines—granted, spiced with their own personal Flava. Each of them touched on old school ways, on male-female relationships, and on the obligatory White audience members and how "we're different . . . but really, we're the same," amongst other similar topics. Of course, such is the stuff of comedy, especially the comedy of My People. Some of the comedians were better at that stuff than others, though. And in this case, Steve Harvey playing concert host while doing his own shtick won the Kings's Race of Champions.

Harvey, a self-proclaimed "country boy" (though all of the Kings were Country, dag!) had both the Charlotte *and* the movie theater audience right in the palm of his hand. He worked the crowd like a master (to say that he reminded me of Johnny Carson in this, is a compliment), and almost everything out of Harvey's mouth was flat-out funny. D. L. Hughley, who followed Harvey, wasn't as "on" as I've seen him in the past. I had never heard this routine before, but it sounded too familiar; too . . . tired. I found myself wishing he'd do his brilliant "Come Back With Me" nostalgia "tour."

Up next was the always-stylish Cedric the Entertainer, and while he couldn't quite top Harvey, he also pumped up the audience. I know I'd pay for a recording of "Peanut Butter . . . No Jam." Closing the bill—in my opinion, a mistake—was Bernie Mac. The thought that kept coming to me while watching Mac was, "what the hell is he so mad about?" The second thought was, " . . . and why should I care?" Not a good thing when you're supposed to be laughing at the jokes. True, I snickered now and then, but Mac never took off for me. And neither did the relatively flat ending.

Unless I miss my guess, Spike Lee should take blame for that virtual thud. There were too many ineffective background bits, and the editing job wasn't great. And can you get less impersonal than to keep showing the auto-tracking camera moving back and forth across the stage? The cold feeling of the shots almost negated the energy that Harvey & Company generated. Still, Lee deserves props if only for bringing this concert to a wide audience. After all, when's the last time you saw a comedy concert released theatrically?

BAMMER'S BOTTOM LINE

"Kings"? Hmmm . . . more like Clown Princes (and Bernie Mac, more a Squire). Still, the foursome did well, with Steve Harvey conducting the "How to Work an Audience" clinic of a lifetime. But what was up with Spike Lee's filming and editing, though. This joint looked downright ugly . . .

GREEN LIGHT

Rat Race

(2001)

RATED PG-13; running time 125 minutes
GENRE: Comedy
WRITTEN BY: Andy Breckman
DIRECTED BY: Jerry Zucker
CAST: Rowan Atkinson, John Cleese, Whoopi Goldberg, Cuba Gooding Jr., Seth Green, Jon Lovitz, Lanai Chapman, Kathy Najiny, Vince Vieluf, Amy Smart, Breckin Meyer

THE DIGEST

A group of ordinary strangers find themselves bound to one another after they are "randomly" selected to compete for two million dollars. There are no rules to the contest, other than the first one who makes it to the location where the money is stored, gets it. The participants are:

Enrico Pollini (Rowan Atkinson). Enrico is

just in Las Vegas on vacation. He is from Italy and suffers from narcolepsy.

Vera Baker (Whoopi Goldberg) and Merrill Jennings (Lanai Chapman). Vera is there to meet the daughter she gave up for adoption at birth and hasn't seen since. Merrill, the daughter, owns her own business and is just a *little* stressed out.

Owen Templeton (Cuba Gooding Jr.) is in Las Vegas hiding out. He made the wrong call on a coin toss for a playoff game. Everyone is talking about it because everyone lost bet money because he blew the call.

Duane Cody (Seth Green) and his brother, Blaine (Vince Vieluf), are small-time cons who keep screwing up.

Randy Pear (Jon Lovitz), wife Bev (Kathy Najimy), and their two children are in Las Vegas on vacation.

Supersquare lawyer Nick Shaffer (Breckin Meyer) is in Las Vegas for a bachelor party. He prides himself on never having done one thing illegal in his entire life. This changes when he become attracted to helicopter pilot Tracy Faucet (Amy Smart).

At the shot of a gun, everyone takes off from Las Vegas to Silver City, New Mexico, hoping to be the first to get their hands on the money. Each participant ends up in some kind of mess on their way to New Mexico and that is where the fun begins.

THE DISH

After the first 20 minutes of this movie, I was ready to get up and leave. I'm so glad I stayed because when the race starts, I swear, I about died. I laughed until I cried. I love slapstick and physical comedy and this had plenty of it. Blaine pierced his own tongue and now it's infected (I know . . . gross), so now he talks with an *extreme* lisp. Suddenly, no one can understand what the hell he is saying. Blaine and his brother, Duane, are really the comedic glue that holds the movie together.

Jon Lovitz also gets high marks from me. It takes a skilled person to make Hitler funny. And Jon managed to do just that. I don't normally care for Jon Lovitz, but his Randy Pear is a force unto himself. He has convinced his wife that he has to drop everything to go to New Mexico for a job. Randy's effort to keep up with that lie and get to the money was priceless. I must admit, as much as I dislike bathroom humor, there is a scene with his daughter that made me cry I laughed so hard.

Whoopi was underutilized, as was Lanai Chapman, who played her daughter. Cuba Gooding Jr. pulled off his comedic turn. I could have done without just about everyone else.

There were some issues though . . . The last 20 minutes were just horrible, but I'm not quite sure how you can end a movie like this, so maybe any ending would have been horrible.

THE BLACK FACTOR

Bams and I had different opinions on this movie, yet I found her Black Factor commentary compelling enough to add it to my review. The words below belong to Bams.

"Some people take issue with my questioning of Black actors acting like buffoons in what is *supposed* to be a comedy.

And up to a point, I agree: all other characterizations being equally buffoonish, a Black actor in a comedy should *not* be held to a different standard by being made unnaturally noble. Indeed, I'd rather see a funny actor of *whatever* race being allowed to be funny, over them being made the hero just to avoid the tricky subjects of race, class, and culture (which, really, doesn't avoid them at all, since folks like me are chompin' at the bit to razz a pedantic, paternalistic filmmaker).

So this BF is purely a jab at Cuba Gooding Jr., and not at the machine that would have him act the fool. He does that to himself without much help. The man is brilliant as a serious actor; I've enjoyed him thoroughly, without pause, in films like *Boyz N the Hood* and *Men of Honor* (see page 101). But please, somebody, spank his agent's ass if Gooding decides to do another comedy, another 'This Moment in Black Buffoonery' created just for him."

THE DIRECTIVE

The Rat Race scored a big piece of comedic cheese. But set your expectations low. Watch it, knowing it will be dumb and that there will be some implausible stuff. If you can manage this, your experience will be enjoyable.

GREEN LIGHT

Bams **Rush Hour 2**
(2001)

RATED PG-13; running time 89 minutes
GENRE: Action/Comedy
WRITTEN BY: Jeff Nathanson
DIRECTED BY: Brett Ratner
CAST: Jackie Chan, Chris Tucker, Zhang Ziyi, John Lone, Roselyn Sanchez, Alan King, Harris Yulin

> We've been on the Chan Boat for years and we sure are glad that American audiences are finally starting to respect Jackie Chan.

THE DIGEST

In *Rush Hour*, Detective James Carter (Chris Tucker) and Detective Inspector Lee (Jackie Chan) saved the daughter of the Chinese consul. After that situation, they need a vacation and decide to relax in Hong Kong. But, alas, there is no rest for the weary. Rather than rest, workaholic Detective Lee keeps taking assignments, and this doesn't sit well with Detective Carter who is bored and wanting some attention. What Carter doesn't realize is that Lee is after the most dangerous gang leader around. Ricky Tan is the former partner of Lee's father and also responsible for the elder Lee's death. It appears that Tan's gang members are responsible for the recent death of two Americans in the American consul's office, and Lee is determined to get to the bottom of it.

Well, it's pretty hard for Lee to get his job

done when he is constantly bombarded with Carter's whining. Lee, trying to kill two birds with one stone, first takes Carter to a nightclub, then to a massage parlor, both of which are frequented by Ricky Tan. Carter, true to form, lets his mouth get them in trouble, as well as thrown off the case by the Secret Service. This, of course, does not stop Lee and Carter. They forge ahead, finally doing battle with Hu Li (Zhnag Ziyi), Tan's vicious bodyguard, *and* finally finding out that there is an American connection that leads them from China to Las Vegas.

THE DISH

I love Chris Tucker and I love this character, but James Carter is going to get real old, real fast. There were no real new elements added to this film. It was *Rush Hour* in a different location. The only real twist was that some of Jackie Chan's lines in the film were Chris Tucker's lines from the first movie, and that was funny. For example, Lee told Carter that he was going to "bitch-slap you back to Africa," and in *Rush Hour* Carter was forever telling Lee that he was going to "bitch-slap you back to China." This movie also had more scenes with Carter and Lee fighting together.

Rush Hour 2 is pretty much standard "popcorn" cinema. Stare at the screen and giggle. Don't expect anything above average, especially with all the plot holes.

May I take this moment to vent? The Motion Picture Association of America needs an enema. This is a PG-13 movie. I would have thought with all the language it would be an R movie. I don't get how they decide what is inappropriate and what isn't.

THE DIRECTIVE

Rush Hour is decent movie, even if the plot got off at a different exit.

GREEN LIGHT

 Shanghai Noon
(2000)

RATED PG-13; running time 109 minutes
GENRE: Action/Comedy
WRITTEN BY: Alfred Gough, Miles Millar
DIRECTED BY: Tom Dey
CAST: Jackie Chan, Owen Wilson, Lucy Liu, Roger Yuan, Xander Berkeley, Walt Goggins, Brandon Merrill

> Jackie's real name is Chan Kwong-Sang or Sing Lung (Cantonese), or Cheng Long (Mandarin).

THE STORY

Set in the late 1800s, *Shanghai Noon* is a fun mix of humor, martial arts, and riffs on and homages to Western flicks ranging from *High Noon* to *Blazing Saddles* to *Butch Cassidy and the Sundance Kid*.

After Princess Pei Pei (Lucy Liu) is kidnapped from Forbidden City, China, and taken to America's western frontier of Carson City, Nevada, Imperial Guard Chon Wang (Jackie Chan) is reluctantly allowed to go to America, along with three other guardsmen, to rescue her. Fate meets him on a train, when Roy O'Bannon (Owen Wilson), a flirtatious train robber with a heart o' gold (and a nose for *finding* gold), crosses paths with Chon and eventually teams up with him to help Chon find the princess.

THE UPSHOT

The word best used to describe *Shanghai Noon* is "fun." Not just funny, though it was definitely that—*Shanghai* worked well because it never took itself too seriously (ya gotta love a Cowboy movie where the Indians *aren't* treated like Noble Savages, and they poke fun at themselves), and neither did its two lead actors characters. And because of its lighthearted approach, I was easily able to ignore plot holes that might otherwise have bugged the daylights out of me.

The trademark of any Jackie Chan movie comes in his high-energy martial arts combined with his usual humorous flair. Chan did not disappoint on either end. Chan is the Dick Clark of martial arts movies. The man must be 105 years old by now (I remember watching him in *The Cannonball Run* when I was a wee pup myself and he looked about the same age even then), but watching him fly around on-screen, doing all his own fighting and stunts, you'd swear that he was still a young thing. And I defy you to find anything cuter than Jackie Chan getting silly after puffing on a peace pipe.

Equally enjoyable, in a different way, was Owen Wilson as Roy O'Bannon. I couldn't help but to see shades of a young Robert Redford in Wilson, though unlike Redford's Butch Cassidy, Roy was a lot more personable and a lot less misogynistic.

But it was the interplay between Roy and Chon (and, of course, between Chan and Wilson), that most impressed me. The "Chinese Drinking Game" they played had me in stitches, as did their early fight scene together. I'd dearly love to see these two actors expand on their great chemistry; who knows—maybe they *could* be the next Paul Newman and Robert Redford buddy team.

The beauty of *Shanghai Noon*, though, is that it doesn't just rely on the two leads to move its story forward. Lucy Liu's princess is no shrinking violet; as headstrong as she is beautiful, she had some fight in her, and she didn't just sit back and let herself get rescued like a damsel in distress. And though Roger Yuan didn't really distinguish himself in what could've been a plum role as bad guy Lo Fong, the same cannot be said of Xander Berkeley (Marshall Nathan Van Cleef); the fun he must've had in playing the marshall in his dueling scenes with Roy was evident during his performance. It's just too bad that he wasn't given more onscreen time.

A couple bits didn't work all that well. I never did get what Wallace's deal was all about; he seemed to be one bad guy too many. Maybe I blinked and missed it—or maybe the meat of their parts were left on the editor's cutting-room floor. And though the tribal chief's daughter (played by model Brandon Merrill) was apparently a throwback to similar female characters in past westerns, I rolled my eyes at how her story played out in the end. Fortunately, these were minor missteps, and they had a negligible effect on my enjoyment of the movie. Usually, thoughts of movie remakes and part twos give me the hives; but I didn't get enough of *Shanghai Noon*. I want more.

THE BLACK FACTOR

I hesitated on addressing the Black Factor—or, more precisely, the "Minority Factor"—in this review; after all, Chan and company took such a whimsical look at the lives of Chinese and Native Americans in the Wild Wild West of yore ("I don't know why they call me the 'Shanghai Kid'; I'm not from Shanghai!") it seems almost wrong to deal with those issues on a more serious basis. Still, I've not been one to back down from examining prejudices—Hollywood's as well as my own.

The lighthearted approach used in dealing with race in this movie didn't mean that it was glossed over; it was just treated subtly, and in my opinion, worked all the better for that subtle treatment. Only once did my BS meter go off (Blacks would be welcome in a saloon in the 1800s, but not Chinese?), and only once was bigotry specifically, directly addressed. The treatment felt right, though issues of Chon's assimilation into Western culture left me vaguely ill at ease.

But more disturbing to me, on a personal level, was my own prejudicial reaction to this movie in a roundabout way, most of which had little to do with *Shanghai*, and more to do with Chan's hit movie *Rush Hour*, costarring Chris Tucker, which I didn't watch for the longest time because I, frankly, didn't feel like seeing Tucker play the sidekick as court jester.

The Diva broached this issue when she said, "Why is it okay for me to spend my money watching a stupid Adam Sandler movie, but not okay for me to watch *Booty Call*?" The question made me stop and won-der the same about my own prejudging of the role of the Black Sidekick like Tucker in *Rush* vs. the White Sidekick like Wilson in *Shanghai*. The self-examination left me somewhat disconcerted; I had to ask myself if there's really a difference in how the characters are written and/or played by their respective actors, and more to the point, whether the difference is an actual, tangible thing, or merely my perception.

I haven't quite decided yet. My heart wants to say that a Tucker, or a Danny Glover, or a (insert Black Actor as Sidekick name here) *is* written or directed differently than would be a Wilson, or a Gene Wilder, or a (insert White Actor as Sidekick name here). But my head tells me that even where there is fault in the writing or direction, there is probably also duplicity on the actor's part. And maybe a bit of some on mine.

BAMMER'S BOTTOM LINE

Shanghai Noon. It's the funniest movie I've seen in a long time; Owen Wilson is a silly charmer, and Jackie Chan is still one baaad mofo. And don't forget: as with most Jackie Chan movies, do *not* leave before you see the outtakes.

GREEN LIGHT

Bams What Planet Are You From?

(2000)

RATED R; running time 100 minutes

GENRE: Comedy

WRITTEN BY: Michael Leeson (based on a story by Garry Shandling)

DIRECTED BY: Mike Nichols

CAST: Garry Shandling, Annette Bening, John Goodman, Greg Kinnear, Ben Kingsley, Linda Fiorentino, Anne Cusack, Camryn Manheim, Nora Dunn, Caroline Aaron, Richard Jenkins, Samantha Smith, Janeane Garofalo

THE STORY

What Planet Are You From? takes the "Men Are from Mars" concept to another level: Harold Anderson (Garry Shandling) is a brother from another planet—a planet of men with no penises (shudder). It should come as no surprise, then, that these dickless men wish to conquer another planet—and which planet would that be? Three guesses, and the first two are wrong.

After putting his planet's men through semi-intensive training on the ways of Earth women, hoping that they'd be easy, fearless leader Graydon (Ben Kingsley) picks Harold as their man. His mission: grab his attachable penis, get an Earth girl knocked up, and something or another mumble mumble about the new superbaby . . . oh yeah, it will become Supreme! Ruler! Of! Earth!

A few things get in the way first, though; mainly, his lame lines fail to impress many women—including a flight attendant he met on the way to Earth—that is, until he meets Susan Hart (Annette Bening) who, he figures, just might be the one. Finding a job at a bank while he's waiting for the child thingy to resolve itself, he also has to deal with his slimy sycophant co-worker Perry Gordon (Greg Kinnear), their boss Don, and FAA inspector Roland Jones (John Goodman), who is committed to proving to his bosses that Harold is from somewhere way the hell out there.

THE UPSHOT

What Planet Are You From? started out slowly and picked up steam as it went along, with some very funny scenes along the way. What really worked about it for me is the sense of *fun* the characters and actors seemed to have with each other, from Susan kickin' it with her girlfriends Liz (Anne Cusack), Alison (Camryn Manheim), and Madeline (Nora Dunn) to the comic interplay between Shandling and the surprisingly funny Bening—and especially Goodman, one of the funniest Big Men in Hollywood. The laughs were easily drawn out of me, even I as sat there determined not to laugh at this movie.

The feel of this comedy is very *Raising Arizon-aish*; stretching the predictable lines men often troll on women and the hook-line-and-sinker way women often respond to them to a comic extreme, you quickly see, through Harold's eyes, just how silly the battle between the sexes really is. But even after the obligatory alien-develops-human-feelings bit, the "yes, dear" relationship, in all its familiarity, seems somehow comforting; at least it did for this old married chick.

I do, however, take slight issue with what I see as two casting flaws. The character most out of place here was Helen Gordon, played to her smoky best by Linda Fiorentino; though Ms. F. did no real wrong in her role, her character seemed to be an unnecessary distraction, an appendage to "prove" how bad Perry was. Still, she delivered one of the best lines of the movie when Harold tells her that the humming sound she heard was coming from his penis, she says, "I guess it doesn't know the words." Rollin', I tell ya; absolutely rollin'.

The second, more problematic, casting flaw involves Janeane Garofalo; as was done in *Dogma* (see page 177) she was included here in a glorified cameo as a nervous airline passenger used as a target for more of Harold's intro-to-Earth bit. She would've been better cast as Roland's wife, Nadine, and *her* minor part should've been played instead by Caroline Aaron (the actress who actually played Nadine Jones).

BAMMER'S BOTTOM LINE
Yeah, I know: I'm as shocked as you probably are to see me give *WPAYF* a green light (especially since I only gave its soul mate, last year's *Galaxy Quest*, a conditional yellow). Hey, every Chick can be wrong once, eh?

GREEN LIGHT

Bams The Whole Nine Yards
(2000)

RATED PG-13; running time 105 minutes
GENRE: Comedy
WRITTEN BY: Mitchell Kapner
DIRECTED BY: Jonathan Lynn
CAST: Bruce Willis, Matthew Perry, Rosanna Arquette, Michael Clarke Duncan, Natasha Henstridge, Amanda Peet, Kevin Pollak, Harland Williams

THE STORY
From the official Web page:

Nicholas "Oz" Oseransky (Matthew Perry) is a nice dentist living in suburban Montreal. His new next-door neighbor, Jimmy "The Tulip" Tudeski (Bruce Willis), is a hit man hiding out from a dangerous Chicago crime family. Despite their differences, Oz and Jimmy have one thing in common: someone's trying to kill them both. For Jimmy, avoiding a couple of hired killers is child's play. But for Oz, it's a whole new ball game.

To stay alive, they're going to have to stick together—Jimmy with his cunning and cold-blooded accuracy and Oz with his dental tools.

THE UPSHOT
The story started out slow (and no, I don't mean "slowly") and ended with a whimper instead of a bang. The storyline was nothing to write home about—we've seen variations of it before—but the *way* it was told is what made this comedy work. It had a very natural flow to it: something that doesn't often happen in comedies, especially

not the sitcom variety. I found myself wondering where the time went, and almost surprised that it was ending so soon. And if, by some stretch of the imagination, *Nine* could technically be labeled a "sitcom," it wasn't like any I've seen before.

A nice touch was the use of jazz throughout; in these days of "soundtracks" being really just a vehicle to promote whichever singers or rappers the producer happens to be in bed wi . . . er, like, it's refreshing to hear music that's actually part of the movie, rather than tacked on to sell CDs.

The actors and their characters, though, were the real story behind *Nine*. During his heyday in the *Moonlighting* TV series and *Die Hard* movies, Willis hogged the spotlight away from his costars. Not so in *Nine*; here, his "Tulip" was much more subdued, but at the same time, for lack of a better word, commanding. There's a noticeable shift partway through the movie, when Jimmy takes on a mean streak and the old hammy Willis starts to come to the fore, but that doesn't last for long, and Willis again blends in with the not-quite-ensemble cast.

Matthew Perry really surprised me; I fully expected his Oz to be a one-dimensional doofus, pratfalling his way across the screen. Well, he did sorta-kinda, but in a charming way. Though Oz became "wise" too easily about halfway through the flick, and his relationship with Jimmy's estranged wife Cynthia worked my nerve, I looked past that, concentrating instead on scenes such as the one where he runs into glass doors—and you haven't lived until you've seen him bounce off a glass door—hey, that was just plain *funny*. Sue me for liking physical comedy; I Loved *Lucy*, too.

Not to be outdone by her sister, Patricia "Gots Ta Fix Mah Teefes" Arquette, Rosanna Arquette just made me wanna smack her character, Sophie, upside the head whenever she opened her mouth and out spilled the phoniest French-Canadian accent I've ever heard. Yeah, I *know* Sophie was *supposed* to be unlikable, but was Rosanna? Also dragging the movie down somewhat was Harland Williams as Buffalo Steve, a "hitter" that Sophie hires, and, surprisingly, Kevin Pollak's Janni Gogolack, leader of the Chicago Hungarian mob that Jimmy ratted on (which is the reason why he moved to Canada in the first place). Janni was basically a one-trick pony in this movie; his shtick was the way he slowly mumbled and "mispronounced" words in supposedly Hungarian. Worth only a quick chuckle or two, it seemed a waste of Pollak's talents. Buffalo Steve was nothing more than (literally?) a stiff; though (I guess) the character was needed to advance the story, there was far too little explanation of what he was there for, to make him work.

THE BLACK FACTOR

So, how did Michael Clarke Duncan acquit himself? Quite well, I thought. His natural "bigness" notwithstanding, my fears of his being typecast as the Big Black Guy were unfounded. Duncan didn't play Figs as larger than life. Yes, he's Big, and yes, he's Black—but neither were really the point here (except inasmuch as a hit man's hetman needs to be foreboding to put the fear in their target). The truth will out in future films, of course, but for now, thumbs up.

But Amanda Peet as Jill, the Dental Assistant With a Twist, came close to stealing the show. Jill had me rollin' in almost every scene she was in, especially after Oz told her about "The Tulip." Peet's enthusiasm was contagious, and seemed to make the other actors performances go up a notch or two. I think I'll be following Amanda Peet around the Big Screen, too.

BAMMER'S BOTTOM LINE

The Whole Nine Yards is in a word: fun. The story was fun for the audience (after the slow start), and the cast and crew seemed to be having fun telling the story. That's a rare combination in movie comedies these days, what with "comedy" being co-opted more and more with "drama" to make "dramedies." Bammer sez, ain't nuttin' wrong with being straight (but intelligently) funny. More comedies oughta try it, dig?

GREEN LIGHT

ever notice how there aren't very many Black people in the future? Anyway . . . some of these movies will scare you while others will fascinate you. Some may even gross you out. Others will upset you, because the group splits up to look for "Johnny," leaving "Jamil" behind. If the brotha is lost, he's on his own . . . y'all catch our drift.

A.I.: Artificial Intelligence
(2001)

RATED PG-13; running time 153 minutes
GENRE: Science Fiction
WRITTEN BY: Steven Spielberg (based on the short story by Brian Aldiss)
DIRECTED BY: Steven Spielberg
CAST: Haley Joel Osment, Jude Law, Frances O'Connor, Sam Robards, Jake Thomas, William Hurt, Jack Angel, Robin Williams, Chris Rock (voice)

THE DIGEST

Somewhere in the not-so-distant future, the polar ice caps melt, which causes most major seaboard cities to be washed away. In an effort to survive, the "gubmint" decides that certain precautions have to be taken. One of the precautions is to require people to get a license in order to have children. They've also created lifelike robots to provide essential functions and services. (The "gubmint" also managed to recreate a U.S. that has only two Black people, a scientist and a "comedian" robot voiced by Chris Rock.) The creator of the artificial intelligence behind the robots, Professor Hobby (William Hurt), has decided to take it a step further. He wants to create a child. Once this child is activated, he/she will love you forever and ever. There is no going back. You can't just shelve this robot or give it to a shelter when you tire of it. The child is yours as if you gave birth to it.

David (Haley Joel Osment) is the first prototype. He is given to an employee of the company, Harry Swinton (Sam Robards), and his wife, Monica (Frances O'Connor), whose own son is sick. A reluctant Monica decides to love David, only to drop him off in a forest when it *appears* that he means to harm her birth son. David then sets off to find the "Blue Fairy," á la *Pinocchio*, to turn him into a real boy, so his mommy will love him. Along the way he meets Gigolo Joe (Jude Law), a robotic prostitute, and they set out to meet the Wizard . . . I mean the Blue Fairy.

THE DISH

Oh Lawd . . . three days later and I still can't wake up. I was bored to tears by *Bicentennial Man* and this was a repeat performance. I wanted to cry and I wanted to feel sad that David longed for his mommy. But my heartstrings refused to be manipulated. I just wasn't feeling it. What I *really* wanted was for him to be turned off and put on a shelf somewhere.

I will give Haley Joel some credit. This was a big role and his acting didn't disappoint, but he was limited by the script. There were so many holes in *A.I.*, and it moved so unbearably slowly, I'm surprised there weren't outtakes of the crew sleeping in between takes. Chris Rock sounded like the rib boy from *I'm Gonna Git You Sucka*; thankfully, his character was promptly disintegrated. Jude Law was amusing as a 'ho, but not enough to save the movie.

THE DIRECTIVE

The intelligence of *Artificial Intelligence* wasn't artificial, it was gone.

FLASHING RED LIGHT

Battlefield Earth
(2000)

RATED PG-13; running time 117 minutes

GENRE: Action/Thriller

WRITTEN BY: Corey Mandell and J. David Shapiro, based on the novel by L. Ron Hubbard

DIRECTED BY: Roger Christian

CAST: John Travolta, Barry Pepper, Forest Whitaker, Kim Coates, Sabine Karsenti, Richard Tyson, Marie-Jose Craze, Kelly Preston

> Travolta has said that he is going to make a part 2. We think that's a crime against humanity and he should be punished accordingly.

THE DIGEST

Circa the year 3000, humans are either living in caves or they are slaves to the Psychlos, a race of aliens that in just nine minutes attacked Earth, making man an endangered species. They've also turned Earth into a mining planet, stripping it of all its natural minerals.

Jonnie "Goodboy" Tyler (Barry Pepper) leaves his cave in search of more food for his village. He is promptly captured and taken to the main human slave camp in Denver. When he is not in the cage, he is trying to escape, which brings him to the attention of Terl (John Travolta), the security chief for the Psychlos. He hates Earth and wants to leave but because he has upset the wrong people, he has to stay on Earth indefinitely. But his biggest mistake isn't

pissing off the wrong people; it's underestimating the humans.

He teaches Jonnie to speak his language. Jonnie then gets a group of rebels together and they plot the taking back of their planet.

THE DISH

To say this movie is bad would be an understatement. It is downright horrible. So much of it was just unbelievable. These yahoos can learn to fly a fighter plane in seven days, but they can't figure out how to brush their nasty teeth? Better yet, how about learning how to make pants.

And the ending was just as implausible. Why didn't anything deteriorate? Where was all the dust? Where was all the rust? It is explained that the atmosphere of the Psychlos home planet is very unstable, but that still doesn't make the implausible method in which they are blown up any more credible. By comparison, sending up a computer virus in *Independence Day* was a work of art.

I wasn't having it and neither was the audience. They laughed at what was supposed to be a dramatic scene within the first two minutes of the movie. Even the effects were horrible. It got to the point where it was so painful to watch this movie that some people got up and left. No joke.

No, I didn't forget about Forrest Whittaker. Bless his heart; I guess he has a house note.

THE DIRECTIVE

If you are the type of person who likes to watch traffic accidents, then *Battlefield Earth* is for you.

RED LIGHT

Bicentennial Man
(1999)

RATED PG-13; running time 145 minutes

GENRE: Drama

WRITTEN BY: Nicholas Kazan (based on the
story by Isaac Asimov)

DIRECTED BY: Chris Columbus

CAST: Robin Williams, Sam Neill, Hallie Kate
Eisenberg, Embeth Davidtz, Oliver Platt,
Wendy Crewson, Lindze Letherman, Kiersten
Warren, Stephen Root, Bradley Whitford,
Lynne Thigpen

THE STORY

Bicentennial Man tells the story of Andrew Martin
(Robin Williams), a robot purchased by the
wealthy Martin family—Sir (Sam Neill), Ma'am
(Wendy Crewson), Little Miss (Hallie Kate
Eisenberg), and Portia (Embeth Davidtz). Andrew is attached to them in one way or another
throughout its existence. Or, maybe more correctly, *his* existence: for as time passes, and with
the help of scientist Rupert Burns (Oliver Platt)
and his perky robot Galatea (Kiersten Warren),
Andrew "evolves" from "one who wishes to
serve" to a creative, cognitive, sentient being.
But does having human body parts make him
human?

THE UPSHOT

Supposedly spanning a 200-year period (hence
the title—though the importance of that passage of time still escapes me, and indeed was one
of the problems with this movie). *Bicentennial
Man* was never quite sure what it wanted to be.

The first part was definitely reminiscent of the
earlier Williams-Columbus collaboration, *Mrs.
Doubtfire*, but that lasted only as long as the piano duet scene with Andrew and Little Miss; the
flickers of *Mrs. Doubtfire* left the screen when the
first generation of Martin children grew up.
From there on, the heaviness set in, and any
thoughts that *Bicentennial* was a comedy were
dashed. At best, it could be called humorous in
spots, heavy on the message; interesting, but
never quite fulfilling.

What went wrong? Some will probably place
the blame for the mostly disappointing results of
Bicentennial Man on Robin Williams; as a zany
comedian who has had some good and not-so-
good turns as a straight actor, Williams is the eas-
iest target to choose. But I will disagree with
those critics who point at Williams; no, I place
the blame squarely on the shoulders of Chris
Columbus. His direction lacks direction; his vision is unclear, and without having a firm grasp
of anything but smarmy sentimentality, it's little
wonder that this movie missed the mark.

Williams definitely reigned in his usual wild
humor, though bits of it strained to peek from
under that cute android suit. He played Andrew
with the necessary subtlety until Andrew, reading
the numerous books that Sir provided for him,
wanted his freedom (there's a bit for the Black
Factor, no?). From there, the movie turned from
being a story involving family interactions to Andrew's One-Robot Crusade; his Forrest Gump—
like trek around the world caused such a dead
spot, you could hear the snores throughout the
audience. Columbus, not Williams, should be the
one burning at the stake for all those snores.

As far as the supporting cast goes, only Sam

Neill, Oliver Platt, and the effusively funny Kiersten Warren made a dent in the movie. As Sir, Neill's performance was understated and welcome; Platt also played it quiet, but that was a good call on his part. For some bizarre reason, Wendy Crewson's Ma'am was all but invisible (and I wish that I could say the same thing for the bratty Miss; maird, I wanna go on a butt-whuppin' spree on some of these movie kids one of these days), and thankfully, the irritating Eisenberg didn't ply her trade for long here. Davidtz was interesting enough. And curses onto Chris Columbus's head for not using the usually wonderful Bradley Whitford more in this flick; he could've easily played Gerald, the Robotics company owner (played by the equally little-used Steven Root). What a waste of opportunity that was; Whitford plays slime like few others in Hollyweird.

Overall, *Bicentennial Man* took too long to get where it got, painted a weird picture of the future (and are cars the only things that'll "change" over that time span, huh Chris?) and left me with more questions than answers. Still, it wasn't half bad for an afternoon's worth of entertainment.

THE BLACK FACTOR

In a futuristic movie spanning 200 years and taking 2 hours and 25 minutes to tell, I recalled seeing only one Black person: character actress Lynne Thigpen (though at least she was the leader of the World Congress—the name alone makes me roll on the floor, laughing).

So how many Blacks are there in outer space? Thigpen, Nichelle Nichols, and LeVar Burton, that guy that played Sisko on one of the "Star Trek" shows . . . and Billy Dee "Calrissian" Williams. Okay, so there's *five* of Us around in the future. Hey, no sweat, we're used to it by now.

BAMMER'S BOTTOM LINE

At 2 hours 25 minutes, *Bicentennial Man* felt longer than *The Green Mile*, and had some plot holes big enough to drive my truck through—but all things considered, Robin Williams acquitted himself well enough. But I do so miss the Funnyman underneath all that makeup.

YELLOW LIGHT

the Diva   **Deep Blue Sea**
(1999)

RATED R; running time 104 minutes
GENRE: Thriller/Horror
WRITTEN BY: Duncan Kennedy and Donna Powers
DIRECTED BY: Renny Harlin
CAST: Thomas Jane, Saffron Burrows, Samuel L. Jackson, Jacqueline McKenzie, Michael Rapaport, LL Cool J

Like Alfred Hitchcock, director Renny Harlin likes to make cameos in his films. See if you can spot him in *Cutthroat Island*, *Deep Blue Sea*, or *Driven*.

THE DIGEST

Dr. Susie McAlester (I prefer the name Dr. Susie Stupid) (Saffron Burrows) is on the verge of finding a cure for Alzheimer's disease. She figured out that sharks don't lose their brain capacity as they get older. So she injects them with hormones and harvests their brain cells. Problem is she made them supersmart and they're super-pissed. (I don't blame them either. I would have an attitude if some was always poking around in my brain cells.) Mr. Franklin (Samuel L. Jackson), the guy that runs the pharmaceutical company that sunk 200 million into this project, wants to pull the plug on the research because one of the sharks gets out and causes some problems. Dr. Susie Stupid invites him out to the lab to show him how close they are to getting the cure for the disease. (*PSSSSTTTT*, Samuel, next time someone wants you to go out into the middle of the ocean during an impending storm to be surrounded by sharks…don't go.) It doesn't take him long to regret his decision.

THE DISH

Bottom line is, we have yet another predictable movie. We know the sharks turn on them. We can figure out who is going to end up in the belly of a shark. We know about halfway through how it's going to progress and end. With few surprises and tons of plot holes, I found myself praying for this movie to hurry up. Actually, what I said was "Kill 'em and get it over with."

To the movie's credit, I will say this much, those sharks were tough. They weren't messing around a'tall. Given the special effects surrounding the sharks, they actually had the best screen time. In fact, they were the best actors. The other actors didn't fare as well. LL Cool J provided the comic relief, but he isn't a comedian. All his jokes fell flat and it was painful to watch him. Samuel Jackson seemed out of place to me in this movie. It was like he was homeboy from *Pulp Fiction*, only this time he was filthy rich and shark bait.

THE BLACK FACTOR

First of all, there were two Black men in this movie, so I knew the "brotha rule" (see page xv) was going to be in full effect. (Darn shame, too. Hollywood just doesn't get it.) Is it that hard to let a Black man live to see the next day? I'll never understand this. It's difficult to discuss this rule without giving away the plot, but let's start with the premise that *somebody* Black has to die and they die in about an hour. Let's continue by stating that it's almost always a Black man. If there isn't a Black man but a Black woman, the rule applies to her. If there are no Black folks at all, then by default it's the minority in the picture. So, knowing all of this, you can imagine how disheartening it is to watch this movie.

THE DIRECTIVE

Horror-movie aficionados should include *Deep Blue Sea* on their list, everyone else should bypass it and go straight to the "E" section in the video store.

FLASHING RED LIGHT

End of Days
(1999)

RATED R; running time 118 minutes
GENRE: Thriller/Horror
WRITTEN BY: Andrew W. Marlowe
DIRECTED BY: Peter Hyams
CAST: Arnold Schwarzenegger, Gabriel Byrne,
    Robin Tunney, Kevin Pollak, Renee Olstead,
    Matt Gallini, Linda Pine, C.C.H. Pounder

THE DIGEST

It's 1979, and a girl child is born in New York City. All is normal except she has the marking of the beast, and it is said that she will be the one to carry the spawn of Satan. Satan (Gabriel Byrne) will appear on earth in 1999 to claim his bride. Evil and Good circle the wagons. The Vatican sends a priest to watch over her, while devil worshipers insinuate themselves into her life. From psychologists to nurses, all of them keep an eye on her.

Fast forward to 1999. Jericho Cane (Arnold Schwarzenegger) is the head of a security firm. He is a bitter ex-cop with a drinking problem. He drinks away the pain of having lost his wife and daughter, who were killed because he testified in some case. He and his partner (a very funny Kevin Pollak) are assigned to provide security for a wealthy stockbroker who just happens to be Satan.

Meanwhile, the girl child, Christine York (Robin Tunney), as she is known, has grown up. Both of her parents are dead and she lives a fairly normal life with her stepmother, but with one exception. She has visions, visions that terrify her.

She has always had them and has tried to suppress them with drugs, but lately things have gotten worse.

As Jericho and Christine's paths cross, he knows that he must protect her. Once he finds her, the movie picks up speed and doesn't stop until the quite predictable end.

THE DISH

Wow! Even though Arnold is playing the same old character and it's chock-full of plot holes and corny one-liners (what Arnold Schwarzenegger film isn't?), I cannot say enough good things about Gabriel Byrne's take on Satan. Hands down, he is the best Satan, ever. Absolutely fabulous!

And how much do I love C.C.H. Pounder? "Eyyyeeeee am Caalllling yoooooooou I know you hear me." Yes, I'm proud to say I own the soundtrack to *Baghdad Café* . While she didn't sing that song, it comes to my mind whenever I see her. C.C.H. is so underappreciated as an actress, I'm thinking of starting my own fan Web site for her. Her role in *End of Days* was remarkable. I was happy to see her working again.

Don't rent this expecting to see an Oscar-worthy movie. Take it for what it's worth: an opportunity to "veg" for two hours. I did.

THE DIRECTIVE

If you liked *The Exorcist*, *The Omen*, and *Rosemary's Baby*, don't miss *End of Days*.

GREEN LIGHT

Evolution
(2001)

RATED PG-13; running time 105 minutes
GENRE: Comedy/Action
WRITTEN BY: Don Jakoby, David Diamond, and David Weissman
DIRECTED BY: Ivan Reitman
CAST: David Duchovny, Julianne Moore, Orlando Jones, Seann William Scott

THE DIGEST

Wannabe fireman Wayne is out in the Arizona desert torching buildings and dummies in order to practice for his test to become a fireman. In the blink of an eye, he is blown out of the area by a falling meteorite. Geology professor–girls volleyball coach Harry (Orlando Jones) and Biology professor Ira (David Duchovny), grab a sample from the meteorite and take it back across town to the local community college.

When they get it back to school, Harry runs off to coach a game, while Ira studies the liquid goo that came out of the meteorite. Ira notices that the cells in the goo are evolving at a very rapid rate, approximately 125 million years in 5 minutes. Harry and Ira are beside themselves, convinced that they will get the Nobel Prize in Science. Meanwhile, the government has sent Allison (Julianne Moore) to head up the scientific investigation of the meteorite, and she has issues with Ira.

This organism is going through the same evolution that brought about humans. When the organisms evolve to the point where they'll need oxygen, human beings, indeed all creatures, will be in danger of extinction.

Can Harry and Ira figure out how to destroy the creatures and save Earth?

THE DISH

Good Lord, this was one stupid-ass movie. It was just like *Ghostbusters*—which was very funny when I was 14. This too would have been funny if I were 14. But I'm not, and neither is over half the population.

There were times when I chuckled. Those were the times I tried to lighten up and enjoy it for its stupidity, but I couldn't manage that for the entire movie. Seann William Scott had me cracking up when he was hunting the dinosaur in the shopping mall; other than that, most of the gags fell flat. Orlando Jones was *mildly* amusing, though I was initially very irritated that he was playing some idiotic clown. As if we need another African-American jackass. But I thought about it, and when was the last time we saw Adam Sandler play someone serious? If being a jackass works for Mr. Jones, then he should go right ahead and do just that. I'll just grin and bear it.

Julianne Moore was painful; almost as painful as David Duchovny. Let's just say, I was relieved when it was over.

THE DIRECTIVE

You should really wait until NBC buys the rights for this one.

FLASHING RED LIGHT

the Diva The House on Haunted Hill

(1999)

RATED R; running time 96 minutes
GENRE: Thriller/Horror
WRITTEN BY: Dick Beebe and William Malone;
     based on the 1958 screenplay by Robb White
DIRECTED BY: William Malone
CAST: Geoffrey Rush, Famke Janssen, Taye
     Diggs, Ali Larter, Bridgette Wilson, Peter Gal-
     lagher, Chris Kattan

THE DIGEST

Stephen Price (Geoffrey Rush) is the amusement-park king. He is very wealthy and loves to throw parties where his guests are scared witless. He is also in a loveless marriage. In fact, he and his wife keep trying to kill each other. His wife, Evelyn (Famke Janssen), wants to throw herself a birthday party, and sends him the guest list. He shreds it and writes his own list with just six people. The list is mysteriously changed, and six random strangers are invited to "The House" instead. No one knows how or why these particular strangers were chosen, but nonetheless, each stranger will receive one million dollars if they live through the night. Those who die will have their million split amongst the survivors.

Sounds easy, right? Wrong. The house they are staying in was once an institution for the criminally insane. And the former residents are up to unspeakable evil.

THE DISH

Why do I torture myself? One of these days, one of the characters in a scary movie I'm watching will go investigating some spooky noise by themselves, and I'll have an aneurysm. The lack of common sense never ceases to amaze me, but I guess that's part of the fun with scary movies. It wouldn't be a scary movie if someone didn't do something ridiculous.

For example, the guests are there for about 10 minutes when the house locks itself. They immediately split up (?!?!?!?!?), and go searching for a way out. While they are searching the basement, weird things begin to happen. The smart ones go back to the main group upstairs. The dumb ones stay down there and get in trouble.

Don't you know that some of the guests kept going *back* into the basement? Look folks, people die when they go downstairs. How hard is it to stay on the couch and read? Grab a chair and crochet a blanket? Do a crossword puzzle? Play charades? Why keep going back? If someone is dumb enough to leave the group, then, BYE! None of this "what's taking so-and-so so long? Maybe we should go find him and make sure he is all right." He's been gone thirty minutes on a five-minute trip. Let the police find his body.

But in fairness to the movie, it did what scary movies are supposed to do. It scared the stuffing out of me on more than one occasion, and I really dug the special effects. As far as the acting goes, Chris Kattan was hilarious. Geoffrey Rush had the difficult task of filling the shoes of Vincent Price, who starred in the original, which he does quite well. I was equally impressed with Famke Janssen's portrayal of his "adoring" wife. The rest of the cast left a lot to be desired.

THE DIRECTIVE

The House on Haunted Hill almost merits a green light. If you consider yourself a connoisseur of horror films, you'll be disappointed. If you are easily scared, then you will love it.

FLASHING YELLOW LIGHT

Jurassic Park III
the Diva
(2001)

RATED PG-13; running time 93 minutes
GENRE: Thriller
WRITTEN BY: Peter Buchman, Alexander Payne, and Jim Taylor
DIRECTED BY: Joe Johnston
CAST: Sam Neill, William H. Macy, Téa Leoni, Alessandro Nivola, Trevor Morgan, Michael Jeter

> Despite the fact that this was a horrible movie, expect to see *Jurassic Park 4* in the next few years.

THE DIGEST

As he was in prequels, Dr. Alan Grant (Sam Neill) is still doing his archeological digs and once again short on money. He has been on the lecture circuit trying to drum up support for his new theories and books, but all the public really cares about is the theme park and the San Diego incident (see *Jurassic Park II—The Lost World*). He is extremely frustrated and thinking of throwing in the towel when Paul (William H. Macy) and Amanda Kirby (Téa Leoni) approach him.

Paul and Amanda are rich thrill-seekers. They have gotten permission from the Costa Rican government to fly over Isla Sorna, the second In-Gen (the company responsible for the first theme park; see *Jurassic Park I*) dinosaur site. They want Alan to be their tour guide; in return they will write him a check for however much he wants for his research. Of course Alan accepts, as long as they are just flying over the site—not landing.

What Alan doesn't know is that they don't have permission but they have every intention of landing. You see, the Kirbys are looking for their 11-year-old son, who was last seen parasailing over the island. Not only do they land on the island, they crash onto the island, and now they must stay alive long enough to find the boy and save themselves.

THE DISH

Children, I have suffered again and I'm hoping that I don't stroke out. Everything that could have gone wrong with this film, did. Let's be real. We don't watch this franchise to see Oscar-winning acting and stories. We watch these *Jurassic Park* movies because of the dinosaurs. They are the biggest attraction. So, what happens when the dinosaurs aren't very menacing? What happens when the plot is horrible? What happens when you pray that one of the characters is eaten alive? What happens when the most vicious dinosaur evokes laughter and not fear? *Jurassic Park III* is what happens.

THE DIRECTIVE

Jurassic Park III is one big stinking pile of dino poopoo.

RED LIGHT

 **The One**
(2001)

RATED PG-13; running time 96 minutes
GENRE: Science fiction/Action
WRITTEN BY: Glen Morgan, James Wong
DIRECTED BY: James Wong
CAST: Jet Li, Carla Gugino, Delroy Lindo, Jason Statham

> Contrary to popular belief, the term "kung fu" doesn't only apply to martial arts. Defined literally, "kung fu" means "hard work." This book, for instance, could be said to have been accomplished through "writing kung fu." Dig that.

THE STORY

The One takes the notion that Somewhere Way the Hell Out There, there's someone just like you and me, and flips it on its ear: here, there are *multiple* universes (the multiverse) with several hundreds of someones like us out there.

For bad guy Yu Law (Jet Li), that old saying, "That which does not kill me, makes me stronger," doesn't quite apply: Law discovers that killing all of his other "me"s is what makes him stronger. He travels through the multiverse seeking out his doppelgangers (I do so love that word) and killing them, thereby taking on their energies, growing stronger, faster, more invincible every time.

To become the last Law standing, Law must go after Gabriel Law (also Jet Li), an unsuspecting sheriff in our universe. As Yu Law comes closer to Gabe's world, Gabe tries to convince his wife, T.K. (Carla Gugino), that something's wrong. But Gabe will need more help than she can give him. That's where Multiverse Agents Roedecker (Delroy Lindo) and Funsch (Jason Statham) come in . . .

THE UPSHOT

Maybe in an alternate universe, someone will save the audience time, and make an action flick that just moves from one action scene to another without even bothering with a plot. Oh wait; that's porn. My bad. *The One* fell into the classic big-budget action flick trap of putting much more into the way it looked and moved, than into the story itself; probably because writer-director James Wong didn't give the story enough time to simmer on the development stove. On the other hand, let's be real: who really goes to see this kind of big-budget film for much besides the *action*? I didn't expect much past the pretty pictures, and my low expectations were met head-on.

And man, did it look good. The "Li vs. Li" fight scenes were spectacular. Li's close-quarters *kata* movements were quite impressive to watch. Likewise, the special effects—computer wizardry—was topnotch. The post-production work that went into making *The One* come across so stunningly on screen raises the bar for the next epic action flick that comes down the pike. But with nothing of any real substance to wrap this movie around, the viewer walks away feeling like they ate a big ball of cotton candy: empty calories on a stick.

BAMMER'S BOTTOM LINE

Any movie where someone gets pimp-slapped with a motorcycle is something you gotta see.

Just don't expect much else from *The One*, an action-packed but story-light flick.

FLASHING YELLOW LIGHT

Bams **Red Planet**
(2000)

RATED R; running time 110 minutes
GENRE: Science fiction
WRITTEN BY: Chuck Pfarrer and Jonathan Lemkin, (based upon a story by Chuck Pfarrer)
DIRECTED BY: Anthony Hoffman
CAST: Val Kilmer, Carrie-Anne Moss, Tom Sizemore, Benjamin Bratt, Simon Baker, Terrence Stamp

THE STORY

The year: 2057. 12 billion people living on Earth. Something's gotta give and, increasingly, it's Earth's natural resources.

> We would like to send the filmmakers on a cruise to Mars. Pass the plate, y'all.

For 20 years, Earth scientists sent unmanned probes to Mars, hoping to stimulate life there, to one day allow some of Earth's citizenry to colonize Mars. When the oxygen levels on Mars start dropping, "Houston" sends a crack team of their top people to Mars to investigate. The team in-

cludes tough-as-nails (but soft inside!) mission commander Kate Bowman (Carrie-Anne Moss); techie Robby Gallagher (Val Kilmer), whom the team teasingly calls their "Space Janitor"; Dr. Quinn Burchenal (Tom Sizemore), a geneticist with science constantly on the brain; Lieutenant Ted Santen (Benjamin Bratt), mission copilot and resident stud; terraforming specialist Chip Pettengill (Simon Baker), picked for the mission as a last-minute replacement; and Dr. Bud Chantillas (Terrence Stamp), former scientist and current seeker-of-light.

And let's not forget AMEE, the robot Wonder Dog; prepped for exploration as well as military mode, AMEE is one terminator that you do not wanna tick off.

THE UPSHOT

Red Planet was, in a word, boring. And in a few more words, it had plot holes wide enough to drive a truck through, uninteresting characters that you were glad to watch die one at a time, a story line that was laughingly thin with weak feints toward having big philosophical discussions, multiple deus ex machinas (one in particular that had the geek in me up in arms; anyone with working knowledge of how modems work, will see what I mean), and the dumbest, most unintentionally funny excuse for an Evil Monster that I've seen in a long time. Oh, but the movie *did* have irrelevant-to-the-scene Sting songs constantly playing in the background, and, proving that it was "modern and hip!," lots of references to the Web. Oooh. I'm impressed.

I give *Planet* credit for almost coming to life near the end (ironic that the more characters died off, the more interesting the movie got), and for avoiding the easy *Matrix* way out by not making Carrie-Anne Moss's character melt around all the flying testosterone (at least, not completely). The movie certainly *looked* pretty enough. And I gotta admit that that Bra-less Space Commander close-up even got *my* attention (must be cold up there, eh, Commander?). But what a waste of Tom Sizemore; hell, of Moss (who had a few sparky moments), and Terrence Stamp, too (Val Kilmer was his usual wooden self).

THE BLACK FACTOR

The good news: there were no Black astronauts in this "futuristic" space flick to test out Diva's "Brotha Rule of Science Fiction" (in which the Black astronaut/scientist/comic relief is usually the first to die). The bad news: there were no Black astronauts in this "futuristic" space flick. The better news: there were no Black actors wasted in this stunningly boring space flick.

BAMMER'S BOTTOM LINE

Director Anthony Hoffman oughta be pimp-slapped for having all that powerful acting ability at his fingertips and leaving it lost in space like that.

YELLOW LIGHT

the Diva **Scream 3**
(2000)

RATED R; running time 86 minutes
GENRE: Thriller/Horror
WRITTEN BY: Ehren Kruger, based on characters created by Kevin Williamson
DIRECTED BY: Wes Craven
CAST: Neve Campbell, David Arquette, Courteney Cox Arquette, Patrick Dempsey, Parker Posey, Scott Foley, Lance Henriksen, Matthew Keeslar, Jenny McCarthy, Emily Mortimer, Deon Richmond, Liev Schreiber

THE DIGEST

Years earlier, there were some gruesome murders in a small town. Sidney (Neve Campbell) survived both outbreaks (*Scream* and *Scream 2*) and is now living in Los Angeles. To her dismay, Hollywood has decided to make a series of movies based on that horrible time in her life. *Stab 3* is the final installment of the series based on those murders, and by living in the hills and barricading herself in the house, Sidney is trying to ignore the fact that her reality is being exploited on screen. To make ends meet, she is answering calls for a woman's crisis line and using a false name.

Meanwhile, in the city . . . The other survivors have gone on with their lives as well. Cotton Weary (Liev Schreiber) is the host of a controversial talk show, Gale Weathers (Courteney Cox Arquette) is a roving reporter for a show similar to *Entertainment Tonight*, and Dewey Riley (David Arquette) is a technical advisor for *Stab 3*. Five minutes into *Scream 3*, the first survivor is killed. No one is too shook up until the third victim is

killed. The survivors race against the clock to figure out who the next victim is going to be and
why the killings have started up again. The kicker
is that the killer appears to be following the script
for *Stab 3*, and there are three copies of it floating
around.

THE DISH

Neither the dialogue nor the plot of *Scream 3* was
engaging. But I did find it amusing to watch the
cast of *Scream 3* interact with the people playing
them in *Stab 3*, especially Parker Posey in her portrayal of Gale Weathers in *Stab 3*. There were also
a few jabs and swipes at classic horror films and
the real lives of the cast members that I found
funny, with the cameo of Carrie Fisher being the
funniest. It was also refreshing to see Patrick
Dempsey as the police officer assigned to the
case.

Other than that, though, the movie was far
too predictable, and I really don't like how severe
they had Courteney Cox looking. She really resembles Margot Kidder in this film, and Margot
needs to eat a meal or two.

THE DIRECTIVE

Even though it wasn't as scary as the first two, I
still wouldn't recommend watching *Scream 3* in
anything but broad daylight.

FLASHING YELLOW LIGHT

 Space Cowboys
(2000)

RATED PG-13; running time 130 minutes
GENRE: Dramedy
WRITTEN BY: Ken Kaufman, Howard Klausner
DIRECTED BY: Clint Eastwood
CAST: Clint Eastwood, Tommy Lee Jones,
    Donald Sutherland, James Garner, James
    Cromwell, Marcia Gay Harden, Loren Dean,
    Courtney B. Vance, Barbara Babcock, William
    Devane, Aleksandr Kuznetsov

THE STORY

A full 40 years after being upstaged by a monkey
for the opportunity to show they had the "Right
Stuff" in outer space, retired Air Force pilots
Frank Corvin (Clint Eastwood), Hawk Hawkins
(Tommy Lee Jones), engineer Jerry O'Neill (Don-
ald Sutherland), and navigator Tank Sullivan
(James Garner) are reunited in "Operation Date-
less" when a Russian satellite, Ikon, malfunc-
tions. Much to the dismay of Dateless's former
Air Force commander, Bob Gerson (James
Cromwell), Frank is found to be the designer of a
system much like the one found in the satellite.
And since the technology he designed is too an-
cient for the current NASA scientists such as
Sarah Holland (Marcia Gay Harden) to figure
out, the ball is in Frank's court, and he plays it.
He'll gladly fix the satellite as long as he and his
Dateless crewmates are allowed to go on that
long-awaited space mission along with reluctant
current astronauts Ethan Glance (Loren Dean)
and Roger Hines (Courtney B. Vance).

And the big question, voiced by both Frank

and NASA Flight Director Eugene Davis (William Devane): just how did that "similar technology" get into a Cold War–era Russian satellite?

THE UPSHOT

I'm an Old Skool kinda Chick, and in Hollywood, there aren't many older than the likes of Eastwood, Jones, Sutherland, and Garner. Each was charming in his own way, none more than Tommy Lee (whose name alone makes me want to make him an Honorary Brother). Tommy Lee Jones puts the Grump in "Grumpy Old Man," and manages to do so without coming off either smarmy or as irritating as one would think his perpetual Good Ol' Boy acting would play. Jones is one of the most talented, natural actors in the business, and it's almost always a pleasure to watch him work, *Rules of Engagement* notwithstanding.

Space Cowboys was Jones's and Clint Eastwood's puppy to play with. Jones's Grump was matched by Eastwood's patented Grimace. Where Jones is at ease with his suthern drrrrawl, Eastwood Emotes through the grit of his teeth; and though age has softened that grit somewhat, Dirty Harry at 70 is still a force with which to reckon. Of the two remaining leads, Donald Sutherland fared much better than James Garner. I saw shades of Sutherland's younger self, notably the laid-back Jerry O'Neill character he played in *The Dirty Dozen.*

And there was love—what, you didn't know that old folks need love, too?—in the most unexpected of places. The brief flirtation scenes with Frank and Mrs. Corvin (Barbara Babcock) were only a teaser for the more unexpected, yet somehow obligatory, romance between Hawk and

Sarah. I didn't have a problem with that per se; if anything, Harden brought out even more of Jones's natural charm but I'd like the name of Marcia Gay Harden's hairdresser. She needs her butt whupped for letting Marcia Gay go out in public looking like that.

I loved *Cowboys'* sense of itself, of how John Glenn and *The Right Stuff* had to be acknowledged, and especially how it never really pushed the age bit too far (well, almost never). What I *didn't* like was the illogic of Cromwell's character Bob Gerson and how he related to the Russian engineer.

The comedic first half of *Space Cowboys* certainly worked better for me than the more serious second half; once the Cowboys blasted into space, my initial estimation of the movie blasted out with them. Still, though, I wish I'd left the theater more excited about what I had just seen, I most def felt entertained . . . and ain't that what it's all about?

THE BLACK FACTOR

I had to chuckle at the way Diva's "Brotha Rule" played out here. Courtney B. Vance may be married to Angela "Born To Be Storm, I Said!" Bassett, but apparently her cachet hasn't done him much good, as far as his Hollywood roles go. Can't fault a brotha for at least showing up on the set though, even if his fairly nonexistent part amounted to not much more than a playful shove to the back of the shuttle by Tommy Lee. (Oh . . . and please, Mr. Vance, bring back your mustache. Your fans will thank you for it.)

BAMMER'S BOTTOM LINE

Space Cowboys was a tuffy for its sense of humor (Tommy Lee Jones and Donald Sutherland kept me laughing), but the serious outer-space stuff left me rather cold, and I spent way too much time straining to hear what was being said. Still, check it out if for no other reason than to see three and a half good old boys give it ye olde college try.

FLASHING YELLOW LIGHT

14

Stop frontin', y'all. You *know* you don't really feel like spending all that time with your badass nieces and nephews. You just use them as an excuse to see the cartoon but you won't admit it. We say, "Who cares?" If you cry every time *Dumbo* and his mother are separated, or when Snow White tells the Magic Mirror that she's an ugmo, don't be afraid to say so! Just let it flow. We won't tell anyone...honest.

Atlantis: The Lost Empire

(2001)

RATED PG; running time 100 minutes

GENRE: Animation (traditional plus some CGI; nonmusical)

WRITTEN BY: Tab Murphy et al

DIRECTED BY: Gary Trousdale, Kirk Wise

VOICES OF: Michael J. Fox, James Garner, Cree Summer, Claudia Christian, John Mahoney, Leonard Nimoy, Phil Morris, Jim Varney, Don Novello, Florence Stanley, Corey Burton, Jacqueline Abradors

THE STORY

Milo J. Thatch (Michael J. Fox) is a cartographer who has grand plans of finding the lost city of Atlantis, the mythical city that even the philosopher Plato believed was washed away by a great tidal wave. Problem is, no one at the museum for which Milo works as a maintenance man, believes in Milo's vision; just as they didn't believe in the vision when Milo's late grandfather Thaddeus had it.

Someone believes in Milo, though—Preston Whitmore (John Mahoney), an eccentric millionaire who finances a journey to the bottom of the sea, sending Milo off with a fearless bunch of explorers to find the lost city. Led by Commander Rourke (James Garner), the crew includes Rourke's smoldering lieutenant, Helga Sinclair (Claudia Christian); gentle giant Dr. Joshua Sweet (Phil Morris); the nastiest Cookie (Jim Varney) this side of New Mexico, and his soul mate, the dirt-lovin' Mole (Corey Burton); as well

as a host of colorful others. Sure, Milo has the vision; but do the others? And if they do find Atlantis, what then?

THE UPSHOT

As with *Dinosaur* (see page 5), I spent an inordinate amount of time picking out the actors' voices instead of watching the movie itself.

I'm sure the actors would like to think they've made some kind of impression upon their audience. For me, they made *some* kind of impression; I'm just not sure it was a lasting one. To be sure, the movie was well drawn, and reminiscent of classic Disney films, such as *Lady and the Tramp* and the original *101 Dalmatians*. But in this ever-evolving, computerized world, is a nod to the past enough? Will *Atlantis* go down in the books as a new classic?

The answer to that, I'm afraid, is "no." Being simply "cute in spots; not too dull," just doesn't cut it; not with more mature kids who've cut their teeth on computer games (and can program computers better than some adults), not with parents who brought their youngsters in to the movie at upwards of $10 a pop, and maybe not even with the wee tots, judging from the loud, restless ones that were in my audience.

Restless, no doubt, because much of *Atlantis* may have gone over their heads. Between the mix of *Tomb Raider*–worthy mystic mumbo jumbo, the high-for-youngsters violence quotient (my inner child cheered at the fist fights), and the lack of Disney-patented singing and dancing creatures (though they weren't at all missed by me), kids may have wondered what the hell their parents dragged them in to see. And while even grownup grumps like me found ourselves chuckling a time or two, and pleasantly surprised at how some of the characters' "movements" seemed to match their vocalizations incredibly well (Fox's Milo, especially), I didn't find that enough to give *Atlantis* my strongest recommendation.

BAMMER'S BOTTOM LINE

Atlantis: The Lost Empire is good for a diversion, but it won't stick to your ribs like a good animated flick should.

FLASHING YELLOW LIGHT

(Bams) Fantasia

2000

RATED G; running time 74 minutes

GENRE: Animation

WRITTEN BY: Don Hahn, Irene Mecchi, David Reynolds; Hans Christian Andersen (story: "The Steadfast Tin Soldier")

DIRECTED BY: James Algar ("The Sorcerer's Apprentice"), Gaetan Brizzi ("Firebird Suite"), Paul Brizzi ("Firebird Suite"), Hendel Butoy ("Pines of Rome," "The Steadfast Tin Soldier"), Francis Glebas ("Pomp and Circumstance, Marches No. 1, 2, 3, and 4"), Eric Goldberg ("Rhapsody in Blue," "Carnival of the Animals"), Don Hahn ("Host Sequences"), Pixote Hunt ("Beethoven's Symphony No. 5, Allegro con Brio")

MUSIC BY: Paul Dukas (from "L'apprenti sorcier"), Edward Elgar (from "Pomp and Circumstance March No. 1"), George Gershwin (from "Rhapsody in Blue"), Ottorino Respighi (from "Pines of Rome"), Camille Saint-Saens (from "The Carnival of the Animals"), Dmitri Shostakovich (from "Piano Concerto No. 2"), Igor Stravinsky (from "The Firebird"), Ludwig van Beethoven (from "Symphony No. 5 in C minor, Op. 67")

VOICES OF: Walt Disney (Mickey Mouse), Wayne Allwine (Mickey Mouse), Tony Anselmo (Donald Duck), Russi Taylor (Daisy Duck)

SEGMENT HOSTS—PERFORMERS: James Earl Jones, Quincy Jones, Angela Lansbury, Steve Martin, Bette Midler, Penn Jillette, Teller, James Levine, Itzhak Perlman, Leopold Stokowski, Deems Taylor

> Never let it be said that Bammer condones illegal substances of any kind, nuh uh. But if one *did* lean toward indulging (for medicinal purposes, of course), *Fantasia 2000* would be my choice for an altered-states companion. But you didn't hear that from me.

THE STORY

A blend of traditional animation artistry and modern-day computer technology, *Fantasia 2000* melds visual delights with grand classical music scores to create a feeling rather than a straightforward, scripted story. Advancing the wish of Disney founder, Walt Disney, 60 years after its original release, that *Fantasia 2000* be a constant "work in progress," the modern version updates the classic segment "The Sorcerer's Apprentice," and adds six new segments, all done by different directors and creative teams, and introduced by famous (but in the grand scheme of things here, insignificant) entertainers as hosts.

THE UPSHOT

If my description of "the story" is woefully lacking, it's because it's hard to describe the beauty of the images and music in words that would make sense. But I reckon it's my job to try. The narrator introduced the first segment, set to Beethoven's "Symphony No. 5," by saying that there are three kinds of music: music that tells a story, music that paints a picture, and music for its own sake—and further saying that the segment that follows is an example of the latter. I would respectfully disagree with that statement; that first segment, with its beautiful colors, seemed an example of all three kinds of "music." Indeed, most of the segments painted a picture that resonated in a way that a traditional storytelling could hardly approach. And if the first segment, with its shapes that morphed smoothly from undefined objects to colorful "butterflies" and beyond, didn't exactly tell a story, I'd hazard to say the remainder of the segments certainly did.

The visual artistry of each segment was well matched by the beautiful music chosen for it. From the surreal image of lighter-than-air whales (set to "Pines of Rome") to the playfulness of a nonconformist flamingo ("Carnival of the Animals"), and especially the wondrous mating of composer George Gershwin's "Rhapsody in Blue" with artist Al Hirschfeld's unique view of New York City, Fantasia 2000 allowed me to relive fond memories of a time where cartoons were fun without being overly hip, cynical, and devoid of inspiration.

The remaining segments were a mixed bag. The classic "Sorcerer's Apprentice" seemed to not have aged as well as I'd hoped (though you couldn't convince the kids in my audience of that; one squealed "it's Mickey Mouse!" in unrestrained delight). Likewise, Donald and Daisy Duck's turn at being helpers for Noah ("Pomp and Circumstance, Marches No. 1, 2, 3, and 4") was less than an unqualified success. And I'm of the opinion that "The Steadfast Tin Soldier" should've remained on that back shelf that host Bette Midler said it lingered on for so long; it was easily the weakest of all the stories. But all these sins were forgiven by way of the breathtakingly bittersweet closing segment, "Firebird Suite." This normally jaded reporter is not ashamed to say that I smiled, I cried, and I cheered, at the end of this magnificent segment.

That each of the seven segments could get my animation-loving attention, was not surprising. That they could grab my interest in their nonverbal storytelling to the point where I didn't want to leave at the end, was a delight—one that I am anxious to repeat again (and again).

If there was a low point to this film, it came with the Obligatory Famous Entertainers' "hosting" segments, in which the likes of Steve Martin, James Earl Jones, Penn and Teller, Bette Midler, and Quincy Jones, among others, served as a reminder that Hollywood thinks very little of its audience—and thus, we viewers need to have actors as cue cards "explain" to us what we're about to see, since we're obviously too unintelligent to either figure it out for ourselves, or read for ourselves what we're about to see.

BAMMER'S BOTTOM LINE

Fantasia 2000 is a visual—and aural—master-piece. True eye candy in every positive sense of the term, it reminded me of all the reasons I loved the fully orchestrated cartoons of the '40s and '50s. Between all the butchering...er, editing... of classic cartoons, and the Saturday morning dreck they currently have to sit through, kids today truly don't know what they're missing.

GREEN LIGHT

Final Fantasy: The Spirits Within

(2001)

RATED PG-13: running time 96 minutes
GENRE: Animation
WRITTEN BY: Al Reinert, Jeff Vintar, Hironobu Sakaguchi
DIRECTED BY: Hironobu Sakaguchi
VOICES OF: MingNa, Alec Baldwin, James Woods, Donald Sutherland, Ving Rhames, Steve Buscemi, Peri Gilpin

> They give good Voice: Peri Gilpin, like the rest of the main cast of television's *Frasier*, has done many voice-over commercials and animated features.

THE DIGEST

It's 2065, and Earth is a complete and total wasteland. Humans have run from terra firma and are living in space, orbiting the mother planet. The key to the rebirth of Earth are spirits, various life forms hidden throughout the planet, that have managed to survive or have become immune to what destroyed the land in the first place—phantoms. Dr. Aki Ross (MingNa); and her mentor, Dr. Sid (Donald Sutherland), are working tirelessly to save the planet by locating these spirits and bringing them together. To complicate matters, she is forced to work with her old flame, Captain Gray Edwards (Alec Baldwin), *and* she has to go head-to-head with a gung-ho General Hein (James Woods) who has a score to settle with the phantoms and practically wants to blow up Earth to get rid of the creatures.

With the help of Captain Gray Edwards and his crew—Sergeant Ryan Whittaker (Ving Rhames), Neil Fleming (Steve Buscemi), and Jane Proudfoot (Peri Gilpin)—Aki sets out to find the remaining two spirits and save Earth.

THE DISH

"Phhhhbt" or however that noise is spelled. What a hunk of junk.

The animation was *awesome*, but this was not enough to save the ridiculous dialogue and the horrible story. Given how beautiful the animation was, this could have easily been one of my favorite movies of all time if the story hadn't royally sucked. I felt like I ate a whole box of nasty Cracker Jacks, didn't get a prize, and now my stomach hurts for nothing. I want my 90 minutes and my gas money back.

Steve Buscemi as Neil Fleming was the one bright spot in the entire movie. Beyond him and the animation, it was pretty unremarkable.

THE DIRECTIVE

Unless you are an animation junkie, don't go near *Final Fantasy*.

RED LIGHT

Monsters, Inc.
(2001)

RATED G; running time 105 minutes
GENRE: Animation
WRITTEN BY: Dan Gerson, Andrew Stanton
DIRECTED BY: Peter Docter, David Silverman, Lee Unkrich
MUSIC BY: Randy Newman
VOICES OF: John Goodman, Billy Crystal, Mary Gibbs, Steve Buscemi, James Coburn, Jennifer Tilly, Bob Peterson, John Ratzenberger, Frank Oz

Monsters, Inc. set a new box-office record for an animated film; it made 62.5 million dollars its opening weekend.

THE STORY

Calvin may have once fretted about scary monsters being under his bed, but in the world of Monsters, Inc., the real fear is when they come out of the closet.

The Fear Factor is actually a manufactured product at Monsters, Inc., the factory where James "Sully" Sullivan (John Goodman) and his Scare Assistant, Mike Wazowski (Billy Crystal), use special portals to produce the screams that produce the power that allows the monsters of Monstrobia to live comfortably. Sully, a good-natured monster, is in fierce competition with Randall Boggs (Steve Buscemi) for most screams collected for the year, and Randall doesn't play well with others. So, just how do these Scary Monsters collect their screams? Why, from the shrieks of children, frightened by the monsters in their closets. Monsters go in, but the number-one rule is, children must never, EVER, come out. Uh oh . . . how'd that little girl (Mary Gibbs) get attached to Sully?

THE UPSHOT

Pixar, creators of *Toy Story* and *Toy Story 2*, put almost as much techie stuff, fun (that "coaster ride" whee!), and feeling into *Monsters, Inc.* as they did in those earlier movies. "Almost," I say, because while *Monsters, Inc.* does share much of the same beauty as its older siblings, there's something a little less warm (compared to *TS*) and deep (compared to *TS2*) about it. And then John Goodman's Obligatory Big Lug kicks in, in a big and delightful way.

Goodman and Mary Gibbs were so appealing together as "Kitty" and "Boo," that I found myself cheering for them at every turn, rooting for them during the Big Fight . . . and fighting back weepiness when things looked bad for them.

The supporting voices were great across the board, too. No one was more surprised than I at Jennifer Tilly's drastically toned-down voice; her Celia didn't screech or whine at all—well, not much anyway—and I found myself rather enjoying her fairly nuanced performance. I had a similar reaction to John Ratzenberger, a two-time *Toy Story* vet, making a brief appearance as the Abominable Snowman. And though I couldn't quite place James Coburn's voice as CEO Waternoose, Steve Buscemi's voice sounded just as slithery as his exquisitely drawn slimy chameleon Randall looked. Somewhat less pleasing, surprisingly enough, was Billy Crystal as Mike, the smartass, one-eyed, helper bug monster. The longer the movie went on (and it did seem rather long, though still enjoyable), the more irritated I got at his constant mugging and wisecracks. Consequently, when the inevitable misunderstanding between Mike and Sully popped up, I kept hoping Sully would put the smackdown on that ol' one eye.

Along with the funny *For the Birds* short, I did manage to catch some of the tie-ins to other movies, as well as the Pixar canon. For extra fun, look for the "Easter Eggs." ("Easter Eggs" are hard to spot items that the creative team includes in a movie to see if discerning viewers are paying attention.) If some of the monsters in *Monsters, Inc.* seem familiar to you, it's probably because you've seen them before in some form in *A Bug's Life* or one of the *Toy Story* movies.

BAMMER'S BOTTOM LINE

I can't wait to watch *Monsters, Inc.* again, just to see if I missed any Easter Eggs.

GREEN LIGHT

 ## Osmosis Jones
(2001)

RATED PG; running time 95 minutes
GENRE: Live action /Animation
WRITTEN BY: Marc Hyma
DIRECTED BY: Piet Kroon, Tom Sito (animation); Peter and Bobby Farrelly (live action)
VOICES OF: Chris Rock, David Hyde Pierce, Laurence Fishburne, Brandy, William Shatner, Ron Howard, Joel Silver. Live Action: Bill Murray, Elena Franklin, Molly Shannon, Chris Elliott

THE STORY

Frank (Bill Murray), a zookeeper, is a misunderstood widower, only his daughter Shane (Elena Franklin) seems to be trying to help Frank find a clue again; Shane constantly fights a losing battle to get Frank to eat healthy, exercise, and generally live right. Frank's equally nasty bud Bob (Chris Elliott) is as codependent as they come; and after Frank loosed himself on Shane's teacher Mrs. Boyd (Molly Shannon), Frank's gettin' no love from that side of the aisle, either.

But Frank has a whole crew waiting in the wings to help him. Actually, they're waiting inside Frank's body: fighting off colds, allergies, Twinkies, and the occasional monkey-handled egg, are a team of hardworking antibodies and white blood cells, the most strident of which is Officer Osmosis Jones (voice of Chris Rock). Due to a bad history old Ozzie has with his Police Chief (Joel Silver), Oz is initially banished to patrolling the boring mouth sector of The City Of Frank; but when cold tablet Drixoral (David Hyde Pierce) is dispatched to fight off what the Chief, Mayor Phlegmming (William Shatner), and the mayor's assistant, Leah (Brandy) think is merely a cold virus, Ozzie is assigned to help Drix relieve Frank's symptoms. What begins as a routine cleanup of the sewer that is Frank, though, soon turns into something else, when Ozzie discovers that a supervirus named Thrax (Laurence Fishburne) is out to terminate Frank.

(*Man, does that look weird typed out.*)

THE UPSHOT

I can describe *Osmosis Jones* in three words: "punny," "nasty," and "PG." The film's PG rating holds the key to its lack of success.

With that PG rating acting as an albatross hanging around its neck, *Osmosis Jones* didn't, *couldn't*, go far enough in making itself funnier to adult viewers. In my audience, you could hear a pin drop as pun after pun fell on deaf ears: the adults thought the humor was merely "cute," and the kidlets had forgotten everything they knew about the "science" of *Osmosis Jones* two weeks after they were taught it in health class.

Too bad, too; I really wanted the film to succeed. Certainly, the cast should have been up for it; with its collection of comics, humorists, and damn fine actors, one would think *OJ*'s success was written in the stars. To be sure, Fishburne tore it up as Thrax, the baddest mutha of a germ this side of Ebola, though I couldn't help but think about the inherent problems with trying to make a seemingly AIDS-like virus funny; that Sir Laurence succeeded, and playfully so, is a testament to just how great an actor he is. Pierce, an equally great

comic actor in his own right (if you've never seen this modern-day Buster Keaton as Niles from *Frasier*, you don't know what you've been missing), made a wonderful Drix, though I was reminded of his similar voice-acting in *A Bug's Life*; the comparison is favorable, but still, too similar.

Bill Murray reinvented his *Caddyshack* character, though Watching Murray Go There Again was distressing, much the same as if, for instance, Steve Martin suddenly picked up his Wild And Crazy Guy shtick again . . . ewww. Still, a slovenly Frank was necessary for *OJ* to work, and my reservations aside, I can think of no better actor to have played this slob than Murray. As for the balance of the cast, I had to be reminded that William "KHAAAAN!" Shatner voiced the Mayor of Frank, so my issues weren't really with him, nor were they with Ron "Opie" Howard's brief punny bit as Tom Colonic, the Mayor's chief rival, or singer Brandy as the Mayor's headstrong assistant, Leah. Even Chris Rock, who normally gets on my nerves in too large a dose, was quite tame as Osmosis Jones.

Aye, there's the rub. Rock *was* tame; *too* tame, methinks. He tried hard, but even with the likes of Fishburne and Pierce helping to class up the joint, he couldn't seem to elevate *Osmosis Jones* beyond its punny nature, saddled with the limitations of its diluted gross-out humor.

BAMMER'S BOTTOM LINE

Diagnosis: too much Farrelly, not enough funny. Look for a few chuckles here and there, a couple of good lines (Fishburne has the best one late in the movie), and a cute riff on Fishburne's *Matrix* (see page 18) but don't expect too much from *Osmosis Jones*. Like I said, too bad.

FLASHING YELLOW LIGHT

The Princess Diaries
(2001)

RATED G; running time 89 minutes

GENRE: Comedy

WRITTEN BY: Gina Wendkos, based on the novel by Meg Cabot

DIRECTED BY: Garry Marshall

CAST: Julie Andrews, Anne Hathaway, Hector Elizondo, Heather Matarazzo, Mandy Moore, Caroline Goodall, Robert Schwartzman, Terry Wayne

THE DIGEST

Fifteen-year-old Mia Thermopolis (Anne Hathaway) is "invisible" and prefers it that way. The popular kids torment her because her hair is a mess, she sucks at sports, and public speaking makes her hurl. All this changes when her grandmother shows up out of the blue. Her deceased father's mother has never thought to contact her, so Mia is a bit suspicious, but interested nonetheless. When she gets to her grandmother's, she is struck by the fact that the house is absolutely beautiful. Grandmother (Julie Andrews), it turns out, is actually the queen of a small European country, and much to Mia's dismay, she herself is a princess and she must learn how to act like one,

for she is the last of her line and must take over the royal duties.

Mia doesn't take too well to "princess school." She has to learn how to sit, eat, dance, and walk like a princess—difficult under the best of circumstances, nearly impossible when you are as clumsy as Mia. Princess school is the least of her worries, though. She must learn to figure out who her true friends are as well as stay true to herself.

THE DISH

G-rated movies are few and far between. I'd love to sing the praises of this movie from the highest mountain for that fact alone, but I can't. This movie sends a very dangerous message to young girls. Mia was not good enough to be a princess until they straightened her hair, plucked her eyebrows, made her wear makeup and heels, and got rid of her glasses. This would have been a much better movie had they allowed Mia to just be herself and still be a successful princess.

What kind of message did this send to all the little girls that were in the audience and adoring this movie? Are these little girls going to run home and pick themselves apart hoping to have a queen for a grandmother? This was irresponsible of the filmmakers, the same folks who brought us *Pretty Woman*—another dangerous movie. (Psssttt . . . Pretty Woman was a 'ho. Don't forget that. No one can work the corner of Hollywood and Vine and land a billionaire.)

I'm glad that there is a cute movie out that everyone in the family can enjoy, but I do want to caution you on the message it sends to little girls.

THE DIRECTIVE

Proceed with caution. The princess in *The Princess Diaries* may need a therapist, not a diary, when everyone is finished with her.

YELLOW LIGHT

The Road to El Dorado
(2000)

RATED PG; running time 85 minutes
GENRE: Animation
WRITTEN BY: Ted Elliott, Terry Rossio
DIRECTED BY: Bibo Bergeron, Will Finn, Don Paul
VOICES OF: Kevin Kline, Kenneth Branagh, Rosie Perez, Armand Assante, Edward James Olmos

THE DIGEST

Tulio (Kevin Kline) and Miguel (Kenneth Branagh) are two Spanish con men. They hang out in the streets shooting craps with loaded dice. In one hand, they win the map to El Dorado, but it is determined that they are cheaters, so they get run out of town. As luck would have it, they stow away on a ship whose crew they manage to con. Then they manage to escape and drift to El Dorado, where Tulio and Miguel are immediately elevated to the rank of gods when the people see them. Why? Because they arrive on a steed and their arrival resembles a painting of the gods.

Songs were a bit bland and maybe a little out of place. I think some of the songs were playing during the wrong scenes.

THE DISH

It was really difficult for me to watch this flick. I was torn between figuring out if it was historically accurate and trying to just enjoy it. I think my problem was that if it was about a mermaid, I'd know without a doubt that it was fantasy. This wasn't about a mermaid. It was about a city of gold built by people who reminded me of the Mayan people. Knowing what the Spaniards did to Mayans and Incas in the name of imperialism has always upset me, and it was this that stopped me from appreciating this cartoon as I should have.

However, there were some things that I did appreciate. The animation was absolutely gorgeous. We've come a long way since "Steamboat Willie" (Disney's first cartoon). Also, the female lead (voice by Rosie Perez) was umm . . . stacked. She had voluptuous hips and thighs. She also had slightly thick lips. I think it's important for little girls to see fairly normal body dimensions. I also liked how the people of El Dorado were drawn ethnically accurately. Yes, we've come a long way since "Steamboat Willie."

THE BLACK FACTOR

Granted, kids may not get this deep, but by having Tulio and Miguel perceived as gods, I think we are further damaging our minority children by reinforcing images of European men as godlike.

THE DIRECTIVE

Watch it with your children, though be warned, the children in my theater were restless, as if *The Road to El Dorado* failed to hold their interest.

YELLOW LIGHT

the Diva **Shrek**
(2001)

RATED PG-13; running time 118 minutes

GENRE: Animation

WRITTEN BY: William Steig (book), Ted Elliott, Terry Rossio, Joe Stillman, Roger S. H. Schulman

DIRECTED BY: Andrew Adamson and Vicky Jenson

VOICES OF: Mike Myers, Eddie Murphy, Cameron Diaz, John Lithgow

THE DIGEST

Shrek (Mike Myers) is a grumpy ogre who spends his days quietly enjoying his swamp. Every morning he wakes up, takes a mud bath, eats a few yummy bugs, then relaxes until dinnertime. His precious daily solitude is interrupted when he finds his beloved swamp overrun by fairy-tale creatures that have been evicted from the kingdom by the evil Lord Farquaad (John Lithgow). What was once a serene swamp has now been taken over by Snow White and the Seven Dwarfs, the Old Woman Who Lives In A Shoe, Three Blind Mice, the Big Bad Wolf, and every other fairy-tale creature you can think of.

Shrek is none too pleased about this, so he sets out to find Lord Farquaad and give him the "what for." Along the way he meets another banished creature, a talking donkey. Donkey (Eddie Murphy) wiggles his way into Shrek's life and invites himself along for the trip, much to Shrek's dismay. Despite Donkey's constant chatter, Shrek comes to grudgingly enjoy his company. Once they reach Lord Farquaad, Shrek makes a deal with him. Shrek will rescue the fair Princess Fiona (Cameron Diaz) from a fire-breathing dragon and, in exchange, Lord Farquaad will allow the fairy-tale creatures back into the kingdom. Shrek rescues Princess Fiona, and soon they find out that they have a lot in common. To their surprise, they begin to have feelings for one another. In order for them to be truly happy, they must decide if they can see past the outside and find the beauty within. They must also learn that you have to give love to receive love.

THE DISH

Shrek is adorable! I wish I had children I could have dragged to the movies with me to see it. It was funny and heartwarming, with important life lessons for all children: Do not judge a book by its cover, and look for the beauty within. And the animation was phenomenal; I was completely dumbstruck by how real the characters looked. Entertaining for kids, there is plenty to keep the adults laughing. The story was well written and flowed very nicely.

I was a little disappointed with Eddie Murphy's character. He was literally and figuratively a jackass. It was the same ole same . . . the wisecracking sidekick. But I ain't mad at him. It's a good movie and at least he wasn't the bad guy. The only hiccup was when Shrek started singing a song called "Hallelujah." It brought the movie to a screeching halt. But it recovered shortly thereafter.

THE DIRECTIVE

A visually stunning animation masterpiece, *Shrek* is one heck of a movie. And it offers the perfect opportunity for parents to spend a little time with their kids.

GREEN LIGHT

Bams Spirit: Stallion of the Cimarron

(2002)

RATED G; running time 82 minutes
GENRE: Animation
WRITTEN BY: John Fusco
DIRECTED BY: Kelly Asbury, Lorna Cook
VOICES OF: Matt Damon, James Cromwell, Daniel Studi

THE STORY

Spirit: Stallion of the Cimarron is the story of a wild horse in the Wild West, told from the viewpoint of the Cimarron stallion, Spirit. Spirit's "thoughts" are voiced by Matt Damon. As White encroachers were wont to do, a group of Army soldiers capture Spirit and present him to the mean ol' Cavalry Colonel (James Cromwell), who

sets out to break Spirit's spirit and run rampant over the rest of the West. This, of course, includes the Native Americans (or as the Colonel called them, the "hostiles"), one of whom—Little Creek—is captured by the Colonel's men. And treated, pretty much, like an animal.

But they don't call him "Spirit" for nothing . . .

THE UPSHOT

With its G rating, the story in *Spirit: Stallion of the Cimarron* is understandably toned down, considering what probably really happened to horses—and Native Americans—back in the day. Still, I could not help but feel a strong sense of déjà vu in watching the *Roots*-reminiscent scenes in *Spirit*. Spirit running free through his land reminded me of Kunta Kinte running free through his. The "capture" scene immediately put me in mind of Kunta's capture; the "breaking" scene, a kinder, gentler version of Kunta's horrific beatdown. And the bridling together of Spirit and Little Creek's horse, Rain, to enable "one of his own" to help tame the spirited stallion? Kunta and Fiddler, redux. Unfortunately, Kunta didn't have a Little Creek to give him a taste of freedom. And of course, the *Roots* version of Kunta's "smithy" led to more dire consequences for Kunta's "hooves."

On a lighter note, the animation in *Spirit* is superb; the "active" backgrounds alone are worth the trip to the theater. Though both traditional and computer animation were used, the film seemed light on the computer mix, which somehow gave it a warmer, more authentic feeling all around. Even the scenes where computers were obviously used to enhance certain effects (the "rapids" scene, for example) were not so overdone that they take you out of the moment.

Spirit may not make you forget *Shrek* or *Monsters, Inc.*, but it doesn't have to; *Spirit* has wonderful imagery and strong action all its own, framed by a great score by Hans Zimmer. Besides, this flick has something the other two don't have: surprisingly easily translatable, "non-English," horse-speak.

And speaking of horses "speaking," props to whatever it was that led the folks behind *Spirit: Stallion of the Cimarron* to *not* make the animals actually sing or talk. That made all the difference in the world; heck, it even made Bryan "Remember *Robin Hood: Prince of Thieves*?" Adams's singing bearable.

BAMMER'S BOTTOM LINE

Spirit: Stallion of the Cimarron is a beautifully drawn and scripted tale of the old West, full of charm and—dare I say it?—spirit.

GREEN LIGHT

Stuart Little
(1999)

RATED PG; running time 94 minutes
GENRE: Comedy
WRITTEN BY: M. Night Shyamalan and Gregory J. Brooker (based on the novel by E. B. White)
DIRECTED BY: Rob Minkoff
CAST: Geena Davis, Hugh Laurie, Jonathan Lipnicki; voices of Michael J. Fox, Jennifer Tilly, Bruno Kirby, Nathan Lane, Chazz Palminteri, Steve Zahn

THE STORY

Stuart Little (voice of Michael J. Fox) is an orphaned mouse who comes to live with the Little Family: Mr. and Mrs. Little (Hugh Laurie and Geena Davis) and little George (Jonathan Lipnicki), who refuses to accept Stuart into the family at first. That sentiment is shared by Snowball the Family Cat (voice of Nathan Lane), who, after being called out by Stray Cat Monty (voice of Steve Zahn), lets Stuart know in no uncertain terms that he will *not* be the pet cat of a mouse. And as is the norm in such setups . . . wackiness ensues.

THE UPSHOT

Some children's stories need to be animated to have their full impact felt. *101 Dalmatians* was one of them; *Stuart Little* falls right into that same category.

Oh, it was pretty enough; the computer animation was good, and there were other nice touches, including the boat race and especially the roadster. But overpowering the animation was the Morality Whiffle Bat: the Moral Of The Story was pounded home over and over again. Well before the first 30 minutes were over, I was tired of Stuart's grin and cloying "there's no place like home!" lines.

The human characters didn't rub me the right way either. George was cute without being overly cute, and Mom and Pop Little were pleasant enough in relating to each other (the "finish each other's sentences" bit worked nicely), but the rest of the Little family just gave me a headache. Perhaps they should have played those characters as camp instead of as sincere eccentrics. And can anybody explain to me why *everyone* in this movie accepted, with no question, a talking mouse? In *Manhattan???* Ya. Right.

The sole saving graces of this flick were the nonanimated but "talking" cats—Snowball, hopped-up-on-catnip alley cat Smokey (Chazz Palminteri), and especially Monty, steal the show. I found myself rooting for the bad guys more often than I normally do.

THE BLACK FACTOR
Two things: The first thing I noticed was the ethnically correct orphanage. And am I the only one who felt the whole "house cat/field cat" situation? I think summa y'all know what I mean.

BAMMER'S BOTTOM LINE
I can't see a reason for anyone older than, say, 10, to choose *Stuart Little* over *Toy Story 2* (see page 323). Still, some kids may find it enjoyable.

YELLOW LIGHT

Disney's Tarzan
(1999)

RATED G; running time 90 minutes
GENRE: Animation
WRITTEN BY: Tab Murphy (based on the story by Edgar Rice Burroughs)
DIRECTED BY: Kevin Lima and Chris Buck
VOICES OF: Tony Goldwyn, Minnie Driver, Glenn Close, Rosie O'Donnell, Lance Henriksen, Brian Blessed, Wayne Knight

THE STORY
Unless you've been hiding under a rock, you've heard it before: White momma, poppa, and wee baby boy get shipwrecked in the jungles of Africa; through the magic of the movies (where'd those tools come from? hmmm . . .), momma and poppa build a tree house to live in, only to be eaten by the big bad cheetah. Wee baby boy is rescued by an ape momma who is grieving after her wee baby ape is eaten by same big bad cheetah. Wee baby boy grows up to fulfill his White Privilege Destiny (sorry, the Africentrist in me pops up at the strangest times) as Tarzan, Lord of the Jungle.

THE UPSHOT
Before sitting in the theater and watching this beautifully shot movie, I was sure that the premise would be the beginning and the end for me. Knowing full well that the '90s sensibility towards not perpetuating negative stereotypes in the movies (she wrote, trying to keep a straight face) would by default keep many of the problems I had with the Tarzan of Johnny Weismuller's time out of this version of the story, I wondered what else is there to

Tarzan, especially for someone not in Disney's targeted demographic? As it turns out, plenty, especially for techheads like me.

From the first shot to the final frame, I couldn't help but notice how *lush*, how artistically *real* this movie is. At times, I got so caught up in how the *background* looked, I forgot to watch what was going on! The technique used to create the stunning visuals, "Deep Canvas," is a technique patented by Disney that took their technicians years to perfect. That and the sheer number of artists that drew the film (whole teams were assigned to draw the main characters, and I got a kick out of seeing the title "rough in-betweeners" during the closing credits) made it more than just another cartoon.

Still, it had its problems. After seeing the realism of the ocean waves, the cheetah and such, I found it terribly startling to hear the apes talking, not to mention seeing the, for lack of a better term, cartoonish, comically drawn Terk and Tantor the Elephant (voices of Wayne Knight and Rosie O'Donnell, respectively). Momma ape Kala (voice of Glenn Close) just seemed too damned gentle for an ape, and I didn't for one moment buy the way she took Tarzan in (though I could definitely feel her broken-heartedness over the loss of her own son). And hearing Close's song meld into a Phil Collins pop hit gave me pains at first, not to mention the mind-numbingly stoopid production number showcasing Rosie O'Donnell's (ahem) musical talents.

Once I reminded myself that this movie was written for little tots, though, I was able to suspend my disbelief a little longer, and even learned something. Tarzan's difficulty with being accepted for his differences was something

that didn't get lost on me, and I especially liked the way it wasn't forced down the audience's throat. And Phil Collins even grew on me after a while.

As for the vocal talent, Tony Goldwyn and Minnie Driver worked well as Tarzan and Jane; Driver, especially, has the kind of voice that is meant for animated movies. Lance Henriksen (voice of Kerchak the Poppa Ape) and Brian Blessed (voice of the dastardly Clayton) complimented Goldwyn and Driver quite nicely. This contrasted starkly with O'Donnell's vocalizing. I could not get past that Noo Yawk Ape thing she had goin' on. Reel it in next time, girl!

THE BLACK FACTOR

Aside from my previously voiced issues with the Tarzan of old, the BF in this movie is that there *was* none, specifically. Whether out of a feeling of sensitivity to Us, or just because the Disney folks didn't want to be boycotted by Blacks Up In Arms, there were no, none, nada, zilch, zero, Blacks to be seen in this movie. Set in Africa. No Blacks in Deepest Darkest Africa? Nope, not one. It took me a while to decide, but in the end, I realized that this was a good thing; better to avoid the whole issue than to tackle it half-assed, as it would surely have been if this movie addressed it at all.

No, I take that back; there was definitely somethin' goin' on for Us: the whole Accept-Others-Who-Are-Different-From-You-Kids! vibe. Unfortunately, it's not kids who need that lesson most . . .

BAMMER'S BOTTOM LINE

Watch *Tarzan*, if only to witness the eye candy.

GREEN LIGHT

(Bill Pullman) shows up with alien shipmates Preed (Nathan Lane), Stith (Janeane Garofalo), Gune (John Leguizamo), and the human female—potential love interest—Akima (Drew Barrymore) with the message that Cale may hold the future of humanity in his hand.

Bams Titan A.E.
(2000)

RATED PG; running time 95 minutes
GENRE: Animation/Science fiction
WRITTEN BY: Ben Edlund, Randall Mc-
  Cormick
DIRECTED BY: Don Bluth, Gary Goldman
VOICES OF: Matt Damon, Drew Barrymore,
  Bill Pullman, Nathan Lane, Janeane Garofalo,
  John Leguizamo, Tone Loc, Ron Perlman

THE STORY

In the year 3028, a bad, bad bunch of aliens known as the Drej inexplicably blast the planet Earth and its inhabitants away like so many buzzing flies. That would be that—except for the fact that someone knew the Drej were coming and evacuated a bunch of Earthlings just before the moment of doom.

One person in on the secret, Tucker (Ron Perlman), asks his good buddy Tek (Tone Loc) to take his young son, Cale (Matt Damon), with him in one of the evacuating ships. Feeling abandoned, Cale grows up with a chip on his shoulder about dear old dad and humans—the few that are left, anyway—in general. Jaded, he feels all the more cynical when another human, Joe Korso

THE UPSHOT

This flick was clearly derivative of many movies, both animated and traditional. In various places, I was reminded of *Star Wars*, *Heavy Metal*, the *Star Trek* movies, and even a Bruce Lee flick or two. But in its lack of developed back story (in spite of the story line presented, the viewer is left wondering why much of the action takes place), it put me in mind of the most disastrous collection of moving images of the century: none other than *Supernova*.

That's not a very fair comparison, to be sure. But *Titan* certainly bit off way more than it could chew, storywise. With this movie's enormous leaps of logic (uh, how did Cale so easily pilot every spacecraft he encountered? *How long* does it take to rebuild an old, dilapidated ship, again?), I felt my eyes rolling faster than a bowling ball down the gutter lane.

Like their voice counterparts in *Dinosaur* (see page 5), the actors don't add much *character* to their characters, and unlike *Dinosaur*, the actors' voices aren't readily distinguishable (though Nathan Lane, bless his sarcastic lil' heart, gave it ye olde college try). This, I think, was to *Titan's* detriment. If one couldn't tell these highly paid actors from Joe Schmo from Kokomo, one would think the producers didn't get their money's worth, eh?

All those things could be forgiven, had the animation been top-notch. With a name like Don Bluth (*The Secret Of NIMH, An American Tail, All Dogs Go to Heaven*) behind it, good animation should've been a given. It should've. It wasn't. Worse, it seemed schizophrenic, with the human and alien characters drawn by Bluth in traditional (for him) cartoon style, but the ships, planets, and various backgrounds obviously computer-animated. This gave the movie a disjointed feeling, with the computer-animated sections overpowering the traditional drawings (note, for example, how stiff the characters look in the windows of the computer-animated spaceships, as if they were stills of dolls sitting in their seats). Anytime the viewer is taken out of the moment by such jarring revelations, that's most def a bad thing.

BAMMER'S BOTTOM LINE
Titan A.E. wasn't bad. Spiritless, lacking in humor, and poorly thought out, sure. But not bad. Anything that includes even a brief movie moment confirming that minorities *are* part of the future, can't be *that* bad, can it?

It's just too bad *Titan A.E.* couldn't make up its mind and go full out either as traditional animation, or hi-tech CGI sci-fi.

YELLOW LIGHT

The Tigger Movie
(2000)

RATED G; running time 75 minutes
GENRE: Animation
WRITTEN BY: Jun Falkenstein (based on the story by A. A. Milne)
DIRECTED BY: Jun Falkenstein
VOICES OF: Jim Cummings, Nikita Hopkins, Peter Cullen, Ken Sansom, John Fiedler, Kath Soucie, Andre Stojka, John Hurt, Tom Attenborough

THE STORY
In this animated rendition of A. A. Milne's Winnie-the-Pooh stories, narrated by John Hurt, Winnie-the-Pooh bear (voice of Jim Cummings) takes a back seat to Tigger (also voice of Jim Cummings). Tigger is an extroverted tiger who bounces his way in and out of the hearts of his friends Pooh, Eeyore the donkey, Piglet, Rabbit, Owl, the human boy Christopher Robin, kangaroo Kanga, and especially Kanga's son Roo, who looks up to his good friend Tigger as a big brother. Tigger's habit of joyfully bouncing all over the place irks the serious Rabbit and tires out everyone but Roo, yet Tigger doesn't let them steal his joy for long. But his joy over being "the only Tigger" turns to sadness when he realizes that being the only one means he's without a family. Seeing him so sad distresses Roo, who enlists Pooh bear and the others to help him find Tigger's family with potentially disastrous results.

THE UPSHOT

There's a cartoon strip called *Calvin and Hobbes* that, like this movie, features a tiger (Hobbes) as one of the main characters (but unlike Christopher Robin from Winnie-the-Pooh books and movies, the human Calvin is a perpetually 8-year-old boy, at times bratty and irritating, though almost always funny). The first few times I read that cartoon strip (mind you, as an adult), I found it incredibly dumb; for the life of me, I couldn't figure out what could possibly be so funny about the little jerk, and why he had a tiger, of all things, following him around, doing equally jerky things to neighbor Suzie and to Calvin's parents. I was just about to write it off as a loss, when one day the paper ran a strip in which Calvin was going on vacation with his parents, and had Hobbes in the back seat with him, and Hobbes was shown to be a *stuffed toy tiger*. Could'a knocked me over with a feather; up to that point, I had no idea that the "live" Hobbes existed only in Calvin's vivid imagination. That single strip not only revealed new layers of Calvin (and Hobbes) to me, it also taught me a lesson the likes of which the phrase "never judge a book by its cover" could never do in its static-ness.

I was only halfway watching this flick, when seemingly out of nowhere, I had one of those "aha!" moments. Maybe it was just a single word spoken; more likely, it happened during one of the scenes when the onscreen pages of the book turned, as if narrator John Hurt was a father reading the story to his children, and I was transported back to a place in time where Winnie-the-Pooh, Tigger, Eeyore, and Christopher Robin were as real to me as Hobbes was to Calvin. And as silly as it sounds, that "aha!" moment washed over me and made the movie come alive. I wasn't able to hold on to it as long as I would've liked, but it stayed with me long enough to make a difference in the way I watched *Tigger*. And the best thing about the Great Revelation was, it allowed me to be comfortable in the knowledge that even if the 37-year-old me couldn't totally relax and let this children's movie *be* a children's movie without the more sophisticated fare like *Toy Story 2* had built-in, at least the kid in me could appreciate the memories of the simple lessons found in *Tigger* about what family really is.

Once I recovered (mostly) from the "aha!," I was able to sit back and enjoy the ride with less distraction. Though most of the obligatory Disney Songs (and what's a Disney movie without obligatory Disney Songs?) made me stir in my seat a few times, I found myself enjoying *Tigger*'s big production number. And though its comparatively "primitive," not very well drawn artwork can't compete with *Toy Story 2* in the eye candy department (except for one noticeably beautiful shot when the sun shines directly on Tigger as he and Roo travel through the Hundred Acre Wood), that same primitive look is faithful to the artwork we've seen countless times during *Winnie-the-Pooh* TV specials. Overall, the nostalgic flavor that came with the look of *Tigger*, worked in its favor.

Also, beyond graphics, *Tigger* didn't compare to *TS2* in its storyline, nuance, "inside gags." But that didn't stop me from enjoying *Tigger* for what it was. In fact, its honest simplicity made me appreciate it for exactly that; the bouncy Tigger, scatterbrained Pooh, hilariously deadpan Eeyore, and sweetly vulnerable Roo, wouldn't have been the same had they been written as more adult-friendly characters. Kids of all ages will appreciate that—but only if they're kids at heart.

BAMMER'S BOTTOM LINE

The Tigger Movie was no *Toy Story 2* (see page 323). It wasn't really even a *Stuart Little* (see page 317) (as cloying as *that* similarly themed movie was, it *did* have its moments). But maybe that's as it should be; there's *gotta* be room in this world for a Pouncing Tigger and a Roo who loves him, right?

GREEN LIGHT

Bams Toy Story 2
(1999)

RATED G; running time 108 minutes
GENRE: Animation
WRITTEN BY: John Lasseter, Peter Docter, Ash Porannon, Andrew Stanton
DIRECTED BY: John Lasseter, Ash Brannon, Lee Unkrich
VOICES OF: Tom Hanks, Tim Allen, Don Rickles, Jim Varney, Wallace Shawn, John Ratzenberger, Annie Potts, Jodi Benson, Joan Cusack, Kelsey Grammer, Estelle Harris, Wayne Knight, John Morris, R. Lee Ermey, David Ogden Stiers

THE STORY

As the taglines so playfully pun, "the Toys are back in town." The old familiar faces (and voices) that many of us grew up with—even if "grew up with" started with the original *Toy Story*—come back to the big screen. Our old pals Andy (Morris) and his "living" toys, cowboy Woody (Hanks), astronaut Buzz Lightyear (Allen), Mr. Potato Head (Rickles), Slinky Dog (Varney), dinosaur Rex (Shawn), Hamm the piggy bank (Ratzenberger), Green Army Men Sergeant (Ermey), and Woody's lady, Bo Peep (Potts, complete with Peep's Sheep), make a return appearance. They're joined by cowgirl Jessie (Cusack), Stinky Pete the Prospector (Grammer), Bullseye the horse (Stiers), Mrs. Potato Head (Harris), Tour Guide Barbie (Benson), and probably the father of the Beanie Baby craze, Al "The Toy Collector" Chicken Man (Knight), and various others in a tale that combines humor, nostalgia, amazing computer animation, and even a lesson or two, for kids of all ages).

Andy shelves Woody after accidentally "breaking" Woody's arm. Meanwhile, Woody's shelf mate, Wheezer the not-squeaking penguin, is destined for the one event toys hate: the yard sale! Woody also accidentally winds up in the "for sale" bin, from which Toy Collector Al steals him. This turns out to be a joyous occasion for Jessie and the Prospector, who belong to Woody's "family," but not for his pals Buzz and company, who, remembering Woody's heroic rescue of Buzz in the original *Toy Story*, set off to do some derring-do of their own. But will Woody want to leave his newfound family to go back to Andy, who may have grown too old to play with dolls anyway?

THE UPSHOT

Toy Story 2 is more than just a "kiddie movie." The attention to detail alone separates it from your average animated cartoon, even those that are as heavily computer-generated. But there's something more going on here.

The original *Toy Story* wowed us (especially us

techies) with its very real-looking computer animation; I know I'm not the only one who had to look more than a few times before realizing that Andy and the other humans weren't real. Still, though there are some moments where you'd *swear* they blended live action with animation (check out Al's nose hairs when he's passed out on the couch after his Cheesy Poofs attack), the animation seems less precise in this movie than in its predecessor. That's not necessarily a bad thing, though; where *Toy Story* was more technically brilliant, *TS2* has a *much* deeper tale, with more compelling characters.

And what a great bunch of characters they were! The large cast was served well enough, with no one character really hogging (oops, sorry Hamm!) the spotlight the way Hanks's "Woody" and Allen's "Buzz" did last go-round. But who would've thought that Mr. Potato Head (careful, Bammer; the kids might be reading) would have a chance to play "house" with his wife? If I had to

choose a weak spot, I'd go with Rex, who bordered on whiny; even some of the kids in my group started rolling their eyes (on the other hand, *my* eyes got a workout when Jessie started in with the obligatory Disney Song—though after she was done, I was okay about it because the song moved the story along in a somewhat necessary fashion).

By the time the movie was over, I wanted to run home and hug my Curious George *non-collector* dolls. Next time I see this movie—and believe me, there'll be a next time—I think I'll bring old Curious with me.

BAMMER'S BOTTOM LINE
Watch *Toy Story 2* for the gee-whiz animation even if you can feel the pull of the folks behind it wanting to impart the moral of the story to the audience.

GREEN LIGHT

15

3 Black Chicks is about more than just passively watching movies; we want to have an effect on them—especially as relates to Black and other "ethnic" film-makers. Our groove is all about letting Hollywood as well as independent filmmakers know that the Black viewing dollar is a *strong* dollar, one to be reckoned with. And we want to let it be known that we won't sit still for just any ol' trash tossed in front of our eyes—not if we can help it, anyway!

Though we're in cinematically challenged areas of the country, we try to see indie films, arts flicks, and limited-release movies as often as we can. But we don't always get it. Come on, now, some of this independent film stuff is just *weird*, y'know?

Black and White
(2000)

RATED R; running time 100 minutes
GENRE: Drama
WRITTEN BY: James Toback
DIRECTED BY: James Toback
CAST: Power, Raekwon, Bijou Phillips, Brooke
   Shields, Robert Downey Jr., Mike Tyson, Ben
   Stiller, Allan Houston, Claudia Schiffer,
   William Lee Scott, Gaby Hoffmann, Kidada
   Jones, Eddie Kaye Thomas, James Toback, Eli-
   jah Wood, Kim Matulova, Joe Pantoliano,
   Sticky Fingaz, Method Man, Garry Pastore,
   Jared Leto, Scott Caan, Stacy Edwards, Marla
   Maples

THE STORY

Of the more clearly defined roles, this is as near
as I can call it:

Mike Tyson (as himself) inexplicably hangs
around dispensing wisdom to neighborhood
Scarface-wannabe Rich Bower (Power), who
hangs with rapper Cigar (Raekwon), for whom
he is trying to get a record deal with Arnie Tish-
man (James Toback, who also wrote and directed
Black and White). He also hangs out with a group
of White kids—chief amongst them Charlie (Bijou Phillips), Charlie's boyfriend Wren (Elijah
Wood), their friend Marty King (Eddie Kaye
Thomas), and Marty's brother Will (William Lee
Scott), who see themselves, and the Black rappers
they hang with, as "Niggas." In the friendly, fa-
milial sense, of course.

But I'm not quite finished: Rich's other pat'na,
basketballer Dean (Allan Houston), finds himself in a jam at the hands of both his White

anthropology-student girlfriend Greta (Claudia
Schiffer) and Mark Clear (Ben Stiller), who offers
Dean a bribe—and then some. And on top of it
all, documentarians Sam Donager (Brooke
Shields) and her gay husband (yes, you read
right), Terry (Robert Downey Jr.), follow the self-
proclaimed "Niggas" around with a video camera, to try to gain some understanding of just
what makes these White kids want to imitate
Thug Life . . . Oy.

THE UPSHOT

The movie opens with White kid Charlie and her
friend Kim (Kim Matulova) being "used" (with
their consent) by Rich as stone freaks and moves
from there to Charlie confronting her white-
bread, upper-middle-class parents with her
"Black" talk, dress, and lifestyle. One gets the
sense that something important is about to be
addressed in the film. What would Mommy and
Daddy do if they knew what their daughter was
doing in the middle of the park just before she
came home?

Had Toback chosen to stick with this part of
the story, or even done a true documentary on the
White kids, *B&W* would've struck a chord in
these times when Black culture or, more precisely,
the subculture of hip-hop is co-opted more by
middle- and upper-class White youth than by
Blacks (many of whom, like Kidada Jones's character, Jesse, are trying to get *out* of the very way of
life these White kids strive to emulate). Charlie
and her cohorts were the most poignant part of
the movie, and truly exploring their stories might
have gone a long way toward really getting down
to the brass tacks of Black and White life, at least
the portion of it represented by those on screen.

Instead, Toback chose to take the easy, patronizing way out by trivializing the White kids, ignoring most of the "Black story," except to (unintentionally) laughably attempt to paint Rich and his crew as mobster-lite thugs, and by inexplicably casting "names" such as Brooke Shields, Ben Stiller, and Claudia Schiffer, in roles that were downright painful to watch. Shields just looks damned goofy in pseudo-dreadlocks and nose ring. The props work against her attempt to come across as an outsider only minimally trying to be accepted. Half-stepping on her part just didn't work; her character should've either been all the way down, or woefully short of the mark. Stiller, obviously slumming, was just as wasted; his character's entire subplot could've been jettisoned to no ill effect, taking Dean and Greta down the drain with him. And every time Schiffer opened her mouth, I wanted to slap it shut; her mere presence offended me in a way that's only understandable when you hear her character's ridiculous advice to Dean—"just be who you are"—not to mention her scene with Stiller. It grinds my gizzards just to think about that tripe again.

There were surprises to be found, however, pleasant and unpleasant. On the down side, I felt sorry for Joe Pantoliano as District Attorney (and Will and Marty's father) Bill King. Throughout his excruciating scene with Stiller, "Joey Pants" looked like he was searching for the quickest exit out of this flick. On the up side was a triple threat: I never thought I'd say this, but Mike Tyson has a future in acting, even if it's just acting as himself. As he did in *Wonder Boys*, Robert Downey Jr. continues to rise above poor material given to him. And as hoodie-rat Charlie, Bijou Phillips stole the show. Full of gruff bravado, Phillips's Charlie was the one character who re-

mained consistently worth watching throughout this movie. Three decent performances out of a movie of tens of bad ones, though, is never a good thing.

BAMMER'S BOTTOM LINE

If you just must see *Black and White*, and I'm sure there will be more than a few of you who just must, don't go into it expecting to learn anything save this: knuckleheads come in all colors. But you knew that already, eh?

YELLOW LIGHT

Cradle Will Rock
(1999)

RATED R; running time 135 minutes
GENRE: Dramedy
WRITTEN BY: Tim Robbins
DIRECTED BY: Tim Robbins
CAST: Emily Watson, John Turturro, John Cusack, Joan Cusack, Hank Azaria, Angus MacFadyen, Cary Elwes, Cherry Jones, Rubén Blades, Philip Baker Hall, Vanessa Redgrave, Bill Murray, Susan Sarandon

THE DIGEST

Cradle Will Rock the movie follows the inception and production of the play of the same name in the 1930s.

Cradle Will Rock is a somewhat preachy social commentary about a union organizer and a prostitute, directed by Orson Welles (Angus Mac-

Fadyen) and John Houseman (Cary Elwes). The characters of the play are both struggling to find their place in society. The prostitute is ostracized for obvious reasons, but with the country in a Depression, she is doing the only thing that she thinks she can in order to survive. The union organizer is risking his life to get "the message" to the people. Both are considered the scum of society. The movie deals with many issues, most specifically the Federal Theater, an offshoot of Roosevelt's "New Deal." Its goal was to take the unemployed and employ them as actors, stagehands, and crews. It also hoped to take plays to all of the small towns in America and support the struggling playwrights. A great success at its height, it employed more than 3,300 people across America. Fortunately for the playwrights, the Federal Theater was run by Hallie Flanagan (Cherry Jones) who passionately believed in the theater and supported all plays, regardless of content, as long as they were good. Unfortunately, this didn't set well with Intake Supervisor, Hazel Huffman (Joan Cusack). Hazel didn't like the fact that Hallie allowed "Negroes" to act in the plays, and she felt most of the plays supported Communism. She testified before the Senate, which caused all the plays to be put on hold indefinitely and the theaters to be closed. This action, the climax of the movie, cost several hundred jobs.

There are other subplots involving the rich: Nelson Rockefeller (John Cusack), William Randolph Hearst (John Carpenter), Gray Mathers (Phillip Baker Hall), and Countess LaGrange (an absolutely fabulous Vanessa Redgrave). In fact, there are so many different stories within the story, the movie itself is challenging but that was part of the beauty.

THE DISH

Cradle Will Rock was rich with characters and stories, and the acting was divine. Rubén Blades as the famous artist Diego Rivera provided many laughs and served, in my opinion, as the conscience of the film. Vanessa Redgrave was a hoot as the kooky Countess. Paul Giamatti, who is my favorite character actor (have you seen *The Negotiator*?), gave a fine performance as Carlo, as did John Turturro as a husband and a father of four trying to make ends meet and deal with the strong sense of pride his Italian family has for Mussolini and the Fascists. And Bill Murray was fabulous as an aging and bitter vaudevillian.

THE DIRECTIVE

A social commentary, *Cradle Will Rock* might be a bit preachy for some folks. But I'm glad I saw it. I'm still blown away by the closing scene. Check it out.

GREEN LIGHT

 **The Crimson Rivers**
(2001)

RATED R; running time 93 minutes
GENRE: Thriller
WRITTEN BY: Mathieu Kassovitz and Jean-Christophe Grangé (based on the novel by Jean-Christophe Grangé
DIRECTED BY: Mathieu Kassovitz
CAST: Jean Reno, Vincent Cassel, Jean-Pierre Cassel, Nadia Ferés

THE DIGEST

Old-school cop Pierre Neimans (Jean Reno) has been summoned to the small town of Guernon, France, to investigate a bizarre murder. A seemingly quiet university librarian is found tortured to death; his hands, feet, and eyes removed. Meanwhile, in another town, about 180 miles away, young Max Kerkerian (Vincent Cassel), a police officer, is investigating the desecration of a cemetery plot that holds a 10-year-old girl who died horribly 20 years before. Each cop is working separately on his case, not knowing about the other. Neimans is trying to figure out this mystery even as another body shows up and Kerkerian is hunting down clues and trying to figure out why someone would randomly desecrate a grave. Eventually they stumble upon each other and work together to solve these gruesome murders.

THE DISH

A French film with subtitles, *Crimson Rivers* was a bit too predictable and some of the plot twists and nuances fell flat. I started getting a bit bored at the midway point, and the end was anticlimactic for me. The following people should stay away: anyone who hates subtitled movies, anyone who abhors violence, and anyone who expects their movies to have spectacularly happy endings. Still, watching Jean Reno (pronounced Jahn RayNO. Y'all didn't know I could parlay voo frahnsay, didya? Okay I can't, but I can try) deadpan his way through this character and seeing the magnificent scenery was enough to endear the film to me.

THE DIRECTIVE

Crimson Rivers is a nice little weekend diversion; especially if you are tired of the same ol' same from American cinema.

FLASHING YELLOW LIGHT

Crouching Tiger, Hidden Dragon
(2000)

RATED PG 13; running time 120 minutes
GENRE: Martial arts/Drama
WRITTEN BY: Hui-Ling Wang, James Schamus, Kuo Jung Tsai (based on the book by Du Lu Wang)
DIRECTED BY: Ang Lee
CAST: Chow Yun-Fat, Michelle Yeoh, Zhang Ziyi, Cheng Peipei, Chang Chen, Sihung Lung, Gao Xi'an, Li Li, Li Fa Feng, Hai Yan, Wang Deming

THE STORY

In 19th-century Qing dynasty China, warrior Li Mu Bai (Chow Yun-Fat), seeking a more peaceful existence, gives his Green Destiny Sword to fellow warrior and the object of his desire, Yu Shu Lien (Michelle Yeoh), asking her to deliver it to Sir Te for safekeeping. Yu Shu Lien does so, but soon afterwards, a stealthy thief steals the sword from Sir Te's camp.

Suspicion falls upon members of the House of Governor Yu, who, along with Madam Yu (Hai Yan), their willful daughter Jen (Zhang Ziyi), and Jen's governess, have come to visit Sir Te in preparations for Jen's arranged marriage to nobility. As Li Mu Bai and Yu Shu Lien set out to find the thief, they discover there's more to Jen than meets the eye, including her involvement with a desert marauder named Lo.

THE UPSHOT

It amuses me somewhat that the fantasylike acrobatics and the English subtitles would be an impenetrable barrier to anyone enjoying *Crouching Tiger, Hidden Dragon* (hereafter, "*CT/HD*"). My amusement aside, *CT/HD* did take some getting used to, I must admit. But the learning curve wasn't at all steep; after only a few minutes, the audience I was in fully got into the spirit of the film, heartily applauding the magnificent combat scenes, laughing during appropriate moments, and generally following the story from start to moving finish.

I've long appreciated the vast talents of Michelle Yeoh (whom I first saw in, of all things, a 007 flick) and Chow Yun-Fat (one of the best things about 1999's *Anna and the King*. They continued to please here. The actors and their char-

acters seemed to effortlessly compliment each other on and off the fighting arena; Yu Shu Lien's strength of presence being a good match for Li Mu Bai's confident nobility. Much more a surprise was the striking Zhang Ziyi as the reluctant bride-to-be, Jen. She was stunning, in every sense of the word, and helped to elevate the *CT/HD* storyline far above the standard "You Killed My Master!" plot of most martial arts flicks.

Much of the credit for the depth of *CT/HD* goes to its brilliant director, Ang Lee, and the equally brilliant camerawork by the cinematographer Peter Pau. Credit, too, to *CT/HD* fight choreographer Woo-Ping Yuen, costume designer Tim Yip, and to YoYo Ma, whose cello provided *CT/HD* with a haunting musical touch. Thought *The Matrix* (see page 18) had it goin' on? You ain't seen nuttin' until you see Chow Yun-Fat walk on water, or Zhang Ziyi knock big bad brutes back into yesterday. And the weapons used throughout this film kept me—a big-time weaponry fan—salivating (and, at one point, laughing; watch for a late scene with Michelle Yeoh and Zhang Ziyi, to see what tickled my funny bone). The lasting beauty of *CT/HD* is that its pageantry, its tender love stories, and its humor are never eclipsed by its awe-inspiring action; each element is as integral as the next.

THE BLACK FACTOR

You'll have to forgive me again. I know that gang involvement is not truly a Black Factor issue, no more so than any stereotypically destructive activity Blacks are disproportionately involved in, but I couldn't help but be struck by the parallels to modern-day street gangs when Lo spoke of his affiliation with the desert gang that he rode with as being "family," and a "noble" part of his life. Realities of gang warfare aside, I wonder how American movie audiences would take to on-going depictions of gang members as sympathetic, even admirable, characters. Not too well, I'd reckon.

Goodfellas and *Godfathers* notwithstanding.

BAMMER'S BOTTOM LINE

Crouching Tiger, Hidden Dragon was as moving a work of art as any I've ever witnessed; a majestic master stroke from Ang Lee that takes martial arts cinema to a whole new level.

GREEN LIGHT

Bams **Heist**
(2001)

RATED R; running time 107 minutes
GENRE: Crime drama
WRITTEN BY: David Mamet
DIRECTED BY: David Mamet
CAST: Gene Hackman, Delroy Lindo, Danny De-Vito, Sam Rockwell, Rebecca Pidgeon, Ricky Jay, Patti LuPone

THE STORY

Just when Joe Moore (Gene Hackman) thinks he got out, Mickey Bergman (Danny DeVito) pulls him back in . . . Joe is a high-stakes thief; Mickey, his not-too-trustworthy fence. When Joe gets "burnt" on a robbery he and his crew, including Bobby Blane (Delroy Lindo), Joe's wife, Fran (Rebecca Pidgeon), and Don "Pinky" Pincus (Ricky Jay), have committed, Mickey withholds Joe's proper payment and offers Joe and his crew a new job instead. For his last hurrah, Mickey asks Joe to do one more job: steal a mint in Swiss gold for a big payoff that will let Joe retire in style.

The catch? As if having to trust Mickey isn't bad enough, Joe will also have to take Mickey's equally untrustworthy nephew, Jimmy Silk (Sam Rockwell), a hardheaded firebrand, along for the ride.

THE UPSHOT

Consider me somewhat schooled. In watching this film, I learned that as great as actors such as Gene Hackman, Delroy Lindo, Danny DeVito, and Ricky Jay may be, it takes a skillful writer like David Mamet to put words into their mouths that sound like something their characters might *actually* say. And it takes an equally skillful director like David Mamet to put it all together in a package that would have its audience happy to see grown folks act again. In *Heist*, the dialogue almost became a character itself, pulled off by veterans in a way that youngbloods (even worthy, skillful youngbloods like Sam Rockwell) would make sound silly by comparison.

Try as they might, Rockwell (a new favorite of mine, whom I first saw in *The Green Mile*, see page 183) and Rebecca Pidgeon didn't pack the same punch. In any other flick, with actors closer to their age, Rockwell and Pidgeon might have smoked their costars; but they were simply out-matched in *Heist*. They couldn't hang with the big guns, but that had more to do with what was asked of their characters than with any flaws the actors may have. I look forward to seeing them both in future films.

BAMMER'S BOTTOM LINE

Twisting and turning until the end, *Heist* is the kind of movie for folks who like their flicks to have style *and* substance in equal measure. The lumpy foursome of Hackman, Lindo, DeVito, and Jay provide welcome maturity in an era when youth is king; and writer-director Mamet shows once again that he knows how to give good story.

GREEN LIGHT

Bams In the Bedroom
(2001)

RATED R; running time 130 minutes
GENRE: Drama
WRITTEN BY: Robert Festinger, Todd Field (based on the story "Killings" by Andre Dubus)
DIRECTED BY: Todd Field
CAST: Tom Wilkinson, Sissy Spacek, Nick Stahl, Marisa Tomei, William Mapother, William Wise, Celia Weston

Tom Cruise's real name is Thomas Mapo-ther. William Mapother, who plays Richard in *In the Bedroom*, is his first cousin.

THE STORY

In a sleepy little coastal New England town, life goes by at a relaxed pace for high school choral teacher Ruth Fowler (Sissy Spacek) and her husband, Dr. Matt Fowler (Tom Wilkinson). In the type of town where everybody knows your name, Ruth and Matt share an easy camaraderie with their middle-aged friends Katie (Celia Weston) and Willis Grinnel (William Wise) and a loving, if somewhat less easy relationship with their only son, Frank (Nick Stahl).

Frank is a college student and budding home designer with a lot of potential. But to Ruth's dismay, Frank is also involved with Natalie Strout (Marisa Tomei), an older woman with two kids of her own. Despite Matt's assurances to the contrary, Ruth is convinced that her boy will be corrupted by his relationship with Natalie, to the point where he'll stop pursuing his education and career. But that's nothing compared to the firestorm ahead for each of them by way of Natalie's angry, not quite ex-husband, Richard Strout (William Mapother).

THE UPSHOT

In the Bedroom is almost three stories in one. The first revolves around Frank and Natalie, with Ruth tsk-tsking over their "older" woman—younger man relationship, while Richard looms in the background as an unrealized threat. The second story is that threat realized. The third story is all Ruth and Matt, and how they and their friends deal with their grief. On the surface, they live their lives in the same quiet, small-town Maine way they always have. But Ruth and Matt's quietude is disturbed, and their lives veer down an unexpected road. For me, this part of the story delivered the payoff.

In a movie overpopulated with multiple shots and mini-scenes where "nothing" takes place, director Todd Field takes his sweet time telling *In the Bedroom*. I spent a lot of time watching quiet non-scenes wondering what the hell the raving Sundance viewers saw in this film (other than it being a "work of art"). But the last scene really took me there. And Wilkinson's tour de force performance more than made up for the overwhelming feeling that I was peeking in on a series of personal lives, which I didn't quite comprehend or, rather, might comprehend better if told in a more straightforward way. "Reflective" is the best adjective I can come up with for *In the Bedroom*; and on reflection, the guts of this film counted for more than I gave it credit for, immediately after leaving the theater.

I've mentioned Wilkinson's performance. Spacek is almost as strong, conveying a powerful message in her silent fury; and as Matt's true-blue friend Willis, William Wise portrays East Coast folksiness without the stereotype so common in movies about folksy East Coasters.

This is not to say that the youngsters were slouches. Nick Stahl didn't quite have enough time to fully form his college son–young lover role to my liking; but as Richard, William Mapother took what might have come across as yet another abusive husband and breathed new life into that role. And though Tomei, who got a lot of grief over winning an Oscar for her non-se-

rious role in *My Cousin Vinnie*, doesn't get a lot of screen time, she worked the time she had to great effect. She and Spacek share a powerful scene late in the movie that made me realize that the Sundance crowd was right, indeed.

BAMMER'S BOTTOM LINE

This film won't suit everyone's tastes. But if you're in the market for serious adult drama, art-film style, you could do a lot worse than *In the Bedroom*.

GREEN LIGHT

Memento
(2001)

RATED R; running time 116 minutes

GENRE: Thriller

WRITTEN BY: Christopher Nolan (based on a short story by Jonathan Nolan)

DIRECTED BY: Christopher Nolan

CAST: Guy Pearce, Joe Pantoliano, Carrie-Anne Moss, Stephen Tobolowsky, Harriet Sansom Harris, Larry Holden, Callum Keith Rennie, Jorja Fox, Mark Boone Jr.

THE STORY

Here's a big one: Joe Pantoliano's character dies in this movie. But—and here's the cool part—that's not really a spoiler. Because *Memento* begins at the end, and ends at the beginning.

Leonard Shelby (Guy Pearce) is a man with a

past that ends at a specific point, an uncertain future, and no real present to speak of. He suffers from severe short-term memory loss, which developed as he was beaten while defending his wife Catherine (Jorja Fox) from being raped and murdered. His loss of his memory, as well as his wife, is so profound that he has to tattoo across his body, the most important bits of information, which he uses as Cliffs notes for seeking vengeance for his wife's murder. Because he can't remember more than a few minutes at a time, he (re)tells everyone he meets the story of Sammy Jankis (Stephen Tobolowsky) and his wife (Harriet Sansom Harris), whom Leonard met when he was an insurance investigator. Sammy had a condition much like Leonard's, though Leonard steels himself to use Sammy as an example of what *not* to do.

Leonard depends on the kindness and honesty of people who are virtual strangers to him; and some of them take advantage of his condition. Teddy (Joe Pantoliano) tries to help Leonard find the mysterious "John G" who, Leonard suspects, was involved in his wife's murder; Natalie (Carrie-Anne Moss) helps Leonard out of pity and empathy, since she also lost her boyfriend, Jimmy (Larry Holden), possibly at the hands of drug-dealer Dodd (Callum Keith Rennie). And even friendly, helpful hotel clerk Burt (Mark Boone Junior) may have it in for Leonard.

THE UPSHOT

Memento is not the first "backwards" film to have been made, though it's certainly the best *I've* ever seen. I won't front: *Memento* had me confused as hell at times. This is definitely not the kind of film you'd want to see when you're just looking for an empty popcorn flick. Every scene potentially includes something critical for understanding the next scene, which is actually the previous sequence, storywise. Look away, and you might miss something vital; miss a note scratched-out "earlier," and you might not understand why its "later" presence is important.

Guy Pierce was convincing as a man who has a tenuous grip on his life, and has to focus on vengeance to give his life meaning; for me, Joey Pants can do no wrong; and I was very impressed with Carrie-Anne Moss. And in supporting roles, Harriet Sansom Harris (who plays the bigger-than-life Bebe in NBC's *Frasier*) and Stephen Tobolowsky were heartbreaking as Leonard's and Catherine's doppelgangers Sammy and his long-suffering wife. But as good as the cast was in *Memento*, the story's the thing; specifically, the story*telling*. And I've never seen it done better.

It's funny; I noticed many audience members talking in hushed whispers during *Memento*. Usually, that bothers me. But I could feel them in their need to discuss what they'd just seen, here. Hell, I'm looking for a *Memento* discussion group myself. I fiercely need to be debriefed.

BAMMER'S BOTTOM LINE

Memento took the audience to a place that, if we've been there before, we certainly haven't been there quite like *this*.

GREEN LIGHT

Mulholland Drive
(2001)

RATED R; running time 147 minutes
GENRE: Mystery/Drama
WRITTEN BY: Joyce Eliason, David Lynch
DIRECTED BY: David Lynch
CAST: Naomi Watts, Laura Harring, Justin Theroux, Ann Miller, Mark Pellegrino, Michael J. Anderson, Dan Hedaya, Angelo Badalamenti, Scott Coffey, Billy Ray Cyrus, Chad Everett, Kate Forster, Melissa George, Monty Montgomery, Brian Beacock, Robert Forster

THE STORY

I knew I was in trouble after I read this movie's screed:

"Along Mulholland Drive, nothing is what it seems. In this complex tale of suspense, set in the unreal universe of Los Angeles, writer-director David Lynch explores the city's schizophrenic nature, an uneasy blend of innocence and corruption, love and loneliness, beauty and depravity. Lynch constructs a puzzle, propelling us through a mysterious labyrinth of sensual experiences until we arrive at the intersection where dreams and nightmares meet."

Oh brudder. Where's my shovel?

THE UPSHOT

I begged for the hours to please hurry up and pass, as I did during this interminably long, infuriatingly goofy, but boy-how-stylish! film. Lovers of Lynch's oeuvre will no doubt try to take me to task for my failure to recognize his greatness! and for my irritation at his refusal to tell a "Straight Story." "How dare you pan His Greatness! Heathen! Populist! Movie lover!!!" Ahh, bite me.

I'll raise up off Lynch for a moment and admit that I did like the lead actors. First-act Rita (Laura Harring) didn't twist my throttle nearly as much as she did when the script was flipped, but her counterpart, Betty (Naomi Watts), worked it very convincingly throughout. Props, too, to whoever that was who sang "Crying." She blew me away with her big, sad voice. As for the males in this film, Justin Theroux's Adam was just this side of "too bizarre," so I didn't mind him overmuch; and Mark Pellegrino as Joe, the not-so-good hit man, added some much-needed humor to *Mulholland Drive*.

If I could have just held on to Betty's story, with a sprinkling of Rita, I might have made it through this flick. But nooooo, Lynch had to throw other weird sh . . . tuff into the mix and make watching this movie close to unbearable for me. Have I told you how much I dislike his vision?

BAMMER'S BOTTOM LINE

But now—just like Lynch, woo-hoo!—I contradict myself. As much as I hated hated hated hated hated *Mulholland Drive*, I have to give it my second-highest rating as in "see it if you like avant-garde weirdness or train wrecks" with the following "viewer discretion" caveats:

If you're into Art Fillums, David Lynch, or surrealism, you'll love it.

If you're anxious to see something different, and don't mind Weird As Hell, give it a shot.

If you're anxious to see something different, but don't want to be jerked around, you'll only tolerate *Mulholland Drive*. Barely.

If the word "surrealism" gives you a brain ache . . . you're really in the wrong room. Your show's two doors down, to the right.

FLASHING YELLOW LIGHT

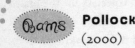

Pollock
(2000)

RATED R; running time 119 minutes

GENRE: Drama

WRITTEN BY: Susan Emshwiller, Barbara Turner (based on the book by Steven Naifeh and Gregory White Smith)

DIRECTED BY: Ed Harris

CAST: Ed Harris, Marcia Gay Harden, Amy Madigan, Jeffrey Tambor, Robert Knott, Bud Cort, John Heard, Val Kilmer, Sada Thompson, Tom Bower, Jennifer Connelly, Sally Murphy, Molly Regan, John Rothman, Annabelle Gurwitch, Isabelle Townsend, Barbara Garrick, Everett Quinton, Stephen Beach, Jill Jackson, David Leary, Donna Mitchell, Frank Wood, Julie Anna Rose

THE STORY

Pollock begins with a scene of a woman bearing a copy of *Life* magazine seeking an autograph from a man who looks like the troubles of the world lie in his steely eyes; then it flashes back to Greenwich Village, New York, in November of 1941, nine years earlier. At that time, Jackson Pollock (Ed Harris) spent as much time drinking, walk-ing through life in a daze, and complaining to his brother Sande (Robert Knott) about the attention his fellow artists were getting ("F*ck Picasso!" he raged), as he did painting, much to the consternation of his pregnant sister-in-law.

Enter abstract artist Lee Krasner (Marcia Gay Harden), who moves rapidly into Pollock's life, his business, and his bed. Impressed with Pollock's work, Krasner soon sets him up with gallery owner Peggy Guggenheim (Amy Madigan), who allows Pollock to work on commission for her gallery. The world doesn't seem to be ready for him, though. He's seen as an original, but that doesn't immediately translate to sales, and he becomes frustrated, and drunk, in waves. Pollock and Krasner eventually move away from the big city, into a more peaceful, if not prosperous, existence on Long Island. But even after he perfects his abstract art style of painting by using thrown and dripped strands of paint in a style called Action Painting, in which the process of painting becomes as important as the finished product—he's still floundering.

That is, until *Life* magazine takes a notice of his work, thrusting him into the limelight. Bringing with it its own, new set of demons . . .

THE UPSHOT

I'll tell you true: for a large part, I just didn't get *Pollock*. Oh, I understood the "starving artist" concept, and the "they don't understand me" concept, and the "tortured soul in another plane of existence" concept, and all. I just don't get folks standing around trying to decide what a given painting "means"; especially one that, let us be for real, here looks like a child made a mess on the canvas. Similarly, I didn't get the gist of what this film was trying to tell the audience, past the madness that comes with coloring outside the lines, so to speak. But most of all, I didn't get what all the people in this cast, especially "names" like John Heard (as Tony Smith), Val Kilmer (Willem DeKooning), and, to a lesser degree, Sada Thompson as Pollock's mother, Stella, had to do with anything in Pollock's life. For all the interaction they had with Pollack, the filmmakers could've easily pared the cast down by half, and spent more time delving into the whys of Pollock's madness and his genius.

All that said, I certainly dug the main performances by Ed Harris, and especially the tour de force by Marcia Gay Harden as Lee Krasner, fellow artiste and, for want of a better term, Jackson's keeper. Harden brought an intensity to the role, especially in her closing scenes, that definitely earned her every ounce of Oscar gold that she got. Combined with good showings by Amy Madigan (Harris's real-life wife) as gallery owner Peggy Guggenheim, and Jeffrey Tambor as art critic Clement Greenberg, and the outstanding directing of Harris himself (I loved his use of quiet shadows throughout; Jackson's and Lee's first love scene was nothing less than a work of art), *Pollock* was an enjoyable, if slightly irritating, peek into a way of life I don't think I'll ever fully understand. I only wish that with as large a cast as this movie had, I could've gotten more of the big picture.

BAMMER'S BOTTOM LINE

I enjoyed *Pollock* more on the strength of stars Ed Harris and especially Marcia Gay Harden, than the overall movie itself. But I appreciated this art flick for its glimpse into the tortured soul of an artist, even though the artist it put me in mind of wasn't entirely sympathetic.

GREEN LIGHT

Bams The Red Violin
(1998)

RATED R; running time 126 minutes
GENRE: Drama/Romance/Mystery
WRITTEN BY: Don McKellar and Francois Girard
DIRECTED BY: Francois Girard
CAST: Samuel L. Jackson, Don McKellar, Carlo Cecchi, Irene Grazioli, Jean-Luc Bideau, Christoph Koncz, Jason Flemyng, Greta Scacchi, Sylvia Chang, Liu Zifeng, Ireneusz Bogajewicz

THE STORY

First things first: If you're not the type that likes films (as Steve Martin said so well in *Bowfinger*, "I don't make *films*, I make *movies!*"), ya might want to exit, stage right. Do so quietly, please, so as not to disturb the other patrons. Okay, now that that business is done....

The Red Violin is the epic tale of a perfect, storied violin that changes hands—and the lives it touches—over the course of three hundred years, several countries, and almost endless cultural upheaval. Drawn in by this film's sumptuous cinematography by Alain Dostie, and held by J. Corigliano's Oscar-winning score, the viewer is transported back and forth in time along with the beautiful violin, from its beginnings in 17th-century Italy, to Vienna in the late 1700s, Victorian England, 1960s China, and finally to an auction house in modern-day Montreal, where the violin meets its "final" destiny.

As the now-defunct Web site for this film once said, "These successive movements, each evoking a different musical style, from Baroque to modern, combine to tell a tale filled with poetry, pageantry, tragedy, romance, adventure, and intrigue."

THE UPSHOT

And that it did, in marvelous ways.

Though not a mainstream flick, it had action, passionate sex, romance, intrigue (if only in how the violin changes hands over centuries), humor, and pathos. It took a couple minutes to get into the story, but by the time the violin moved on to Vienna, I was hooked.

The storytelling was done beautifully, both in the narration and in the filming itself. And the flashbacks were done well and made perfect sense, leaving the viewer wanting to know more and more about what happens next. As it went back (forward?) to present-day Montreal, scenes were repeated from different viewpoints; the shifts in focus were done subtly enough so as not to confuse the viewer, but didn't insult the viewer's intelligence. The events that took place in each vignette tore at my heart (especially the one in Vienna, with Christoph Koncz as Kaspar Weiss; I just wanted to take that poor boy home with me!), made me laugh, made me angry in turn—but not in a manipulative way. Each one was like a puzzle that fit almost perfectly near the end.

Strangely enough, Samuel Jackson—who I'd pay to hear do a read-through of the phone book—didn't work for me. He was too intense and seemed not to belong. Otherwise, the actors were equally outstanding, each in his or her own right; having the overall story told in small vignettes helped to make each segment's featured players get the highlight they need. Standouts include the aforementioned Koncz, Jason Flemyng as Fredrick Pope (the passionate "devil"), Sylvia Chang as Xiang Pei and her own mother, and Ireneusz Bogajewicz (Cesca the tarot reader). The violin itself didn't impress me, and the supposed "secret" about it was pretty transparent from the start.

Do you get the vibe that I liked this film? "Liked" isn't strong enough.

THE BLACK FACTOR

My Issues: Samuel L. Jackson; more specifically, his character's actions in this film.

Of all the actors in this film, at first viewing, Jackson sticks out like a sore thumb. Point blank, it felt like he did not belong there. Don't get me wrong, but his was the only role that didn't synch for me. And don't go assuming that it's because he's Black; that wasn't it. It's because he's so GOTdam intense—which, ironically enough, seems to be exactly why he was cast in the role.

For me (until I read the story on the site, anyway), both his unreasonable, Jules-like anger, and his out-and-out thievery in the end, were misplaced. After reading the story, though, I found both explained; still, it changed the timbre of the movie *as a movie* for me. Having gone to see the movie primarily because he's in it, I left the theater bothered by his actions within it, and feeling that something just wasn't right. Maybe if it wasn't for the situation I'm about to Dish about, I would've been able to Feel him more immediately; who knows . . .

BAMMER'S BOTTOM LINE

With *The Red Violin*, I may have finally found my movie-review niche: foreign artsy-fartsy films. Whoda thunkit?

GREEN LIGHT

State and Main
(2000)

RATED PG-13; running time 106 minutes
GENRE: Comedy
WRITTEN BY: David Mamet
DIRECTED BY: David Mamet
CAST: William H. Macy, Philip Seymour Hoffman, Rebecca Pidgeon, Alec Baldwin, Sarah Jessica Parker, David Paymer, Julia Stiles, Jim Frangione, Clark Gregg, Charles Durning, Patti LuPone

THE STORY

The cast and crew of the late 19-century period piece *The Old Mill* look for a new location in which to film their flick; it seems like the antics of its horny star Bob Barrenger (Alec Baldwin) led to the crew leaving its first location set in New Hampshire in a bit of a hurry. This causes big problems for the movie's put-upon director, Walt Price (William H. Macy), who has to clean up after Bob again when Bob casts his eyes upon Carla (Julia Stiles), a local teenager who lives in the movie's new location: Waterford, Vermont.

But Bob's attractions are just the tip of Walt's problems. He also has to contend with a cantankerous producer; the town's mayor (Charles Durning) and his wife (Patti LuPone); Bob's leading lady Claire Wellesley (Sarah Jessica Parker), who chickens out of a key scene; as well as Joseph Turner White (Philip Seymour Hoffman), a somewhat naive writer who falls for local playwright Annie Black (Rebecca Pidgeon), much to the chagrin of Annie's politician fiancé, Doug Mackenzie (Clark Gregg). This is supposed to be the part where I say "And wackiness ensues," but there's this truth-in-advertising thingy . . .

THE UPSHOT

The wretchedness of *State and Main* upsets me mightily. It *should* have been a witty comedy. Instead, I got to witness a train wreck, saved only by a charming, unknown (to me, anyway) actress by the name of Rebecca Pidgeon (Annie), a few great lines (especially the final, mumbled bit by Alec Baldwin), and a fairly decent end scene: alas, all a day late and a dollar short. *State* didn't earn my complete wrath, as witnessed by my not giving it a full red light, because, taken individually, the performances weren't really all that bad.

The most painful waste of all for me was that William H. Macy, an actor I'd love to thank for his brilliance to date, got suckered . . . uh, was convinced to participate in this film. But I reckon I shouldn't be too harsh. Macy, who got the lion's share of the movie's lines, worked hard at his craft; were he an unknown, auditioning for a one-man play, I'd certainly cast him on the strength of his performance here. Similarly, David Paymer (strangely cast against type as an in-your-face producer), and Philip Seymour Hoffman—two actors I also look forward to watching—bit deep into their juicy roles.

Thankfully, Alec Baldwin and Sarah Jessica Parker were reduced to second-string parts (ironic, since the movie-within-a-movie had them playing the stars of the show they were filming), and Charles Durning (Mayor Bailey) wasn't called on to play the wacky backwoods politician again (*O Brother, Where Art Thou?*, see page 224). And, except for a few hokey bits, writer-director David Mamet pretty much laid off the Wise Local Yokels routine; I guess this was a good thing, though not hearing much of a Vermont dialect in the locals' speech, left something to be desired.

No, the individual parts were fairly harmless; it's when they were made into a whole, that *State and Main* became unbearable to watch. It seemed full of aborted plot lines (did somebody forget about Uberto and the window?), devoid of anything remotely funny. And nothing was more egregious than that godawful background music. It seemed to drone on endlessly throughout the movie, driving me mad with every note.

BAMMER'S BOTTOM LINE
Was *State and Main* supposed to be a cautionary tale about the soullessness of show business folk? Or the importance of being pure and true?

Or a statement about second chances? Sorry, I was too busy praying for an end to the *pain* to notice. Or care.

FLASHING RED LIGHT

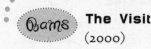

The Visit
(2000)

RATED R; running time 107 minutes
GENRE: Drama
WRITTEN BY: Jordan Walker-Pearlman (based on the play by Kosmond Russell)
DIRECTED BY: Jordan Walker-Pearlman
CAST: Hill Harper, Obba Babatundé, Billy Dee Williams, Rae Dawn Chong, Marla Gibbs, Phylicia Rashad, Talia Shire, David Clennon, Tim DeZarn, Glynn Turman

THE STORY
Alex Waters (Hill Harper) is an Angry Black Man. Sentenced to 25 years to life for a crime he insists he did not commit, Alex expresses his rage and hostility to his counselor, Dr. Coles (Phylicia Rashad), and to the parole board members who hold his life in their hands. But most of his anger is reserved for his brother, Tony (Obba Babatundé), who first left Alex when he went off to college when they were younger—and who abandoned Alex in prison for ten months before visiting him for the first time.

Even in his anger, Alex needs Tony's help. He asks Tony to convince their loving mother,

Lois (Marla Gibbs), and seemingly unfeeling father, Henry (Billy Dee Williams), to come visit him in prison so that Alex can tell his parents some disturbing news. And Tony has a bit of news for Alex, in the person of Alex's childhood friend Felicia McDonald (Rae Dawn Chong), who may have even more in common with Alex now that he's in prison, than she did when he was free.

THE UPSHOT

No histrionics here. *The Visit* whispers where lesser films might shout, yet its message is heard just as clearly. And its messengers amaze; *The Visit* was an extraordinary blend of talented cast and top-notch crew, who combined to work their magic in a way that completely floored me. Granted, I've come to expect solid performances from Obba Babatundé and Hill Harper, and they both delivered, in spades. Babatundé's performance as Tony improved over the span of the movie, and his stirring oration in the climax, touched me. Likewise, Harper made his mark as Alex, proving that he's not just another pretty face (in many scenes, literally).

And the women, Rae Dawn Chong (Felicia), Marla Gibbs (Lois), and Phylicia Rashad (Dr. Coles), handled their demanding roles admirably. But the absolute showstopper was Billy Dee Williams. Billy Dee "Lando Calrissian" Williams. Billy Dee "Colt-45" Williams. Billy Dee "Don't Let The Smooth Taste Fool Ya" Williams. Yes, *that* Billy Dee. If I had to single out one performance from this remarkable ensemble, his would stand head and shoulders above the rest; it resonated in very real ways for me, some of which I'll go through in the "Black Factor" below. Suf-

fice it to say, I owe you a sincere apology, Mr. Williams; I didn't know you had it like that.

The delights of *The Visit* extend well beyond the well-gelled cast. Writer-director-producer Jordan Walker-Pearlman's soulful feel for this story was excellently realized in his realistic dialogue, and in his collaboration with cinematographer John Demps; some of Demps's shots (especially the dream sequences; *especially* the sequence with Alex and his father) were simply breathtaking.

Add to this an achingly beautiful musical score (by Ramsey Lewis, among five others), appearances by Talia Shire, David Clennon, Tim DeZarn, and Glynn Turman as parole board members, and a relevant, true story told without compromise—and you'll understand why I urge you to see this movie .

THE BLACK FACTOR

Bear with me while I address a segment of the nonmonolithic Black community that's only now starting to be addressed in mainstream films: the upwardly mobile, increasingly successful Black family and its patriarchal representative in *The Visit*, father Henry Waters.

I took Henry's feelings of betrayal (in Alex's "allowing" himself to be incarcerated) to heart, so much so that I felt compelled to stop the tape and discuss Henry's issues with my husband. Call it luck, call it a blessing—call it what you want, but my husband and I find ourselves in a position where our sons have come through the gauntlet that is young Black manhood relatively unscathed. I have long taken the hard stance that I'll spend a fortune to send them to college, or help them become and stay gainfully employed—but I won't spend a penny to get them out of jail. In watching Henry, in hearing his anger and lack of compassion for Alex's plight (justified or not; that's not the point for now), I was taken aback. It definitely made me at least contemplate my rigid attitude; my failure to easily forgive human weakness.

BAMMER'S BOTTOM LINE

Full of surprisingly strong yet understated performances—in front of and behind the camera—*The Visit* tells a powerful tale of redemption and the freedom that comes from forgiveness—especially forgiveness of self. If you care anything about quality Black cinema—beyond the lip service all too often paid by so many of us (y'all know who we are)—rent and recommend this one, again and again.

GREEN LIGHT

have you ever watched a movie that lowered your IQ ten points for every second you sat there? One that made you throw your popcorn at the screen? (And you know how bad that is—movie popcorn costs an arm and a leg these days!)

Has a movie ever been so bad, it made you start cussin' after it's over? How about *during* the movie? Have you ever been so disgusted with a flick, you asked for your money back on the way out—and you didn't pay to see it? Have you ever left in the middle of a movie? During the opening credits???

Guess what? We've done all of the above, and more! And if you watch any of the movies in this chapter, you'll be tempted to do one or all of the above, too. Don't say we didn't warn ya . . .

The Animal
(2001)

RATED PG-13; running time 83 minutes
GENRE: Comedy
WRITTEN BY: Tom Brady and Rob Schneider
DIRECTED BY: Luke Greenfield
CAST: Rob Schneider, Colleen Haskell, John C. McGinley, Edward Asner, Michael Canton, Louis Lombardi

THE DIGEST

Marvin (Rob Schneider) aspires to move from police-evidence clerk to full-fledged officer, like his beloved father. He has taken the police academy physical test four times, yet he never seems to pass it, which makes him the laughingstock of the police station.

Everyone walks all over him and treats him like dirt. Even the woman of his dreams, Rianna (Colleen Haskell from *Survivor*), doesn't know he is alive. All this changes when, left alone at the station, he answers a call for a robbery in progress. On the way to the robbery, he has a nearly fatal car accident. He is abducted by the strange Dr. Wilder (Michael Caton), who saves his life by replacing all of his damaged organs with those of various animals.

All of a sudden, Marvin is superstrong; can't stop eating, has unquenchable sexual urges, and a heightened sense of smell. He finally has the abilities to become a police officer and he now has the courage to pursue Rianna. The only obstacles in his way are Sergeant Sisk (John C. McGinley) who is jealous of Marvin and will not stop until Marvin is kicked out of law enforcement, and a rash of odd crimes in the night, with the perpetrator fitting Marvin's description. Marvin must struggle to prove his innocence and pray that Rianna sticks by his side or it's all for nothing.

THE DISH

What in the hell were they thinking? I thought *Deuce Bigalow* was flippin' hilarious, but this crap? I don't think so. I can't even get mad at Colleen Haskell for her "acting," because she's not an actress, and the truth of the matter is, she was almost the best thing about the movie and that's a shame.

The *worst* thing in this movie was the reverse-racism diatribes by Miles (Guy Torry). His character was upset because he could get away with stuff because he was Black. He felt that White folks were making up for slavery by letting him do whatever he wanted. This could have been funny, but his delivery and the sheer stupidity of his complaints killed it.

THE DIRECTIVE

A rabid beast that should be put to sleep, this movie was (to semiquote "Dr. Evil") rigosh-darndiculous.

RED LIGHT

Bait
(2000)

RATED R; running time 120 minutes
GENRE: Action/Comedy (yeah right)
WRITTEN BY: Tony Gilroy, Adam Scheinman, Andrew Scheinman
DIRECTED BY: Antoine Fuqua
CAST: Jamie Foxx, David Morse, Doug Hutchison, Robert Pastorelli, Kimberly Elise, Tia Texada, Mike Epps

THE DIGEST

Alvin Sanders (Jamie Foxx) is your basic screw-up. He has risked his probation by stealing shrimp. Not just any shrimp, but Jumbo Prawns, "Rolleyes." He, of course, gets caught and is sent to Rikers, where he is put in the same cell as John Jaster (Robert Pastorelli) who has been arrested for his part in an armed robbery that netted 43 million in gold bars. John dies in jail and the gold is not found.

Meanwhile, the "gubmint," more specifically Agent Clenteen (David Morse), hatches this brilliant plan to let Alvin out early and implant him with a tracking device, hoping that his cellmate talked and revealed where the gold is. The "gubmint" agents also work overtime to keep Alvin out of trouble since he can't seem to do that himself.

THE DISH
BORING!!

Jamie Foxx is a talented actor but I'm more than tired of seeing him play buffoons. I thought he was *wonderful* in *Any Given Sunday* (see page 172). But enough is enough. Okay, Samuel and Denzel get all of the "good" roles, but you know what? Pay off your bills and save up your money and don't take any more roles until you get something decent. And another thing that irritates me: the types of roles that Tia Texada and Mike Epps keep getting. I don't want them to be stereotyped as the triflin' Black male and the smart-mouthed "Ay Popee" Latina. It's enough to make you scream. And finally, the thing that made me want to throw my drink at the screen: the character of Bristol (Doug Hutchison). He acted and sounded just like John Malkovich. Why? John does just fine. He doesn't need someone to parrot him in a movie.

THE DIRECTIVE

YAWN. If you've seen *In the Line of Fire* and *Enemy of the State* then you've already seen this movie, except those were actually good.

RED LIGHT

 **Bats**
(1999)

RATED R; running time 91 minutes
GENRE: Horror
WRITTEN BY: John Logan
DIRECTED BY: Louis Morneau
CAST: Lou Diamond Phillips, Dina Meyer, Bob Gunton, Leon, Carlos Jacott, David McConnell, Marcia Dangerfield

THE DIGEST

The movie starts out with two teenagers who are "parking." His window is rolled down while they are talking, and something brushes his arm. So what does he do?!?!?! He gets out of the car. He gets back in the car, and a bat begins tearing through the car's roof to get at him and his girlfriend. Does he start the car and attempt to drive off? Nope. That'd be too logical. He and chickiepoo are served up as dinner.

Sheila (Dina Meyer) is a "batologist" (I didn't make that one up); Jimmy (Leon) is her assistant. They are called in to help figure out what happened. When they go into the coroner's office and see the bodies, Sheila gets an attitude because "bats don't do this." Well, normal bats don't, anyway. What has happened is that the government has genetically altered two bats, and they're superstrong, smart, and ugly. And they've escaped from the lab and infected a bunch of normal bats. So now there are thousands of meat-eating bats attacking this little town.

The government comes in and promptly gets its ass thoroughly kicked. Sheila, Jimmy, and the sheriff (Lou Diamond Phillips) save the day by freezing the bats with a refrigerator unit while they are chest-high in bat doodoo. End of story and end of the longest 90 minutes I've had in a while.

THE DISH

This was a horror movie all right…horrible. This movie was bad. BAD. BAD. On the plus side, an important rule is broken. The brotha makes it through the end. It's a shame he was written as a complete buffoon, but I guess a brotha needs to work. On the minus side, this movie sucks. No pun intended.

THE DIRECTIVE

Shaving the corns off of your toes would be time better spent than watching *Bats*.

RED LIGHT

 Bringing Out the Dead
(1999)

RATED PG-13; running time 132 minutes
GENRE: Drama
WRITTEN BY: Paul Schrader (based on the novel by Joe Connelly)
DIRECTED BY: Martin Scorsese
CAST: Nicolas Cage, Patricia Arquette, John Goodman, Ving Rhames, Tom Sizemore, Marc Anthony, Mary Beth Hurt, Cliff Curtis, Nestor Serrano, Cynthia Roman, Afemo Omilami, Cullen O. Johnson, Arthur J. Nascarella

> For those of you who keep getting Ving Rhames and Michael Duncan Clarke mixed up, here's a hint: Ving is the bal'-headed one.

THE STORY

Frank Pierce (Cage) lost his religion after working as a Noo Yawk paramedic for so long, he burnt out. A major contributing factor in his burnout was his inability to save the life of a young homeless girl named Rose, whom he now sees everywhere he looks, like a ghost, haunting him. Having no such trouble (being haunted, that is), are his partners for a day: Larry (Goodman), the paramedic who has seen no food he could not eat; Marcus (Rhames), a preachin' paramedic with a thing for the disembodied; sultry voice of the (female) dispatcher (voiced by Queen Latifah; the male dispatcher was Scorsese himself); and Tom (Sizemore), a ruffneck paramedic whose take-no-prisoners attitude finally drives Frank to . . . something or another. In the midst of all this ensuing wackiness, Frank picks up on Mary Burks (Arquette), a woman whose father had a heart attack on Frank and Larry's . . . ah, forget it.

THE UPSHOT

I can't get it up for *Bringing Out the Dead*, a story with no, zero, none, zilch, nada, redeeming features. Not a one. To believe that the director behind this is the same man who brought us *Goodfellas*, *Raging Bull*, and *Taxi Driver* would cause me to lose faith in the Power of Movies.

Whatever Cage earned for this flick, he needs to give it back. And I'm sorry; all of the Neato Gee Whiz special effects in the world couldn't have put *this* Humpty Dumpty together again.

Its story was nowhere to be found, and Cage's spirit was off contemplating his next flick. But what of the supporting cast? Well, as with many movies today, they were the only things holding up this disappointing series of moving images. Goodman played his usual big jolly goofball, but amongst the big names, the real joys were to be had in Sizemore and his "Sure, I'll save you—right after I kick your ass, you worthless piece of slime" paramedic; the always delightful Rhames and his powerful command of whatever character he plays; and his surprising foil, the artist I'd

most love to meet, Queen La—who had the line of the night when, as the dispatcher, she said one of the patients she was dispatching the paramedics to, was "hearing celebrity voices."

BAMMER'S BOTTOM LINE

I sentence thee, Arquette, to a dentist's appointment. And as for you, Nick, try to hook up that Superman movie that is still in development. Can't be much worse than *Bringing Out the Dead*.

RED LIGHT

 Brokedown Palace
(1999)

RATED PG-13; running time 101 minutes
GENRE: Drama
WRITTEN BY: David Arata
DIRECTED BY: Jonathan Kaplan
CAST: Claire Danes, Kate Beckinsale, Bill Pullman, Daniel Lapaine, Lou Diamond Phillips

THE STORY

After graduating high school, two Hollywood cookie-cutter friends—Alice (Claire Danes), the bad one; and Darlene (Kate Beckinsale), the easily led one—decide to chuck their plans to go to Hawaii for their last hurrah, and go to Thailand instead. There, they hook up with Nick Parks (Daniel Lapaine), a rad Aussie doode who rescues the damsels in distress after they get into a sticky wicket; on his invitation, they decide to fly with him to Hong Kong. Unfortunately for them, some bad stuff is found in their carry-on luggage. Wackiness ensues, and they get to visit Thailand's free bed 'n' board hotspot ("you can check in, but ya can't check out!"). You guessed it: the Broke-down Palace.

THE UPSHOT

From the start, this movie was telegraphed, leaving absolutely no surprises. And worse, the whole premise struck me as just plain stoopid. Let's start with the setup: here's two young ladies, out to have fun before settling down, right? And instead of going to Hawaii on their own, they pick—Thailand? Now, I'm sure that Thailand is a lovely place, but come on; at least you coulda come up with a better, more subtle, hook than that, guys! The Just Say No To Drugs neon light was flashing right off the bat, the infamous Whiffle Bat Of Bad Storytelling, that is.

It also doesn't help that we are given very little back story to work with; nothing much to grab onto to feel these girls, except Alice's vocal flashbacks as told via cassette tape and delivered to Yankee Hank, a "sleazy barrister" living in Thailand, played unevenly by Bill Pullman (*Independence Day*). Lou Diamond Phillips (*La Bamba*), as a surprisingly uncaring—and equally unconvincing—U.S. embassy official, Jacqueline Kim (*Volcano*) as Hank's lawyer-wife Yon Green, and Paul Walker round out the main cast.

There was plenty for me to dislike about this movie: The editing was bad, the storyline was worse, the ending painfully unbelievable—but of all the things I despised about it, what I hated most was the execution (if you could call it that) by the two leads themselves. Visions of *Dawson's Creek* kept running through my mind as if I were

in WB (the non-Ghetto version) Land, with some MTV thrown in for good measure. And I found it criminal that they'd try to pass off two pampered princesses as prisoners in hell. Their transformation into the big bad world of inmate life is weakly noted by a new haircut, and they survive time in the hole with only slightly more muss and fuss (their makeup finally gets washed off, their hair is scruffy, and they break a nail or two). This weakly played version of prison life reminded me more of *The Breakfast Club* than of anything remotely approaching something to be feared and avoided at all costs.

THE BLACK FACTOR

I saw precious little in this movie that would specifically appeal to a person of color; nothing, certainly, that would convince most of Us to dig deep for the ducats. There *was* an obligatory Jamaican who befriended the girls—after all, what's a drug movie without the obligatory Jamaican included for good measure? And that, for those who missed it, was sarcasm.

The other small bit of BF present was BF in reverse: Eddie Murphy once said, if Hollywood ever made a serious horror film starring Blacks, it'd be over in about two minutes—because when the Creature yelled "Get Out," We'd be gone before the last syllable. Well, the same principle applies here; I couldn't honestly see this kind of thing happening to your generic (yet, nonmonolithic) Black kid. Mostly because that Ugly American/White Privilege thingy just don' work too well with Us.

BAMMER'S BOTTOM LINE

Don't spend a penny on *Brokedown Palace*; TV's *Prisoner: CellBlock H* was more believable than this tripe. Heck, *Charlie's Angels* did better chicks-behind-bars segments than this brokedown movie.

RED LIGHT

 Dungeons and Dragons
(2000)

RATED PG; running time 100 minutes
GENRE: Action/Fantasy
WRITTEN BY: Topper Lilien, Carroll Cartwright
DIRECTED BY: Courtney Solomon
CAST: Jeremy Irons, Justin Whalin, Marlon Wayans, Thora Birch, Zoe McLellan, Kristen Wilson

THE DIGEST

The Empire of Izmer is undergoing a change. While it's been run for a long time by the elite magic users, the Mages, the new Empress Savina (Thora Birch) a Mage herself, wants to end the inequality between the classes. She wants Mages and Commoners alike to be equal, but she faces a challenge in the person of Profion (Jeremy Irons), a power-hungry evil Mage who doesn't want to be equal with those beneath him. He also wants control of the empire. For whoever controls the empire also controls the Gold Dragons. The controller of the dragons is the most powerful of all Mages. If he gets a hold of the scepter that controls the Gold Dragons, the only thing the empress can do is find the mythical and mightier Rod of Savrille.

Two hapless thieves, Ridley (Justin Whalin) and Snails (Marlon Wayans), find themselves thrust in the middle of the quest when they, along with a student Mage named Marina (Zoe McLellan), witness the death of a Mage who is helping the empress. They then set off to find the legendary Rod of Savrille, hopefully in time to save the empire.

THE DISH

Where do I begin? Let's start with Marina. It has been a long time since I witnessed acting this bad. I'm sure Zoe McLellan tried her best, but her best wasn't good enough. She was just plain horrible. Now let's discuss Snails. It must seem like I have it out for Marlon Wayans. He can't act his way out of a paper bag. Throughout the entire movie he was a total buffoon. This is the same type of role that Spike was getting at in *Bamboozled*. "Awww Boss, how come you always get the girl and I always get the . . . whatever." Snails was a mental midget compared to Ridley. Snails doesn't want to do something and Ridley tricks him by insisting that he couldn't do it anyway. A 5-year-old wouldn't fall for that. It was painful to watch. It made me think about all of the movies from the '40s that depict Black men as easily fooled children. It was "massah and slave," and it was disgusting. But you know what? Now that I think about it, I'm not going to single out Marina and Snails. Everyone, including Jeremy Irons, more or less sucked.

THE DIRECTIVE

Though the fight scene between the dragons was very cool, there is nothing else about this movie worth seeing. *Dungeons and Dragons?* More like dragging dung.

RED LIGHT

Felicia's Journey
(1999)

RATED PG-13; running time 116 minutes
GENRE: Thriller
WRITTEN BY: Atom Egoyan
DIRECTED BY: Atom Egoyan
CAST: Bob Hoskins, Arsinee Khanjian, Elaine Cassidy, Sheila Reid, Ali Yassine

THE DIGEST

OK. I'm going to try and explain this . . . this . . . this . . . "film" I saw.

Joey Hilditch (Bob Hoskins) is a chef for an industrial factory. Through flashbacks, we find out that his mother was a famous French chef with her own television show in the '50s. Joey also has a secret. He victimizes women, but no one knows he is victimizing women, because he picks girls that no one will miss. You don't even find out that he has an "issue" until halfway through the movie, and even then you never see him actually commit a crime.

Felicia (Elaine Cassidy) is a nice Irish girl who has fallen in love with a nice Irish boy. He leaves Ireland to find work in England. He tells her that he works at a lawnmower factory. The truth is, he actually joined the British army, which is a big no-no if you are Irish. Felicia finds out that she's pregnant and travels to England to find him and tell him. She shows up in England with nothing but a knapsack and some cash. Along the way she crosses paths with Hilditch. He befriends her and begins to manipulate and control her. Eventually, he attempts to kill her. He lets her go after a Black Jehovah's Witness. She gets him to let go of his demons, after which he does something unthinkable.

THE DISH

Children, I want you to think long and hard for a few minutes about someone you dislike with a passion. This is the person you wouldn't spit on if they were on fire. This is the same person for whom you should rent *Felicia's Journey*.

This was the most mind-numbing waste of celluloid that I've ever come across. There were some critics out there raving about this film. They gave it four stars. Don't listen to them! Run! You will be begging for your 116 minutes and your money back. Trust The Diva on this one. I was in a theater with 300 folks. Two, count 'em, two people thought this was a good movie. The rest of us were ready to confess our crimes and beg for forgiveness, as long as we didn't have to see this movie again.

THE DIRECTIVE

Save yourself the grief unless you appreciate torture.

RED LIGHT

Gun Shy
(1999)

RATED R; running time 102 minutes
GENRE: Comedy/Action
WRITTEN BY: Eric Blakeney
DIRECTED BY: Eric Blakeney
CAST: Liam Neeson, Oliver Platt, Sandra Bullock, Jose Zuniga, Mitch Pileggi, Richard Schiff, Mary McCormack, Frank Vincent

THE DIGEST
Charlie Mayough (Liam Neeson) is an undercover Drug Enforcement Agent. He has been given the task of taking down a Colombian drug cartel and the local mob. During phase one, both he and his partner are raped with guns and his partner is killed. He is saved in the nick of time by his fellow officers. Because of this experience, he is terrified to go back into the field, but his superiors insist he goes back one more time.

While posing as an accountant, he sets up a money-laundering scheme between mob representative Fulvio Nesstra (Oliver Platt) and two Colombians. When he is not trying to set them up, he is begging for retirement, in group therapy, or burning the nose hairs of innocent bystanders with his flatulence. His therapist, tired of being blasted with his foul smells, recommends a G.I. specialist. It is here that he meets Nurse Judy (Sandra Bullock) who is determined to save Charlie from himself. She sets out to cure him of his fear, which, in her opinion, will cure him of his stomach ailments.

THE DISH
I won't give away too much. If you are going to torture yourself and watch this movie, you might as well have some surprises. Thirty minutes into this movie, *I* was plotting revenge against the cast and crew, as well as Buena Vista executives.

Well, maybe not *all* of the characters. As usual, Oliver Platt creates an unforgettable character. He plays a hardnosed wise guy, when in reality he just wants to be a gardener and live in Italy. Everyone else pretty much takes the back burner.

THE DIRECTIVE
I'd rather be shot then have to see *Gun Shy* again.

RED LIGHT

 Highlander: Endgame
(2000)

RATED R; running time 85 minutes
GENRE: Action
WRITTEN BY: Gregory Widen (characters); Eric Bernt, Gillian Horvath, Bill Panzer (story); Joel Soisson (screenplay)
DIRECTED BY: (Douglas Aarniokoski)
CAST: Adrian Paul, Christopher Lambert, Bruce Payne, Lisa Barbuscia, Ian Paul Cassidy, Adam "Edge" Copeland, Damon Dash, Sheila Gish, Jim Byrnes, Peter Wingfield, Donnie Yen

THE STORY

The main characters in the *Highlander* series and movies are an unknown quantity of immortals who walk the earth in anticipation of the Quickening (a gathering of immortals in which they go head to head), with the end result being only one immortal left standing. After all, there can be only one. Some immortals—including the MacLeod kinsmen—see these duels as a necessary evil.

Particularly Connor MacLeod, whose latest love is done in by a mysterious stranger. Hoping to be rid of the curse of immortality, Connor hides away in Sanctuary (the one place where immortals do not do their dastardly deeds). But the big kahuna Immortal, Jacob Kell (Bruce "Needs A Membership In Overactors Anonymous" Payne), knows no such boundaries. He seeks revenge on Connor for Connor's having killed his "unarmed" priest father centuries ago, when Kell Senior helped to burn Connor's mother at the stake when the Kells discovered that Connor was . . . oh, must this madness go on???

THE UPSHOT

After sitting through the torture that was this gag-inducing movie, I feel sorriest for those faithful *Highlander* fans of both the original movie starring Christopher Lambert as Connor MacLeod of the Clan MacLeod, and the follow-up TV series starring Adrian Paul as his kinsman, Duncan MacLeod—fans who waited all these years for the lightning that once was *Highlander* to strike again. And this lame, long-form (emphasis on "long") version of a bad music video is the thanks they get?

The original *Highlander* movie was something of a cult hit. Christopher Lambert always struck me as someone whose acting was probably best served when done in his mother tongue, but the whole concept from the first movie was fun enough to give in to, and served as fuel for many similar types of flicks that followed. Parts two and three were utter bollocks, but they were easily forgotten because those of us who liked the series, simply replaced the conflicting bits of fodder with new canon from the series creators. It also helped when Lambert made periodic guest appearances on the series. So, for a while, all was well.

As with many syndicated TV series, holes began to develop in the show's structure, and, after a while, *Highlander* the series fell off my radar. I kept up with it just enough to know that there was supposedly a movie "in the works," and I waited for something to come of it. After I saw this travesty, the wait continues.

Highlander: Endgame is such a weak piece of sh . . . detritus, I hate mentioning it in the same breath as the cheesy-but-fun series and original movie. This version had one of the most lame plots possible: a superimmortal, after all this time? And suddenly, Duncan also has this riot chick pop up from seemingly out of nowhere, as part of his distant, secret past? That'd be like . . . like . . . like Captain Kirk suddenly finding himself with the son he never knew he had. Give me an effin' break, will ya?

The only thing, and I do mean the *ONLY* thing that saved this flick from the red-light dustbin, is its use of mostly effective "flashbacks," similar to those done in the series. But can someone explain once and for all why Adrian Paul always seems to get a thicker brogue the further back in time Duncan goes?

THE BLACK FACTOR
All that, and Diva's Brotha Rule (see page xv) is in full effect too? Will the madness *ever* end? Sheesh!

BAMMER'S BOTTOM LINE

What a horrible ripoff! Highlander fans, y'all deserve better than this dreck. But please, Hollywood. I hope the term "endgame" is a promise, not an idle threat. Man, did *Highlander: Endgame* blow.

FLASHING RED LIGHT

The Ladies Man
the Diva

(2000)

RATED R; running time 84 minutes
GENRE: Comedy
WRITTEN BY: Tim Meadows, Dennis McNicholas, and Andrew Steele
DIRECTED BY: Reginald Hudlin
CAST: Tim Meadows, Karyn Parsons, Billy Dee Williams, Lee Evans, Will Ferrell

THE DIGEST

Leon Phelps (Tim Meadows), the self-proclaimed "Ladies Man," spent his youth in the lap of luxury. Left on the doorstep of the Playboy mansion, he was raised by all of the Bunnies and enjoyed a close relationship with the man of the house (who looks a lot like Hugh Hefner). When Leon breaks the rules and sleeps with, a woman that the man was in love with, he finds himself on the streets.

Now on his own, he survives the only way he knows how—by using women. He endears himself to Lester (Billy Dee Williams), the owner of a local bar. It is at Lester's bar that Leon meets Julie (Karyn Parsons), a jilted bride who has come to the bar to drown her sorrows. Leon tries to pick her up and fails, but he makes her laugh. Julie is also a radio producer and feels that the world could benefit from Leon's advice. Thus a popular radio show is born. His advice usually boils down to "do it in the butt," but the people of Chicago love him or love to hate him. After one too many FCC violations, Leon is kicked off the air, Julie with him, and they must find another gig.

In the midst of all of this, Leon is still sleeping with all kinds of women, particularly *married* women. He soon finds out that there is a support group of husbands who have all caught Leon with their wives. They vow to kill him. Unemployed and doing his best to avoid a bunch of angry husbands, Leon is also looking for a mysterious rich lady who wants to be his sugar mama. How is he going to get out of this mess?

THE DISH

Not every *Saturday Night Live* skit deserves to be a feature-length film. *The Ladies Man* is funny for about 10 minutes, every couple of months. It is *not* funny for 84 *straight* minutes. On the plus side, it was nice seeing Billy Dee Williams and Karyn Parsons who played Hilary Banks on *The Fresh Prince of Bel-Air*.

THE DIRECTIVE

We are begging you . . . no more *Saturday Night Live* skits on the big screen unless they are *really* good.

RED LIGHT

 Me, Myself & Irene
(2000)

RATED R; running time 118 minutes

GENRE: Comedy

WRITTEN BY: Bobby Farrelly, Peter Farrelly, Mike Cerrone

DIRECTED BY: Bobby Farrelly, Peter Farrelly

CAST: Jim Carrey, Renée Zellweger, Chris Cooper, Robert Forster, Richard Jenkins, Mongo Brownlee, Anthony Anderson, Jerod Mixon, Danny Green, Michael Bowman, Traylor Howard, Rob Moran, Lin Shaye

> See if you can spot Jim Carrey in a small role in *Peggy Sue Got Married*.

THE STORY

Charlie (Jim Carrey), a mild-mannered Rhode Island motorcycle cop, stands by while the world walks over him, especially his two-timing wife Layla who cheats on him with Chante Jackson (Tony Cox), the Black chauffeur at their wedding. Even when his "triplet" kids, Jamaal (Anthony Anderson), Lee Harvey (Mongo Brownlee), and

Chante Jr. (Jerod Mixon) come out looking remarkably more like Chante than him. Charlie just grins and bears it. But when Layla leaves him, Charlie eventually snaps into two personalities: his mild, sexually repressed self, and "Hank," the angry, sexually hungry, (and no longer) suppressed side of him that Charlie "buried" inside when Layla ditched him.

There's also a dirt-dumb subplot involving Irene (Renée Zellweger), the target of Charlie *and* Hank's affection. I can't be asked to describe anything else about this inane movie. I'd really like to forget it ever happened, actually.

THE UPSHOT

Going into this flick, I knew it was a Farrelly Brothers production—and all that implies. Shakespeare it ain't; I can dig that. I understood well in advance that the gross factor would be high in *Irene*. "Gross" I could deal with. "Jackass-stupid" and "unreasonably mean-spirited," however, pisses me off to no end.

Irene has no redeeming factors and I spent more time getting irritated by the grating music, the illogical plotline, the foolishly empty characters, the bad acting, Zellweger's nails-on-a-blackboard voice, and the crappy "special effects" (that cow looked like a reject from the *Jaws* mechanical animals pile) than in noticing any semblance of good within its long reels of film. The sound of silence—in the theater, and from the screen in between moments of slapstick hijinx—was deafening. And remember, this was *supposedly* a comedy. Oops.

The only tolerable thing about this whole movie—Jim Carrey's amazingly agile body and the way he can contort it—was tempered by the knowledge that he's been there/done that before. All the Clint Eastwood voice-channeling in the world can't make up for the fact that Carrey has quickly become a one-trick pony, recycling the same characterization over and over, ad nauseum. I kept thinking to myself, "He gets paid $20 mil for *this*? Where do I sign up for Clown Lessons???"

Wasted potential grinds my gizzards. *Recycled* waste served up as a fresh dish causes me to paint yellow lights red. I want that two hours of my life refunded to me, dammit.

THE BLACK FACTOR

In this day and age of so-called Political Correctness (about as stoopid a term as "color-blindness"), one must be careful not to get one's hackles raised when the group with which one closely affiliates—be it Blacks, women, paraplegics, Catholics, World War II vets, soccer moms, what have you—is targeted in a flick like *Irene*. The thin-skinned amongst us might be read'ta take up arms, crosses, bazookas, what have you, to protest Those Bad People Who Made Fun Of Us.

Me, I don't consider myself all that thin-skinned. So, when much fun was made of Chante and the chip on his shoulder for being Black, a chauffeur, and a dwarf, I barely batted an eye (but take note, Farrelly bros: Chante is a girl's name, ka peach?) When that ho' Layla tongued (ewww) Chante right in front of Charlie, I almost lost my lunch, but my temper was intact. Even the "one-drop rule" joke made of Charlie's "triplet" (uh huh) sons, elicited not much more than a roll of my big brown eyes.

But when the brothers Farrelly implied that the only thing Charlie's smart Black sons got out of watching Richard Pryor was the ability to toss around cuss words like lettuce in a salad . . . well, them's fightin' words, buster.

BAMMER'S BOTTOM LINE

Irene begs the question: is Jim Carrey a grossly overpaid but misunderstood clown with a Lucille Ball–like gift for physical humor (and little else), or does he just have an unholy fixation with his ass?

RED LIGHT

The Messenger: The Story of Joan of Arc
(1999)

the Diva

RATED R; running time 148 minutes
GENRE: Drama
WRITTEN BY: Luc Besson and Andrew Birkin
DIRECTED BY: Luc Besson
CAST: Milla Jovovich, John Malkovich, Faye Dunaway, Pascal Greggory, Vincent Cassel, Tchéky Karyo, Richard Ridings, Desmond Harrington, Dustin Hoffman

Milla Jovovich was married to Luc Besson, the writer and director, at the time this was filmed. We really wish directors would stop casting their spouses.

THE DIGEST

The king of France and the king of England signed a treaty. The terms stated that when the king of France died, the king of England would rule both England and France. The problem is that they both died within a few weeks of each other, leaving the monarchy to an infant English king. France wasn't having it. So began the war. England was kicking France's butt. The French were disillusioned and moral was low.

Meanwhile, little Joan is running around the church having confession several times a day, along with visions. She claims that an angel speaks to her and has given her a mission. But she doesn't know what it is yet. By the time Joan is 19, people know her very well. France is still fighting England and, according to French folklore, a maiden from Orleans will lead the French army to victory. Well, that fits Joan to a T.

After picking the would-be King Charles VII out of a crowd, Joan demands an audience with him. He is impressed enough to grant her the audience. He gives her an army, which she leads to victory, securing him the throne. He then turns his back on her and allows the English to toast her.

THE DISH

After 90 minutes of this two-and-a-half-hour film, *I* wanted to be burned at the stake. I thought, "Just burn her already so I can go home." Prior to watching this movie, I really dug ole Joanie. If I were to use this film to get a clear picture of who Joan was, I'd say she was completely nuts. This film showed her to be a weird religious fanatic who had one too many magic mushrooms.

A period piece, this film showed off the English and French mores of the day. Dental hygiene was not a primary concern. How can you kiss someone with black and rotten teeth?!?!? One soldier was going to kill a prisoner for his grill (grill is slang for teeth). Eewww! But I don't blame him! I was like, "Steal the grill! Steal the grill! Go 'head on and get you some new teeth." And the "fashions"! The French women used to shave their hair halfway back. So they had this big huge cranium staring at you. And the table manners! They had bowls and spoons but would still eat off the table. I can only imagine how funky they were.

But I digress. As far as the movie goes, I was irritated that 90 percent of the cast didn't even *try* to be authentic. John Malkovich played King Charles and he didn't even attempt an accent. He could have at least called his son "Louwee." Here he is, the king of France, sounding like he just left Kansas for the first time in his life. The same with Dustin Hoffman. Faye Dunaway was the only one who was halfway believable.

THE DIRECTIVE

As portrayed in *The Messenger*, my girl Joan was a few fries short of a Happy Meal in this one.

RED LIGHT

Superstar
(1999)

RATED PG-13; running time 81 minutes
GENRE: Comedy (and this is debatable)
WRITTEN BY: Steve Koren
DIRECTED BY: Bruce McCulloch
CAST: Molly Shannon, Will Ferrell, Elaine Hendrix, Emmy Laybourne, Glynis Johns, Mark McKinney, Harland Williams

THE DIGEST

Based on a long-running *Saturday Night Live* skit, *Superstar* tells the story of Mary Katherine Gallagher (Molly Shannon) who has one dream in life, and that is to be French-kissed. She decides that the only way to accomplish this is to become a superstar. So she makes it her life's mission to do so. This entails auditioning for the school talent show in which the winner will get a part as an extra on a film. That's the entire film, folks. There are the jocks and the geeks. And, of course, a misunderstood rebel. Same old same. *Nothing* remarkable at all.

You might get a kick out of Mary licking trees and stop signs, but I wasn't impressed. If you want to impress me, lick a pole in the winter. This movie could have been a fifteen-minute skit on *SNL* and I would have been more than thrilled.

THE DISH

Children, your mission—should you choose it— is to bring me the head of Lorne Michaels, the SNL executive who greenlighted this movie. And the kicker? People, especially kids, loved this movie. They were cracking up.

I've been watching *SNL* since it debuted, but I'll never understand why they choose the skits they do to make into feature-length movies. It boggles the mind. Some are good, but the others just plain stink, including *Superstar*. I like the Mary Katherine Gallagher skits but not enough to watch her for 81 minutes. And to top it all off, she had the audacity . . . the unmitigated gall . . . the nerve to sing *my* favorite song from the movie *Fame*, "Out Here On My Own." I'm so unbelievably through. Nothing is sacred anymore. First they frisk Diana "Boss" Ross (whom I have *no* love for, but she *is* a Diva and, as such, is entitled to *not* have her boobies squeezed in public by an overzealous security guard). Now this. What is a Diva to do? I haven't been this through since Whitney Houston lost her mind and married that Bobby "I Should Have Never Left New Edition" Brown.

THE DIRECTIVE

Wait until *Superstar* comes on TBS one Sunday afternoon and even then don't watch it unless you can't change the channel.

RED LIGHT

The 13th Warrior
(1999)

RATED R; running time 102 minutes

GENRE: Horror/Horrible

WRITTEN BY: William Wisher and Warren Lewis, based on the novel *Eaters of the Dead* by Michael Crichton

DIRECTED BY: John McTiernan

CAST: Antonio Banderas, Diane Venora, Omar Sharif, Vladimir Kulich, Dennis Storhøi, Maria Bonnevie, Mischa Hausserman, Sven Wollter, John DeSantis, Asbjørn Riis

THE DIGEST

Antonio Banderas plays a privileged young poet in Baghdad. After falling for a very beautiful and married woman, he is banished from the country to serve as ambassador to all the nearby countries. He travels around learning about other peoples and tribes and teaching them about Baghdad.

After being chased by a group of nomads, he happens across some Norsemen. They begin to have a cultural exchange during which the Norsemen are summoned back home to rid the land of threatening "creatures." They consult a medicine woman who tells them that only 13 can go, and Antonio must be the 13th. So he packs up and heads up north. (Let me pause right here . . . Ain't no way in the world someone is going tell me I need to go off and fight some monsters and I don't question it, especially when I don't speak the language. How am I supposed to understand "RUN"?)

Here is where it gets corny and clichéd. They go there, try to save the town, and lose a few men. Fight. Lose some more men. The director throws in a few scenes to show that Muslims were technologically advanced. More fights ensue as do more losses. There is an obligatory romp in the sack. After more fighting, they all begin to pray. And then a triumphant battle, another death, the end of the story.

THE DISH

O-Dare most foul. This movie pretty much stunk. The Internet Movie Database has this film listed under Action/Thriller/Horror. Well, there ain't no real action, ain't no real thrills, and the horror is that this movie didn't go straight to video. I've come to the conclusion that Michael Crichton runs hot or cold. There is no in-between with him. Either it's really good or it's really bad.

I'm not sure what went wrong with this movie. I think part of the problem is that everything was *almost* good. The entire time I was watching, I kept thinking about how it was just on the edge of being a pretty cool movie. It just never quite got there. It was frustrating. The only saving grace is that Antonio is cute as a button. That and the cameo appearance of Omar Sharif.

THE DIRECTIVE

Stay home and watch the WWF. It's the same thing except they don't fight with swords.

RED LIGHT

1. Eleven.
a. No. Spielberg was not nominated.
b. Best Actress: Whoopi Goldberg; Best Supporting Actress: Oprah Winfrey and Margeret Avery; Best Art Design; Best Cinematography; Best Costume; Best Makeup; Best Original Score; Best Song; Best Screenplay (based on another medium).
c. ZERO.
2. False—Sidney Poitier won in 1963 for *Lilies of the Field* and Denzel Washington won in 2002 for *Training Day*.
3. Hattie McDaniel—Best Supporting Actress, *Gone With the Wind* (1939)
    Sidney Poitier—Best Actor, *Lilies of the Field* (1963)
    Lou Gossett Jr.—Best Supporting Actor, *An Officer and a Gentleman* (1983)
    Denzel Washington—Best Supporting Actor, *Glory* (1989)
    Whoopi Goldberg—Best Supporting Actress, *Ghost* (1990)
    Cuba Gooding Jr.—Best Supporting Actor, *Jerry Maguire* (1997)
    Halle Berry—Best Actress, *Monster's Ball* (2001)
    Denzel Washington—Best Actor, *Training Day* (2001)
4. He lied about his age. He was only 14, almost 15, when production started in 1976.
5. Joel Schumacher—no, he isn't Black. Some of his more famous work:
    Flawless (1999)
    8MM (1999)
    Batman & Robin (1997)
    A Time to Kill (1996)
    Batman Forever (1995)
    The Client (1994)
6. 2.5 million.
7. William Foster produced and directed *The Railroad Porter* in 1912, seven years before Oscar Micheaux.
8. Dorothy Dandridge.
9. One, for *The Color of Money* (1987). He was given an honorary Oscar in 1986.
10. Helen Hayes, Rita Moreno, and Barbra Streisand.

11.

ACTOR	NUMBER OF MOVIES	TOTAL GROSS	AVERAGE GROSS PER MOVIE
Harrison Ford	29	$3,152,046,380	$108,691,254
Samuel L. Jackson	50	$2,666,776,287	$53,335,526
Tom Hanks	28	$2,539,049,055	$90,680,341
James Earl Jones	32	$2,294,634,129	$71,707,317
Eddie Murphy	24	$2,243,624,811	$93,484,367

12.

TITLE	YEAR RELEASED	TOTAL GROSS
Titanic	1997	$600,788,188
Star Wars	1977	$460,988,007
*ET: The Extra-Terrestrial**	1982/2002	$431,088,297
Star Wars: Phantom Menace	1999	$431,088,297
Jurassic Park	1993	$357,067,947
Forrest Gump	1994	$329,693,974
Harry Potter and the Sorcerer's Stone	2001	$317,503,512
The Lion King	1994	$312,855,561
Lord of the Rings: The Fellowship of the Ring	2001	$309,471,992
Return of the Jedi	1983	$309,205,079
Independence Day	1996	$306,169,255
The Sixth Sense	1999	$293,501,675
The Empire Strikes Back	1980	$290,271,960
Star Wars: Attack of The Clones	1980	$287,529,000
Home Alone	1990	$285,761,243
Shrek	2001	$267,652,016
How the Grinch Stole Christmas	2000	$260,031,035
Jaws	1975	$260,000,000 (estimate)
Monsters, Inc	2001	$253,157,707
Spider-Man	2002	$252,103,000

13. *Spider-Man*—$114,844,116.

14. Name the actor: John Ratzenberger.
Name the sitcom: *Cheers.*
Name the trilogies: *Star Wars, Superman.*
Name the recent movies: *Monsters, Inc.; Toy Story 1&2; A Bug's Life.*

15. *Heat* (1995). They never worked together on screen in *Godfather 2*. De Niro was playing a

Figures includes box office from the re-release.

young Vito Corleone; Pacino was playing his grown son. Therefore, the two actors never were on screen together. *Heat* was the first time they worked face to face. Some claim that you never see both of them in the same shot in *Heat*, but it's clear that they are working with one another.

16. Bob Fosse.

17. John Grisham
A Time to Kill (1989 book; 1996 movie)
The Firm (1991 book; 1993 movie)
The Pelican Brief (1992 book; 1993 movie)
The Client (1993 book; 1994 movie)
The Chamber (1994 book; 1996 movie)
The Rainmaker (1995 book; 1997 movie)
[*The Runaway Jury* (1996) should be in theaters in 2003.]

18. Whoopi Goldberg.
Denzel Washington graduated from Fordham University.
Angela Bassett went to Yale on a full scholarship and completed her B.A. in Afro-American Studies and went on to earn an M.F.A. in Drama.
Samuel L. Jackson went to Morehouse and was kicked out in 1969 for staging a protest about the lack of Black members on the board of trustees. He returned to the school in 1972 and completed his degree.

19. Tony Curtis was born Bernard Schwartz. Jack Lemmon and Harrison Ford both use their birth names. Kirk Douglas is the son of Russian immigrants and changed his name from Issur Danielovitch Demsky.

20. Anthony Quinn. His grandfather was an Irishman living in Mexico. His grandmother and mother were both Mexican nationals. His parents were married on a train filled with rebels and that is also where he was conceived in 1915.

21. Drew Barrymore. Her grandfather John Barrymore, along with his brother Lionel and sister Ethel, are considered to be among the greatest actors who ever lived. Barrymore siblings, parents, uncles, aunts, and grandparents were all very famous stage actors through the 1800s and early 1900s. With the birth of cinema, the Barrymore siblings became matinee idols and some of the most sought-after performers.

22. Tommy Lee Jones and Al Gore were roommates for four years.

23. Tom Hanks, for his roles in *Philadelphia* and *Forrest Gump*. Spencer Tracy accomplished the same feat in 1938 and 1939.

24. Dorothy Dandridge—*Carmen Jones*
Diana Ross—*Lady Sings the Blues*
Cicely Tyson—*Sounder*
Diahann Carroll—*Claudine*

Whoopi Goldberg—*The Color Purple*
Angela Bassett—*What's Love Got to Do With It?*
Halle Berry—*Monster's Ball*
25. *Sudden Impact.*

African Queen 196

A.I.: Artificial Intelligence 290

Ali 38

All About Eve 60

All the Pretty Horses 197

Almost Famous 144

Along Came a Spider 93

American Beauty 74

An American in Paris 218

An Officer and a Gentlemen 53

Anchors Aweigh 220

Angel Eyes 198

The Animal 344

Any Given Sunday 172

Art of War 94

Atlantis: The Lost Empire 306

Auntie Mame 62

Baby Boy 109

Bait 345

Bamboozled 111

Bats 345

Battlefield Earth 291

A Beautiful Mind 234

Bedazzled 261

Behind Enemy Lines 145

Best in Show 262

The Best Man 113

Bicentennial Man 292

Big Momma's House 2

Birth of a Nation 95

Black and White 326

Black Belt Jones 114

Black Caesar 115

Black Heat 116

Blade II 96

The Blair Witch Project 3

Blair Witch 2: Book of Shadows 236

Blazing Saddles 263

Bless the Child 235

Blow 77

Boiler Room 75

Bowfinger 265

The Bone Collector 98

Bridget Jones's Diary 146

Bring It On 99

Bringing Out the Dead 346

Brokedown Palace 347

The Brothers 117

Bucktown 119

Castaway 237

Charlie's Angels 199

Chicken Run 4

A Christmas Story 260

The Cider House Rules 175

Coffy 120
The Contender 200
Cornbread, Earl and Me 121
Corrina, Corrina 201
Coyote Ugly 202
Cradle Will Rock (1999) 327
The Crimson Rivers (2001) 329
Crouching Tiger, Hidden Dragon 329

Days of Wine and Roses 238
Deep Blue Sea 293
Dinosaur 5
Disney's 'Tarzan' 318
Dogma 177
Don't Say a Word 239
Double Jeopardy 7
Double Take 63
Down to Earth 64
Dr. Dolittle 2 6
Driving Miss Daisy 40
Dungeons and Dragons 349

End of Days 295
Erin Brockovich 8
E.T. the Extraterrestrial 20th Anniversary 9
Eve's Bayou 122
Evolution 296

The Family Man 179
Fantasia 307
Felicia's Journey 350
15 Minutes 180
Fight Club 78
Final Fantasy: The Spirits Within 309
Finding Forrester 124
Flawless 240
For Love of the Game 148
Foxy Brown 125

Frequency 181
Friday Foster 126

Galaxy Quest 266
Ghost 41
Girl, Interrupted 204
Gladiator 11
Glory 42
Gone in 60 Seconds 12
The Green Mile 183
The Grinch 13
Guess Who's Coming to Dinner 44
Gun Shy 351
Guys and Dolls 221

Hanging Up 205
Hannibal 242
Harlem Nights 127
The Haunting 243
Head Over Heels 267
Heartbreakers 268
Heist 331
High Fidelity 185
Highlander: Endgame 351
His Girl Friday 150
Hollow Man 244
Hollywood Shuffle 128
The House on Haunted Hill 297
How High 66
The Hurricane 45

I Am Sam 151
Ice Age 15
I'm the One that I Want 269
In The Bedroom 332
In Too Deep 129
The Insider 245

Jerry Maguire 47
Josie and the Pussycats 222
Jurassic Park III 298
Just Visiting 270

Keeping the Faith 152
Kingdom Come 67
A Knight's Tale 143

The Ladies' Man 353
Lady Sings the Blues 48
The Last Castle 247
Lara Croft: Tomb Raider 256
Legally Blonde 271
The Legend of Bagger Vance 100
The Legend of Drunken Master 272
Let's Do It Again 130
Light It Up 132
Lilies of the Field 50
The Long Kiss Goodnight 206
The Lord of the Rings—
    The Fellowship of the Ring 16
Lost Souls 248
Love and Basketball 134

Magnolia 79
The Matrix 18
Me, Myself & Irene 354
Meet the Parents 274
Memento 333
Men of Honor 101
The Messenger: The Story of Joan of Arc 355
Mickey Blue Eyes 32
Miss Congeniality 19
Monster's Ball 51
Monsters, Inc. 310
Moulin Rouge! 223
Mulholland Drive 335

Music of the Heart 154
The Mummy Returns 21
Mystery Men 275
Mystery, Alaska 83

Notorious C.H.O. 276
Nurse Betty 207
Nutty Professor II: The Klumps 68

O Brother, Where Art Thou 224
Ocean's 11 22
An Officer and a Gentleman 53
The One 299
On the Town 226
The Original Kings of Comedy 278
Osmosis Jones 311
Our Song 69

The Patriot 85
Pay It Forward 186
Pearl Harbor 23
A Piece of the Action 108
The Perfect Storm 25
Planet of the Apes 26
Play It to the Bone 249
Pollock 336
Price of Glory 156
The Princess Diaries 313
Proof of Life 158

A Raisin in the Sun 61
Random Hearts 208
Rat Race 279
Red Planet 300
The Red Violin 337
Remember the Titans 103
The Replacements 159
The Road to El Dorado 314

Romeo Must Die 161
The Rookie 163
The Royal Tenenbaums 187
Rules of Engagement 366
Rush Hour 2 281

Saving Grace 209
The Score 189
Scream 3 310
Serendipity 164
Shaft 2000 136
Shane 166
Shanghai Noon 282
The Shawshank Redemption 54
Shrek 315
Singin' in the Rain 227
The Sixth Day 251
The Sixth Sense 251
Sleeping with the Enemy 87
Sleepy Hollow 253
Space Cowboys 302
Sparkle 70
Spider-Man 28
Spirit: Stallion of the Cimarron 316
Star Wars Episode II: Attack of the Clones 29
State and Main 339
Stigmata 254
Stir of Echoes 255
The Straight Story 167
Stuart Little 317
Superstar 357
Sweet Sweetback's Baad Asssss Song 137
Swordfish 88

The Talented Mr. Ripley 89
The Tigger Movie 321
The Thirteenth Warrior 358
The Thomas Crown Affair 190
Three Kings 168
Titan A.E. 360
Toy Story 2 323
Training Day 56
Turn It Up 138

U-571 90
Unbreakable 33
Uptown Saturday Night 139

Vanilla Sky 191
Vertical Limit 257
The Visit 340

West Side Story 229
What Lies Beneath 211
What Planet Are You From? 285
What Women Want 169
What's Love Got to Do with It? 57
Whipped 192
Willy Wonka and the Chocolate Factory 71
The Whole Nine Yards 286
The Wiz 230
Woman on Top 212
The Wood 140
The World Is Not Enough 32

X-Men 35